Auditing: Principles and Practice

Auditing

Principles and Practice

F Clive de Paula
CBE, TD, FCA, JDipMA, CBIM

and **Frank A Attwood**
BSc(Econ), FCA, ACIS

Partner, Robson Rhodes
Chartered Accountants

Pitman

PITMAN BOOKS LIMITED
128 Long Acre, London WC2E 9AN

PITMAN PUBLISHING INC
1020 Plain Street, Marshfield, Massachusetts

Associated Companies
Pitman Publishing Pty Ltd, Melbourne
Pitman Publishing New Zealand Ltd, Wellington
Copp Clark Pitman, Toronto

Sixteenth edition 1982

British Library Cataloguing in Publication Data
De Paula, F. Clive
Auditing: principles and practice.—16th ed.
1. Auditing
I. Title II. Attwood, Frank A.
657'.45 HF5667
ISBN 0-273-01778-0

Text set in 10 on 12pt VIP Times, printed and bound in Great Britain at The Pitman Press, Bath

Contents

Preface to the sixteenth edition

In April 1980 the first Auditing Standards and Guidelines, developed by the Auditing Practices Committee of the Consultative Committee of Accountancy Bodies, were published by the Councils of the English, Irish and Scottish Institutes of Chartered Accountants and by the Association of Certified Accountants. The Standards do not herald any change in fundamental objectives: they do no more than codify best practice such as we have described in previous editions of this text. They do however serve as a useful and timely reminder of the requisite basic procedures, and we seek in this new edition to provide the auditor with practical assistance in implementing the underlying principles.

In dealing with the Auditing Standards and Guidelines, we have drawn on the booklet which we were asked to write for the English Institute entitled *Auditing Standards: from Discussion Drafts to Practice*, which was published by the Institute immediately after the issue of the First Discussion Drafts of the Auditing Standards. This booklet was intended to give practical illustration of how the Standards might work and thereby assist the debate which led up to the finalization of the definitive Standards.

Accordingly we hope the book will be of assistance both to the practitioner wishing to review his audit procedures against the requirements of the Standards, and to the student preparing for his professional examinations in auditing.

This new edition also provides us with the opportunity to bring our text up to date in respect of the numerous changes in legislation and professional pronouncements with which the auditor must be concerned: viz. the recent Companies Acts and important Statements of Standard Accounting Practice dealing with Stocks and Work-in-Progress, Group Accounts, Deferred Taxation, and Current Cost Accounting. The auditor is only beginning to appreciate what this latest accounting convention is going to imply, but we hope we are able to be of practical assistance in highlighting the areas where attention will be required. For this, and for many other illustrations of procedural documentation which we have used, we are indebted to the partners of Robson Rhodes, who have allowed us to draw freely upon documentation used within the firm's own practice, and in particular we are grateful to Mr P. R. Lemanski, MA, FCA, for his assistance with the chapter dealing with computer auditing. Any failings of the book, however, remain our responsibility.

It has also given us great pleasure to have been writing this book during the centenary year of the Institute of Chartered Accountants in England and Wales. To mark the achievement in reaching this proud age the Institute has published 'Accounting Thought and Education: Six English Pioneers', by J. Kitchen and R. H. Parker, and one of those pioneers chosen was the late F. R. M. de Paula, CBE, FCA, the original author of this book. To see him described as 'a standard bearer in the movement for fuller disclosure and greater comprehensibility in financial reporting' has given us heart in our task.

In this edition, we have broken new ground by the inclusion of a chapter on the subject of Audit Committees. There has been a good deal of public and professional discussion about these committees, which have become a familiar part of the public company scene in North America; but, so far, not much practical guidance as to the role which they might play in UK companies, or as to how they might set about their work. We have therefore drawn on practical experience of Audit Committee work in the UK in the hope that this may be helpful to anyone venturing into what is, for all of us, a very new field

Finally, the book contains numerous references to the material contained within the Members' Handbook of the English Institute and we are grateful for permission to quote from this and also to reproduce in full as an appendix the Auditing Standards. We would also like to express gratitude to the Controller of Her Majesty's Stationery Office for permission to reproduce the relevant parts of the Companies Acts.

1 Introduction to auditing

Historical Development

The practice of auditing, in a primitive form, can be traced back to ancient times, but auditing as it exists today was established only in the latter part of the nineteenth century.

In this country, during the nineteenth century, industrial enterprise was greatly expanded and the evolution of the mechanized factory involved the provision of finance far in excess of that required by industry under the old-fashioned hand methods.

Originally individual concerns were owned and financed by either a sole proprietor or a partnership, and naturally under this type of organization the finance and credit available was limited to that which the owners themselves could provide and influence. For this reason, therefore, the capital available for industry was strictly limited.

The introduction of the joint stock company greatly widened the possibility of raising capital for industry. As the liability of each shareholder was limited, it was possible to offer shares to the public and thus there became available to industry and commerce a vast new supply of capital. Thus in course of time the joint stock company largely took the place of the small privately owned business.

Under the company form of organization the shareholders as a body delegate the management of the undertaking to a board of directors, and periodically the board submits to the shareholders the accounts of the company in order that the members may see the financial position and the profit or loss of the undertaking in which they are interested.

In these circumstances the need arose for some means by which the shareholders as a body might be satisfied that the accounts, presented to them by their board of directors, did show an objective view of the financial position and results of the company. It was for this reason, therefore, that the practice developed of appointing auditors whose duty it was to verify on behalf of the shareholders the accounts of the directors and to report thereon to the shareholders. Obviously it is impracticable and impossible for every shareholder of a company to examine the books and records of a company and therefore the shareholders as a body appoint auditors to act for them.

Under the early Companies Acts, the auditors appointed were one or two of the shareholders of the company. As, however, the chosen auditors commonly had no technical qualifications, they were probably not able to carry out a very effective audit — nor were they paid anything for the work they did, although a later Act did provide for them to employ a clerk to do some work, whose remuneration should be provided by the company.

It was the Companies Act 1900 which first made it legally compulsory for every company to appoint independent auditors, as we now know them, and provided for their remuneration. It was undoubtedly the rapid increase in the number of joint stock companies which took place at this time and the compulsory professional audit thus provided for in the Companies Act 1900 that gave a great impetus to the development of the accountancy profession.

Position of Auditors under the Companies Acts

Pursuant to the Companies Acts 1948 and 1967, every company in this country is required to have its accounts audited by professional accountants. Their appointment, and removal, are provided for in the Companies Acts: 1948 — Sections 159 to 161; 1967 — Section 13; 1976 — Sections 13 to 17. The appointment is made by the shareholders as a body and the auditor is, therefore, acting as their agent to audit the accounts of the directors, who themselves are merely agents of the shareholders, on whose behalf, and for whose benefit, the directors carry on the business. This fact must be clearly appreciated and borne in mind by the auditor. For, though in the course of his work he is constantly brought into contact with the directors, who conduct the business, he is not acting for them at all. He is appointed to act as a check upon the directors and to ensure on behalf of the shareholders, who are the proprietors of the business, that the directors carry on the undertaking honestly for the benefit of the shareholders and render to them true and fair accounts.

It is, however, of interest that, although the auditor is appointed by the shareholders, for whom he acts, the shareholders themselves appear to have no right of communication with the auditor whom they have appointed. If a shareholder has any question on the accounts upon which the auditor has reported, the shareholder cannot discuss the matter with the auditor. The law provides only for the shareholder to receive the auditor's report. There is, therefore, the slightly unusual situation of a 'principal' and 'agent' between whom there is no form of communication (other than the auditor's report).

The directors of a company, or the company in general meeting, are empowered to appoint auditors to fill a casual vacancy, and, failing this, the power to make the necessary appointment rests with the Trade Secretary. In these cases, the auditor acts as the agent of the shareholders in exactly the same way as if he had been appointed at the annual general meeting.

Section 14(1) of the Companies Act 1976 provides that 'every company shall at each general meeting of the company', where accounts are laid before the company, 'appoint an auditor or auditors to hold office from the conclusion of that meeting until the conclusion of the next general meeting of the company' where accounts are received. An auditor, however, may be removed during his term of office by ordinary resolution of the company.

Section 15 further provides that if a resolution is to be proposed at a general meeting of a company appointing as auditor someone other than the retiring auditor, special notice must be given to the company. The company must in turn send a copy of the notice both to the newly proposed auditor and to the auditor who is to retire or be removed. The latter may then make written representations which the company (unless the representations are defamatory) should distribute to its members; or if the distribution is not made, the auditor can have the representations read out at the general meeting. The auditor is entitled to attend the meeting and to receive all notices about any such meeting to which a member would be entitled.

If an auditor wishes to resign, he must under Section 16 give the company written notice, which must include either 'a statement to the effect that there are no circumstances connected with his resignation which he considers should be brought to the notice of the members or creditors of the company, or a statement of any such circumstances'.

The auditor has further powers under Section 17 in that he can deposit a written requisition with the directors of the company to convene an extraordinary general meeting to discuss the circumstances of his resignation and to send his resignation statement to all members entitled to attend the meeting. If the statement is not so sent it should be read out at the meeting. The auditor may attend the meeting himself and should continue to receive notices of, and be able in his capacity as auditor to speak at, other meetings of the company. Directors failing to take reasonable steps to convene the meeting within twenty-eight days of the auditor's requisition are liable to a fine.

In the past, cases arose in which conscientious auditors who carried out their duties properly, and in consequence came into conflict with the directors, were not re-elected at the annual general meeting, the directors nominating someone else for the appointment without giving any notice beforehand to anyone.

The position of auditors in relation to directors who wish to displace them was usefully brought out in The City of London Real Property Co. Ltd affair in 1963. A difference of opinion arose between the board of that company and its auditors and the directors proposed to replace the auditors by another firm.

The Institute of Chartered Accountants in England and Wales considered that the proposal raised issues of such fundamental importance that it issued a statement dealing with the displacement of auditors and, *inter alia*, emphasizing:

'The auditors of a company are appointed to represent the shareholders in accordance with the requirements of the Companies Act and have a statutory duty to make a critical review of the accounts submitted by the directors and to report to the shareholders whether those accounts show a true and fair view and comply with the requirements of the Act.

If the auditors disagree with such accounts to any material extent their duty is to say so in their report and to specify the material respects in which they disagree.

The fact that the auditors disagree, if they do so, is not a justification for their displacement unless the reasons for their disagreement are such that the *shareholders* no longer have confidence in the judgement, competence or conduct of the auditors as their representatives.

Confidence between directors and auditors, whilst obviously desirable, is not indispensable for the adequate performance by the auditors of their onerous duties on behalf of the shareholders; indeed in some circumstances the performance of those duties may lead inevitably to differences of opinion between the directors and auditors and to a report to this effect by the auditors to the shareholders.

The existence of such a possibility is among the reasons why auditors are appointed. The work of auditors and their freedom to perform it with a sense of complete independence can only continue as long as it is generally accepted that the issue by auditors of a report expressing disagreement with the directors of a company of which they are auditors does not of itself provide a reason for the removal of the auditors from office. The purpose implicit in the appointment of auditors under the Companies Act would be defeated if there were to grow up a practice of displacing auditors whenever a disagreement between them and the directors of a company occurs on a matter of accounting principle.'

Subsequently in 1963 the board of The City of London Real Property Co. Ltd, in the light of the considerable opposition aroused, withdrew its resolution. The Companies Act 1976 has now strengthened the relationship between shareholders and auditors.

The remuneration of the auditors, in the same way as their appointment, rests entirely with the shareholders, except where, as a matter of convenience, the directors act for the shareholders in the case of the appointment prior to the first annual general meeting, or where a casual vacancy occurs. Again in these latter circumstances the remuneration fixed by the directors only holds until the next annual general meeting. Nevertheless, it is common practice for shareholders in general meeting each year to delegate to the directors the power to fix the remuneration of the auditors.

Qualifications of an Auditor

Section 161 of the Companies Act 1948, and Section 13 of the Companies Act 1976, provide that an auditor, legally competent to exercise a company audit function, must be a member of a recognized body of accountants. Section 161 further specifies that none of the following persons shall be qualified for appointment as auditor of a company:

(*a*) An officer or servant of the company.
(*b*) A person who is a partner of, or in the employment of, an officer or servant of the company.
(*c*) A body corporate.

The principle underlying these provisions is that an auditor shall be in an independent position, and so no director or officer of the company can be appointed, or be in a position to exert influence over an auditor.

The above provisions now apply to all limited companies, since the Companies Act 1967 abolished the status 'exempt private company'. These companies were previously allowed to have unqualified auditors or auditors who were partners of directors.

It was not uncommon in the past to find, say, one partner of a firm of accountants acting as director or secretary of the company, and another partner as auditor. In these circumstances the auditor might find himself in conflict with his partner who was a director of the company. The provisions of Section 13 now make such appointments illegal.

Although an officer of the company cannot be appointed as auditor, it is of interest that an auditor appointed under Section 159 of the Companies Act 1948 becomes an officer of the company, and as such has responsibilities and liabilities which are considered in later chapters.

Qualifications required by an auditor are many and varied. First of all, he must have a complete and thorough knowledge of bookkeeping, accountancy and costing. An auditor in course of time is called upon to deal with many different systems of bookkeeping in many different businesses, and unless he understands exactly how such accounts should be prepared, he cannot audit them. Therefore, he must know his subject and be able to apply his knowledge to any set of circumstances. He must thoroughly understand practical business, and be able to grasp the technical details and the business methods of any concern whose accounts he is called upon to audit. A knowledge of accountancy is essential, but that alone will not make a competent auditor, for the art of auditing is quite apart and distinct from accountancy. Many beginners seem to think that, provided they are able to follow the system of bookkeeping and that the trial balance agrees, everything must be in order, and the auditor has only to check the preparation of the profit and loss account and balance sheet and to sign his report. The agreement of the trial balance in itself proves nothing, not even the arithmetical accuracy of the books.

In addition to his technical knowledge, he must be above all things a man possessed of both strength of character and tact. He must not be easily led and influenced by others but, knowing what his duty is, he must do it in spite of direct or indirect pressure. In the long run the reputation he will thus gain for absolute integrity will prove of far greater value to him. An auditor must also be methodical and painstaking and he must be endowed with considerable perseverance, for it is essential that the work should be thoroughly and carefully done. He must never pass any item unless he understands its nature and is absolutely satisfied that it is in order. If he is not, he must make intelligent and exhaustive inquiries until he has ascertained the exact state of affairs. One of the greatest dangers is to pass entries which are not completely understood, because the auditor is fearful of displaying ignorance by asking questions. If he cannot ascertain for himself, he should, without fail, ask for the necessary information. Should he affect to possess knowledge which, in fact, he does not, he inevitably will make mistakes which will be far more damaging to his reputation than would be the case if he asked for information upon, for instance, technical details of which he has not had previous experience. An auditor must be practical, and if asked for professional advice, must appreciate the practical requirements and circumstances of the business, and thus avoid making recommendations which, though perhaps theoretically perfect, are entirely unfitted to the circumstances of the particular business. However, the auditor cannot insist upon his recommendations being carried out; his only sanction is his report.

Finally to revert to the question of independence: it has already been mentioned that the development of the accountancy profession has partially resulted from the shareholders' need for an objective review of the accounts prepared by the directors, and it has been explained how the Companies Acts seek to regulate the appointment and protect the position of auditors so that their independence may be assured. This is a subject which has received considerable attention first in the United States of America, and now within this country, both from the professional bodies and from individual firms within those bodies. It is also one which has seemed the more urgent following other criticisms of auditors, to which we refer later. In consequence, the Institute of Chartered Accountants in England and Wales issued in October 1979 a revised 'Guide to Professional Ethics', which stipulates that 'a member in practice should be, and be seen to be, free in each professional assignment he undertakes of any interest which might detract from objectivity'. No doubt this will serve to help clarify the attitudes required of an auditor, but there is far more to independence than can ever be ensured by regulation or legislation, for it is a function of the professional ethics of the individual auditor.

The Explanatory Notes attached to the Guide are, however, of particular interest in focusing on an area seen as a topical problem and 'directing the attention of each member to the over-riding importance in his professional life of integrity and objectivity'. The particular difficulties envisaged are twofold:

(*a*) where there is financial involvement with the affairs of a client such that could affect objectivity in the reporting function, and

(*b*) where a conflict of interest could arise, especially in circumstances of the provision of other financial services to audit clients.

It has for some time been widely questioned whether the close association of executive directors of a company with most appointments of auditors did not impair the auditors' objectivity in their reporting to shareholders whom they actually represent. This problem is perhaps particularly acute in the case of public companies where the directors may often be quite separate from shareholders, and also where audit fees may be particularly large and attractive. The Explanatory Notes to which we refer aim 'to give helpful guidance in cases where the objectivity of a member may be questioned as a consequence of an actual, or seeming lack of independence'. We summarize below the principal points of this guidance:

(*a*) A practice should not become dependent on any one client connection for too great a part of its income, recommended not to exceed 15% of gross fees.

(*b*) Care should be taken to ensure that objectivity is not endangered in consequence of any personal relationship.

(*c*) There should generally be no beneficial holdings of shares in an audit client by any partner or staff in a practice, nor by the spouse or minor child of a partner.

(*d*) Where shares are held by a trust of which a partner or the spouse of a partner in the practice is a trustee, the shareholdings should be disclosed in the financial statements and where possible the audit review should be undertaken by another partner.

(*e*) Neither a practice nor a partner should be involved with loans to or from clients, other than banking institutions.

(*f*) Goods and services should not be accepted from a client save on terms no more favourable than those available to employees of the client.

(*g*) A client should be informed in writing of the amount of any commission receivable by a practice in consequence of any advice given to that client.

(*h*) Appointments should not be accepted where conflicts of interest seem likely to occur, but where they do arise there should be full disclosure followed by appropriate disengagement.

(*i*) Other services beyond audit performed for audit clients should not extend to performance of executive functions or to making executive decisions.

(*j*) In cases where a practice is concerned in the preparation of accounting records for an audit client, it must be ensured that the client accepts responsibility for such record keeping and that this is seen as distinct from the execution of the audit function.

Before leaving the question of independence, we would refer also to the developing role of the audit committee — the functions of which we explore in more detail in chapter 12 — as a potentially important means of 'distancing' the auditor from executive directors. Audit committees have not thus far been greeted with much official enthusiasm in the UK, yet we believe they offer considerable scope for an improved audit function from the points of view of both the auditor and his larger client company.

Main Objects of an Audit

Originally the work of professional accountants was confined largely to the checking of the arithmetical accuracy of the detailed records in books of account, the agreement of the trial balance, and the preparation of accounts; in fact, to what may be described as 'accountancy work', but nowadays a very large part of a professional accountant's work is that of auditing. The difference between accountancy and auditing is not always clearly understood, it being thought that if accounts are prepared by a professional accountant, he necessarily guarantees their accuracy. This, however, is far from being the case.

If an accountant is instructed merely to prepare accounts from a set of books, the work involved would be that of agreeing the trial balance, and thereafter preparing the profit and loss account and the balance sheet. He would not check the books themselves, except in so far as would be necessary to agree the trial balance, and he would not report that the position shown by the balance sheet was a true and fair one. All he could say would be that the balance sheet was in accordance with the books. Accountants are often called upon to deal with figures in this way, but when doing so, they should be particularly careful to point out to their clients that they are not carrying out an audit, for an audit is quite distinct and apart from accountancy.

An audit does not entail the preparation of the accounts at all, but denotes something much wider, namely:

> 'the independent examination of financial statements of enterprises, where such an examination is conducted with a view to expressing an opinion on whether those statements give a true and fair view and comply with the relevant statutes'.

This then is the main object of an audit in accordance with the Companies Act 1967, to report whether, in the opinion of the auditors, the balance sheet and profit and loss account give a true and fair view. In making this report they are also required, by Section 14(4), to form an opinion:

'(*a*) whether proper books of account have been kept by the company and proper returns adequate for their audit have been received from branches not visited by them; and

(*b*) whether the company's balance sheet and . . . profit and loss account are in agreement with the books of account and returns.'

In addition, 'if the auditors fail to obtain all the information and explanations which, to the best of their knowledge and belief, are necessary for the purposes of their audit, they shall state the fact in their report' (Section 14(6)).

In the past, the detection of fraud was also regarded as being a major part of an auditor's function, and indeed probably is still so regarded by many of those who employ auditors. However, leading professional opinion, set out by the Auditing Practices Committee in the Explanatory Foreword to 'Auditing Standards and Guidelines', would no longer regard its discovery as being more than a by-product of the proper application of the audit procedures necessary to enable the expression of an opinion on the accounts under examination:

'The responsibility for the prevention and detection of irregularities and fraud rests with the management, who may obtain reasonable assurance that this responsibility will be discharged, by instituting an adequate system of internal control'.

'The auditor should recognize the possibility of material irregularities or fraud which could, unless adequately disclosed, distort the results or state of affairs shown by the financial statements. The auditor should, therefore, plan his audit so that he has a reasonable expectation of detecting major misstatements in the financial statements resulting from irregularities or fraud'.

Whilst an audit cannot be a substitute for internal controls over transactions exercised at the time, nevertheless an assessment of these controls must be made by the auditor so that he can determine the volume of detailed checking necessary to enable the discharge of his primary audit function. This also then provides the opportunity for a service to management in pointing out deficiencies in internal control and making recommendations for improvements.

The basic approach to which we shall be returning in later chapters is thus that auditors should aim to reduce their detailed checking to the minimum consistent with the system of internal control and the state in which they find the records. If their inquiries and tests satisfy them that the system is sound in principle and is carried out in practice then no useful purpose is served by extensive detailed checking. If on the other hand the system is not sound or is not properly carried out then the auditors must first reach a conclusion as to the nature of the shortcomings before they can decide upon the nature and extent of the detailed checking which they should undertake.

Auditing Standards and Guidelines

Interestingly, and perhaps surprisingly, in spite of the legislative background to the development of auditing since the nineteenth century, the form and extent of the detailed audit work required to support an audit opinion has never been prescribed. Until recently, this was primarily a question for the individual auditor's professional judgement, and the only recommendations made as to how such judgement should be exercised were contained in 'Statements on Auditing' issued by the Institute of Chartered Accountants in England and Wales (see Appendix A). Over the last decade, however, in parallel with the promulgation of Statements of Standard Accounting Practice and with the development of Statements of Auditing Standards in the United States of America, there has been pressure to set Auditing Standards in the UK. This pressure has been further reinforced during the last five years or so by criticisms of audit procedures expressed by Department of Trade Inspectors.

The consequences of these circumstances have been twofold: firstly, the establishment with effect from 1 January 1980 of the Joint Disciplinary Scheme to investigate, in cases of public interest, the competence and conduct of members, and secondly, the publication in April 1980 by the Auditing Practices Committee of the Consultative Committee of Accountancy Bodies of the first Auditing Standards and Guidelines (Appendix B).

Auditing Standards may be seen as having the same objective in relation to audit practice as Accounting Standards to the preparation of accounts: 'the narrowing of areas of difference and variety in practice'.

Previously, as we have said, auditors have developed their practical skills from a number of sources: statements by the professional bodies, formal professional training, case law, Department of Trade reports, practical experience of course, and even from well-known auditing texts!

However, each auditor had been left to develop his own approach and procedures for all types of audit assignment, and to establish 'good practice' for himself. The codification arising from the Standards now aims to set out what is best practice.

As the Chairman of the Auditing Practices Committee said in an introductory letter to them: 'Auditing Standards and Guidelines are, of course, only the codification of existing best practice, but I believe that they will provide for each member a yardstick by which he may judge not only the general level of his work, but also the suitability of the action he proposes to take in a particular case. That is not to suggest that Auditing Standards and Guidelines can ever replace the judgement of the individual member. Only the member carrying out the audit can decide when he has adequate evidence for the purpose of arriving at the opinion expressed in his audit report.'

The Standards presently issued are as follows:

(*a*) The Auditor's Operational Standard, covering:
- (i) planning, controlling and recording
- (ii) accounting systems
- (iii) audit evidence
- (iv) internal controls
- (v) review of financial statements.

(*b*) The Audit Report, covering any opinion on whether the financial statements give a true and fair view.
(*c*) Qualifications in Audit Reports, covering the situation where the auditor has to qualify his report by referring to material matters about which he has reservations.

In addition, each Standard is followed by Guidelines on procedures by which it may be applied, and on its application to specific items appearing in financial statements. The Guidelines also describe techniques currently being used in auditing. They are not meant to be definitive and do not form part of the Standards.

Previous Auditing Statements (Appendix A) are also accorded the same status as Auditing Guidelines except to the extent that these former may have been expressly withdrawn. Further Guidelines are expected to be issued from time to time.

The Auditing Standards have been suggested to offer the following benefits:

(*a*) the demonstration that self-regulation by the profession does work;
(*b*) an improvement of the image of auditors and audit work in the eyes of the public;
(*c*) a reduction in the differences which currently exist between audit reports, thereby enabling users better to understand the message the auditor wishes to convey;
(*d*) a set of principles which will help the auditor, when combined with his professional judgement, to choose the relevant audit tasks to perform;
(*e*) an aid in persuading clients that the procedures which the auditor wishes to carry out really are necessary!

It is the approach depicted by the Standards and Guidelines, stemming as they do from best practice, we describe in the chapters which follow. Meanwhile the reader may be helped to assimilate the audit approach envisaged by a diagrammatic representation of the interface between the Standards and audit tasks and their objectives in the context of a systems based audit where it is proposed to place some reliance on internal controls.

The general audit approach

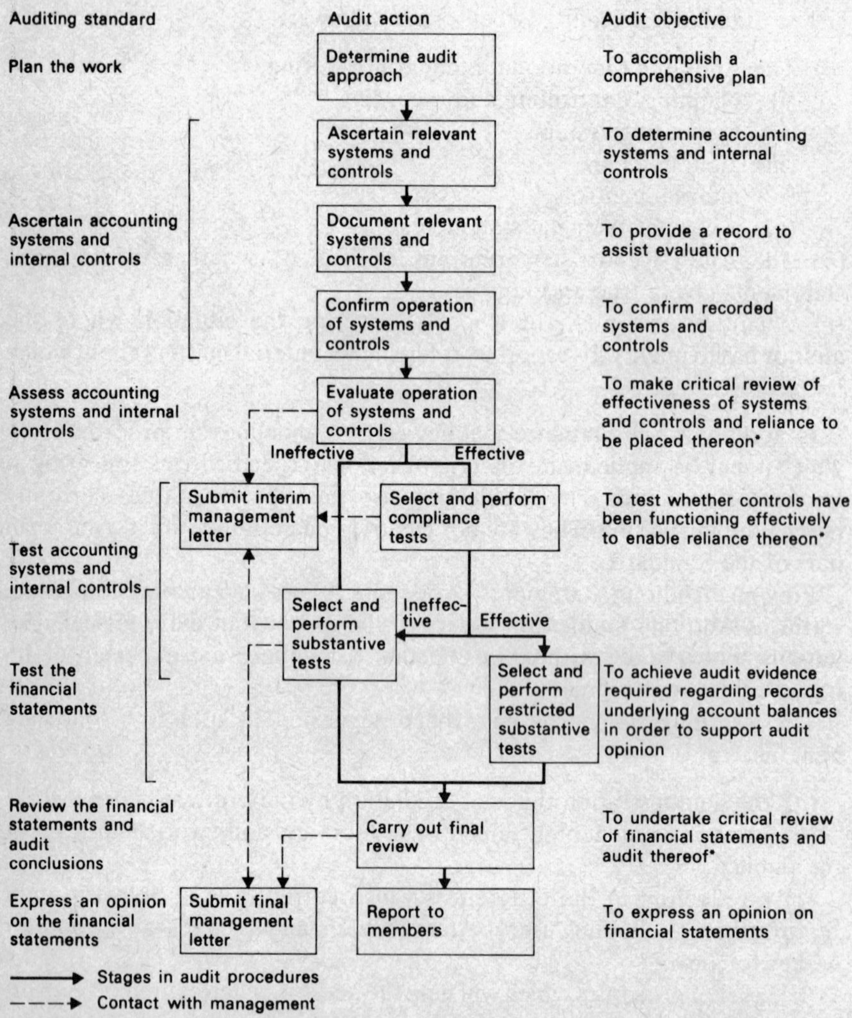

*A secondary objective of this audit action is to recommend to management improvements in systems and controls and in accounting procedures and practices.

2 Audit plans and reports

Audit practice has developed over the years towards giving increased recognition to the importance of internal check within a company's system in determining the level of audit tests. This has been accompanied by a tendency to place greater emphasis and reliance upon the auditor's appraisal of systems, and to spend less audit time on the examination of detailed transactions. At the same time, however, the auditor's dependence on a reduced scale of audit tests has made the planning of those tests more important. Further, pressures to provide higher standards of service to clients, and the increasing cost of providing such services, now necessitate a business-like approach to the organization of audits generally.

Letters of Engagement

The use of engagement letters has been an important development providing the opportunity for auditors to place on record their understanding of the responsibilities of management in relation to internal control and fraud — both of which, of course, are of fundamental importance to auditors — and at the same time define their audit objectives and responsibilities. It is important, where auditors are involved in the provision of accountancy services to clients, that the client be made to differentiate clearly between the audit function and other accountancy work undertaken.

Even more important is the situation where accounts are being prepared for which no audit responsibility is being taken, as for instance with a sole trader, partnership or unincorporated body. It is essential for the client to realize that no audit has been done, and this must also be made evident to third parties who may see such accounts.

A suggested engagement letter for company clients, following the lines of Statement V.16 issued in 1969 by the English Institute, is as follows:

Outline engagement letter

To the Chairman/The Managing Director/The Finance Director/The Secretary of XYZ Ltd

Dear Sir

(New appointment)
Following our appointment as auditors of XYZ Ltd (and its subsidiary/ies — ABC Ltd), we set out below our responsibilities as auditors of the company/companies and our understanding of the further service you require us to perform.

OR

(Existing appointment)
Following our discussion with you, we write to confirm our mutual understanding of our responsibilities as auditors of XYZ Ltd (and its subsidiary/ies — ABC Ltd), and our understanding of the further services you require us to perform.

Audit

Our function as auditors under the Companies Acts 1948 and 1967 is to examine and report on the accounts presented to us by the directors. As auditors we are not responsible for the preparation of the accounts, nor for the maintenance of the accounting records of the companies, which duties are imposed on the directors by the Companies Acts. Any accounting services we provide are distinct from our function as auditors.

We shall, as required by law, report to the members whether in our opinion the accounts of the company/companies which we have audited give a true and fair view of the state of the company'/companies' affairs at the date of the balance sheet, and of the profit or loss for the period ended on that date, and whether these accounts comply with the Companies Acts 1948 and 1967.

The regulations of the Institute of Chartered Accountants in England and Wales further require us to report:

(*a*) whether the accounts show a true and fair view of the source and application of funds for the period, and
(*b*) if the accounts do not comply in any significant respect with relevant Statements of Standard Accounting Practice.

In arriving at our opinion we are required by law to consider the following matters, but only to report on any in respect of which we are not satisfied:

Whether proper accounting records have been maintained so as to:

(*a*) disclose with reasonable accuracy, at any time, the financial position of the company at that time;

(*b*) enable the directors to ensure that the company's financial statements give a true and fair view of the company's state of affairs and profit or loss;

(*c*) contain:

— entries from day to day of all sums of money received and expended and the matters in respect of which the receipt and expenditure takes place,

— a record of the assets and liabilities of the company,

— where the company's business involves dealing in goods,

(i) statements of stock held by the company at the end of each financial year of the company, and

(ii) all statements of stocktakings from which this is derived,

(iii) statements of all goods sold and purchased showing the goods and the buyers in sufficient detail to enable the goods, buyers and sellers to be identified. (This is not required in the case of goods sold by way of ordinary retail trade.)

Whether the balance sheet(s) and profit and loss account(s) are in agreement with the accounting records;

Whether we have obtained all the information and explanations which we think necessary for the purposes of our audit.

In accordance with normal professional practice, our audit will be planned primarily to enable us to express our opinion. It should not be relied upon to disclose defalcations or other irregularities, but their disclosure, if they exist, may well result from the audit tests we undertake.

The work we shall do to enable us to form our opinion will include:

(*a*) keeping under review the system of bookkeeping, accounting and internal control;

(*b*) making such tests and enquiries as we consider necessary for the purposes of our audit. These tests will *inter alia* include those of the day-to-day operations and the verification of assets and liabilities (including attendance to observe your stocktaking procedures), but their precise nature and extent will vary according to our assessment of the company's/companies' system of internal control.

It is our normal practice to bring to the attention of the directors any material weaknesses in, or observations on, the company's accounting and internal control system which emerge in the course of our work referred to in the previous paragraph. You will appreciate, however, that the establishment and maintenance of appropriate accounting records and an adequate system of internal control remains the responsibility of the directors.

Accounting

You require us to assist with certain accounting services, namely:

(*a*) to prepare final accounts for approval by the Board from draft accounts prepared by your staff;
(*b*) to prepare consolidated accounts for approval by the Board;
(c) to type and print the accounts and directors' report.

(To be amended to suit actual arrangements with client)
You also require us to assist you with certain accounting services. You have agreed that your staff will be responsible for the preparation of the accounts up to the trial balance and management accounts stage but that we shall then prepare the final accounts for your approval.

OR

(To be used for clients where no accounting (or taxation) services are required)
You do not require us to provide any accounting (or taxation) services. However, by arrangement, we shall be pleased to give advice and provide such services on request.

Taxation

You require us to assist you with the following taxation services:

(*a*) to compute the provisions for taxation to be included in the accounts;
(*b*) to prepare the company's/companies' tax computations and to submit them to and agree them with the Inland Revenue.

Your staff will deal with all matters required by statute to be completed by officials of the company/companies, including returns for the purposes of VAT and PAYE and the completion of forms P11D and CT61, but we shall be pleased to advise on any of these, or other taxation matters if so requested.

Other services (as appropriate)

We shall be pleased to provide, if requested, ancillary services such as:

(*a*) Reports on profits and wages for the purposes of your consequential loss insurance.

(*b*) Accountants reports in support of (for example) grant claims.
(*c*) Assistance with secretarial services.
(*d*) Management accounting services including reviews of the company's/companies' bookkeeping, costing and budgetary control systems.
(*e*) Investigations and reports for special purposes.

Fees

Our fees are based upon the degree of responsibility and skill involved and the time necessarily occupied on the work. Unless otherwise agreed, fees will be charged separately for each class of work mentioned above.

(Here outline method of billing appropriate to the circumstances)
It is our normal practice to render interim accounts of charges and to receive payment on account as work progresses. In respect of audit work, we propose to bill you following the completion of our systems-review/interim-audit. For taxation work, we propose to bill you half-yearly.

We shall be grateful if you will kindly acknowledge receipt of this letter. If the contents are not in accordance with your understanding of our agreement, we shall be pleased to receive your further observations and to give you any further information you require.

May we conclude by saying that although our function as auditors is laid down by statute, we believe that an audit should also be of service to clients, from which they benefit. (We believe this to be the position with your company/companies and we hope that this will continue in future.)

Yours faithfully . . .

It is appreciated that with an existing client it may not be easy to submit such a letter without prior discussion, but advantage should be taken of any change in the situation which would facilitate its introduction, and certainly additional services requested by the client should be suitably recorded as they arise.

Once a letter of engagement has been initiated, it should then be examined regularly to ensure that it always reflects the current terms of engagement, clearly and fully setting out the auditors' role and thereby eliminating the risk of misunderstandings with clients. The relationships of a practicing accountant with his client are rarely static and it is therefore an essential first step of planning an audit to review the terms of the engagement letter to ensure that they are still appropriate.

Client Timetables

Whilst the engagement letter may formalize the auditors' responsibilities to the client, in practice problems will continue to recur regarding the responsibility for specific tasks associated with the preparation of audited accounts. Many of these may be clarified by the initiation of a regular planning meeting with the client before starting each year's audit, to deal with such matters as a discussion of the client's current business situation, and any points outstanding from the previous audit, such as a review of accounting systems developments following the previous year's management letter (see below). The opportunity should also be taken to discuss detailed arrangements for the audit visits and any specific audit points likely to cause problems.

An important preparation for such a meeting is to ensure that all specific points requiring attention will be discussed and, rather than relying on general discussion to bring these out, the auditor would be well advised to undertake the necessary preparatory work himself and produce an appropriate agenda for the meeting.

The matters likely to be covered would include the following.

Agenda for Audit Planning Meeting

1. Consideration of current trading circumstances and business developments since the previous financial statements.
2. Consideration of any problems arising during the previous audit and any recommendations to management made following previous audit.
3. General review of principal accounting systems, state of internal control, and any known areas of difficulty.
4. Consideration of accounting policies generally, and specifically in relation to Statements of Standard Accounting Practice.
5. Consideration of timetable for completion and audit of the financial statements.
6. Agreement of dates for the detailed review and testing of internal controls and the audit of transactions for the year.
7. Agreement of detailed timings for:

(*a*) Physical stocktakings;

(*b*) Circularization of debtors and creditors for verification purposes;

(*c*) Agreement of intra-group balances;

(*d*) Letters of authority to be sent by the client regarding information required from third parties;

(*e*) Inspection of documents (e.g. title deeds, share certificates), statutory books and minutes;

(*f*) Internal certificates to be obtained by the client and made available to the auditors (e.g. cash floats, employee loans);

(*g*) Certificates to be obtained from third parties (e.g. stocks in hands of third parties);

(*h*) Certificates to be obtained from the client (e.g. directors' emoluments);

(*i*) Valuations of specific assets (e.g. properties, unquoted investments), including availability of required additional information.

Such a meeting also provides an opportunity to agree the nature and extent of the audit schedules which will be required and which of them will be prepared by the client rather than the auditors. In that many of the problems of audit planning relate specifically to timing, discussion of a programme of audit schedules provides an opportunity for auditors to influence client work timetables and thereby improve the allocation of audit staff. It should also serve to reduce the overall time spent on the preparation and audit of the accounts by focusing attention on the general extent of tasks to be done, thus enabling these tasks to be marshalled better. Whilst it is recognized that the extent of formalized planning required for the small assignment will be less elaborate than that for the larger one, nevertheless every well-run audit entails some planning.

Set out below is a specimen timetable for the completion of the preparation and audit of a company's accounts; such a timetable should be discussed with the client before starting the audit and then kept under review throughout the audit with all deviations being noted and explained as they occur:

Specimen timetable for the preparation and audit of the company's accounts

Client	Schedule...........	*Date due*	*Date received* (and any comments)
Job timetable	Prepared by .... Date........		
	Reviewed by .... Date........		
Accounting date			
General			
1 (*a*) Year-end trial balance, before taxation and other adjustments to be available.			
(*b*) Company to notify the auditors in writing of any appropriations to reserve or any proposed dividends.			
(*c*) Adjustments to trial balance, to include tax provisions, and extension to final trial balance to be complete.			
(*d*) First draft of company's accounts to be available.			

Client	Schedule...........		*Date due*	*Date received* (and any comments)
Job timetable	Prepared by	Date........		
	Reviewed by	Date........		
Accounting date				
(*e*) Company to supply the auditors with a draft of the proposed directors' report. (*f*) Auditors to notify clearance of accounts, or any changes. (*g*) Final copies of accounts and the auditors' report to be available.				
Taxation **2** Company/auditors to compute the tax charge on current profits.				
Creditors and accrued expenses **3** (*a*) Bought ledger to be closed. (*b*) Balances at year-end to be proved with control account and scheduled for the auditors. (*c*) Detailed schedules of goods received but not invoiced and accrued expenses to be prepared by the company and made available to auditors. (*d*) Sales-ledger credit balances to be extracted and listed, together with explanations. (*e*) Balances due to other group companies to be agreed at the year-end and made available to auditors to enable direct confirmation with companies concerned.				
Capital commitments and contingent liabilities **4** (*a*) Company to prepare schedules of outstanding capital commitments and other capital sanctions at the end of the year and deliver this to auditors. (*b*) Company to instruct its solicitors to confirm direct to the auditors any outstanding claims and other litigious matters of which they are aware and in which the company is, or may become, involved.				
Fixed assets **5** (*a*) Company to provide schedules of fixed assets, additions and deletions during the year, together with relevant dates.				

Client .... Schedule...........	Date due	Date received (and any comments)
Job timetable — Prepared by .... Date........ ; Reviewed by .... Date........ ; Accounting date		
(*b*) Company to provide summary of fixed assets and depreciation, including movements during year, supported by detailed schedules showing depreciation calculations.		
Stock and work-in-progress **6** (*a*) Company to let auditors have a copy of detailed instructions for the counts. (*b*) Reconciliations between stock records and financial records to be completed and summary handed to auditors. (*c*) Company to review for obsolete and slow-moving items; and a copy of report to management thereon, together with any authorization for disposal or other write-off to be handed to auditors.		
Debtors and prepayments **7** (*a*) Sales-ledger balances at year-end to be proved with control accounts and made available to auditors. (*b*) Schedule of bills receivable at year-end to be made available to auditors. (*c*) Schedule of miscellaneous sundry accounts receivable to be made available to auditors. (*d*) Schedule of debit balances on bought ledger, together with explanation of each item, to be made available to auditors. (*e*) Provision for bad debts to be reviewed at year-end in light of latest information and statement setting out provision and how derived to be made available to auditors. (*f*) Balances due from other group companies to be agreed at the year-end and made available to auditors to enable direct confirmation with companies concerned.		
Bank balances and cash **8** (*a*) Cash book to be closed promptly at close of business.		

Client .... Schedule	*Date due*	*Date received* (and any comments)
Job timetable Prepared by .... Date........		
Reviewed by .... Date........		
Accounting date		
(*b*) Bank reconciliations to be prepared and made available to the auditors.		
Profit and loss account schedules **9** (*a*) Auditors to inform the company what profit and loss account schedules they need. (*b*) Agreement on the responsibility for the preparation of these schedules to be reached before the year-end. (*c*) Company to provide such schedules as agreed.		
Directors' emoluments **10** Company to prepare a schedule setting out the directors' emoluments in detail for the year and make this available to auditors.		
Letter of representation **11** Letter confirming amounts appearing in the accounts (see Chapter 9) to be obtained from the directors at the conclusion of the audit: (*a*) auditors to provide suitable draft for consideration. (*b*) final letter to be completed, signed by the managing director and the chief accountant, and returned to auditors.		

Audit Timetables and Budgets

If an audit is to be controlled in an efficient and business-like way, then, besides persuading clients to plan their work, the auditors too must pay sufficient advance attention to the preparation of their plans.

As a minimum, these plans should document the following points:

(*a*) the overall audit timetable, setting out the dates agreed with the client for the commencement and completion of the work;

(*b*) in general terms, the audit tasks to be undertaken;

(*c*) an assessment of the skill required for each audit task and the level of staff most appropriate, together with arrangements for the supervision of staff and review of their work;

(*d*) an assessment of the time required to complete each audit task by such a member of staff;

(*e*) a summary of the staff required to complete the audit within the given timetable;

(*f*) the allocation of the appropriate members of staff with the requisite experience and special skills;

(*g*) an evaluation of the audit budget;

(*h*) arrangements for adequate briefing of audit staff regarding the company's affairs and the audit work they are to carry out.

The preparation of such a plan enables the early agreement of fees between the auditor and the client, always desirable from the points of view of both parties; and both for this reason and because one year's plan is widely used in the preparation of next year's, any significant variations between budgeted and actual performance should be analysed. Where such variations are due to poor performance by the client's staff, these should be reported to the client immediately. Where it is due to poor performance of the audit staff, then the appropriate training of the individuals should be initiated.

The timetable prepared for these purposes should also provide for phasing the audit over the year, as an alternative to carrying out the audit all at one time, thus helping to spread the workload, easing time pressures generally, and improving control over audit progress.

The opportunities for phasing an audit are likely to be threefold:

(*a*) Interim audit, generally covering the assessment and testing of internal control, together with detailed checking of transactions. In the case of a large client, such interim audit work may involve several similar visits during a year, or even a continuous attendance by audit staff.

(*b*) Advance year-end work to deal with the verification of certain balance sheet items prior to the end of the financial year. Suitable items, where the client's internal control is adequate, might include debtors, creditors and stocks.

(*c*) Final audit, largely confined to the audit of the accounts and concentrating on a review of the profit and loss account, together with verification of the balance sheet.

The main danger of audit phasing is likely to be that of insufficient link-up between staff involved in the various phases of such an audit. It is, of course, most important that any balance sheet implications of matters coming to light when checking transactions should be properly taken into account when planning the year-end work. For instance, the testing of sales credit notes during the interim audit may reveal some delay in their issue. This must put the auditors on notice to inquire into parallel circumstances at the year-end. To provide a basis for this follow-through, it is essential that sufficient conclusions are recorded at each stage of the audit, and it is important that their filing within the audit working papers be systematized, so as to ensure that due attention is later given to those conclusions.

Audit Files and Working Papers

The main purpose of preparing and maintaining audit working papers is to have on permanent record full details of the information obtained, the methods used, and the work carried out by the auditor. It is on the basis of the evidence provided by his working papers that he must make a decision on the form and content of his report to the proprietors on the financial statements under review, a decision which at some later date he may have to justify.

This main purpose may be subdivided into the following objectives of working papers:

(*a*) To ensure that the audit work is conducted methodically and systematically and to provide continuity where audit staff changes occur;

(*b*) To enable the accounts to be reviewed and evaluated independently by persons other than those who carried out the detailed audit work;

(*c*) To record all material aspects of the accounts and to disclose the audit tests applied and the information and explanations received in relation thereto.

Furthermore, each working paper schedule should indicate:

(*a*) the client to which it refers;
(*b*) its subject matter;
(*c*) the relevant accounting date;
(*d*) any important points of principle or matters of judgement to carry forward for further attention;
(*e*) by whom the working paper was prepared, and on what date;
(*f*) the disposal of points carried forward;
(*g*) by whom the working paper was reviewed, and on what date.

To enable their objectives to be achieved, it is advisable to adopt a standard index for working papers, facilitating reference and review, and care should be taken to ensure a chain of cross-referencing within the working papers, from trial balance to final accounts via lead summaries and supporting schedules.

In fact it is customary for the audit working papers to be split between two files, one containing those relating specifically to the year under review (the current working papers file) and one containing more permanent records likely to be required from year to year (the permanent audit file). It must not be overlooked, however, that the details on the permanent audit file will change as time goes by, and will require up-dating each year.

The contents of the permanent audit file will vary from client to client, but a suitable form of index to cover most cases would be as follows:

Permanent File Index

General

1. Brief description and history of business, copies of investigation reports, etc.
2. Addresses of Registered Office, other offices and factories, together with note of their size and functions and instructions to staff on how to get to each location.
3. Organization chart of directors, secretary, senior executives, accounting personnel, indicating name and telephone number of primary client contact (updated as necessary from year to year).
4. Copy of letter of engagement and any amendments or additions thereto limiting or increasing the scope of the work undertaken.
5. Copy of memorandum and articles of association, and amending resolutions.
6. Copies of important agreements, service contracts etc.

Group structure

1. Details of parent companies.
2. Details of subsidiary companies.
3. Details of fellow subsidiaries.
4. Details of associated companies.
5. Make-up of consolidation adjustments reflecting above relationships.

Accounting systems

1. Details of accounting policies.
2. List of books of account maintained.
3. Code of accounts.
4. Copy of client's accounting instructions.
5. Accounting systems documentation.
6. Assessment of internal controls.
7. Copies of management letters and notes on subsequent action taken by client.
8. Authorities and specimen signatures.

Share capital, reserves and long-term loans

1. Details of issued share capital.
2. Details of reserves.
3. Copies of loan stock and debenture trust deeds.

4. Details of mortgages and charges.
5. Details of share options.

Fixed assets

1. Details of freehold and leasehold premises.
2. Summary of other fixed assets.
3. Details of depreciation policies.
4. Details of leasing and hire-purchase agreements.
5. Copies of professional valuations.

Financial history

1. Tabulated balance sheets, sources and application of funds, and profit and loss accounts for recent years, noting significant features.

2. Tabulations of relevant financial ratios for recent years, with explanations of material fluctuations.

Miscellaneous

1. Banking arrangements and facilities.
2. Guarantees held and given.
3. Insurance cover: details of risks and extent of insurance.
4. Pension arrangements.

The current working papers files, on the other hand, should relate only to the accounts in respect of the period under review and should contain schedules supporting these accounts and a record of the audit work done. Variations between clients make a rigid system of filing such working papers undesirable in that the constraints so imposed may cause important information to be omitted simply because there was nowhere to file it. However, some degree of standardization is desirable to ensure a methodical approach, and the following is put forward as a comprehensive system of indexing allowing sufficient flexibility.

Current Working Paper File Index

A. General review notes and points forward, including copy of management letter, letter of representation and certificates of directors' emoluments.
B. Accounts.
C. Analytical review (including forecasts, budgets, etc.).
D. Trial balance, journal entries.
E. Minutes.
F. Post-balance-sheet events, contingencies and commitments.
G. Share capital and statutory books.
H. Reserves.
J. Taxation, including copy of previous year's computation.

K. Debentures, secured loans and unsecured loan stock.
L. Creditors and accrued expenses, including direct verifications.
M. Fixed assets and depreciation.
N. Investments (including subsidiary and associated companies).
P. Inter-company balances (group and associated companies).
Q. Stocks and work-in-progress, including physical stocktaking observation reports.
R. Debtors and prepayments, including direct verifications.
S. Bank and cash balances (and bank overdrafts), including direct verifications.
T. Consolidated accounts.
U. Profit and loss account details, including:

Detailed trading and profit and loss account.
Internal management accounts, including budget and prior-year comparatives.
Forecast (budget) for following year and supporting cash flow forecast.
Details of transaction tests executed.

Z. Other working papers, including sundry notes and minor queries disposed of.

It is essential that working papers contain adequate notes of verifications obtained, work done generally, and the conclusions ultimately derived, thus facilitating review of the audit without need for verbal clarification. The working papers must provide a record of all material aspects of the accounts and they must indicate the means by which constituent figures were derived and the reasons for any decisions taken at the time of the audit.

In this way, should questions arise in the future, the auditors will be in a position to show exactly what work was performed, what queries were raised, what explanations and information were received, and by whom these latter were given. The importance of this will be appreciated later, when the question of an auditor's liability is considered. It must be remembered that, should anything be amiss, it may emerge years after the work was performed, when perhaps those who were in charge are no longer available, so that, if proper records were not kept, auditors might find themselves in a position of considerable difficulty and danger.

To guard against this we would recommend the adoption of a formalized system for evidencing the control and supervision of an audit as it progresses. We set out below a suggested means of achieving this, by the use firstly of a 'file control schedule', and secondly of a 'file review checklist'. By these means the staff undertaking the detailed audit work will be subject to the discipline of reviewing the completeness of their own work, listing outstanding points for further consideration, before passing their working papers through for final review. In turn, that reviewer is provided with an 'aide memoire' of those major aspects of an audit which he should ensure have received adequate consideration.

The degree of day-to-day supervision required by the reporting partner in any particular audit will depend on the complexity of the assignment and the experience and proficiency of the audit staff. It follows that the details of a review will vary from one assignment to another. Nevertheless the final responsibility rests with the reporting partner and accordingly he may wish to adopt a form of audit completion checklist to ensure that all significant audit procedures have been followed.

FILE CONTROL SCHEDULE — Schedule No.

Client:

Accounting date: — *Date* — *Intls.*

Before passing for review, senior should indicate as follows:

— File indices amended to final form
— All audit schedules, working papers and audit programmes complete, including extent of work done and conclusions reached (except for points listed)
— All queries cleared (unless referred to reviewer)
— Audit notes for reviewer's attention listed
— Draft accounts cross-referenced to schedules
— Accounts agreed to trial balance and post-trial balance journal adjustments
— Companies accounts checklist completed
— Review for presentation and disclosure completed
— Analytical review of trading results completed
— All necessary third-party confirmations obtained
— Following certificates drafted:
(*a*) representation
(*b*) directors' emoluments
— Management letter drafted
— Time records completed, variances explained, fee/scale comparison prepared
— Permanent file reviewed and updated
— Points forward from last audit cleared
— Points forward to next audit listed

REVIEWED BY

FILE COMPLETION CHECKLIST Schedule No.

Client:

Accounting date:

	Tick as appropriate	
	Yes or N/A	Refer to note
Permanent file		
— Engagement letter appropriate to the current circumstances of the assignment		
— Specimen signatures updated. Notes made of changes in business organization, resources, etc.		
Current files — interim		
— Systems notes/flowcharts updated		
— Systems properly evaluated; significant strengths and weaknesses highlighted		
— Compliance/substantive tests tailored to evaluation; level of testing appropriate		
— Tests recorded in adequate detail as to work done, results, and conclusions drawn; signed off for completion and review		
— Adequate audit coverage of computer procedures		
Current files — final		
— File control schedule signed off; all matters included therein satisfactorily completed		
— Audit programme suitable; signed off for completion and review		
— Level of testing appropriate — related to conclusions drawn from interim work		
— Schedules and working papers initialled and dated; clear evidence of work done and conclusions drawn		
— Tax position reviewed		
— Adequate review of accounts of associates and subsidiaries; consolidation working papers reviewed		
— Trading, profit and loss account schedules adequate and not excessive		
— Analytical review completed; satisfactory explanation of trading result in terms of prior		

	Tick as appropriate	
	Yes or N/A	Refer to Note
year, budgets, management accounts, gross profit changes, etc.		
— Letter of representation appropriately worded		
— Management letter(s) constructive		
— Time records reviewed; adverse variances analysed; remedial action noted for next year		
Financial statements		
— Companies Accounts checklist completed		
— Reviewed for adequacy of disclosure, propriety of accounting policies, and fairness of presentation		
— Post-balance-sheet events reviewed; disclosed as necessary		
Financial position		
— Future financing requirements reviewed		
— Short-term borrowing repayments adequately covered		
— Working capital position adequate; bank overdraft facilities reviewed		
— Going-concern assumption appropriate		
Audit report		
— Audit report appropriate		
— The expression of any qualification is:		
(*a*) clear as to the nature and degree of our reservations		
(*b*) clear as to the effect on the financial statements		
(*c*) referred, where appropriate, for second opinion or review panel		
Completion		
— All notes and queries cleared; all outstanding audit matters satisfactorily concluded		
— Audit procedures properly followed; sufficient evidence on file to support audit opinion		
— Points forward for next year include notes on		
(*a*) any areas in which the efficiency or cost effectiveness of audit procedures might be improved		

	Tick as appropriate	
	Yes or N/A	Refer to Note
(*b*) any respects in which we can improve the planning and organization of this assignment — Any points of special interest or difficulty noted for further discussion.		

Signed off for completion

.... **Date** ....

Reporting to Shareholders: Statutory Points

In the interests of a thorough and efficient audit, it is imperative that the audit objectives are kept in view throughout and that auditors consciously weigh the relevance of each audit task to these objectives. It is for this reason that the end-product of an audit, the auditors' report to shareholders, is introduced so early in this book, before any consideration of audit procedures, so that it may be kept in view throughout.

The auditor's reporting duty is primarily governed by statute, but the general considerations set out in the Auditing Standards must also be considered.

Auditors are required to state expressly whether in their opinion the accounts on which they are reporting give a true and fair view and have been properly prepared in accordance with the provisions of the relevant Companies Acts. If they are unable to report affirmatively in the required respects they must say so.

Auditors are required also to form an opinion whether:

(*a*) proper accounting records have been kept by the company;

(*b*) proper returns adequate for their audit have been received from branches not visited by them;

(*c*) the accounts are in agreement with the accounting records and returns;

(*d*) in the case of a holding company submitting group accounts, that the group accounts have been properly prepared in accordance with the provisions of the Acts so as to give a true and fair view of the state of affairs and profit or loss of the company and its subsidiaries so far as concerns members of the company.

It is the auditors' duty to report on these matters only if, in their opinion, these requirements have not been complied with. The absence of any comment in their report is therefore equivalent to a positive statement by the auditors that they have investigated and satisfied themselves on all these matters. Likewise their report must state, if such is the case, the fact that they have not obtained all the information and explanations which, to the best of their knowledge and belief, were necessary for the purposes of their audit.

The auditors also have a specific duty to include in their report statements giving the particulars required under certain sections of the Acts if the accounts themselves fail to do so, i.e.

(*a*) Companies Act 1948:
Section 196 — Particulars of directors' remuneration
Section 197 — Particulars of loans to officers

(*b*) Companies Act 1967:
Section 6 — Particulars of directors' emoluments
Section 7 — Particulars of directors' emoluments, the right to receive which have been waived
Section 8 — Particulars of salaries of employees receiving more than £10 000 a year

(*c*) Companies Act 1980:
Sections 54–56 — Particulars of transactions involving directors.

Further, following the Companies Act 1976, the auditor needs to consider the extent of compliance with Section 12 thereof dealing with the maintenance of accounting records, a term adopted in place of 'books of accounts' to enable records to be kept in computerized form.

Prescribed accounting records to be kept are more closely defined by the 1976 Act. The records:

(*a*) must disclose with reasonable accuracy, at any time, the financial position of the company at that time, and
(*b*) must enable the directors to ensure that the company's financial statements give a true and fair view of the company's state of affairs and profit or loss;
and they must contain:

(*c*) entries from day to day of
(i) all sums of money received and expended by the company,
(ii) the matters in respect of which the receipt and expenditure takes place;
(*d*) a record of the assets and liabilities of the company;
(*e*) where the company's business involves dealing in goods,

(i) statements of stock held by the company at the end of each financial year of the company,
(ii) all statements of stocktakings from which (i) is derived,
(iii) statements of all goods sold and purchased showing the goods and the buyers in sufficient detail to enable the goods, buyers and sellers to be identified. This is not required in the case of goods sold by way of ordinary retail trade.

If the auditor is of the opinion that the accounting records have not been properly maintained, or that the accounts are not in accordance with those records, then he must qualify his report accordingly. In the absence of comment, the auditor is again assumed to be satisfied in this respect.

The Unqualified Report

The Audit Report Standard contained within the Auditing Standards sets out *inter alia* the following general considerations:

(*a*) The audit report should 'identify those to whom it is addressed and the financial statements to which it relates'.

(*b*) The auditor should refer expressly in his report to the following matters:

— 'Whether the financial statements have been audited in accordance with approved Auditing Standards.
— Whether in the auditor's opinion the financial statements give a true and fair view of the state of financial affairs, profit or loss and, where applicable, source and application of funds, and
— any matters prescribed by relevant legislation or other requirements.'

Further, where reporting on financial statements in which, in order to avoid giving a misleading view, there has been a material departure from a Statement of Standard Accounting Practice (SSAP), it is suggested that the auditor should refer to the departure in a separate paragraph in his report and state that he concurs with it. Such a reference in the audit report is regarded as an 'emphasis of matter', which does not constitute a qualification of the opinion.

The suggested wording of an unqualified report is shown below:

'*Auditors' report to the members of* ....

We have audited the financial statements on pages .... to .... in accordance with approved Auditing Standards and have carried out such procedures as we considered necessary.

In our opinion the Financial Statements (which have been prepared under the historical cost convention as modified by the revaluation of certain assets) give a true and fair view of the state of the company's financial affairs at 31 December 19........ and of its profit and source and application of funds for the year then ended and comply with the Companies Acts 1948 to 1981.'

Form of report

The form of report now proposed represents a change to a more positive style of reporting. The Standard requires the auditor to refer specifically to matters which, at the moment, are assumed to be satisfactory unless stated otherwise. In particular, the audit report includes a statement as to whether the audit has been carried out in accordance with approved Auditing Standards and whether the auditor has carried out such procedures as he considered necessary. However, no statement is required as to whether the financial statements have been prepared in accordance with generally accepted accounting policies, this continuing to be assumed by the use of the words 'true and fair view'.

The fact that the suggested form of report does not, however, form a part of the Auditing Standard itself leads us to infer a concern to retain a degree of flexibility in order to meet new circumstances as they arise and to allow for some freedom of expression, rather than to prescribe a precise form of words.

This proposed form of report can conveniently be considered in two separate parts: firstly, an explanation of the scope and nature of the audit and, secondly, an expression of opinion.

'Scope' paragraph

The 'scope' paragraph enables the audit report to identify clearly the financial statements to which it relates. This is best done by referring to page numbers on which those statements are set out. If, unusually, the auditor needs to refer to information presented on other pages (for example, in the directors' report), he should identify in his report the specific paragraphs to which he is referring. It is a basic principle of any report that it should explain the scope and nature of the examination on which it is based. Auditing Standards set out 'the basic principles and practice which auditors are expected to follow' (Auditing Standards, Explanatory Foreword, para. 3). Compliance with them gives the auditor a basis from which to express an opinion and it is informative for the reader to know that the examination has been performed in accordance with these Standards. However, the Standards do not prescribe the means by which they might be implemented. It is for the auditor to decide how best to apply the Standards in his particular context and thus he should further inform the reader that he 'carried out such procedures as he considered necessary'.

Comparative figures

The suggested report does not cover the question of the extent to which comparative figures are brought within the scope of the auditor's opinion. It may be that strictly the auditor's opinion extends to the comparative figures only if that fact is specifically stated in his report. However, it should be remarked that even where the scope of an opinion is not expressly stated to cover the comparative figures many readers are believed to assume that it does. Where the previous year's figures have not been audited, or where they have been audited by other auditors, or have been the subject of a qualified opinion, the auditor should consider whether it would be appropriate for these facts to be disclosed in the notes to the financial statements. There may be some circumstances in which the auditor may wish to draw attention to such matters in a separate paragraph of his report — possibly by way of an 'emphasis of matter'.

'Opinion' paragraph

In the 'opinion' paragraph the auditor is presently required to give an opinion as to whether the accounts give a true and fair view and as to whether they comply with the Companies Acts of 1948 to 1981. We would suggest to the reader that this requires that he consider whether the accounts have been prepared in accordance with acceptable accounting policies. These, however, are nowhere codified in a single source of reference. They may emanate from pronouncements of the accountancy bodies or they may become acceptable through common business usage. Moreover, the term might be said to embrace not only broad accounting principles but also the various conventions, rules and procedures which combine to define accepted accounting practice at any particular time.

Acceptable accounting policies

'Acceptable accounting policies' is therefore a phrase which is not capable of precise definition. Statements of standard accounting practice certainly provide the core but they are not comprehensive. It is quite likely that a business will have cause to adopt accounting policies in areas which are not presently covered by definitive standards but which nevertheless might have a material bearing on the determination of the result for the year and which would therefore require disclosure as accounting policies. This is not to say that the problem is a new one. Auditors have always had to form a view as to whether the adopted accounting policies are acceptable; but whether accounts are presented in conformity with acceptable accounting policies is clearly a matter of opinion, not of fact. In forming his opinion, the auditor must judge whether the chosen principles are (*a*) acceptable and (*b*) appropriate in the circumstances.

In determining the acceptability of a particular policy, the auditor should have regard *inter alia* to policies commonly adopted in particular industries or to policies for which there may be authoritative support. However 'acceptable', nevertheless it should be noted that an accounting policy can still be inappropriate to the particular circumstances of the business. A particular instance is the case where compliance with an SSAP would result in a misleading view. Whilst all significant accounting practices must, of course, be fully disclosed, and whilst acceptable accounting policies provide the framework for showing a true and fair view, nevertheless disclosure *per se* does not guarantee truth and fairness. What is appropriate in the circumstances is for the auditor to judge. In areas where it is acknowledged that alternatives exist, it is quite possible — and, it is suggested, quite acceptable — for the auditor to conclude that more than one accounting policy is appropriate in the particular circumstances; thus a 'fair' presentation might take a variety of forms.

Accounting conventions

This point is further illustrated by the choice between the accounting conventions under which financial statements may be drawn up. Accordingly the Explanatory Note to the Auditing Standard lays down that the auditor should refer to the particular convention used in preparing the financial statements, 'to avoid misunderstanding'. Such misunderstanding is most likely to arise where the financial statements include current-cost statements. In this case the auditor may find it necessary to specify in his report the particular convention adopted in order to make it quite clear that his opinion on the truth and fairness of the statements is given within the context — and limitations — of the cost convention adopted.

As to the question of auditor's reports on current-cost statements, much will depend on whether they are supplementary or part of composite primary accounts. In the former case it will be customary for the report to be presented as an additional paragraph to the report on the 'primary' statements. Here a suitable form of wording would include a term such as 'properly prepared'. In the latter case, however, it will be necessary for the report on the current-cost information to include an opinion on the overall truth and fairness of the statements.

Departures from SSAPs

A further matter touched upon by the Explanatory Note deals with the circumstances which may arise in which a departure from standard accounting practice is necessary in order to give a true and fair view. In these circumstances it is recommended that the auditor refer to the departure in a separate paragraph in his report and to state that he concurs with it.

However, three points should be noted. Firstly, such a reference does not constitute a qualification and the auditor should not quantify the effect of the departure. Secondly, the auditor should draw attention to it only if it has a material effect on the financial statements. Thirdly, the auditor must be satisfied that the alternative policy adopted is acceptable. Although not required to say so expressly, his acceptance of it is implicit in the unqualified opinion which follows the explanatory paragraph in his report.

Emphasis of matter

An 'acceptable' departure from an SSAP is one example of what may be described as an 'emphasis of matter'. Although this phrase may be new to the auditor's reporting terminology, it describes a practice which has been in use for some time, i.e. the need to emphasize a particular matter regarding the financial statements while nevertheless intending to express an unqualified opinion. There is a danger, however, that references to specific aspects of the accounts, although made for emphasis, will be misread as qualifications. The auditor must exercise great care, therefore, in the use of this reporting technique and the Explanatory Note to the Standard explains that it is only 'in rare circumstances' that 'the reader will obtain a better understanding of the financial statements if his attention is drawn to important matters'.

In considering such emphasis, the auditor must be mindful that his function is to report on the truth and fairness of the financial statements as presented by management. It is management's responsibility to prepare and present those financial statements and to ensure that the information which they disclose is adequate. If, in the auditor's view, the information disclosed is insufficient to give a true and fair view then he should qualify his opinion. It follows, therefore, that the auditor's only purpose in using emphasis can be to give greater prominence to important matters which are already contained in the financial statements. Where the auditor does decide to make use of such emphasis,

(*a*) it should be presented as a separate paragraph of the report; and

(*b*) the auditor should avoid the use of any phrases which 'link' his opinion to the matters emphasized: for example to open the opinion paragraph with the words 'with this explanation' effectively 'qualifies' the opinion.

The Explanatory Note suggests the introductory phrase 'we draw attention to . . .', but consideration is still needed as to the siting of the subsequent paragraph in the report. If the emphasis paragraph precedes the auditor's opinion, the auditor may consider that there is danger of such a reference being misconstrued as a qualification. It may be that this risk would be reduced if the opinion paragraph preceded the matters to be given emphasis.

Date of audit report

One last matter for further consideration in the context of the unqualified report is the date on which the audit report should be signed. Clearly this must be after the accounts have been formally approved by management; but it should also be as near as possible to the date on which the accounts are issued — not least because this minimizes the intervening period during which there might occur a significant post-balance-sheet event. As a general rule, it is suggested that the date of the auditor's report should be timed as closely as possible to the date on which he completes his field work (including final review procedures such as those relating to post-balance-sheet events), and it would be desirable for the timing of the completion of the audit and the formal Board approval and issue of the accounts to be so arranged as to be, as far as possible, coincidental.

Qualified Reports

If the auditor is not satisfied upon any points, or there is any information which, in his opinion, should be placed before the shareholders, he must qualify his report accordingly, and make any such matters clear therein.

It is the duty of the directors to prepare the accounts, and the auditor has no right himself to alter such accounts in any way. If dissatisfied upon any point, his duty is confined to dealing with the matter in his report, and in this way laying the facts before the shareholders. In the same way, if the system of bookkeeping is bad, the auditor cannot insist upon alterations; but if it is so bad that reliable accounts cannot be prepared, then, in such circumstances, he should report to this effect to the shareholders.

In those cases in which an auditor has decided that he must make reservations in his report, the choice of the wording of the qualification is a matter of vital importance. It is regarded by boards of directors as being a serious matter to be compelled to issue accounts with a qualified audit report. The strongest pressure probably will be directed towards persuading the auditor to give an unqualified report, an invariable argument being that a qualified report will have a serious effect upon the affairs of the company, and this may sometimes be the case. The auditor will be fully aware of this fact, but the whole purpose of his appointment is that he shall report to the shareholders in clear terms if he is not satisfied that the accounts exhibit a true and fair view of the state of the financial affairs and profit or loss of a company.

If an auditor has definitely decided that he must qualify his report, the directors may endeavour to persuade him to adopt wording which will soften the qualification. This course is fraught with great danger as it is exactly in these circumstances that it is imperative that the auditor should make the position, as he sees it, absolutely clear to the shareholders. In fact, that is the whole purpose of his office.

The Companies Acts lay down no specific requirements as to the manner in which auditors should report when they judge it necessary. The broad principle must be that a qualifying statement should be direct and informative. It should be so phrased as to leave the reader in no doubt as to its meaning on the view formed by the auditor on the implications for the accounts. It should:

(*a*) be as concise as is consistent with clarity;
(*b*) be specific as to the items and facts and as far as possible the amounts involved;
(*c*) within the limits of the information available to the auditor, make clear its effects on the accounts; and
(*d*) express the auditor's opinion without possibility of misinterpretation.

The object should be to give in clear and unequivocal terms such information as will, in the auditor's opinion, provide the information required by the Act and ensure that the accounts will then present a true and fair view.

The nature of the circumstances giving rise to a qualification of opinion will generally fall into one of two main categories described by the Auditing Standard dealing with Qualifications in Audit Reports:

Uncertainty — 'Where there is an uncertainty which prevents the auditor from forming an opinion on the matter.' (Examples would include major litigation, the long-term outcome of contracts or doubts about the ability of the enterprise to continue as a going concern.)
Disagreement — 'Where the auditor is able to form an opinion on a matter but this conflicts with the view given by the financial statement.' (Examples would include departures from acceptable accounting practices, disagreement as to facts or amounts included in the financial statements, disagreement as to the manner or extent of disclosure of facts or amounts, or failure to comply with relevant legislation.)

The Auditing Standards recommend the forms of qualification which should be used in different circumstances. These are shown on p. 50.

Nature of circumstances	Material but not fundamental	Fundamental
Uncertainty	'Subject to' opinion	Disclaimer of opinion
Disagreement	'Except' opinion	Adverse opinion

These are elaborated:

(*a*) In a 'disclaimer of opinion' the auditor states that he is unable to form an opinion as to whether the financial statements give a true and fair view;

(*b*) In an 'adverse opinion' he states that in his opinion the financial statements do not give a true and fair view;

(*c*) In a 'subject to' opinion the auditor effectively disclaims an opinion on a particular matter which is not considered fundamental;

(*d*) In an 'except' opinion the auditor expresses an adverse opinion on a particular matter which is not considered fundamental.

Purpose of the Standard

The purpose of the Standard is to promote a better understanding of qualified audit reports by the consistent usage, wherever possible, of common terminology. A frequent criticism of qualified reports is that they leave the reader in doubt as to their real meaning. The auditor may be clear as to his intent, and may take great care over the drafting of his report, yet the substance of what he is saying is misunderstood. In the Auditing Practices Committee's words: 'the principles set out in the Standard are intended to make qualified audit reports more understandable by developing a consistent use of language . . .'.

In order to illustrate the need for such a standard, consider the following example which is not untypical of the sort of qualified report which has been published with some regularity:

> 'The financial statements set out on pages . . . to . . . have been prepared on the basis of the company as a going concern which assumes the continued support of the company's bankers.
>
> 'In our opinion these financial statements give a true and fair view . . .'

'What', the reader may well ask, 'am I supposed to make of that? Is the company about to "crash"? Or is the auditor telling me no more than what I know to be a fact of commercial life, that many companies are dependent in some degree on bank finance? He has not qualified his opinion. Maybe I should not worry. But why has he made the reference at all? He must have thought the matter to be important. I am not sure what he is trying to tell me.'

To the informed reader the auditor is clearly expressing some uncertainty. Yet he has done no more than arouse the reader's enquiry. He has pointed to a problem, but has given the reader no help in assessing the extent of that problem. The statement appears to be by way of explanation, but hints at something more. If there is real uncertainty as to whether the going-concern concept is appropriate, the auditor should express his opinion subject to that uncertainty. Preferably, he should give the reader some means of assessing the extent of the uncertainty. It is this sort of ambiguity which the Standard seeks to reduce. It focuses on what are thought to be the two prime reasons why qualified audit reports are often misunderstood: firstly, because of a failure to distinguish clearly between, on the one hand, matters to which the auditor is merely drawing attention and, on the other, matters about which he has reservations; and, secondly, because the inconsistent use of basic terminology in audit qualifications makes it difficult for the reader to assess the seriousness of the reservation which the auditor is expressing.

Where there is a departure from the short form of unqualified audit report merely in order to draw attention to a particular matter, the opinion in the report will still be unqualified. 'Emphasis of matter' has already been discussed. Otherwise the approach taken is to provide the basic framework within which an auditor might find the general means of expression appropriate to the particular circumstances. Accordingly we deal, in turn, with the distinctions drawn in the table above, i.e. the question of materiality, circumstances of uncertainty and disagreement, and alternative forms of qualification.

Materiality

It remains an over-riding principle of reporting that a qualification is only required where the matters at issue are material. The interpretation of 'materiality' is dealt with in more detail in chapter 5. However, the auditor should report on *all* material matters about which he has reservations: qualifying on what, in his view, is the most important single item does not relieve the auditor of his duty to qualify on other — possibly unrelated — items of significance.

Given that the matters in question are material, the auditor must then exercise his judgement in a second respect, i.e. as to whether the items in doubt or disagreement are so fundamental as to affect the presentation of the true and fair view. What is 'fundamental' will also be a matter for judgement. A general rule suggested is that a matter is likely to be fundamental if the effect, or potential effect, is such 'as to undermine the view given by the financial statements taken as a whole'. Where the matter is not thought to be fundamental — that is, where the element of uncertainty or disagreement is limited — the auditor should be able to report that in his opinion, subject to the specific item of uncertainty or except for the specific item in disagreement, the financial statements present a true and fair view. However, where the matter is judged to be fundamental, the auditor should either disclaim any opinion on the accounts or issue an adverse opinion.

Circumstances of uncertainty

The circumstances which give rise to uncertainties may be described as those where management makes an estimation which, although not unreasonable in the circumstances, is not susceptible to objective assessment by the auditor. It should be emphasized, nevertheless, that the auditor has a duty to form a view wherever possible and the fact that an item is surrounded by an element of uncertainty should not be used by the auditor as a means of avoiding this responsibility. This applies particularly where the uncertainty relates to the value at which an item is stated. Thus: 'Inherent uncertainties will not normally include instances where the auditor is able to obtain adequate evidence to support estimates and use his experience to reach an opinion as to their reasonableness, for example as regards collectability of debts or realizability of stock'.

Circumstances giving rise to uncertainties are also described as including those in which a limitation is placed on the scope of the audit, which is discussed further below.

Circumstances of disagreement

Circumstances which might give rise to a difference of opinion between the auditor and those who have prepared the accounts are described as including (*a*) disagreement as to the facts or amounts disclosed in financial statements, or as to the manner or extent of disclosure, and (*b*) departures from acceptable accounting practices, or failure to comply with statutory or other requirements.

Departures from SSAPs

The difficulty associated with defining 'acceptable accounting policies' has already been referred to. However, where the accounting practice in question is the subject of an SSAP, the auditor's duty is quite clear: all significant departures from SSAPs should be referred to in the auditor's report. If the auditor does not agree with the departure, he should qualify his opinion. If the auditor does agree with the departure, he should not qualify his opinion but should draw attention to the departure by way of an 'emphasis of matter'. Where the practice in question is not the subject of an SSAP the auditor must exercise his judgement whether the adopted policy is (*a*) acceptable, (*b*) appropriate to the circumstances, and (*c*) adequately disclosed and explained in the financial statements.

As to the general matter of disclosure, the Companies Acts lay down certain minimum requirements. However, what further information is required in any one case in order to achieve a true and fair presentation of the facts will be a matter of judgement in the particular circumstances.

Disclaimer of opinion

Section 14 of the Companies Act 1967 requires an opinion one way or the other from the auditor and does not appear to envisage circumstances in which the auditor is unable to form an opinion. Nevertheless it has always been acknowledged that in extreme circumstances this is a possibility. The form of disclaimer now proposed (' . . . we are unable to form an opinion . . .') therefore is not new. However, it is now envisaged that the circumstances in which a disclaimer of opinion will be appropriate will be limited to those in which both (*a*) uncertainties exist and (*b*) the uncertainties are so pervasive as to affect the financial statements as a whole.

In the Auditing Guidelines on Audit Report one of the Examples illustrates a suitable form of report in circumstances where the uncertainty surrounding an item in the financial statements is of such significance as to prevent the auditors from giving any opinion. The 'opinion' paragraph, which follows a paragraph of explanation, reads as follows:

> 'Because of the significance of this matter, we are unable to form an opinion whether the financial statements give a true and fair view.'

However, a disclaimer of opinion deprives the reader of any assurance whatsoever and should therefore be regarded only as 'a measure of last resort'. In many cases the uncertainties which exist can be limited to specific items on which the reader can be given sufficient information to enable him to make a reasonable assessment of what the effect of the uncertainties might be. In these cases, full disclosure should enable the auditor to make an appropriate reference in his report and to issue a 'subject to' opinion, without resorting to a disclaimer.

Adverse opinion

The alternative adverse opinion should also be given only in extreme circumstances. It is appropriate only where (*a*) there is disagreement and (*b*) the area of disagreement is so extensive and/or material that, in the auditor's opinion, the financial statements ' . . . do not give a true and fair view'.

Qualified opinion

A qualified opinion is indicated by the use of the phrase 'except for' or 'subject to'. 'Except for' is used where there is a difference of opinion regarding a particular accounting principle or a matter of disclosure. 'Subject to' is used where there are uncertainties regarding specific items in the financial statements. In either case the matters giving rise to qualification will not be so fundamental as to require either a disclaimer or an adverse opinion.

Limitations in scope

The circumstances in which 'uncertainties' can arise also includes any limitation on the scope of the auditor's examination which he has not been able to circumvent by alternative procedures. In this case, the examination cannot be said to have been carried out in accordance with approved Auditing Standards. Qualifications of this nature can arise *inter alia* because of deficiencies in the system of internal control. This can present a major problem for the auditor of the small proprietary company where controls may be absent or unreliable. It is generally acknowledged that 'many of the controls which would be relevant to the large enterprise are not practical, appropriate or necessary in the small enterprise'. In these circumstances, although the auditor may rely on the close involvement of management, he should recognize that management can override controls. As a result, the auditor may have to carry out extensive substantive testing and review of margins to compensate for inadequate controls. However, he will still have to consider carefully whether he is able to obtain adequate assurance that the accounting records do reflect all the transactions of the enterprise. The Explanatory Note to the Auditing Standard dealing with Qualifications in Audit Reports offers the following guidance:

> 'In many situations it may be possible to reach a conclusion that will support an unqualified opinion. . . There will be other situations where the evidence available to the auditor is insufficient to give him the confidence necessary for him to express an unqualified opinion but this uncertainty is not so great as to justify a total disclaimer of opinion. In such situations the most helpful form of report may be one which indicates the need to accept the assurances of management as to the completeness or accuracy of the accounting records. Such a report should contain a "subject to . . ." opinion.'

Reporting to Management: the 'Management Letter'

An important secondary audit objective to bear in mind throughout is the provision of constructive assistance to management in the form of systems recommendations and advice on matters of financial management.

It is now generally accepted practice for auditors to report to management on matters coming to their attention during the course of the audit. The primary purpose of such reports is to bring to management's attention weaknesses in internal control and other unsatisfactory accounting procedures and practices, and to suggest remedial action. The reports place on record the more important matters discussed between the auditors and management, thus clarifying the responsibility of management for any event stemming from failure to rectify the matter. Weaknesses reported may not be so serious as to prevent an unqualified audit report, but they will have raised an extension of the level of audit testing in the areas affected and their correction would therefore both reduce the risk of errors and irregularities and save time and cost in future.

In general such reports should be sent at least once a year, but this may be insufficient where interim audit work is undertaken during the year, in which case the auditor has a responsibility to draw control weaknesses to the attention of management at the earliest opportunity.

All matters should be discussed with management at the appropriate level before writing the report, and the final written report should only deal with the more important matters. The tone of the report should always be constructive and helpful and care should be taken to avoid an irritable catalogue of the company's shortcomings. It should be made clear that the comments did not result from any special survey but that they came to the auditors' attention during the course of normal audit procedures and therefore cannot be relied upon to deal exhaustively with all weaknesses and errors in the accounting procedures and records.

In the case of the smaller company, many of the matters dealt with will often relate to internal control, to the difficulties of adequately segregating staff duties, and to recommendations for alternative means of providing a satisfactory degree of control. If, in the auditor's opinion, such internal control weaknesses can only be corrected by increasing staff numbers, this should still be reported. Thereafter it will be a matter for management judgement and decision whether the costs of improving internal control would be likely to exceed the benefits to be derived. However, before recommending the employment of further staff in such a situation it is important not to overlook the alternative controls which may often exist, or be capable of implementation, through the close supervision of trusted senior management.

The report should deal with, but not necessarily be limited to, the following matters, if material:

(*a*) weaknesses in the system of internal control, together with recommendations for their improvement;
(*b*) any breakdowns in systems occurring during the year, together with a summary of the nature and amounts of material errors discovered;
(*c*) additional audit time involved as a result of systems weaknesses and any failure of the client to adhere to timetables previously agreed;
(*d*) points arising on accounting practices which the auditors consider require modification or further consideration by management;
(*e*) suggestions generally to improve the financial and accounting efficiency of the client's operation.

It is suggested that each main topic be clearly set out in the management letter and that the comments under each heading should deal separately with:

(*a*) the facts being reported;
(*b*) the effect of what is reported;

(*c*) the auditor's recommendation for improvement;
(*d*) the action proposed by management during discussion.

The report may also refer to previous reports, and should comment on any failure to implement previous recommendations. To avoid the need for this, it is advisable to follow-up reports to management if no satisfactory written response is received, by arranging a meeting to discuss points arising, for the level of such response is frequently a function of the auditor's own reporting and his inability to make the points he considers of importance seem so to management.

3 Recording systems

Introduction to Systems Audits

It has already been explained that the basic approach of modern auditing procedures is founded upon 'systems auditing' designed to achieve its audit objectives by the examination, evaluation and testing of the client's accounting procedures so that the auditor can assess the degree to which he considers it safe to rely on the accuracy of the figures produced to him. The adoption of this approach to the audit of a company's accounts entails the following stages, as set out in the Auditor's Operational Standard (the work having been planned, controlled and recorded, perhaps along the lines we suggested in the last chapter):

(*a*) ascertaining and recording the accounting control systems, and proving by means of a small sample of tests that these systems do appear to operate as described;
(*b*) where it is intended to place any reliance on internal control, evaluating the efficiency of that internal control by means of identifying points of apparent strength and weakness within the accounting systems described;
(*c*) constructing and executing a programme of audit work in the light of this evaluation, designed to obtain audit evidence by assessing the level of confidence which can be placed in the accounting data produced by the systems. The extent of the work set out in such an audit programme needs to be reconsidered in the light of any reassessment of the initial systems evaluation which may be necessitated as a result of the findings arising from this detailed testing;
(*d*) obtaining further audit evidence by verifying the final balance sheet and reviewing the financial statements as a whole.

Each of these stages will be considered in more detail in this and subsequent chapters.

Ascertainment and Recording of Systems Information

Wherever companies have sufficient staff to allow any segregation of their duties, they should be encouraged to document their control systems themselves, for the lack of such documentation is in itself a weakness which can lead to confusion amongst their staff and may well lead to the informal adoption of short cuts which, in fact, albeit inadvertently, by-pass the prescribed control points. However, clients are not always willing or able to do this themselves; and as systems audits are dependent upon examination of the accounting systems in operation, it is essential in these circumstances that the auditor document these systems himself so as to ensure that his working papers contain sufficient information to make a proper evaluation as to their adequacy as a basis for the preparation of accounts. To a considerable extent the auditor is dependent on the records produced within the accounting system, and if the auditor has to use the accounting system to assist him to form an opinion, then it follows that he must derive sufficient confidence in it for this purpose, and therefore he must assess its adequacy. Furthermore, the auditor has a responsibility to make such an assessment in his consideration of his client's compliance with the requirements of the Companies Act 1976 concerning the adequacy of accounting records.

Where the client's own documentation is inadequate for audit purposes then the relevant information must be obtained verbally by the auditor from the appropriate departmental head or other senior officials. Before commencing his inquiries the auditor must thoroughly familiarize himself with the client's business, so that he may ask the right questions and ensure that the information and explanations he is given are comprehensive of all relevant aspects. When the information given has been recorded, the auditor must then make a practical examination of it by means of a small sample of 'walk through' tests. That is to say, three or four transactions of each type should be traced through each stage of the system so as to ensure that the auditor appears to have been given accurate information about what the system actually is, and that he has correctly understood and documented this information.

Once the accounting systems have been recorded, and until there has been a major change in them, they will need only to be corroborated at subsequent audits by again taking a small sample of transactions and once more checking them through the systems, or otherwise observing the system in operation.

There are for practical purposes three main methods of documenting systems information, which will be dealt with in turn:

(*a*) systems notes;
(*b*) descriptive questionnaires;
(*c*) flow charts.

Systems Notes

Systems notes involve the compilation of a narrative description of accounting routines, in itself a simple operation. However, a general criticism of such systems notes as are frequently found on audit files is that they are badly compiled, neither fully detailed nor adequately cross-referenced, with the result that they are difficult to understand subsequently and it becomes impossible to identify the controls within the systems from the notes — the very purpose for which they were compiled. In addition, it is not always easy to detect if any part of the system has been omitted.

A disciplined approach to writing systems notes does, to some extent, enable these weaknesses to be overcome and the remedy is in the adoption of a formalized method of recording, with standardized layout and, perhaps, symbols. For instance:

(*a*) The systems should be clearly identified at the head of the page, with a reference number and description, and the date at which operative.

(*b*) Each operation should be sequentially listed, and numbered for purposes of subsequent identification and cross-referencing.

(*c*) Each operation should also be categorized, by use of a standard symbol, to indicate its type, for instance, as between an operation, a check and a filing process.

Thus comprehensive narration can be ensured in a format which facilitates identification of controls.

Alternatively a form may be designed along the following lines:

(*a*) Descriptions of operations should be listed down the centre of the form.

(*b*) To the left of the operation description, input documents should be identified, together with their source, volume and frequency.

(*c*) To the right, output documents should be similarly specified.

(*d*) In each case, all documents should be cross-referenced.

(*e*) Each system description should be supported by a note of the personnel concerned with its operation and details of the records retained within the relevant department, their volume, filing sequence, etc.

In this case the control points are less readily identifiable, but the inter-relationship and inter-dependence of different systems is better highlighted.

Descriptive Questionnaires

Questionnaires used for audit purposes are generally referred to as ICQ (Internal Control Questionnaires), and their purpose is to assist in the evaluation of the various types of internal checks operating within a company. This function of evaluation will be returned to in the next chapter, but in dealing with recording systems it should be borne in mind that an ICQ can be drafted in such a way as to call for descriptive answers to questions which serve to describe the systems in operation. The preparation of such an ICQ involves the following steps:

(*a*) Breaking down each section of the system into appropriate sections.
(*b*) Phrasing questions calling for detailed description of the systems.
(*c*) Additionally posing questions to assist in the identification of the various controls.

Examples of questions dealing with goods-received procedures for a purchase system, which would be suitable for inclusion in a descriptive questionnaire, are as follows:

(*a*) Is the receipt of goods at all locations recorded?
(*b*) By what means is such receipt recorded?
(*c*) Who prepares receiving records?
(*d*) How many copies are there of receiving records and to whom are these passed?
(*e*) Are receiving records prenumbered?
(*f*) What system is there for ensuring that all goods received have been properly ordered?
(*g*) How are receiving records controlled to ensure that invoices are obtained for all goods received?
(*h*) Are goods received examined for quantity and quality?
(*i*) What evidence is there for such examination?

Although such an ICQ is comprehensive, its very bulk can inhibit the exercise of initiative by its user and, by itself, it does not evaluate the significance of weaknesses.

Flow Charts

Flow charts probably represent the most satisfactory method of recording important accounting systems, consistent with a disciplined approach to systems audits. A flow chart is a method of representing systems graphically by showing:

(*a*) A record of documents in existence and their movements.
(*b*) A record of the operations performed and their sequence.
(*c*) A record of check procedures built into internal control systems, at which stage these are performed, and by whom.
(*d*) How staff duties are segregated.
(*e*) How accounting procedures relate to other facets of the business.

The symbols set out on page 63 are suggested as suitable for flowcharting for audit purposes (other than computer systems where certain other symbols have become accepted as standards), and a series of specimen flowcharts for a simple purchasing system is shown to illustrate the above points (pp. 64–71).

The disciplines of this technique ensure that the flowchart will highlight strengths and weaknesses in internal control in a way which systems notes or descriptive questionnaires rarely can. Thus the flowchart, besides fulfilling its primary purpose of providing a record of an accounting system, will assist the auditor in evaluating internal control.

In preparing flowcharts, the following points should be borne in mind:

(*a*) The charts are to feature a movement of documents and information, in space and time:

Horizontal lines indicate movement in space.

Vertical lines indicate movement in time.

(*b*) Each chart should be headed with the name of the client, the general desciption of the operation, the date and the initials of the person who has prepared the chart.

(*c*) The chart should start in the top left of the paper and finish in the bottom right.

(*d*) A column on the left-hand side of the paper should provide a brief narrative explanation of each operation and the consecutive operation number. The rest of the chart should be divided according to the departments/persons involved.

(*e*) The lines should be:

(i) ———— solid: to show the flow of a document.

(ii) – – – – broken: to indicate a flow of information, which should be horizontal.

It is essential to differentiate between these two flows. Thus information flows include:

— posting of a ledger;
— checking of one document with another, or preparation of one document from information contained in another.

(*f*) The flowcharts should not indicate movements of goods.

(*g*) As an operation is rarely carried out on a document while it is being transferred from one department to another, it follows from (*a*) above that symbols should only appear on a solid vertical or on a broken horizontal flow-line.

(*h*) It is important that not too much information be put on one chart. Where it is necessary to use more than one chart, a connector symbol should be used. Where a document is transferred from one chart to another, it should be 'ghosted' by a broken line symbol, as shown above, to indicate on the new chart what the document is.

(*i*) Copy documents, preferably actual documents, should be attached where necessary.

(*j*) A key should be provided where symbols or abbreviations used on a flowchart are not expressed in generally accepted terminology.

From an audit point of view, the purpose of the flowchart is not only to chart the client's accounting system, but also to highlight the weaknesses in internal control. Consequently, it is essential that a proper distinction be made between:

(i) an operation,
(ii) a check.

The greater the preponderance of checking operations, the more appropriate it may be to reduce audit tests or switch them to other areas.

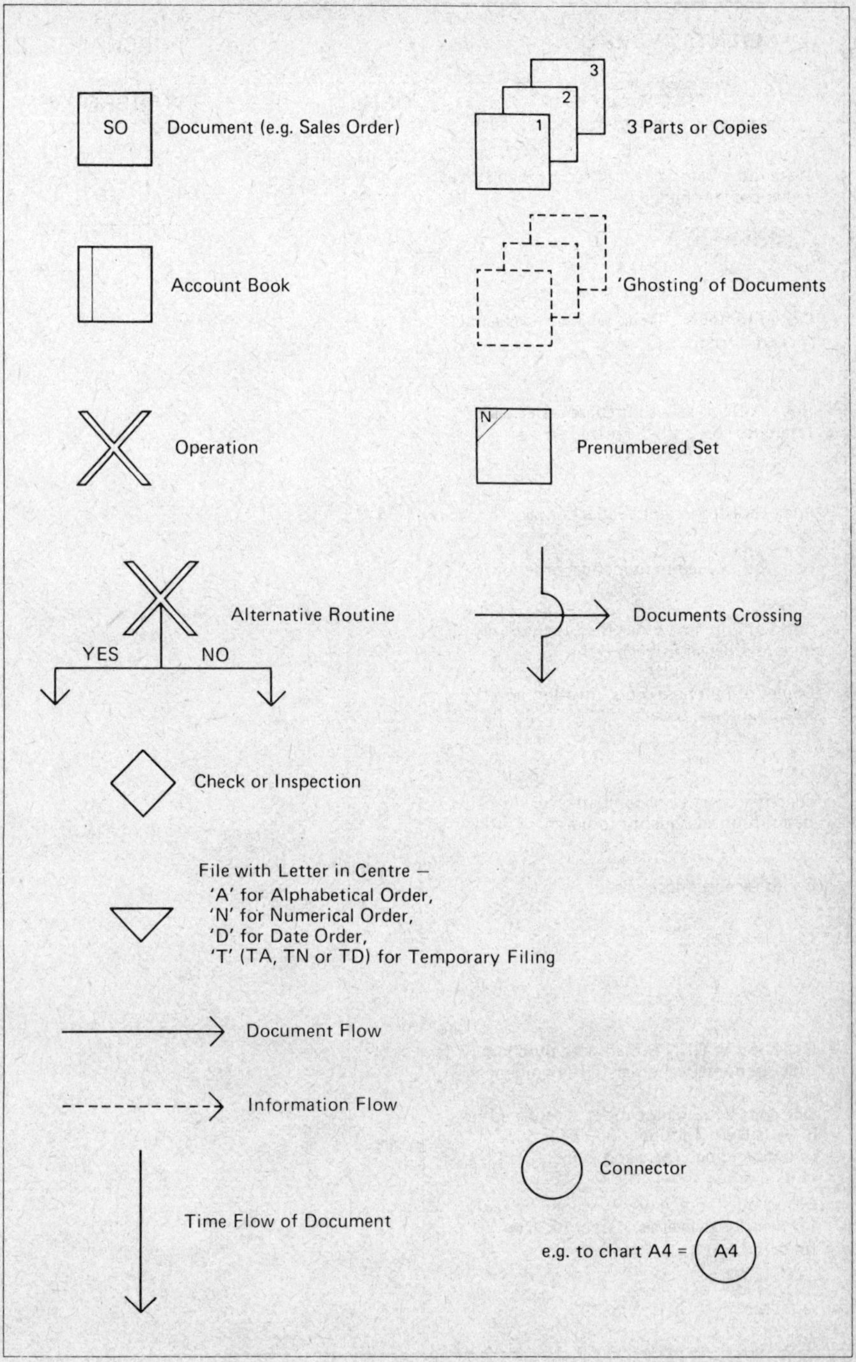
SO
Document (e.g. Sales Order)
3
2
1
3 Parts or Copies
Account Book
'Ghosting' of Documents
Operation
N
Prenumbered Set
Alternative Routine
YES
NO
Documents Crossing
Check or Inspection
File with Letter in Centre –
'A' for Alphabetical Order,
'N' for Numerical Order,
'D' for Date Order,
'T' (TA, TN or TD) for Temporary Filing
Document Flow
Information Flow
Connector
Time Flow of Document
e.g. to chart A4 =
A4

CLIENT: XYZ LTD.		PURCHASES 1
NARRATION	**OP.No.**	**WAREHOUSE**
Warehouse Manager raises req'n when stocks reach predetermined re-order levels.	1	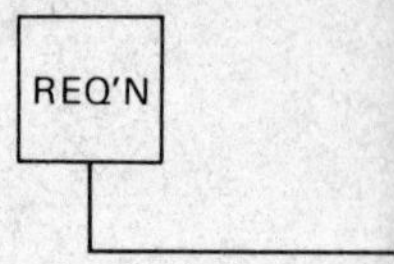
Passed to Buyer's Dept. where it is checked for authorisation.	2	
Buyer's Dept. raises purchase order with reference to supplier's price lists.	3	
Price list filed in alphabetical order.	4	
Requisition filed in numerical order.	5	
Copy of purchase order filed temporarily in date order in Buyer's Dept.	6	
Copies of purchase order filed temporarily in alphabetical order.	7	
On arrival goods are compared for quantity, description and quality to purchase order.	8	
Goods received note raised.	9	
One copy of GRN is filed with purchase order in numerical order (GRN sequence).	10	
One copy of purchase order is returned to Buyer's Dept. for updating of file of outstanding orders and is then filed in date order.	11	
File of outstanding orders scanned weekly for overdue deliveries, if overdue Dept. follow up with supplier.	12	

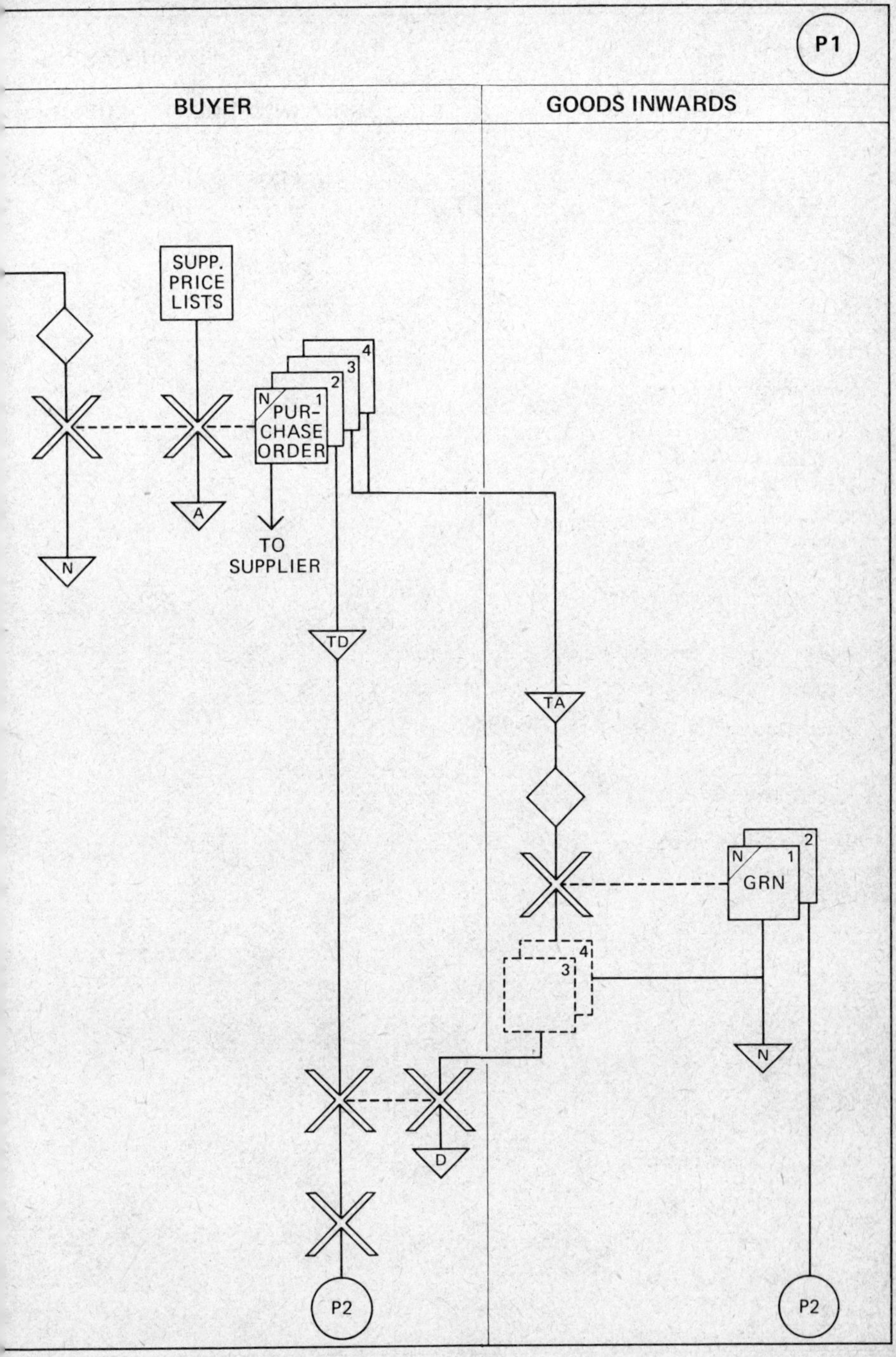
P1
BUYER
GOODS INWARDS
SUPP. PRICE LISTS
N
A
N
1
PUR-CHASE ORDER
2
3
4
TO SUPPLIER
TD
TA
N
1
GRN
2
3
4
N
D
P2
P2

CLIENT: XYZ LTD. PURCHASES 2

NARRATION	OP. No.
Goods inwards note checked with purchase order.	13
Filed in numerical order.	14
Invoice stamped with grid for approvals and given sequential number.	15
Temporarily filed in alphabetical order.	16
Temporarily filed in alphabetical order.	17
Invoice checked with GRN	18
Filed in numerical order.	19
Casts and extensions checked.	20
Posting prelist prepared.	21
Invoices posted to bought ledger.	22

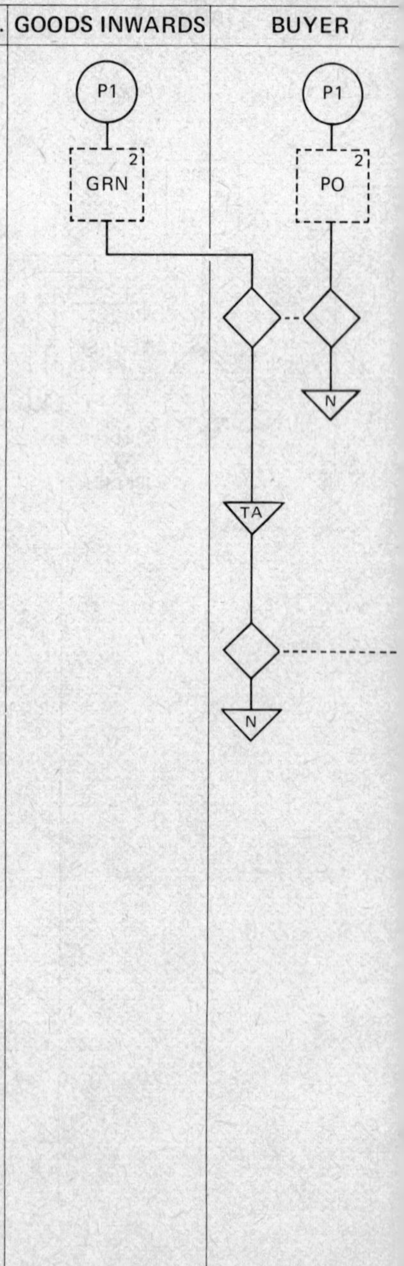

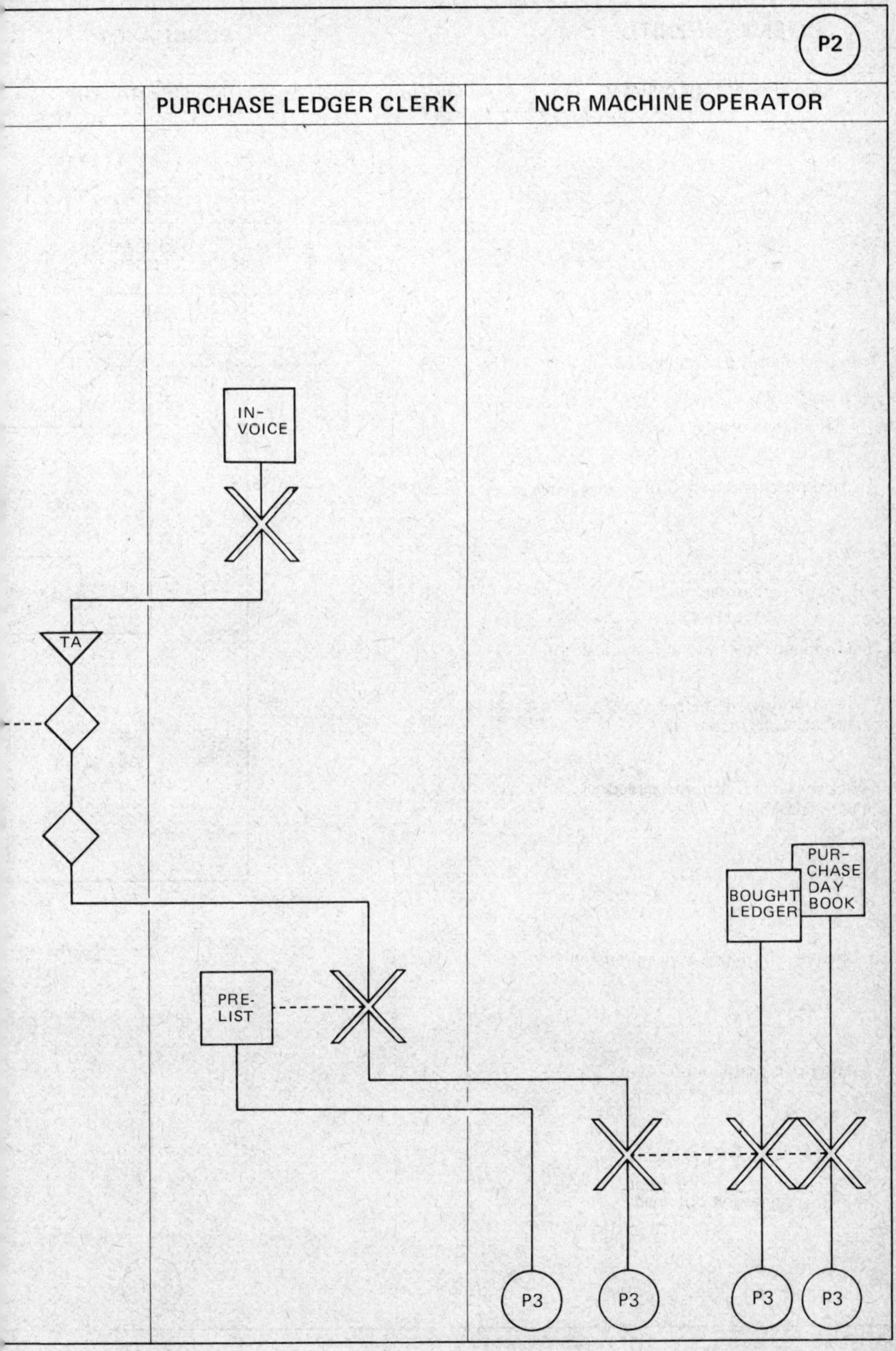
P2
PURCHASE LEDGER CLERK
NCR MACHINE OPERATOR
IN-
VOICE
TA
PRE-
LIST
BOUGHT
LEDGER
PUR-
CHASE
DAY
BOOK
P3
P3
P3
P3

CLIENT: XYZ LTD. PURCHASES 3

NARRATION	OP. No.
Pre-list agreed to total posted.	23
Filed in date order.	24
Total purchases posted to general ledger.	25
Filed in date order.	26
Statements sorted to alphabetical order.	27
Temporarily filed in alphabetical order.	28
Bought ledger accounts agreed with statements.	29
Cheque remittance advice prepared.	30
Cash book written up.	31
Cheque signatures obtained.	32

NCR MACHINE OPERATOR

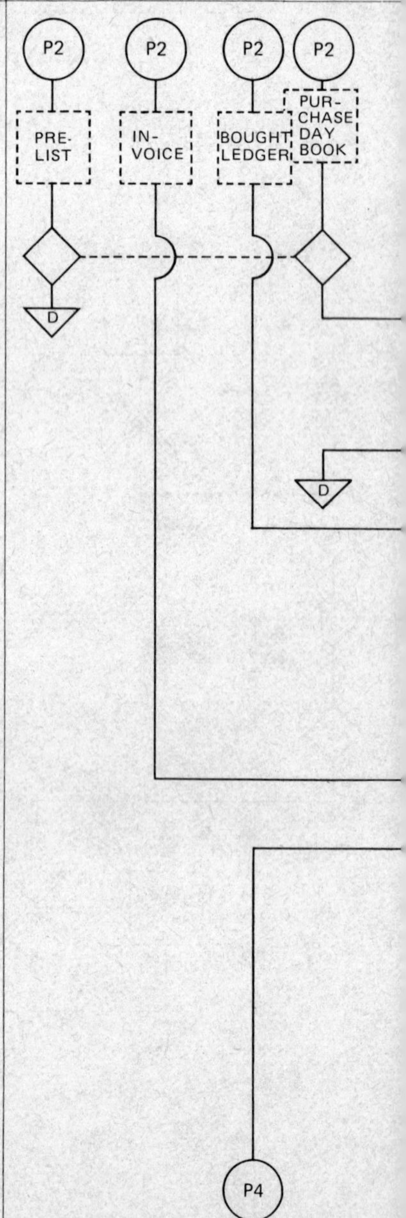

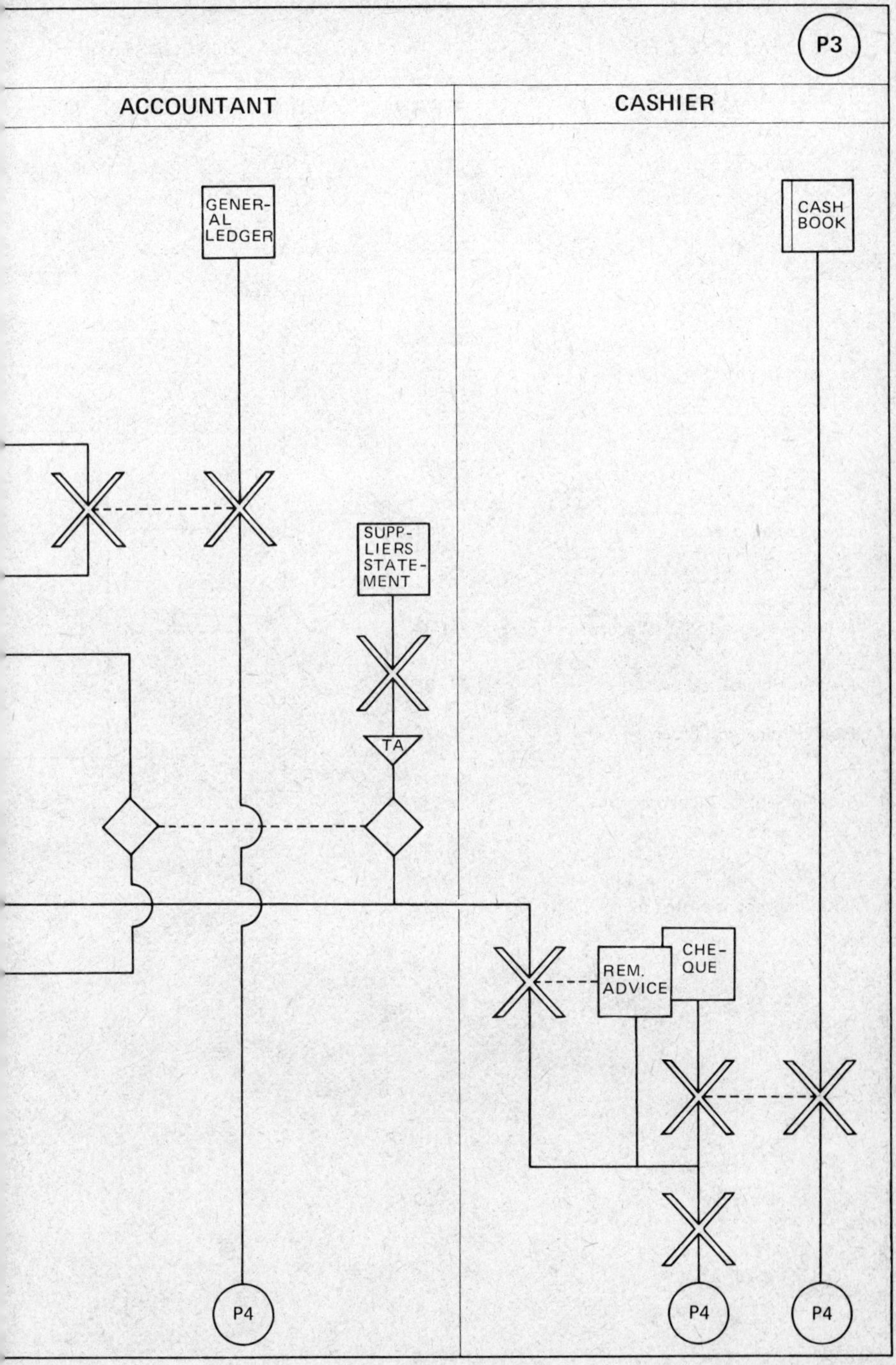
P3
ACCOUNTANT
CASHIER
GENER-AL LEDGER
CASH BOOK
SUPP-LIERS STATE-MENT
TA
CHE-QUE
REM. ADVICE
P4
P4
P4

CLIENT XYZ LTD. PURCHASES 4

NARRATION	OP.No.	NCR MACHINE OPERATOR
Cash posted to ledger.	33	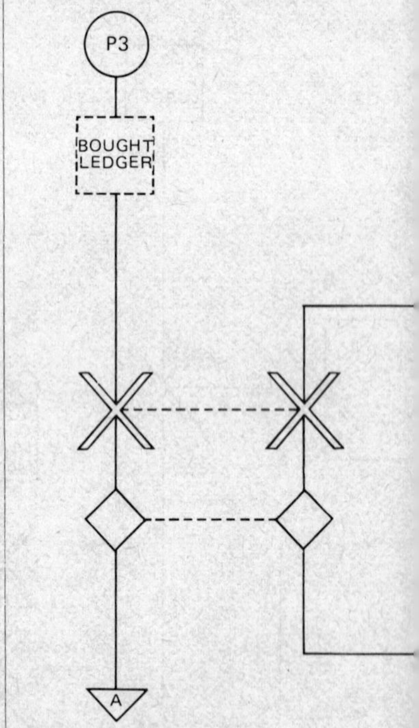
Cash book agreed to total posted to ledger.	34	
Filed in alphabetical order.	35	
Filed in numerical order.	36	
Filed in alphabetical order.	37	
Cash book totals posted to general ledger.	38	
Filed in date order.	39	
Filed in date order.	40	

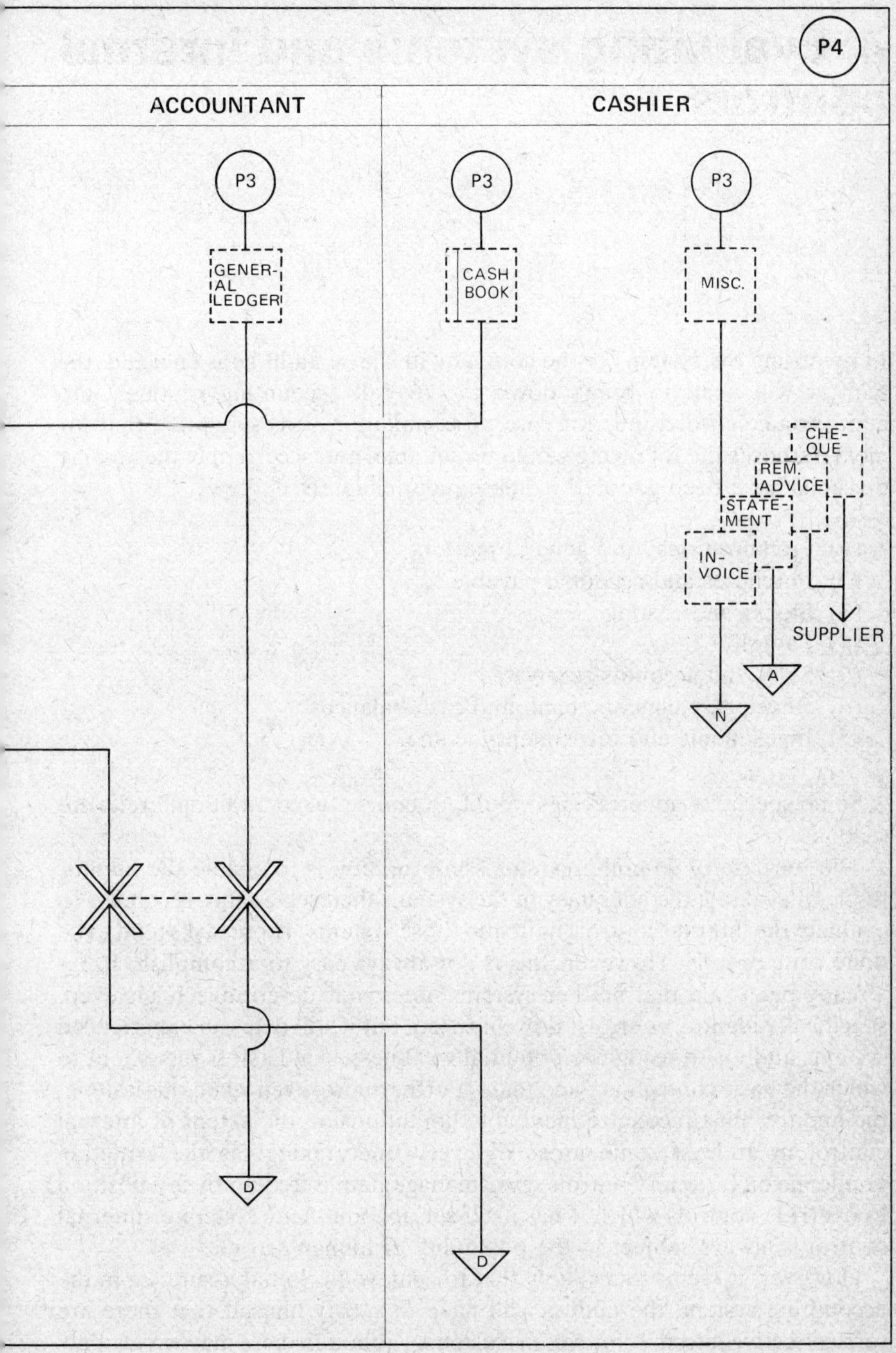
P4
ACCOUNTANT
CASHIER
P3
P3
P3
GENER-
AL
LEDGER
CASH
BOOK
MISC.
CHE-
QUE
REM.
ADVICE
STATE-
MENT
IN-
VOICE
SUPPLIER
A
N
D
D

4 Evaluating systems and internal controls

In recording the systems of the company in whose audit he is engaged, the auditor will need to break down the overall accounting routines into appropriate sub-divisions for ease of assimilation. It is suggested that for most purposes the following would be suitable, and accordingly these same divisions have been adopted in subsequent chapters:

(1) Organizational and general matters
(2) Purchases and accounts payable
(3) Stocks and costing
(4) Payroll
(5) Sales and accounts receivable
(6) Receipts, payments, bank and cash balances
(7) Investments and investment income.

Some specialist undertakings would, of course, need additional relevant sections.

The purpose of compiling systems information is to enable the auditor firstly to evaluate the adequacy of the systems themselves and, secondly, to evaluate the internal controls built into those systems. These tasks tend to be done concurrently. However, this is not always easy to accomplish. It has already been said that neither systems notes, nor descriptive ICQs even, specifically identify controls; flowcharts do, but it still takes an experienced systems auditor to recognize potential weaknesses and assess the extent to which the basic controls are adequate. Furthermore, even when this is done, the auditor must recognize inevitable limitations on the extent of internal control in at least some areas of every undertaking: as the Auditing Guideline on Internal Controls says, 'management is frequently in a position to override controls which it has itself set up', and, 'any system of internal control is always subject to the possibility of human error'.

However, it seems to us likely that to achieve his initial assurance in the accounting system, the auditor will have to satisfy himself that there are some effective internal controls in existence, although these may vary widely as to type.

Management Controls

One of the elements of control which the auditor should be looking for is management supervision and review.

An important feature of effective internal control is that directors should review the company's financial operations and position at regular and frequent intervals by means of interim accounts and reports, operating summaries and other appropriate financial and statistical information. Comparison with results for previous periods may indicate discrepancies that call for further examination or, where budgetary control is in use, attention will be drawn to material variances and explanations required. In addition to regular reviews of this nature management may from time to time call for special reviews of particular items such as stocks, or the operation of the wages department; these constitute yet another instrument of control. In smaller firms examinations of the nature indicated may be carried out by the owner or manager personally. Managerial supervision and reviews of this nature are an essential element in any effective internal control system.

To some extent it is possible for management to delegate this function, especially as regards detailed examinations and special reviews, and hence the existence in some large organizations of an internal audit department, made up of specially assigned staff with a principal accounting objective of assuring management of the efficient and effective design and operation of internal checks within accounting systems.

It may be seen then that the independent external auditor and the internal auditor have some common objectives. However, it must be emphasized that there are also fundamental differences:

(*a*) *Scope*. The extent of the work undertaken by the internal auditor is determined by the management, whereas that of the independent auditor arises from the responsibilities placed on him by statute;

(*b*) *Approach*. The internal auditor's approach is with a view to ensuring that the accounting system is efficient, so that the accounting information presented to management throughout the period is accurate and discloses material facts. The independent auditor's approach, however, is governed by his duty to satisfy himself that the accounts to be presented to the shareholders show a true and fair view of the profit or loss for the financial period and of the state of the company's affairs at the end of that period;

(*c*) *Responsibility*. The internal auditor's responsibility is to the management whereas the independent auditor is responsible directly to the shareholders. It follows that the internal auditor, being a servant of the company, does not have the independence of status which the independent auditor possesses.

Many large organizations today have an internal audit department. The Auditing Guideline dealing with 'Internal Controls' provides help as to the extent to which the external auditor is able to place reliance on the work of the internal auditor in drawing up his own programme. In essence this will depend on his assessment of the effectiveness of the internal audit function. In particular the external auditor will be concerned with:

'(*a*) the degree of independence of the internal auditor from those whose responsibilities he is reviewing;

(*b*) the number of suitably qualified and experienced staff employed in the internal audit function;

(*c*) the scope, extent, direction and timing of the tests made by the internal auditor;

(*d*) the evidence available of the work done by the internal auditor and of the review of that work;

(*e*) the extent to which management takes action based upon the reports of the internal audit function.'

However it may be seen as axiomatic that the existence of an internal audit function will tend to serve to reduce the level of testing which the external auditor requires to carry out.

Organizational Controls and Segregation of Duties

The company's organization chart must be reviewed for the extent to which authority and responsibility has been appropriately allocated in a clear reporting structure to those with sufficient ability to fulfil their function within the internal control system. In particular the auditor will wish to assess the extent to which the division of duties between members of the staff has been arranged in a manner to lessen the risk of errors and defalcations. It is suggested that a segregation of staff duties questionnaire should be drawn up to supplement the flowcharts, thus providing a résumé of 'who does what' and serving to highlight areas of poor organizational control, possible conflict of duties, and areas where family relationships could serve to vitiate the effectiveness of the division of duties.

Using the divisions above, the following specimen questions indicate what is required to serve this purpose:

The more that the functions indicated above can be seen to be separated, then the more effective is the existence of internal check upon which the auditor may still seek to place reliance.

1. Organizational and general matters

	Name and position	*Completed by*
Who:		
1.1 is responsible for the use of the company seal?		
1.2 is responsible for the custody of the company minute book?		
1.3 ensures that transfer documents are in order?		
1.4 is responsible for the custody and issue of share and loan certificates?		
1.5 is responsible for share and loan registers?		
1.6 checks dividend warrants?		
1.7 signs dividend warrants or controls pre-signed warrants?		
1.8 authorizes the issue of duplicate dividend warrants?		
1.9 prepares dividend bank reconciliations?		
1.10 keeps the nominal ledger?		
1.11 keeps the journal?		
1.12 is authorized to make journal entries?		
1.13 raises requests for capital expenditure?		
1.14 sanctions capital expenditure?		
1.15 maintains records of outstanding sanctions and orders?		
1.16 maintains registers of fixed assets?		
1.17 is responsible for custody of documents of title?		
1.18 determines depreciation rates?		
1.19 authorizes disposals of assets?		

	Yes/No	*Comment/reference to other controls*	*Completed by*
1.20 Are 1.1 to 1.5 above the responsibility of separate individuals?			
1.21 Are 1.6 to 1.9 above the responsibility of separate individuals?			
1.22 Are 1.10 to 1.12 above the responsibility of separate individuals?			
1.23 Are 1.14 to 1.19 above the responsibility of a separate individual from 1.17 above?			
1.24 If not, are there adequate compensating controls?			

2. Purchases and accounts payable

	Name and position	*Com-pleted by*
Who: 2.1 raises requisitions for orders? 2.2 approves requisitions? 2.3 places orders with suppliers (i) for goods? (ii) for services? 2.4 receives goods onto premises? 2.5 approves invoices? 2.6 keeps the accounts payable ledgers? 2.7 checks calculations on invoices? 2.8 codes invoices?		

	Yes/No	*Comment/reference to other controls*	*Com-pleted by*
2.9 Are 2.2 to 2.8 above the responsibility of separate individuals? 2.10 Is 2.6 above the responsibility of a separate individual from 1.10–1.12? 2.11 Is 2.5 above the responsibility of a separate individual from 1.14 and 1.17? 2.12 If not, are there adequate compensating controls?			

	Name and position	*Com-pleted by*
Who: 3.1 is responsible for custody of stocks? 3.2 is responsible for keeping physical stock control records? 3.3 is responsible for keeping financial stock control records? 3.4 approves stock issues? 3.5 approves scrap sales and other disposals? 3.6 is responsible for periodic counting of stock? 3.7 authorizes the amendment of physical stock records following counts?		

3.8 authorizes the amendment of financial stock records following counts? 3.9 reviews stocks and stock levels, etc.?			

	Yes/ No	*Comment/reference to other controls*	*Com- pleted by*
3.10 Are 3.1 to 3.3 above the responsibility of separate individuals? 3.11 Are 3.4 and 3.5 above the responsibility of separate individuals? 3.12 Are 3.6 to 3.8 above the responsibility of separate individuals? 3.13 Is 3.9 above the responsibility of an individual not involved in the custody of stocks or stock records? 3.14 If not, are there adequate compensating controls?			

Contracts	*Name and position*	*Com- pleted by*
Who: 3.15 is responsible for authorizing acceptance of a contract? 3.16 is responsible for authorizing amendments to a contract? 3.17 is responsible for keeping the contract cost ledger? 3.18 authorizes cost transfers in the cost ledger? 3.19 is responsible for periodic contract valuations? 3.20 keeps the records of progress monies received?		

	Yes/ No	*Comment/reference to other controls*	*Com- pleted by*
3.21 Are 3.15 and 3.16 above the responsibility of the same individuals? 3.22 Are 3.17 and 3.18 above the responsibility of separate individuals?			

	Yes/ No	*Comment/reference to other controls*	*Completed by*
3.23 Are 3.19 and 3.20 above the responsibility of separate individuals? (*Note:* Normally, 3.15, 3.16, 3.18 and 3.19, will be the collective responsibility of more than one person. It is essential to support the brief answers above with full notes of the precise authorization/checking procedures and of the level of Authorizing Authority of each individual concerned.			

4. Payroll

	Name and position	*Completed by*
Who:		
4.1 keeps records of engagements, terminations, etc.?		
4.2 authorizes or approves clock cards, timesheets, etc.?		
4.3 calculates the payroll from such supporting documents?		
4.4 checks these calculations?		
4.5 authorizes changes in rates of pay?		
4.6 makes up wages envelopes?		
4.7 distributes wages?		
4.8 has custody of unclaimed wages?		
4.9 approves payrolls before wages distribution?		

	Yes/ No	*Comment/reference to other controls*	*Completed by*
4.10 Are 4.1 to 4.7 above the responsibility of separate individuals?			
4.11 If not, are there adequate compensating controls?			

5. Sales and accounts receivable

	Name and position	*Completed by*
Who:		
5.1 approves customers' credit limits?		
5.2 approves customers' orders?		

5.3 dispatches goods?			
5.4 raises invoices?			
5.5 receives returned goods?			
5.6 approves credit notes?			
5.7 keeps the accounts receivable ledger?			
5.8 is responsible for credit control?			
5.9 authorizes writing-off bad debts?			

	Yes/ No	*Comment/reference to other controls*	*Com-pleted by*
5.10 Is each of the above the responsibility of a separate individual?			
5.11 Are 5.7 and 5.9 above the responsibility of separate individuals from 1.10 to 1.12?			
5.12 If not, are there adequate compensating controls?			

6. Receipts, payments, bank and cash balances

	Name and position	*Com-pleted by*
Who:		
6.1 opens the mail?		
6.2 makes the first listing of remittances received?		
6.3 records receipts in the cash book?		
6.4 reconciles the cash book with till rolls, receipt books, etc. for cash sales?		
6.5 prepares bank paying-in slips?		
6.6 banks receipts?		
6.7 approves cash discounts?		
6.8 prepares cheques and records payments?		
6.9 signs cheques?		
6.10 has custody of any facsimile signatures?		
6.11 is responsible for custody of petty cash?		
6.12 approves petty cash payments?		
6.13 carries out checks of petty cash balances?		
6.14 prepares bank reconciliations?		
6.15 checks bank reconciliations?		

	Yes/ No	*Comment/reference to other controls*	*Com-pleted by*
6.16 Is the responsibility for 6.3 and 6.8 above separate from that for 1.11 to 1.18, 2.5, 3.5, 4.1 and 4.5 to 4.8, and 5.7 and 5.9?			

	Yes/No	Comment/reference to other controls	Completed by
6.17 Is the responsibility for 6.3 and 6.8 above separate from that for 6.11, 6.14 or 6.15 above? 6.18 Is the responsibility for 6.1 and 6.2 above separate from that for 5.2 and 5.7, and from 6.3, 6.6 and 6.7 above? 6.19 Is the responsibility for 6.7 above separate from that for 5.7? 6.20 If not, are there adequate compensating controls?			

7. Investments and investment income

	Name and position	Completed by
Who: 7.1 is responsible for authorizing purchases and sales? 7.2 checks prices of transactions? 7.3 has custody of documents of title? 7.4 keeps investment registers? 7.5 keeps financial records of investment income? 7.6 checks to ensure that income is properly received?		

	Yes/No	Comment/reference to other controls	Completed by
7.7 Are all the above the responsibility of separate individuals? 7.8 Are 7.5 and 7.6 above the responsibility of separate individuals from 6.3 and 1.10? 7.9 If not, are there adequate compensating controls?			

Accounting Controls

These should ensure:

(*a*) that all transactions have been authorized and approved;
(*b*) that all those so authorized and approved are then included;
(*c*) that all transactions are correctly recorded;
(*d*) that all records have been accurately processed into the accounts.

To assist in their evaluation it is possible to design a shorter form of ICQ than the descriptive one, comprising a check list of questions pertinent to the identification of controls. It is suggested that such questions in turn be segregated between fundamental 'key' questions and supporting subsidiary questions influencing the answer to each key question. The extent of this influence will vary depending upon the particular circumstances, but most of the key questions should be relevant to most businesses other than some specialist undertakings.

To ensure that the auditor properly understands the system with which he is concerned and that it is he rather than the client who critically appraises the internal controls, it is recommended that the auditor himself answers the subsidiary questions and refers to the client's staff only if further clarification then becomes necessary. Having answered questions concerning related detailed internal controls, the auditor is then in a position to give a considered and reasoned answer to the key questions, based on an understanding of the strengths and weaknesses of the system. All answers to key questions should be supported by explanations and appropriate cross-references both to the relevant flowcharts and subsidiary questions, for it is on these that the initial levels of audit testing will be based and it is essential, therefore, to identify those areas requiring particular attention.

For this reason it is also recommended that each system be dealt with comprehensively in turn, rather than adopting a work method whereby, for instance, flowcharts for all systems are prepared before the evaluation of any of them is commenced. Better, having recorded a system, that the auditor should proceed to answer the subsidiary and key questions relating to it and, based on his resultant assessment of the controls, proceed to draw up the programme of audit tests for that area.

However, many of the internal controls which would be relevant to large businesses will be inappropriate or unnecessary in the case of smaller businesses. As a result the ICQ set out below may, for businesses below a given size, prove over-elaborate as a basis for evaluating a limited system of control.

For this reason, and in the interests of an efficient and cost-effective audit, a checklist of Minimum Controls may be preferable in respect of such smaller businesses.

As a general guide, it is suggested that this approach might be appropriate on the audit of businesses which are distinguished by:

(*a*) a limited number of accounting or office staff (perhaps up to 4 or 5) and, in consequence, the absence of many of the formal internal control duties that would be appropriate in larger businesses, and

(*b*) the close personal involvement of the manager and/or proprietor in the conduct or supervision of day-to-day transactions.

The Minimum Controls Checklist (MCC) can adopt the same key-question concept as is used in the full Internal Control Questionnaire (ICQ). The difference between the two documents is primarily one of scale: the MCC anticipates a less sophisticated system and is therefore shorter; the subsidiary questions within it are designed to highlight the aspects of control which are of particular relevance to the smaller business. Examples of both the ICQ and MCC are set out below.

Specimen Internal Control Questionnaire

The following specimen ICQ indicates the form of key and subsidiary questions which will assist the auditor to identify the strengths and weaknesses in a client's systems. Whenever answering a subsidiary question adversely, i.e. acknowledging a weakness in internal control, the auditor should pay particular attention to the possibility of the existence of a compensating control at a different point in the accounting system. It is important that the ICQ should be carefully reviewed, once completed, for it will have an important bearing on the nature and extent of audit testing, which we discuss in the next chapter, and on the matters to be reported in the management letter to which we have attended in Chapter 2.

ICQ1. Organizational and general matters

	Yes/ No/ N/A	*Comment/reference to flowcharts, systems notes, etc.*	*Completed by*
1.1 Is the business effectively managed and properly administered?			
(*a*) Are accurate and timely management accounts (and/or other reports of business performance) produced on a regular basis?			
(*b*) Are financial plans, budgets and cash-flow forecasts maintained?			
(*c*) Is a comparison made between actual and forecast/budgeted results and are significant variances analysed and explained?			
(*d*) Do management appear to be fully appraised of the performance of the business?			
(*e*) Are management decisions properly minuted?			
(*f*) Are there adequate procedures to			

	Yes/ No/ N/A	Comment/reference to flowcharts, systems notes, etc.	Com- pleted by
ensure that all decisions are implemented? (*g*) Are there any non-executive directors on the board and is their function specified? (*h*) Is there an audit commitee? (If so, obtain copy of its 'constitution' or terms of reference.) (*i*) Is there a proper definition of duties and responsibilities at all levels? (*j*) Are accounting procedures laid down (by manual, etc.) and how are they monitored? (*k*) Is there an internal audit department? If so: (i) to whom is it responsible? (ii) are regular reports submitted by the department to the Board? (*l*) Is an up-to-date organization chart maintained? (*m*) Are there adequate stand-by arrangements in force to cover staff sickness, etc. or loss of accounting records (by fire, etc.)?			
1.2 Can the secretarial and statutory records be improperly manipulated or misappropriated?			
(*a*) Is the company seal kept in safe custody and its use controlled? (*b*) Is the supply of blank share certificates controlled? (*c*) Is the register of members, debenture holders, etc. agreed with the issued share or loan capital and the dividend/interest payments? (*d*) Are share and debenture records subjected to a transfer audit? (*e*) Are dividend/interest payments made through a separate account and the balances checked against unclaimed warrants? (*f*) Are all registers required by law			

	Yes/ No/ N/A	*Comment/reference to flowcharts, systems notes, etc.*	*Com- pleted by*
maintained by the company and up-to-date?			
(*g*) Is the company's file at the Companies' Registry maintained up-to-date?			
1.3 Can fixed assets be acquired or disposed of without proper authority or recording?			
(*a*) Is capital expenditure over certain limits subject to authority?			
(*b*) Is disposal of fixed assets subject to special authority?			
(*c*) Is there a capital expenditure/disposal budget and, if so, is it regularly compared with actual expenditure authorized and incurred?			
(*d*) Are records maintained for capital works carried out by the company, including the allocation of overheads?			
(*e*) Is a register of fixed assets maintained and is this checked regularly against the actual assets?			
(*f*) Are records maintained for fixed asset disposal/scrappings, etc.?			
(*g*) Is the register of fixed assets regularly reconciled to the nominal ledger?			
(*h*) Are rates of depreciation laid down and are they adequate in the particular circumstances? Or excessive?			
(*i*) Are profits on disposal of fixed assets within the group segregated?			
(*j*) Are documents of title kept in safe custody?			
1.4 Does the company maintain adequate insurance cover over all aspects of its business?			
(*a*) Does the company maintain adequate insurance cover in respect of: (i) consequential loss			

	Yes/ No/ N/A	Comment/reference to flowcharts, systems notes, etc.	Completed by
(ii) employer's liability (iii) public liability (iv) fire, burglary and theft (v) cash and goods in transit (vi) any other cover relevant to the type of business transacted? (*b*) Is cover periodically reviewed and updated in the light of current results and values? (*c*) Have all the required declarations by the company and/or certificates by third parties been submitted to the insurers? (*d*) Are persons handling cash or high value stocks covered by fidelity bonds?			
1.5 Are transactions with related parties (i.e. with group, associated and other affiliated companies or with businesses under common control) undertaken otherwise than at arms length?			
(*a*) Is there a properly defined group structure? (*b*) Are there adequate procedures for the disclosure of interests of shareholders, directors and employees in other undertakings? (*c*) Is the transfer of funds between such undertakings properly authorized and, as regards overseas transfers, in accordance with any exchange controls in the countries concerned? (*d*) Are trading transactions and transfers of fixed assets between such undertakings in accordance with laid down procedures and on an arms length basis? (*e*) If transactions are undertaken on other than at arms length basis: (i) is their effect on trading results/asset values quantified and assessed?			

	Yes/ No/ N/A	Comment/reference to flowcharts, systems notes, etc.	Com-pleted by
(ii) are they approved by the Board?			
1.6 Can improper entries be made in the nominal ledger?			
(*a*) Is the nominal ledger kept in safe custody?			
(*b*) Can unauthorized persons make entries in the nominal ledger?			
(*c*) Is the nominal ledger regularly cast and balanced?			
(*d*) Are all journal entries subject to authorization by a responsible official?			
(*e*) Are all journal entries supported by proper documentation?			
(*f*) Do the nominal ledger accounts provide sufficient analysis over headings appropriate to the business, so as to facilitate the preparation of financial statements and management reports?			

ICQ2. Purchases and accounts payable

2.1 Can goods or services (other than occupancy charges) be ordered without being authorized?			
(*a*) Are purchase requisitions prepared and approved by responsible officials?			
(*b*) Are there any limits of authority operating over the ordering of goods/services?			
(*c*) Are blank purchase orders issued only to personnel responsible for buying?			
(*d*) Are purchase orders:			
(i) issued for all purchases of goods and services?			
(ii) pre-numbered, and all numbers accounted for?			

	Yes/ No/ N/A	Comment/reference to flowcharts, systems notes, etc.	Completed by
(iii) completed with specifications of prices and terms? (*e*) Are purchase orders valued and compared with existing budgets or other management information? (*f*) Is there adequate control over the recharge of staff purchases?			
2.2 Can liabilities for goods or services be incurred but not recorded?			
(*a*) Are all goods received at a central receiving point? (*b*) Are goods-received records: (i) made out immediately on receipt of goods? (ii) on pre-numbered forms? (iii) all accounted for? (iv) used to update stock records? (*c*) Are goods examined on arrival as to quantity and quality and, if so, how is this evidenced? (*d*) Are copies of the goods-received records given to: (i) purchasing department? (ii) accounts department? (iii) stock records department? (iv) other departments (give details)? (*e*) Are there any records prepared for services received? (*f*) Are goods-returned records: (i) made out immediately on return of goods to suppliers? (ii) on pre-numbered forms? (iii) all accounted for? (iv) used to update stock records? (*g*) Are returned goods properly authorized?			

	Yes/ No/ N/A	*Comment/reference to flowcharts, systems notes, etc.*	*Completed by*
2.3 Can liabilities be omitted, wrongly recorded or wrongly charged?			
(*a*) Are purchase orders regularly reviewed for items for which no invoices have been received and are these investigated?			
(*b*) Are goods-received records regularly reviewed for items for which no invoices have been received and are these investigated?			
(*c*) Does the system ensure that all invoices received and approved are processed through the accounting systems?			
(*d*) Are suppliers' statements reviewed for items which have not been processed into the accounting system?			
(*e*) Are purchase ledger balances regularly reconciled with suppliers' statements and outstanding items investigated?			
(*f*) Are debit balances in the purchases ledger regularly reviewed?			
(*g*) Are goods-returned records regularly reviewed to ensure all credit notes have been received?			
(*h*) Is there an adequate system to ensure that invoices are processed into the correct accounting classification, with particular reference to fixed-asset accounts?			
2.4 Can goods or services be paid for without being received?			
(*a*) Are suppliers' invoices and credit notes:			
(i) serially numbered immediately on receipt?			
(ii) all accounted for?			
(iii) correlated with purchase order for type, quality and price?			

	Yes/ No/ N/A	Comment/reference to flowcharts, systems notes, etc.	Com- pleted by
(iv) correlated with goods received (or returned) records for type and quantity? (v) checked for casts and calculations? (vi) checked for correct accounting classification? (vii) initialled for work done? (viii) approved by a responsible official? (*b*) Are invoices and credit notes recorded only when authorized? (*c*) Are the purchase ledger balances regularly agreed with the control account? (*d*) Is there adequate control over deliveries direct to customers?			

ICQ3. Stocks and costing

3.1 Can stocks be misappropriated or mislaid? (*a*) Is there proper security covering the handling and storage of stocks? (*b*) Are stocks stored in an orderly manner and readily identifiable? (*c*) Are there satisfactory controls over the documentation covering the receipt and issue of goods? (Refer also to questions dealing with sales and credit procedures.) (*d*) Are perpetual stock records maintained and if so, is the recording function separated from that for the handling of goods? (*e*) Are there regular stocktakings and proper control over the adjustment of physical discrepancies? (*f*) Do the stock records facilitate the identification and reconciliation of physical discrepancies? (*g*) Is there control over allowances			

	Yes/ No/ N/A	Comment/reference to flowcharts, systems notes, etc.	Completed by
made for shrinkage from whatever cause?			
(*h*) Are there adequate procedures for the identification and segregation of obsolete, damaged and slow-moving stocks?			
(*i*) Is there control over the disposal of obsolete, damaged and slow-moving stock?			
(*j*) Are there adequate controls over stocks held by third parties or on behalf of third parties?			
3.2 Can work in progress be overstated or understated?			
(*a*) Is there an acceptable and consistent basis for charging materials, direct labour and overheads?			
(*b*) Are inter-departmental transfers of (i) materials (ii) partly finished work (iii) completed work all subject to documentary control?			
(*c*) Do the work-in-progress records properly identify: (i) each separate stage of production; (ii) the amount of materials, labour and overheads charged to each job?			
(*d*) Is the work-in-progress subject to periodic physical checks which are reconciled with book records?			
3.3 Does the costing system provide adequate controls with the financial records?			
(*a*) Is the cost-accounting system integrated with the financial records?			
(*b*) Are cost variances properly analysed and explained on a regular basis?			
(*c*) Are standard costs kept under			

	Yes/ No/ N/A	Comment/reference to flowcharts, systems notes, etc.	Completed by
proper review by management and are they reliable?			
3.4 Do the stock records adequately segregate raw materials, work-in-progress and finished stocks and do they provide for movements between these categories to be properly recorded?			
(*a*) Are there physical counts at points of transfer between areas?			
(*b*) Is there an acceptable and consistent basis for charging overheads into valuations and does this basis make proper allowances appropriate to the stages of manufacture?			
Contracts:			
3.5 Does the system ensure that contracts accepted are within the capabilities of the business and are economically viable?			
(*a*) Do the methods of estimating and preparing quotations ensure that all the items and/or stages of the contract are correctly costed?			
(*b*) Is allowance made in the quotation for known or expected price rises?			
(*c*) Does the company ensure that all contracts make adequate provision for the effects of inflation?			
(*d*) Are estimates and quotations reviewed by a senior official of the company?			
(*e*) Is the method of financing contracts sufficient to ensure cash flow is adequate for the duration of contracts?			
(*f*) Are specific warranties and indemnities, penalty terms and conditions reviewed and agreed by a senior official(s) as being reasonable and attainable?			

	Yes/ No/ N/A	*Comment/reference to flowcharts, systems notes, etc.*	*Completed by*
(*g*) Do contracts always include specific maintenance periods and conditions of release? (*h*) Are there any limits to the authority of those responsible for accepting contracts on the company's behalf? (*i*) Are contract price adjustments (other than those specified in the original contract) and variation orders subject to the same controls and authority as the original contract? (*j*) Are quotations checked by a senior official to ensure that the proposed work falls within: (i) the technical capability of the company? (ii) the anticipated capacity of the company at the time when the contract will have to be undertaken? (*k*) If some of the contract work has to be put to subcontract, are quotations received from subcontractors before the submission of the main quotation; and is there an authorized list of approved subcontractors? (*l*) Is the procedure for putting names on the list of approved subcontractors subject to authorization by a senior official? (*m*) Are contracts and contract variations agreed with subcontractors by a senior official?			
3.6 Are contract costs correctly allocated, recorded and controlled?			
(*a*) Are there adequate controls in the following systems to ensure that costs are allocated to the correct contract? (i) Purchase invoice processing? (ii) Subcontractors' certificates? (iii) Payroll? (*b*) Is there an acceptable and consis-			

	Yes/ No/ N/A	Comment/reference to flowcharts, systems notes, etc.	Com- pleted by
tent basis for allocating overheads to contracts? (*c*) Are the contract cost ledger balances regularly agreed with the control account? (*d*) Is there written authority for any transfers of costs between contracts or to close contract records? (*e*) Is the use of plant charged to contracts carefully controlled? If plant is operated as a cost centre, are there procedures for: (i) Physically controlling plant? (ii) Calculating the daily rate at which it should be charged to contracts? (iii) Recording plant movements between contract sites? (iv) Controlling plant operating costs?			
3.7 Is contract performance adequately monitored and regularly reviewed? (*a*) Are valuation procedures carried out regularly and are they adequate with regard to: (i) Measuring procedures adopted for work done and materials on site? (ii) Recording of work carried out against variation orders? (iii) Recording of rectification work carried out and/or to be carried out? (*b*) Are valuations regularly compared to estimated and actual costs to date? (*c*) Are 'costs to complete' forecasts regularly prepared and reviewed in relation to contract value? (*d*) Are visits arranged to the major contract sites at the financial year-end to ensure that the valuation procedures are being satisfactorily carried out?			

	Yes/ No/ N/A	*Comment/reference to flowcharts, systems notes, etc.*	*Com-pleted by*
(*e*) Is the work of sub-contractors controlled to ensure that it complies with the terms of the main contract?			
(*f*) Are the procedures adequate for warning senior management if any penalty clauses in a contract are likely to be invoked by the customer?			
3.8 Are progress monies receivable adequately controlled and properly recorded?			
(*a*) Are there satisfactory procedures for ensuring that monies due in accordance with the contract terms are applied for as and when they become receivable?			
(*b*) Are overdue progress monies followed up promptly?			
(*c*) Is the contract manager/quantity surveyor notified of monies which are seriously overdue?			
(*d*) Are retention monies due recorded separately from monies received?			
(*e*) Are progress monies received recorded in such a way as to be separately identifiable from other amounts due?			
(*f*) Are penalty clause deductions suffered recorded separately from outstanding progress accounts?			

ICQ4. Payroll

4.1 Can employees be paid for work not done?			
(*a*) Are time clocks supervised by a responsible official?			
(*b*) Are time records and piece-work sheets and other source documents:			

	Yes/ No/ N/A	Comment/reference to flowcharts, systems notes, etc.	Com- pleted by
(i) controlled by persons independent of the payroll department, (ii) approved by a responsible official before being processed? (*c*) Are time records, piece-work sheets and other source documents checked before processing by the payroll department for: (i) appropriate authorization as to their correctness, (ii) casts and calculations? (*d*) Are proper controls exercised over adjustments for lateness, sickness and absenteeism (holidays, etc.)? (*e*) Are separate payroll bank accounts operated, credited with the exact amount required, and regularly reconciled? (*f*) Are adequate safeguards operated over wages and salaries paid to employees in cash, and over unclaimed wages? (*g*) Are adequate controls operated over the processing of payrolls into the accounting records?			
4.2 Can the payroll be inflated in any way?			
(*a*) Are individual personal records (including contracts of employment) maintained independently of the payroll department? (*b*) Are written authorizations required for all: (i) employees added to the payroll, (ii) changes in rates of pay, (iii) employees taken off the payroll? (*c*) Is the payroll section effectively notified by the personnel department of any changes? (*d*) Are payrolls checked: (i) with clock cards or other rele-			

	Yes/ No/ N/A	Comment/reference to flowcharts, systems notes, etc.	Completed by
vant time records, (ii) for salesmen's commission based on periodic sales, (iii) for correct rates applied, (iv) for casts and calculations?			
(*e*) Are payrolls and payroll summaries approved and initialled by a responsible official?			
(*f*) Are all payments for casual labour approved and made against proper documentation?			
(*g*) Are payrolls periodically checked against the independent personal records?			
(*h*) Is written authorization required for overtime, and are the rates clearly laid down?			
(*i*) Are movements between successive payrolls reconciled in terms of numbers and values?			
(*j*) Are wages and salaries regularly compared with budgets, costing records or other management information and significant variances investigated?			
(*k*) Are payroll deductions reconciled with the nominal ledger?			
(*l*) Is the cash for payrolls kept entirely separate from any other sources of cash (e.g. sales, petty cash)? Are all payroll deductions settled by cheques?			
4.3 Can other errors occur in payroll calculations?			
(*a*) Are there proper authorizations for all payroll deductions other than statutory deductions?			
(*b*) Does the system provide adequate safeguards for dealing with PAYE and other statutory deductions and are these reconciled regularly?			
(*c*) Are the gross wages or salaries and			

	Yes/ No/ N/A	Comment/reference to flowcharts, systems notes, etc.	Completed by
total tax deducted agreed with PAYE returns to the Inland Revenue? (*d*) Is the issue of luncheon vouchers satisfactorily controlled?			

ICQ5. Sales and trade debtors

5.1 Can goods be dispatched to a bad credit risk? (*a*) Are orders accepted only from customers whose credit worthiness is acceptable? (*b*) Is reference made to the age and amount of debtors' balances prior to further goods being dispatched to them? (*c*) Are goods only dispatched against approved orders? (*d*) Is there any credit insurance? 5.2 Can goods be dispatched but not invoiced, or vice versa? (*a*) Can dispatches go unrecorded? (*b*) Are there adequate safeguards over the security and access to stores, dispatch areas and other locations where goods are held? (*c*) Are dispatch notes: (i) pre-numbered (ii) controlled to ensure that all have been accounted for, (iii) checked against goods dispatched? (*d*) Does the customer acknowledge receipt of the goods? (*e*) Are dispatch notes correlated with: (i) sales invoices, (ii) stock records? (*f*) Can goods be invoiced without a dispatch note?			

	Yes/ No/ N/A	Comment/reference to flowcharts, systems notes, etc.	Completed by
(*g*) Is there an adequate system for processing partly completed customers' orders?			
(*h*) Are dispatches in respect of cash sales (including sales to staff) properly controlled?			
(*i*) Is the sale of scrap effectively controlled?			
(*j*) Are modifications made by the customer to his original order properly controlled, and invoiced?			
5.3 Can sales be invoiced but not recorded in the accounts?			
(*a*) Are invoices pre-numbered?			
(*b*) Is there an independent sequence check of the ledger-posting copies of the invoices?			
(*c*) Are there satisfactory procedures for spoilt and cancelled invoices?			
(*d*) Is there control over 'sale or return' goods?			
5.4 Can invoicing errors occur?			
(*a*) Are invoices prepared from approved price lists? Is there control over sales or trade discounts on terms different from approved price lists?			
(*b*) Are customers' orders numbered and checked against invoices?			
(*c*) Are invoices checked with dispatch notes?			
(*d*) Are invoices checked arithmetically?			
(*e*) Is there an independent check of amounts recharged for freight, insurance, etc.?			

	Yes/ No/ N/A	Comment/reference to flowcharts, systems notes, etc.	Completed by
5.5 Can debtors' accounts be improperly credited or returns, etc. not be recorded in accounts?			
(*a*) Are credit notes: (i) prepared from approved price lists and/or checked against original invoice values, (ii) issued against approved documentation and authorized by a senior official. What are the limits of such authorizations? (iii) checked with goods returned documents, (iv) checked arithmetically, (v) pre-numbered and checked sequentially?			
(*b*) Are cash discounts: (i) checked to be in accordance with approved terms, (ii) checked arithmetically, (iii) where found to be excessive, followed up with the customer?			
(*c*) Are transfers between accounts or between sales and purchases ledgers authorized? If so, by whom, and are such transfers and the resulting balances agreed with customers/ suppliers?			
(*d*) Are goods-returned documents: (i) pre-numbered and checked sequentially, (ii) checked to credit notes, (iii) checked to stock records, if appropriate?			
5.6 Are accounts receivable properly controlled?			
(*a*) Are statements sent out on a regular basis?			
(*b*) Is there adequate control over, and identification of, accounts subject to			

	Yes/ No/ N/A	*Comment/reference to flowcharts, systems notes, etc.*	*Com- pleted by*
factoring agreements? (*c*) Are statements to customers controlled to prevent falsification, suppression or interception prior to mailing? (*d*) Are accounts receivable followed up if payment is not received promptly? (*e*) Are ledger balances: (i) periodically extracted, (ii) agreed with an independent control account, (iii) aged, (iv) reviewed by a responsible official? (*f*) Are bad-debt recoveries controlled by a responsible official and bad debts pursued even after being written off? (*g*) Are there satisfactory controls over ledger postings covering proof of entries, additions in day books and ledgers, independent control accounts, etc.? (*h*) Are any of the sales invoices factored, or pledged as security in any way?			

ICQ6. Receipts, payments, bank and cash balances

6.1 Can monies be received but not properly recorded? (*a*) Is incoming mail controlled to prevent misappropriation between arrival on premises and opening by authorized officials? (*b*) Is mail opened in presence of at least two employees? (*c*) Is there rotation of duties on mail opening and are these duties kept strictly separate from cashiers and staff responsible for the maintenance			

	Yes/ No/ N/A	Comment/reference to flowcharts, systems notes, etc.	Completed by
of ledgers, payment of wages, etc.?			
(*d*) Are records of over-the-counter cash receipts subject to independent controls?			
(*e*) Are all cheques received immediately stamped 'not negotiable — A/C payee only'?			
(*f*) Are all remittances received through the post: (i) listed in the mail room immediately on receipt, (ii) entered onto bank paying-in records, (iii) banked intact as soon as possible?			
(*g*) Are remittances received by other employees (e.g. travellers)? If so, are these receipts adequately controlled?			
(*h*) Are the remittances to the bank independently scrutinized against the bank statement?			
(*i*) Are pre-numbered receipts given for all cash received? If so, is there control over unused receipt books?			
(*j*) Are all cash-received sheets and cash books checked to prove that casts and cross casts are correct?			
(*k*) Is there adequate control over the accounts classification of receipts?			
6.2 Can unauthorized payments be made?			
(*a*) Are cheques crossed, marked 'A/C Payee' and 'Not Negotiable' before being signed?			
(*b*) Are unused cheque books kept in controlled custody?			
(*c*) Are at least two signatories required on cheques and are they governed as to authorized limits as to value?			
(*d*) Are cheques drawn only against			

	Yes/ No/ N/A	Comment/reference to flowcharts, systems notes, etc.	Completed by
authorized vouchers, remittance advices, etc.?			
(*e*) Are supporting documents produced to each cheque signatory before payment is made?			
(*f*) Is there adequate check that proper discounts are being obtained where possible?			
(*g*) Are the authorized vouchers, etc. immediately stamped 'paid' or otherwise cancelled to prevent duplicate payment?			
(*h*) Are cheques mailed without being returned to the drawers of these cheques?			
(*i*) Do any cheques carry pre-printed signatures?			
(*j*) Are cheques ever signed in blank?			
(*k*) If mechanical cheque signers are used, is such use adequately controlled?			
(*l*) Is there control over: (i) cheques drawn for cash, (ii) payments on account or in advance of delivery?			
(*m*) Are all cash payments sheets and cash books checked to prove that casts and cross casts are correct?			
(*n*) Are all direct debits and standing orders on bank statements checked for accuracy and authority?			
(*o*) Is there adequate control over the accounts classification of payments?			
(*p*) Is there proper control of cheques cashed for members of the staff?			
6.3 Can cash and bank balances (and negotiable instruments) be misappropriated?			
(*a*) Are bank reconciliations prepared at least monthly and regularly checked by a senior official other than those			

	Yes/ No/ N/A	Comment/reference to flowcharts, systems notes, etc.	Completed by
responsible for receipts and payments? (*b*) Are items more than one month old contained in the reconciliation statement thoroughly investigated to establish that they are genuine? (*c*) Are checks imposed on the sequential numbering of cheques, etc. issued and are all spoiled cheques retained and cancelled? (*d*) Are transfers between bank accounts authorized by a senior official? (*e*) Is petty cash subject to an imprest system? Is the float reasonable for the size of business and not excessive? (*f*) Are all negotiable instruments in hand subject to adequate control? (*g*) Are petty-cash balances independently counted and reconciled, on an irregular basis? (*h*) Are cash payments made only against authorized vouchers? Are vouchers then cancelled to prevent duplicate payment? (*i*) Are IOUs permitted only on the specific authority of a senior official?			

ICQ7. Investments and investment income

7.1 Are all purchases and sales of investments authorized, in accordance with the company's policy, and properly recorded in the accounts? (*a*) Are all purchases and sales authorized or approved by responsible officials? (*b*) Is a proper record maintained of all orders to brokers to buy and sell			

	Yes/ No/ N/A	Comment/reference to flowcharts, systems notes, etc.	Completed by
investments and are brokers' accounts regularly reconciled?			
(*c*) Are all records of purchases and sales checked with authorities?			
(*d*) Are investment records regularly agreed with the nominal ledger accounts?			
(*e*) Are gains or losses on disposal properly calculated?			
(*f*) Is the value of securities: (i) only written down or off on the authority of a responsible official, (ii) reviewed periodically for any changes?			
(*g*) Is the company's entitlement to bonus or rights issues properly recorded and checked against other sources (e.g. Extel cards)?			
7.2 Can documents of title be lost or misappropriated?			
(*a*) Are documents of title physically safeguarded and their location recorded?			
(*b*) Does the system ensure that securities not received promptly are followed up?			
(*c*) Are all investments registered in the name of the client?			
(*d*) Are documents of title subject to periodic physical inspection?			
(*e*) Can documents of title be released other than on authorized written instructions?			
(*f*) Do officials responsible for the purchase or sale of investments or the custody of documents of title have access to the investment records or the nominal ledger?			
(*g*) Are any documents of title pledged as security in any way?			

	Yes/ No/ N/A	Comment/reference to flowcharts, systems notes, etc.	Completed by
7.3 Is all income due received or otherwise accounted for? (*a*) Is income mandated directly to a bank account? (*b*) Are records of income independently checked with other sources, e.g. published accounts, Extel cards? (*c*) Does the system ensure that all income receivable in respect of securities sold 'ex-dividend' is received? (*d*) Is all income received in respect of securities sold 'cum dividend' properly accounted for to the purchaser? (*e*) Is there a proper system for claiming income on bearer shares?			

Specimen Minimum Controls Checklist

In planning the audit of a small business it will not normally be possible to place so much reliance on internal controls as would be the case for a large business with a more comprehensive system. In the small business, however, the absence of many of the more formal sources of control may be compensated for by the close personal involvement of management on the day-to-day operations.

It is for this reason, in the modified specimen checklist set out below for businesses of this type, the final question in each section requires an assessment as to how far the manager/proprietor supervision effectively compensates for what would otherwise be regarded as weakness in the system. In answering this question it will be necessary to assess *inter alia* whether the manager/proprietor exercises that supervision consistently and with sufficient diligence. This assessment should be made critically, and with an awareness that their close personal involvement in itself makes it easier for management to override controls and to exclude totally from the records transactions which a proper segregation of duties should ensure are included.

MCC1. Supervision, organization and general matters

KEY QUESTION: Is the business conducted in an orderly and profitable manner, including the maintenance of adequate accounting records?			
Subsidiary questions	*Yes/ No*	*Comment/reference to systems notes, etc.*	*Completed by*
1.1 Are the accounting records: (*a*) kept up to date and balanced monthly? (*b*) sufficient to satisfy the minimum requirements of the Companies Act 1976? (*c*) kept in safe custody? 1.2 Are journal entries authorized only by the manager/partner? 1.3 Is a suitable record of fixed assets maintained, periodically checked against assets, and reconciled with the nominal ledger? 1.4 Are investments adequately accounted for and bought and sold only on the authority of the manager/partner? 1.5 Are statutory books and documents of title kept in safe custody? 1.6 Is there adequate insurance cover (particularly fidelity insurance in respect of employees handling cash or desirable goods)? 1.7 Has the division and rotation of duties been developed to the fullest possible extent within the framework of the business? 1.8 Are all staff required to take holidays and are standby arrangements adequate to cover holiday and sickness periods? 1.9 What is the relationship of the manager/partner to the business (e.g. age, length of service, shareholding, relationship to other shareholders/employees, etc.)? 1.10 What is your assessment of the efficiency with which the commercial			

Subsidiary questions	*Yes/ No*	*Comment/reference to systems notes, etc.*	*Com- pleted by*
and accounting aspects of the business are conducted? 1.11 Are budgets used to monitor business performance? 1.12 Are adequate financial statements available to the manager/partner on a regular basis? (Describe form and content: append specimen.) 1.13 Does the manager/partner appear to take a direct and active interest in the financial affairs and reports which are available to him?			

MCC2. Purchases and creditors

KEY QUESTION: Is there reasonable assurance that all liabilities are: (*a*) incurred for the purposes of the business, and (*b*) fully and properly recorded?

Subsidiary questions	*Yes/ No*	*Comment/reference to systems notes, etc.*	*Com- pleted by*
2.1 Are all orders evidenced in writing? 2.2 Are purchase orders: (*a*) pre-numbered and all numbers accounted for? (*b*) approved by the manager/partner? (*c*) reviewed for items for which no invoices have been received? 2.3 Is the receipt of goods evidenced in writing? 2.4 Are goods-received records: (*a*) pre-numbered and all numbers accounted for? (*b*) compared with copy purchase orders? 2.5 Are suppliers' invoices: (*a*) checked with purchase orders? (*b*) checked with goods-received records?			

Subsidiary questions	*Yes/No*	*Comment/reference to systems notes, etc.*	*Completed by*
(*c*) checked for calculations? (*d*) initialled for work done? (*e*) approved by the manager/partner and authorized for processing? 2.6 Are purchase ledger balances regularly reconciled with: (*a*) suppliers' statements? (*b*) the control account? 2.7 Does the extent of manager/partner involvement and/or supervision in this area effectively compensate for any basic control weaknesses noted above?			

MCC3. Stocks and work in progress

KEY QUESTION: Is there reasonable assurance (*a*) that stocks cannot be misappropriated or mislaid, and (*b*) that the records fairly state the cost of all work-in-progress?			
Subsidiary questions	*Yes/No*	*Comment/reference to systems notes, etc.*	*Completed by*
Stocks 3.1 Are goods stored under proper security and in an orderly manner? 3.2 (*a*) Are perpetual stock records maintained? (*b*) If not, are stocks periodically estimated on the basis of gross-profit tests? 3.3 (*a*) Is the record (or estimate) of stock periodically checked against physical quantities? (*b*) Are material differences always investigated/explained? 3.4 Is the person responsible for the receipt, storage and issue of goods independent of any responsibility for the purchases, sales and stock records?			

Subsidiary questions	*Yes/ No*	*Comment/reference to systems notes, etc.*	*Com- pleted by*
Work-in-progress 3.5 Are inter-departmental transfers of (*a*) materials, (*b* partly finished work, (*c*) completed work all subject to documentary control? 3.6 Do the work-in-progress records properly identify: (*a*) each separate stage of production? (*b*) the amount of materials, labour and overheads charged to each job? 3.7 Does the extent of manager/partner involvement and/or supervision in this area effectively compensate for any basic control weaknesses noted above?			

MCC4. Wages

KEY QUESTION: Is there reasonable assurance that wages are paid only for work done and that the payroll cannot be inflated?			
Subsidiary questions	*Yes/ No*	*Comment/reference to systems notes, etc.*	*Com- pleted by*
4.1 Are individual personnel records maintained? 4.2 Are adequate time and/or piece-work records maintained? 4.3 Is the payroll independently checked for calculations and casts? 4.4 Are all changes in (*a*) employees and (*b*) rates of pay authorized only by the manager/partner? 4.5 Is a separate cheque drawn for the exact amount of net pay? 4.6 Does the manager/partner review and approve the payroll before signing the cheque? 4.7 Is the person preparing the payroll independent of any responsibility for the payment of wages?			

Subsidiary questions	*Yes/ No*	*Comment/reference to systems notes, etc.*	*Com-pleted by*
4.8 Are any amounts being drawn gross, without deduction of PAYE, either through petty cash or the payroll? If so, is it acceptable for Inland Revenue purposes?			
4.9 Does the extent of manager/partner involvement and/or supervision in this area effectively compensate for any basic control weaknesses noted above?			

MCC5. Sales and debtors

KEY QUESTION: Is there reasonable assurance: (*a*) that all goods leaving the premises are invoiced, (*b*) that all invoices are recorded and, (*c*) that debtors' accounts are not improperly credited?			
Subsidiary questions	*Yes/ No*	*Comment/reference to systems notes, etc.*	*Com-pleted by*
5.1 Credit control: does the manager/partner approve all new customers before goods are dispatched to them?			
5.2 Are all orders recorded?			
5.3 Are delivery notes:			
(*a*) pre-numbered and all accounted for?			
(*b*) prepared for all goods leaving the premises?			
(*c*) correlated with order forms?			
(*d*) correlated with invoices?			
5.4 Are invoices pre-numbered and all accounted for?			
5.5 Are credit notes pre-numbered and all accounted for?			
5.6 Are discounts, allowances and bad-debt write-offs authorized only by the manager/partner?			
5.7 Are statements:			
(*a*) sent out monthly to all customers?			

Subsidiary questions	*Yes/ No*	*Comment/reference to systems notes, etc.*	*Com-pleted by*
(*b*) reviewed by the manager/partner before mailing them himself? 5.8 Are sales ledger balances listed and reconciled with the control account monthly? 5.9 Does the listing include an age analysis and is this reviewed by the manager/partner? 5.10 Does the extent of manager/partner involvement and/or supervision in this area effectively compensate for any basic control weaknesses noted above?			

MCC6. Receipts

KEY QUESTION: Is there reasonable assurance that all monies received are fully and properly recorded?			
Subsidiary questions	*Yes/ No*	*Comment/reference to systems notes, etc.*	*Com-pleted by*
6.1 To what extent does the business: (*a*) sell goods or services for cash? (*b*) deal in 'desirable' products or services (which although generally invoiced on credit terms can, in fact, be sold or converted directly for cash)? 6.2 Does the manager/partner open and check the contents of all incoming mail? 6.3 Are all cheques stamped 'A/C PAYEE only'? 6.4 Are over-the-counter takings controlled by cash-register tapes/counter receipts, etc.? 6.5 Are all receipts banked (*a*) regularly (*b*) intact?			

Subsidiary questions	*Yes/ No*	*Comment/reference to systems notes, etc.*	*Com- pleted by*
6.6 Is the record of receipts independently checked against bank statements? 6.7 Is the 'cashier' totally independent of any responsibility for the sales or nominal ledger? 6.8 Does the extent of manager/partner involvement and/or supervision in this area effectively compensate for any basic control weaknesses noted above?			

MCC7. Payments

KEY QUESTION: Is there reasonable assurance that monies cannot be put to improper use?			
Subsidiary questions	*Yes/ No*	*Comment/reference to systems notes, etc.*	*Com- pleted by*
7.1 Are all payments (except sundry expenses) made by cheque? 7.2 Are all cheques signed: (*a*) by the manager/partner? (*b*) only after they have been properly completed (i.e. never in blank)? (*c*) only on the evidence of supporting documentation? (*d*) only after that documentation has been approved and cancelled? 7.3 Are all cheque numbers accounted for? 7.4 (*a*) Is petty cash subject to an imprest system? (*b*) Does the manager/partner approve all items above a set limit? 7.5 Does the manager/partner prepare, or review in detail, regular bank reconciliations? 7.6 Are those responsible for prepar-			

Subsidiary questions	*Yes/ No*	*Comment/reference to systems notes, etc.*	*Com- pleted by*
ing cheques or handling cash totally independent of any responsibility for: (*a*) approving or authorizing invoices for payment? (*b*) maintaining purchases and nominal ledgers? 7.7 Does the extent of manager/partner involvement and/or supervision in this area effectively compensate for any basic control weaknesses noted above?			

Whenever major changes occur in the way a business operates, careful consideration should be given as to whether the use of the MCC will continue to be appropriate. As businesses grow in size, so the level of internal control should correspondingly increase. The position should be appraised afresh each year in order to establish whether the control systems have become sufficiently comprehensive for them to be better assessed by completing a full ICQ. Similarly, a significant expansion in the size of a business which is not matched by an increased level of formal controls should cause a careful reappraisal of the extent to which management supervision can continue to be effective as an alternative.

This assessment of the efficacy of managerial supervision is particularly important, as it follows that failure to comply with the minimum controls specified by the checklist must entail reference in the audit report to accounting inadequacies. This matter of the appropriate form of audit report in the circumstances of the smaller business has been one which has beset the development of Auditing Standards. Whilst we do not believe substantial reliance on managerial supervision automatically has to lead to a form of audit report disclaimer, nevertheless we do not wish to underestimate the number of occasions where such involvement can throw into question the existence of essential and verifiable accounting controls.

In such circumstances the decision may be taken to adopt a non-systems based approach to the audit, i.e. not to rely on internal controls, but rather to follow the 'vouching' approach to the work. This may often be associated with the auditor receiving instructions to undertake extensive accountancy work too, but the audit work must be clearly identifiable as being a separate responsibility.

However, even in these circumstances where the audit concentrates on extensive vouching of transactions and substantiation of year-end balances,

Annual evaluation and test of internal control

Name of client:

Accounting period:

KEY QUESTION:								
Preliminary evaluation		Audit tests						
Overall conclusion		C/S†	Sample and population size	Description	Results/ conclusions	Audit schedule	Work done by Intls	Date
Ref*	Reasons*							
Evaluated by	Date		Tests designed by	Date				
Reviewed by	Date		Approved by	Date	Reviewed by	Date		

* List (by reference to supporting documentation) the major strengths and weaknesses of the system which support this conclusion.

† Indicate whether (C)ompliance or (S)ubstantive test.

the requirement for proper accounting records remains, and this implies the need still to consider a minimum level of controls.

Evaluation of Internal Control

The record of the systems and the information obtained from completing either the Internal Control Questionnaire or the Minimum Controls Checklist provides the basis for a preliminary evaluation of the extent of internal control within the system. Such evaluation should be of each key control question. It will be this preliminary evaluation which will determine the nature and extent of the audit tests planned: as such it is critical to the efficiency and effectiveness of the audit and its importance cannot be too greatly emphasized.

Accordingly it should be formally documented, listing—with reference to supporting documentation — the major strengths and weaknesses in a system, and then recording an overall conclusion. Moreover it will be at these major strengths and weaknesses that the subsequent audit testing will be directed, and it may therefore be convenient to devise audit documentation in a manner to facilitate this approach.

A suggested format is set out opposite which combines evaluation of internal control with an audit programme to test the critical areas.

5 Auditing transactions

Planning Audit Tests

Having recorded the systems of accounting and internal control and assessed the strengths and weaknesses, the auditor is then in a position to plan the nature and extent of the audit tests he proposes to execute in relation to the company's accounting transactions. The tailoring of the audit programme in this way to the individual demands of different accounting and control systems is fundamental to the concept of systems audits, and again it may be seen how it is dependent upon the care with which the systems evaluation has taken place. A distinction will be drawn between compliance tests, to be applied where internal controls are to be relied upon, and substantive tests. It is important to make this distinction correctly because the nature of the subsequent audit approach may be dependent upon it. In this connection the Planning Audit Tests diagram set out may be of assistance as a reminder of the general audit approach outlined in Chapter 1.

Planning audit tests

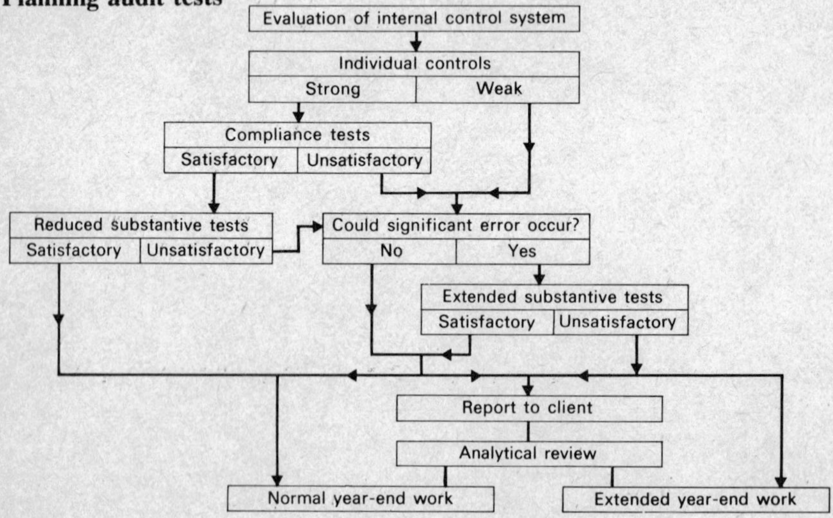

The distinction is also well illustrated in 'True and Fair' (Issue 12, Summer 1979, the bulletin of the Auditing Practices Committee), by two examples of the different types of test. Firstly a compliance test: 'to satisfy yourself with reasonable confidence that no goods *can* be dispatched without being invoiced'. This is contrasted with a substantive test 'to satisfy yourself that no material amounts of goods *have* been dispatched without being invoiced'.

Compliance Tests

Compliance tests are explained in the Auditing Guideline on Internal Controls:

> 'The auditor is not entitled to place any reliance on an internal control based solely on his preliminary evaluation. He should carry out compliance tests to obtain reasonable assurance that the controls on which he wishes to rely were functioning both effectively and throughout the period. It should be noted that it is the control which is being tested by a compliance test, and not the transaction which may be the medium used for the test. For this reason the auditor should record and investigate all exceptions revealed by his compliance testing, regardless of the amount involved in the particular transaction.'

It concludes:

> 'If compliance tests disclose no exceptions, the auditor may reasonably place reliance on the effective functioning of the internal control tested.'

It is submitted that the auditor will then be able to limit his substantive tests on the relevant accounting information.

Compliance tests are therefore designed to test that the key aspects of the controls have operated so that the auditor is able to rely upon the information being produced by the system. For this reason his tests should be concentrated on those aspects of the control system which are fundamental to its efficient and accurate operation. However, if the results of the compliance tests are unsatisfactory, if for instance, one number of the company's staff is not adequately performing the control function delegated to him, then the system, notwithstanding the initial evaluation, must be regarded in practice as being weak and, as an alternative, appropriate tests must be designed to evaluate the materiality of that weakness.

The programme of compliance tests will need to be written out by senior staff responsible for the audit because this whole approach of tailoring the work to the different requirements of individual systems precludes the use of any master audit programme suitable for use under a variety of circumstances.

This programme will record the exact details of the work to be performed by the audit staff, columns being provided in order that the persons who are occupied in performing each part of the checking may add their initials as and when they complete it.

If an audit programme is drawn up in this way, the auditor can be certain that all the necessary audit work is planned in a systematic manner after careful consideration of all the circumstances of the case. He may then be certain that the audit staff will cover the whole of the ground, and in future years, the staff engaged upon the audit can see by reference to the programme exactly what work has previously been performed. Further, reporting partners can see at any time what part of the work has been completed, and what remains to be done. In a large practice, unless some such method is adopted, the reporting partners would of necessity lose a very large amount of control, and be very much in the hands of their staff. Then the efficiency of the audit would depend, not upon the skill and competence of such partners, but upon the skill and competency of the member of staff in charge of the particular audit.

An objection to the programming of audit tests is that the staff may lose a sense of responsibility, and consequently carry out the work in a mechanical manner. It should be impressed upon them, therefore, that the programme set out is the basis upon which the audit is to be conducted, and that they must use their intelligence when carrying it out. They should be encouraged to recommend additions and improvements to the audit programme. It should constantly be borne in mind that experience shows that serious discrepancies in accounts are frequently revealed by unprogrammed investigations and inquiries.

The greatest danger in practical auditing is that the work may become mechanical. Most businesses are in a process of continual change, and this process inevitably extends to the accounting system. These changes will be disclosed by the continual review of the system of internal control, and the audit programme must be regularly modified to ensure that it, too, is kept up to date.

For this reason it is important that the audit programme, besides recording the actual test carried out, should be cross-referenced to the appropriate questions in the internal control questionnaire and should clearly identify any errors or weaknesses found during the execution of the tests, as those may affect the overall view taken of the adequacy of the internal control. Thus, if the compliance tests have disclosed exceptions which indicate that the control being tested was not operating properly in practice, the auditor should determine the reasons. He needs to assess whether each exception is only an isolated departure or is representative of others, and whether it indicates the possible existence of errors in the accounting records. If the explanation he receives suggests that the exception is only an isolated departure, then he must confirm the validity of that explanation, for example by carrying out further tests. If the explanation or the further tests confirm that the control being tested was not operating properly throughout the period, then he cannot rely on that control. In these circumstances the auditor should determine whether he can seek to rely on an alternative control and carry out compliance tests on that, or whether he is unable to restrict his substantive testing.

Substantive Tests

The Auditing Guideline on Audit Evidence states that:

> 'Audit tests may be classified as "compliance", or "substantive" according to their primary purpose. Both purposes are sometimes achieved concurrently. Substantive tests are thus tests of transactions and balances, and other procedures such as an analytical review, which provide audit evidence as to the completeness, accuracy and validity of the information contained in the accounting records or in the financial statements.'

The nature, extent and timing of the substantive tests are determined by the degree of reliance which the auditor can place on the operation of internal controls.

Where there are no controls on which to place reliance, or where the auditor has decided that it will be more efficient to disregard the existence of internal controls, he will similarly need to design and carry out substantive tests in such a way as to obtain reasonable assurance that material error or omission has not occurred.

Substantive tests must therefore be adopted in relation to items which are material to the validity of the accounts and may need to be extended where compliance tests have proved the controls to be weak.

Designing substantive tests appropriate to individual circumstances often calls for some ingenuity on the part of the auditor; but the nature of the resultant detailed tests of transactions will generally fall into one or more of the following broad classifications and should be recorded in a programme similar to that used for compliance tests.

Vouching approach

Vouching means the examination of the transactions of a business, together with documentary and other evidence of sufficient validity to satisfy an auditor that such transactions are in order, have been properly authorized, and are correctly recorded in the accounting records. By this means the auditor goes behind the accounting records and traces the entries to their source, and it is in this way that he can ascertain the full meaning and circumstances of the various transactions. In the absence of an effective internal control system, the entries in the records may show only such information as the client's accountant chooses to disclose, and such information may be purposely, or unintentionally, contrary to the true facts. Therefore, only by examining external evidence can an auditor possibly ascertain the real state of affairs.

The vouching approach has its place in every audit, but extensive vouching should be restricted to circumstances of weakness and should only be adopted with caution and after careful consideration of what it will achieve. This method of audit testing is very time-consuming and the auditor must always be wary lest, even after extensive vouching, the state of the control systems is such that he is still unable to derive assurance as to the accuracy of the recording of other transactions which he has not actually vouched.

Examination of management information

This would include the detailed review of management accounts, together with their comparison with budgeted results and actual financial statements for comparable periods in prior years, from which the auditor would follow up any unusual features disclosed.

Similarly he would undertake appropriate ratio analysis of figures connected with the area of weakness, the resultant ratios being compared with those expected and those being achieved by comparable companies within the same industry group.

Extended balance-sheet audit work

Especially in the absence of a satisfactory system of internal control, the auditor may find the most effective form of substantive test, and in some cases the only practicable one, to be the extension of his audit work on the final accounts figures. For instance, if the key control question 'Can goods be dispatched to a bad credit risk?' receives an affirmative answer, then the most effective audit test will be an extension of the year-end balance sheet work necessary to verify the adequacy of the provision for bad and doubtful debts.

Such applications of substantive testing to year-end balances and financial statements will be matters to which we shall return in later chapters.

Suggested Tests for Auditing Transactions

Set out below are examples of typical audit tests which may be appropriate to the key control questions outlined in chapter 4. It should be now appreciated that these are merely guidelines, and any selection of these tests will need to be augmented by additional work specifically designed for the precise circumstances under review.

In drawing up detailed tests it will always be helpful to refer to the Auditing Guideline on Audit Evidence. This suggests that audit tests fall into the broad categories of:

inspection — reviewing or examining records, documents or tangible assets

observation — looking at an operation or procedure being performed by others with a view to determining the manner of its performance
inquiry — seeking relevant information from knowledgeable persons inside or outside the enterprise, whether formally or informally, orally or in writing
computation — checking the arithmetical accuracy of accounting records or performing independent calculations.

It further puts forward the following general presumptions concerning the reliability of audit evidence:

'documentary evidence is more reliable than oral evidence;
evidence obtained from independent sources outside the enterprise is more reliable than that secured solely from within the enterprise;
evidence originated by the auditor by such means as analysis and physical inspection is more reliable than evidence obtained from others'.

From this we may conclude that the most effective audit tests will involve the *auditor* obtaining *documentary* evidence from *independent* third parties; the least effective may be those which rely on oral evidence obtained within the company; and accordingly the detailed audit programme should be constructed with this in mind.

Organizational and general matters

Client: Accounting date:			Prepared by: Reviewed by:	Date: Date:	
Audit tests	*Details of tests*	*Audit schedule*	*Errors, etc.*	*Work performed By*	*Date*
General 1. Obtain a copy of organization chart. 2. Consider internal control effected by division of duties. 3. Consider actual results against budget and ascertain reasons for major variances. 4. Examine reports of internal audit department and note points for particular attention. 5. Check that accounting procedures laid down are satisfactory and are being maintained. 6. Test specific areas of laid-down accounting procedures.					

Client:			Prepared by:	Date:	
Accounting date:			Reviewed by:	Date:	
Audit tests	*Details of tests*	*Audit schedule*	*Errors, etc.*	*Work performed By*	*Date*
Secretarial 1. Check records of use of seal from minute book and note any points affecting audit. 2. Extract and agree schedules of members and debenture holders to total issued capital, etc. 3. Reconcile unclaimed dividend/interest account. 4. Examine minutes, noting approval and any points affecting audit. 5. Inspect all statutory books and confirm up to date.					

Client:			Prepared by:	Date:	
Accounting date:			Reviewed by:	Date:	
Audit tests	*Details of tests*	*Audit schedule*	*Errors, etc.*	*Work performed By*	*Date*
Fixed Assets 1. Check compliance with rules laid down for authorizing capital expenditure or disposals. 2. Check actual costs, etc. against budgets and ascertain reasons for major variances. 3. Consider correctness of records (including overhead allocation) of capital works carried out by company. 4. Examine asset register, vouch movements and note periodic check by company. 5. Test existence of assets. 6. Check depreciation calculations.					

7. Check reconciliation of asset register to nominal ledger.					

Client:			Prepared by:	Date:	
Accounting date:			Reviewed by:	Date:	
Audit tests	*Details of tests*	*Audit schedule*	*Errors, etc.*	*Work performed By*	*Date*
Insurance 1. Obtain a schedule of insurance policies and the extent of cover, and review for adequacy and completeness. 2. Check that all required declarations and certificates have been submitted.					

Client:			Prepared by:	Date:	
Accounting date:			Reviewed by:	Date:	
Audit tests	*Details of tests*	*Audit schedule*	*Errors, etc.*	*Work performed By*	*Date*
Group trading 1. Obtain a schedule of all group, associated and other affiliated companies. 2. Enquire into relevant interests in other concerns with which the company has dealings. 3. Check that all transfers of funds have been properly authorized and recorded and that the relevant statutory and other requirements have been complied with. 4. Test transactions and note and inquire into any that appear to be on other than arm's length terms. 5. Inquire into any expenditure made for or by, and income received for or by, such concerns and test with relevant documentation.					

Client:		Prepared by:	Date:		
Accounting date:		Reviewed by:	Date:		
Audit tests	*Details of tests*	*Audit schedule*	*Errors, etc.*	*Work performed By*	*Date*
Nominal ledger 1. Test nominal ledger casts. 2. Test extraction of trial balance and casts. 3. Examine nominal ledger for unusual entries. 4. Examine journal entries and authorizations. 5. Test journal postings to nominal ledger. 6. Vouch sample of journal entries.					

Purchases and accounts payable

Client:		Prepared by:	Date:		
Accounting date:		Reviewed by:	Date:		
COMPLIANCE TESTS *Audit tests*	*Details of tests*	*Audit schedule*	*Errors, etc.*	*Work performed By*	*Date*
1. Test sequence of purchase orders. 2. Test approval of purchase orders. 3. Test adherence to authority limits. 4. Test sequence of goods-received records. 5. Test sequence of goods-returned records. 6. Test authorization of adjustments to purchase ledger balances. 7. Test that purchase invoices are serially numbered. 8. Test sequence of purchase invoices. 9. Test correlation of purchase invoices with purchase orders and goods-received records.					

10. Test correlation of credit notes with goods-returned records. 11. Test that casts and calculations on purchase invoices have been checked. 12. Test that purchase invoices have been coded for accounting classification purposes. 13. Test that VAT has been correctly segregated. 14. Test that purchase invoice 'grid' has been initialled for work done. 15. Test approval of purchase invoices for processing into accounting system.					

Client: Accounting date:			Prepared by: Reviewed by:	Date: Date:	
SUBSTANTIVE TESTS *Audit tests*	*Details of tests*	*Audit schedule*	*Errors, etc.*	*Work performed* *By*	 *Date*
1. Test purchase orders in relation to nature of company's business. 2. Select sample of goods-received records and: (*a*) note whether goods received have been checked as to quantity and quality; (*b*) check against suppliers' advice notes; (*c*) trace copies of purchasing, accounts and stock records department. 3. Test goods-returned records to stock records. 4. Review: (*a*) outstanding purchase orders; (*b*) outstanding goods-received records; (*c*) outstanding goods-returned records. 5. Examine reconciliations of purchase ledger balances with suppliers' statements.					

Client:			Prepared by:	Date:	
Accounting date:			Reviewed by:	Date:	
SUBSTANTIVE TESTS *Audit tests*	*Details of tests*	*Audit schedule*	*Errors, etc.*	*Work performed* *By*	 *Date*
6. Review debit balances in purchase ledger. 7. Check purchase invoices to purchase orders and goods-received records for relevant details. 8. Check purchase invoice codings for accounting classification purposes. 9. Test casts and calculations on purchase invoices. 10. Select sample of purchase invoices and test postings to: (*a*) personal account; (*b*) control account; (*c*) nominal account. 11. Agree list of balances to control account. 12. Review nominal accounts for expenses for unusual items. 13. Inquire into procedures for identification of liabilities secured by reservation of title. 14. Test procedures relating to recording purchases subject to reservation of title.					

Stocks and costing

Client:			Prepared by:	Date:	
Accounting date:			Reviewed by:	Date:	
COMPLIANCE TESTS *Audit tests*	*Details of tests*	*Audit schedule*	*Errors, etc.*	*Work performed* *By*	 *Date*
1. Observe physical security over stocks. 2. Test recording of stock movements. 3. Test authority for stock adjustments. 4. Test authority for dumping of stocks.					

5. Test recording of stock movements relating to third parties. 6. Test authority for stock movements. 7. Inspect cost-variance analyses. 8. Test identification of stocks held subject to reservation of title.					

Client:		Prepared by:		Date:	
Accounting date:		Reviewed by:		Date:	
SUBSTANTIVE TESTS *Audit tests*	*Details of tests*	*Audit schedule*	*Errors, etc.*	*Work performed* *By*	 *Date*
1. Examine selected stock records, vouch movements and count stock balances. 2. Examine calculations supporting shrinkage allowances. 3. Confirm stock reports from third parties and stock records. 4. Vouch cost records with underlying documentation. 5. Test transfer of information from cost records to financial records.					

Client:		Prepared by:		Date:	
Accounting date:		Reviewed by:		Date:	
COMPLIANCE TESTS *Audit tests*	*Details of tests*	*Audit schedule*	*Errors, etc.*	*Work performed* *By*	 *Date*
1. Test sample of time records, etc. for: (*a*) approval by responsible official; (*b*) check of casts and calculations. 2. Test authority for payment of casual labour. 3. Observe wages distribution for adherence to procedures.					

Client:			Prepared by:	Date:	
Accounting date:			Reviewed by:	Date:	
COMPLIANCE TESTS *Audit tests*	*Details of tests*	*Audit schedule*	*Errors, etc.*	*Work performed* *By*	 *Date*
4. Test authorizations for payroll amendments. 5. Test control over payroll amendments. 6. Examine evidence of checking of payroll calculations. 7. Examine evidence of approval of payrolls by a responsible official. 8. Examine evidence of independent checks on payrolls. 9. Inspect payroll reconciliations. 10. Examine explanations for payroll expense variances. 11. Test authorities for payroll deductions. 12. Inspect reconciliations of payroll deductions.					

Client:			Prepared by:	Date:	
Accounting date:			Reviewed by:	Date:	
SUBSTANTIVE TESTS *Audit tests*	*Details of tests*	*Audit schedule*	*Errors, etc.*	*Work performed* *By*	 *Date*
1. Select sample of time records, etc. and test casts and calculations. 2. Test sample of personnel records for: (*a*) rates of pay; (*b*) authorization of changes in rates of pay; (*c*) leavers' and joiners' personnel details. 3. Select payrolls and:					

(*a*) check to time records, etc.;					
(*b*) test to personnel records;					
(*c*) test casts and calculations;					
(*d*) vouch deductions.					
4. Vouch sample of payroll reconciliations.					
5. Test totals of cheques drawn to net pay due.					
6. Test controls over unclaimed wages and vouch signatures for receipts to personnel records.					
7. Test postings of payrolls to nominal accounts.					

Sales and accounts receivable

Client:		Prepared by:		Date:	
Accounting date:		Reviewed by:		Date:	
COMPLIANCE TESTS *Audit tests*	*Details of tests*	*Audit schedule*	*Errors, etc.*	*Work performed* *By*	 *Date*
1. Test approval of orders for creditworthiness.					
2. Test sequence of dispatch notes.					
3. Test customer acknowledgements of receipt of goods.					
4. Test correlation of dispatch notes with sales invoices.					
5. Test correlation of sales invoices with dispatch notes.					
6. Test sequence of sales invoices.					
7. Test postings of sales invoices to personal and nominal accounts.					
8. Test that invoices quote customers' order numbers.					
9. Test evidence of arithmetical check on sales invoices.					

Client:			Prepared by:	Date:	
Accounting date:			Reviewed by:	Date:	
COMPLIANCE TESTS *Audit tests*	*Details of tests*	*Audit schedule*	*Errors, etc.*	*Work performed* *By*	*Date*
10. Test that VAT has been correctly segregated.					
11. Test sequence of credit notes.					
12. Test correlation of credit notes with goods-returned documents.					
13. Test authorization of credit notes.					
14. Test evidence of arithmetical check on credit notes.					
15. Test authority for bad-debts written-off.					
16. Test sequence of returned-goods documents to credit notes.					
17. Test correlation of returned-goods documents to credit notes.					
18. Test postings of credit notes to personal and nominal accounts.					
19. Test authorization of transfers between personal accounts.					
20. Test debtors ageing analysis.					

Client:			Prepared by:	Date:	
Accounting date:			Reviewed by:	Date:	
SUBSTANTIVE TESTS *Audit tests*	*Details of tests*	*Audit schedule*	*Errors, etc.*	*Work performed* *By*	*Date*
1. Review selected credit limits.					
2. Check that credit limits have not been exceeded.					
3. Examine stores and dispatch security.					

4. Select sample of sales invoices and: (*a*) check to customer order; (*b*) note whether details agree to dispatch records; (*c*) check prices against independent sources; (*d*) check extensions and casts; (*e*) check postings to personal and nominal accounts.				
5. Select sample of credit notes and: (*a*) check to returned-goods documents; (*b*) check prices; (*c*) check extensions and casts; (*d*) check authorization; (*e*) check postings to personal and nominal accounts.				
6. Test cash discounts in accordance with approved terms and for arithmetical correctness.				
7. Check sample of bad-debts written-off against external evidence.				
8. Agree list of balances to control account.				
9. Observe procedures for dispatch of statements to debtors.				
10. Review follow-up procedures for recovery of bad-debts written-off.				

Receipts, payments, bank and cash balances

Client:			Prepared by:	Date:	
Accounting date:			Reviewed by:	Date:	
COMPLIANCE TESTS *Audit tests*	*Details of tests*	*Audit schedule*	*Errors, etc.*	*Work performed* *By*	 *Date*
1. Attend mail-opening procedures.					
2. Test control medium for cash receipts for independent check to bank lodgements.					
3. Test sequence of any pre-numbered receipts for cash.					
4. Test authority for cash discounts.					
5. Test evidence of arithmetical check on cash-received records.					
6. Inspect current cheque books for: (*a*) restrictive endorsements; (*b*) sequential use; (*c*) controlled custody; (*d*) any signatures in blank.					
7. Test cancellation of paid vouchers.					
8. Test evidence of arithmetical check on card payment records.					
9. Examine evidence of authority for current standing orders and direct debits.					
10. Examine evidence of regular bank reconciliations.					
11. Examine evidence of independent check of bank reconciliations.					
12. Examine evidence of follow-up of outstanding items on bank reconciliations.					

13. Test petty cash vouchers for approval. 14. Test cancellation of paid petty cash vouchers. 15. Test evidence of arithmetical check on petty cash records. 16. Examine evidence of independent check of petty cash balance.					

Client:		Prepared by:		Date:	
Accounting date:		Reviewed by:		Date:	
SUBSTANTIVE TESTS *Audit tests*	*Details of tests*	*Audit schedule*	*Errors, etc.*	*Work performed* *By*	*Date*
1. Test mail-room listings of receipts to: (*a*) bank paying-in records; (*b*) cash-received records; (*c*) bank statement; and confirm prompt banking. 2. Test control medium for cash receipts to bank lodgements. 3. Vouch miscellaneous receipts. 4. Test rates and calculations of cash discounts. 5. Test casts and cross casts of cash-received records. 6. Test postings of cash-received to: (*a*) personal account or nominal account; (*b*) control account(s). 7. Vouch miscellaneous cash payments outside purchase ledger system. 8. Test casts and cross casts of cash payment records.					

Client:		Prepared by:	Date:		
Accounting date:		Reviewed by:	Date:		
SUBSTANTIVE TESTS *Audit tests*	*Details of tests*	*Audit schedule*	*Errors, etc.*	*Work performed* *By*	*Date*
9. Test postings of cash payments to: (*a*) personal account or nominal account; (*b*) control account(s). 10. Vouch sample of returned cheques. 11. Check selected bank reconciliations in detail. 12. Vouch transfers between bank accounts and reimbursements of petty cash. 13. Vouch sample of petty-cash payments and sundry petty-cash receipts. 14. Test casts and cross casts of petty-cash records. 15. Count and reconcile petty-cash float. 16. Test petty-cash postings. 17. Test that exchanged cheques are banked promptly.					

Investments and investment income

Client:		Prepared by:	Date:		
Accounting date:		Reviewed by:	Date:		
Audit tests	*Details of tests*	*Audit schedule*	*Errors, etc.*	*Work performed* *By*	*Date*
1. Test purchases and sales with evidence of authority and confirm prices with contract notes. 2. Test agreement of investment records with					

nominal ledger at dates throughout period.					
3. Test nominal ledger postings and casts.					
4. Test calculation of gains or losses on disposal.					
5. Check authority for writing-down or -off investments.					
6. Test holdings against external sources for entitlement to bonus and rights issues.					
7. Examine security of documents of title.					
8. Inspect documents of title to confirm that registered in name of client.					
9. Examine evidence of checks carried out by client.					
10. Test authorization for release of documents of title.					

Sample Selection

Having decided upon the nature of the audit tests to be applied in the individual circumstances, it remains to decide upon the extent of those tests and the method to be adopted for the selection of the given sample. Broadly there are two ways of selecting an audit sample, either by the use of random selection techniques or otherwise by the exercise of personal judgement in a number of ways.

Random selection techniques

Although the auditor bases his opinion on the results of many tests, nevertheless each test contributes to his opinion on the assumption that the sample tested is representative. Wherever a sample of less than 100% is taken, there is, however, the possibility of the sample selected not being representative of the population. Moreover, mere avoidance of personal bias through a haphazard choice of items does not provide a random sample. The requirement is that each item in the population must have an equal probability of being selected, but this cannot easily be met.

Theoretically, a truly random sample could be obtained by shuffling the entries to be audited and then drawing the required number of items to be tested. However, the practical problems which would be involved can readily be seen, and these may be avoided by employing random-number tables, consisting of lists of digits which have been tested for randomness by the use of statistical techniques. Having obtained a starting point in the tables by haphazard selection, one should proceed systematically down the vertical columns of numbers, discarding those outside the limits of the population, until enough random numbers have been obtained to satisfy the required sample. If, for any reason, too many items are ever obtained in a sample, they can only be discarded in reverse sequence of selection and not on the basis of those appearing at the end of, say, a numerical order list.

The most common problem arising from the use of random-number tables is the need to be able to identify each item in the population by a discreet number. However, an exact knowledge of the population size is not always necessary and an approximation can be achieved which will enable each item to be identified if selected. For example, where there is a fairly consistent number of items on each page and where the number of pages is known, the random numbers drawn should include sufficient digits firstly to identify the page and secondly to identify the item number on the page. In such a situation it is vital that the maximum number of items appearing on any page is allowed for, so that every item does stand an equal chance of being selected.

Fixed-interval selection

Where random selection is not practicable, the best alternative is fixed-interval selection (systematic sampling) which may be employed without undue risk of corrupting the sample. This technique involves the selection of every *n*th item, where *n* is the result of dividing the population by the sample size and then selecting at random the first item to be sampled. To ensure that the full sample size is obtained, the interval should be rounded down to the nearest whole number.

This method of selection does have two disadvantages of which the user should be aware:

(*a*) there is a danger that unrecognized time-cycles in the population might give rise to a bias which would corrupt the sample;

(*b*) a sample selected by this means cannot be subsequently extended should the need arise.

Stratification

Where it is desirable that emphasis should be placed on a certain part of the population and that any sample should be biased towards items of that type, then stratification of the population can be used. Its most common application is to enable the concentration of audit testing on the higher value items in a population, in order to ensure that items, outside the samples selected, which could contain errors, are less likely to be material in relation to the objectives of the audit test.

Block sampling

This involves the selection of a defined block of transactions for audit testing, such as all items within a particular period, or all items of a particular type.

Sample Sizes

Having established the nature of the detailed audit checking to be undertaken and the means of selecting the items to be checked, we are still left with the problem of determining the size of the sample to be selected.

Most commonly in practice this too remains a matter for judgement, exercised by the auditor on the basis of his experience and influenced in the individual circumstances by the following factors:

(*a*) the relative importance of the control to be tested;
(*b*) the overall adequacy of internal control in the area as a whole;
(*c*) the size of the population;
(*d*) the extent to which there are to be other audit tests in the same area.

Judgement samples, however, lack two important features: their size cannot be determined objectively, and their results cannot be evaluated objectively. In the light of this and of the objective of sampling, which is to enable the auditor to express an opinion on a total population of items by examining only a part of them, there has therefore been a growing trend towards the use of statistical sampling techniques, a mathematical method of determining sample size and evaluating sample results.

If the auditor is to use statistical sampling techniques, then he must familiarize himself with some basic terminology.

'*Confidence*'—any test of less than 100% of a population must inevitably involve a certain degree of risk that the sample will not be truly representative of the population from which it was drawn. This degree of risk is expressed in terms of confidence in the results.

'*Precision*'—similarly, the projection of sample results across an entire population causes a loss of precision. This is usually reflected by quoting the results not as a specific figure, but rather falling within a range.

These two factors are closely related since a given result can always be expressed to a high degree of precision and a low degree of confidence, or alternatively to a low degree of precision with a high degree of confidence. Thus a given result might be expressed either as giving 90% confidence of accuracy within the range ±2%, or as giving 99% confidence of accuracy within the range ±10%. The choice lies between greater accuracy with less confidence or greater confidence of a lower degree of accuracy. To increase both requires a larger sample size. Before a sample size can be determined, therefore, decisions need to be taken as to the degrees of precision and confidence required, after which published tables are available to show how many items will need to be examined without disclosing error to achieve the specified levels.

In this context, the numerical sampling guidelines below may prove useful.

Overall adequacy of internal control	Relative importance of this control: Major	Medium	Minor	Population
Good	85	45	30	Less than 5000
Medium	100	55	35	
Poor	135	70	45	
Good	95	50	35	5000 +
Medium	115	60	40	
Poor	150	75	50	

These tables have been compiled on the basis that:

(*a*) The overall adequacy of internal control determines the confidence level to be used:

Good 85%
Medium 90%
Poor 95%

(*b*) The relative importance of the control to be tested determines the maximum acceptable error rate:

Major ±2%
Medium ±4%
Minor ±6%

N.B. These tables cannot be used for population sizes of less than 500.

It will emerge that it is the finite size of the sample which is important rather than the size of the population. For example, to achieve 95% confidence of accuracy within the rate ±2%, the sample size required from a population of 500 would be 135, whereas this would only increase by 15 to 150 were the population infinite. Where this sample size is broadly acceptable, then for practical purposes an infinite population can be assumed and such a sample of 150 can be employed. This is commonly less than would be checked as a result of judgement sampling on a large audit. Where this is not the case, then the auditor may care to reflect on the adequacy of his existing sample sizes. Numerical sample sizes referred to so far have been on the footing that the sample would be error-free. Where this is not the case, then more work remains to be done. Firstly the items containing errors need to be carefully vouched, and secondly the sample size relating to other items of that type needs to be extended so that the auditor may better assess the likelihood of similar errors recurring to a material extent.

However, all conclusions derived so far will remain in terms of the number of errors rather than their value, for such evaluation is a separate and complex exercise whose application to auditing is not yet universally accepted by either accountants or statisticians. Suffice it to say for these purposes that means are available by which the auditor may attempt to evaluate the likely magnitude of the misstatement of the figures in the accounts arising from the errors discovered by his statistical sample. Nevertheless, the 'quality' (or rather the heinousness) of the individual error may still be of critical significance to the auditor; as may be also the pattern, rather than the number, of a quantity of errors.

A particular statistically based approach, however, which may be of practical assistance, particularly with regard to the balance-sheet audit, is that of cumulative monetary sampling. Hitherto we have been dealing with numerical sampling, that is the sampling of a number of documents the result of which will tell us, within certain limits, the number of documents to which errors apply. However, this does not give any direct evidence as to the value of the extent of error and hence this form of sampling is more useful in compliance testing, where value is of secondary importance since that is not the objective of the tests. By contrast, cumulative monetary sampling is suited to balance-sheet audit work, as the impact of the errors found can be expressed in value terms.

The basis of the method is probably easiest to illustrate with a simple example:

— assume the sum of £10 000 is taken as the auditor's judgement of materiality, then
— he selects as the first item in his sample that which causes the cumulative monetary total in the area being tested to equal or exceed £10 000
— he selects as the second test the item which brings the cumulative monetary total over £20 000, and so on.

It follows from a cumulative monetary sampling approach that all items greater than the materiality limit will be selected for testing automatically, and that otherwise an item's chance of selection is exactly proportionate to its relationship to the materiality limit.

It remains then to evaluate the results of the monetary sampling, by

— listing the total value of each item in which an error has been found
— listing the amounts of the errors, differentiating those occurring in items greater than the materiality limit
— multiplying up the error value for those items below the materiality limit

— adding in the error value of the items greater than the materiality limit
— ranking the adjusted errors by size, dealing separately with errors of over- and under-statement
— calculating the precision-adjusted error by reference to tables of precision-adjustment factors.

At this stage it will be possible to calculate the revised precision which is the maximum possible error in the population, and to estimate the likely actual error. These data will need to be considered by the auditor in conjunction with his view of materiality so that he may decide how the results of testing his statistical sample bear upon his audit opinion.

The question which the auditor normally asks himself when drawing up his audit programme is 'how much work must I do reasonably to ensure that the transactions I have examined are representative of the whole population of similar transactions?' This is fundamentally a statistical question and it should be considered whether it may not best be answered in statistical terms. However, it must be remembered that statistical sampling techniques are merely aids; they still leave the auditor with the major decisions of principle, and they are in no way a substitute for the alert, inquiring approach and the flair which distinguishes a good auditor.

Materiality

Our initial description of the first stages of obtaining audit evidence would not be complete without introducing the concept of materiality, as the Auditing Standards contain several references to the subject and references to the materiality or significance of an item also appear with some frequency in the Companies Acts and in Statements of Standard Accounting Practice. Moreover its consideration is germane to the ensuing chapters dealing with the audit of the profit and loss account and balance sheet.

A set of financial statements summarizes a mass of facts, and those who prepare and report on them have to extract from all that information those items which have a real bearing on the true and fair view. Not to disclose an important fact or figure may give a misleading view to the financial statement; conversely, the overall view can be obscured by the inclusion of too much detail. A true and fair view can take a variety of forms. There are degrees of latitude involved in the preparation of financial statements, the acceptable parameters of which are dictated by judgements as to materiality. Materiality is fundamental to the whole audit process and it has many aspects from an auditor's point of view. It influences the extent of his field work, the scope and thrust of his detailed audit tests, and the way in which he will substantiate particular assets and liabilities. It also has a bearing on his evaluation of any errors or discrepancies disclosed by his audit work.

Thus the extent to which the auditor will increase his substantive tests will depend largely on his evaluation of the significance of the way in which the error has arisen.

We also have to be concerned with materiality in the accounting disclosure and reporting sense, and particularly in so far as it has a bearing on the principles of presentation in financial statements. For this purpose, the English Institute's Statement V.10, 'The Interpretation of "Material" in relation to accounts', offers the following definition:

> 'A matter is material if its non-disclosure, misstatement or omission would be likely to distort the view given by the accounts or other statement under consideration.'

Matters which may require decisions as to materiality in this sense include the following:

— whether an error should be corrected before financial statements are issued;
— whether an item should be separately disclosed;
— whether an accounting policy needs disclosure and explanation;
— whether the fact, and financial effect, of a change in accounting policy needs to be disclosed and explained;
— whether the auditor should draw attention in his report to a departure from acceptable accounting policies.

It should be noted that the English Institute preface their definition of materiality by describing the word as requiring a 'wide interpretation according to the variety of circumstances which can arise' and therefore that it is 'not possible or desirable . . . to give a precise definition of such an expression'.

In other words, the materiality of an item is relative to the circumstances surrounding it and it is therefore essentially a matter of judgement. That judgement must be based on professional experience, an awareness of the particular circumstances, and with regard for the needs of the readers of the financial statements. As far as the auditor is concerned, his judgement as to materiality must be grounded in a sound knowledge of the business of the company upon which he is reporting.

The auditor's judgement will always be personal and highly subjective, but there is room for making that judgement more than purely arbitrary. Whilst it must be stressed that the intention throughout is not to eliminate the need for professional judgement — which would be both impossible and undesirable — but merely to guide it, nevertheless attempts have been made to provide specific definitions of materiality in percentage forms.

A percentage limit requires some basis against which to calculate the percentage. If the materiality of an item is to be assessed in the context of the overall view of the financial statements, then in the great majority of cases it will be judged in terms of its impact on profits. In so far as profits are an important indicator of performance, and of primary significance to the readers of financial statements, net profit would seem to be the most appropriate basis against which to measure the materiality of an item.

Profits, however, can be unstable. Consequently, the same amount might — because of a change in profitability — be judged material in one year and immaterial in the next. Similarly, low profits or losses may give rise to unacceptably small materiality limits. A better basis for comparing materiality of an item might therefore be the average or 'normal' profits for a number of years. Normal profits would be before extraordinary items and before taxation.

Perhaps the most useful percentage levels suggested are in the proposals contained in a Statement issued by the Institute of Chartered Accountants in Australia in August 1974. This document might be thought to provide a convenient working guide to practical materiality decisions and can be summarized as follows:

(*a*) When considering the materiality of an item, it should be compared with an appropriate base amount. The following base amounts should be used:

(i) profit and loss account items should be compared with the operating profit for the current year or with the average operating profit for the last five years, whichever is the more relevant measure of profit having regard to the trend of business over that period;

(ii) balance sheet items should be compared with the lower of:

— total share capital and reserves, and

— the appropriate balance sheet class total.

(*b*) The above comparison should be guided by the following percentage limits:

(i) an amount of 10% or more of the appropriate base amount should be presumed to be material unless there is evidence to the contrary;

(ii) an amount of 5% or less of the appropriate base amount should be presumed to be immaterial unless there is evidence to the contrary;

(iii) the materiality of an amount which lies between 5% and 10% of the appropriate base amount is a matter of judgement depending upon the circumstances.

In general there are two broad factors relating to the materiality of any item, both of which will usually be considered together, but each of which might have particular bearing on the final decision: firstly, the nature or characteristics of the item in question; secondly, its amount. While percentage guidelines may be helpful, they should neither predicate nor dictate judgement. In the final analysis, the materiality of an item can only be assessed in terms of its impact on the overall view given by the financial statements in the light of existing circumstances. Some of the more general matters which might influence decisions as to materiality are described below.

Recurring or non-recurring: An item of a non-recurring or exceptional nature or arising from unusual circumstances is likely *prima facie* to be of more significance than an item arising out of the ordinary activities of the business.

Statutory requirement: The permissible margin of error on items subject to the disclosure requirements of the Companies Acts will often be very small. Indeed for items such as directors' and auditors' remuneration or investment income, there can be very little latitude at all. Matters such as these are believed to be of particular relevance to the readers of financial statements and any error or misstatement might be regarded as material even though its impact on the overall true and fair view may be trivial.

Degree of estimation: The value of an item may be capable of precise measurement (for example debtors, cash balances and monetary amounts in general) or it may be based on estimates and assumptions (such as stock or depreciation). The degree of latitude permissible in the former case is likely to be narrower than in the latter.

Material in principle: Even though the amount involved is insignificant, it may be necessary to regard an item as material because of a departure from some acceptable accounting policy. For example, describing as extraordinary an item which is manifestly not so might be regarded as a material distortion of the overall view, even if the amount involved is insignificant. Similarly, a change in accounting policy might, in a particular case, be expected to have a major impact on the results of future periods—and may therefore require disclosure—even though the effect on the current year is negligible.

Trend: When assessing the materiality of the amount of an item the overriding test is its effect on the reported earnings or net worth of the business. However, the amount involved should also be judged in the light of the relevant trend, since it might be said that the reported earnings of a company for any one period are *per se* of less importance than the trend of that company's profits over a number of periods. To the extent that readers of financial statements can be said to regard the trend of profits as important, any materiality decision must also be viewed in that context.

Related amounts: The emphasis on the trend of results suggests that the materiality of an item might be assessed in a wider context; it should also, however, be viewed in the narrower context of its relationship with other amounts which appear in the financial statements. Thus the materiality of an item might be judged in terms of the corresponding amount for the previous year or in terms of the caption or class of which it forms part.

Critical points: An item which would otherwise be regarded as insignificant might, if corrected or disclosed, have a critical impact on the overall view. A minor adjustment might have the effect of turning a small profit into a small loss, or of revealing as marginally insolvent what would otherwise have appeared to be marginally solvent. Similarly an amount can assume disproportionate significance and this may have particular bearing on the matter of disclosure, especially where the reader might have expected the amount to be far greater than in fact it is.

Matters such as these go to emphasize that there are many aspects to any one materiality decision; that more is called for than the strict application of percentage guidelines; and that it is the exercise of professional judgement in specific circumstances which is required. Whatever the final decision, the auditor would be well advised to place a well-documented note of his conclusion, together with the reasons which support it, on the audit file.

6 Computer auditing

In recent years there has been a rapid development in the use of computers as a means of producing financial information. This development has created certain problems for the auditor in that although general audit principles have not been affected, he has nevertheless had to revise his approach and use specialized audit procedures and techniques.

The intention of this chapter is to outline the various key controls and other factors which need to be taken into account in evaluating internal control within electronic data processing (EDP) systems, and to draw attention to the modifications in audit procedures which may be required in certain circumstances. It is not a manual intended to provide the knowledge to develop EDP specialists, but rather a 'guide book' for the informed generalist.

General Considerations

It must be emphasized, from the outset, that the objectives of an audit are not affected by the introduction of computerized systems. Further, since the auditor will generally wish to minimize the extent of verification work by identifying the control procedures upon which he can rely, his approach to the audit of a computerized system will be similar to that used for manual systems. Thus, the auditor will follow the same basic steps of ascertaining, recording, evaluating and testing the system of internal control, regardless of whether the systems under review are computerized or not.

The major differences in the audit of EDP systems are the unique problems which exist within a computer environment. An effective evaluation of these problems and the review of these control procedures will force the auditor to change his traditional audit methods.

Before discussing these control procedures in detail, it is essential to understand the major problems which can arise in an EDP environment:

(*a*) Where several systems are operating within the same computer installation, a potentially dangerous concentration of duties can occur. Whereas previously the major accounting functions would be undertaken by different personnel, the effect of computerization is to channel all these functions through one group of staff.

(*b*) Significant aspects of internal control are removed from those staff who have traditionally controlled the accounting function. Responsibility for this control now passes to staff who are often untrained in accounting procedures.

(*c*) Many of the informal controls which operate in any manual system disappear completely. The manual 'reasonableness' test, which will always exist to some extent in any clerical system, often cannot be programmed into a computer system.

(*d*) The impact of poor systems design and programming errors can be significant. Thus, the computer will continue to process information in accordance with its prescribed set of instructions, regardless of whether or not the instructions are correct.

(*e*) Poor systems design can lead to a lack of audit trail, particularly following the development of 'management by exception' and real-time/on-line systems. In this respect, it is worth noting that changes to operational systems are usually far more difficult to implement in an EDP environment than in a manual system.

(*f*) For output to become readable to the human eye it must first be interpreted by the client's staff (i.e. by the programming section). Thus, information held on a magnetic file may be manipulated before printing takes place and, perhaps more significantly, can be interpreted differently on two separate reports.

EDP Controls and their Evaluation

The control techniques which may be used to control the EDP function fall into two broad classifications:

(*a*) *Organizational controls*, which apply to the computer department as a whole, and which are used to regulate its activities. As such, these controls (or their lack) apply to all, rather than specific systems operated within the department, and are likely to have a significant impact on the system of internal control.

(*b*) *Application controls,* which should verify the information processed through a specific application, e.g. payroll, sales ledger, stock control, etc. Such controls include software validations written into the constituent computer programs as well as the system of user checks which verify processing on an independent basis.

It should be emphasized that, in general terms, no single control procedure is likely to resolve any one computer problem. Instead, the objective should be to establish a system (or 'maze') of control which, although theoretically capable of being broken in some way, should minimize the risk of error (either deliberate or accidental) passing undetected. As with all controls, they must be cost-effective (i.e. their cost must be compared with an evaluation of the risk they are aimed at preventing or containing).

In broad terms, any evaluation of the system of internal control must include a review of the whole system of control which, in turn, would involve the review of all computerized and manual procedures. Thus, in his assessment of a weakness in internal control, the auditor must review all aspects of the system to ensure that, for example, an identified weakness in the computer processing area is not, in fact, adequately compensated for by an independent manual control procedure (or vice versa).

Any weaknesses highlighted by this review should be carefully assessed as to their potential significance on the financial accounts under review, and therefore on the audit opinion.

The degree of reliance which the auditor may place on computerized or manual control procedures is dependent on each system of control. Thus, for example, the auditor may be able to place reliance on control procedures built in to specific application programs, if his review of the computer installation indicates that access to, and amendment of, such programs is effectively controlled. Alternatively, the auditor may perhaps choose not to place any reliance on organizational controls, on the grounds that the system of internal control outside of the computer department would detect any processing errors.

In practice, the auditor would normally rely on a combination of organizational, programmed and manual control procedures. It should also be emphasized that whilst, in theory, the auditor may be able to rely solely on the user controls operating outside the computer system, this situation is unlikely to occur frequently since it implies a fairly basic computer system coupled with a strong level of control, which is unlikely to be adhered to in practice. For example, a user review of a payroll exception report detailing all pay rates over a certain value would not be sufficient as a control in itself unless the user procedures involved a full review of all payslips to ensure that all employees over the prescribed rate actually appeared on the exception report (since no reliance *per se* could be placed on the integrity of the program which produced the report in question).

Where, in any given system, the auditor places full reliance on the system of user controls to the exclusion of any computer procedures, he should still have regard to the controls over the computer installation. This is because any major disruption of the existing computer facilities can have a significant impact on the daily operation of the business and, in some extreme cases, may call its continued viability into question; e.g. a prolonged failure to send out sales invoices may cause a drain on financial resources so serious as to drive a business into insolvency.

Having evaluated the system of internal control, the auditor must exercise his professional judgement as to how any weaknesses may be resolved. Thus, whilst the objective of control does not vary from one installation to the next (these objectives being to ensure the validity, accuracy and completeness of the company's financial records), the methods by which they are achieved will vary from client to client. For example, small installations generally suffer from an ineffective segregation of duties between the systems development and day-to-day operations functions; the auditor is therefore required to determine any compensatory controls which may exist and, in the absence of such controls, to recommend to management practical ways of resolving this weakness. Matching the controls against the size of installation has become of particular significance in more recent years, which have witnessed the remarkable growth of small business machines.

Evaluating the Installation

The audit review of the computer installation seeks to establish whether there are any weaknesses in the control of the installation itself. The effect of such weaknesses (and indeed the controls themselves) must then be evaluated to determine:

(*a*) whether they are likely to have a material effect on the validity of the information processed through the installation;

(*b*) the degree of reliance the auditor can place on any programmed control procedures identified in subsequent reviews of individual applications. In the extreme case, where there is no effective control over the installation, the auditor may decide that subsequent application reviews are of no practical value since he would be unable to rely on the integrity of the application programs, and therefore on their built-in control procedures. In such cases, the auditor must determine whether there are any procedures exercised outside the EDP department, which would compensate for these weaknesses.

Organizational controls may be analysed as follows:

1. Segregation of duties;
2. System development and maintenance controls;
3. Control over the operation of the computer;
4. Controls to safeguard the computer records;
5. Controls to ensure the continued existence of the data processing (DP) facility.

The following section considers each of these control areas in turn, and specifies the control techniques which may be used to achieve them.

Segregation of duties

In any system, whether it is computerized or not, there must be a fundamental segregation of duties which seeks to place the following responsibilities with independent officials:

(*a*) initiation and authorization of transactions;
(*b*) recording of transactions;
(*c*) custody of assets;

To achieve this division of responsibilities, it is clear that the EDP department, when used to maintain accounting records, must be independent of the users who initiate and authorize transactions and who have custody of assets. Historically, in traditional batch-type mainframe installations, this segregation has been relatively easy to achieve. However, two major developments have threatened the isolation of the EDP department:

(*a*) The development of on-line/real-time systems where data entry is performed directly by the user departments via terminals. In some installations, the effective segregation of duties should be enforced by a system of software checks (e.g. passwords) which restrict terminals to those functions and responsibilities applicable to the department(s) which use them (see below);
(*b*) The emergence of small business computers which are fully integrated within the user organization and specifically preclude the existence of a separate EDP department. Problems specific to small business computers are discussed later in this chapter.

Internally, the EDP department should be organized such that the three major disciplines of operations, development and control are undertaken by independent personnel. This segregation would normally involve separating:

(*a*) data control;
(*b*) data preparation and conversion;
(*c*) job scheduling and review;
(*d*) operations;
(*e*) program/file library maintenance;
(*f*) software maintenance;
(*g*) systems;
(*h*) programming.

It should be emphasized that the full division of duties as listed above will usually be found in large installations only. Smaller installations, for example, rarely employ a file librarian, and frequently combine the activities of system development and programming. However, the above division of duties should be borne in mind since it represents the optimum definition of theoretical control in a traditional EDP environment. Note, however, that the distinction between some of these functions does not exist in many on-line/real-time systems.

Division of duties separates the important EDP functions and should minimize the risk of fraudulent manipulation of computer-based records. Additionally, it is essential that the organizational structure be designed to ensure that there is adequate review of all departmental activities. This review function is discussed in more detail below, but its importance must be emphasized since it is the fundamental control which ensures that installation standards (i.e. the prescribed procedures and controls) are adhered to.

Given an adequate number of staff, the internal segregation of EDP functions has been generally easy to achieve in the batch-type mainframe installation. In such cases, for example, all processing work is undertaken within the computer area. Thus, by controlling physical access to this area, and ensuring that the operators only accept work via the operations manager, it is a relatively easy task to ensure that only authorized jobs are processed through the machine, thus preventing unauthorized activities. However, with the introduction of on-line terminals, operation of the computer cannot be so easily isolated. Thus, a user could process data, or a programmer may be able to effect program amendments, through terminals located in their own offices.

Where there is an ineffective segregation of duties, EDP and user management must resort to other compensating procedures to restrict the use of terminals, control computer operations through review techniques and monitor the validity of the data processed through the installation.

Software development controls

This area covers the development, implementation and maintenance of all system and application software. Fundamental to these controls is the use of 'standards', which establish the procedures to be followed in order to ensure a measured approach to each phase of development and maintenance projects. Standards in themselves imply a system of review since, only by reviewing the work performed, can an assessment be made of whether the prescribed standards have been adhered to.

1. *Control to ensure proper and accurate systems development*
The following steps, explained in detail below, should be undertaken for each major development project.

Feasibility studies should be carried out before new systems are authorized and undertaken in order to:

(*a*) define the problem;
(*b*) evaluate alternative procedures;

(*c*) estimate likely cost and cost savings;
(*d*) establish a realistic time for project completion.

The basic objective of this phase is to establish that the proposed solution is viable and also the most suitable to the business.

System specifications should be produced to confirm user requirements and to act as a guide for programming staff. Their contents will include:

(*a*) an overview of the system;
(*b*) a description of each processing step;
(*c*) file layouts;
(*d*) specimen input documents;
(*e*) specimen output reports.

In the detailed specification (which must be complemented by outline or 'functional' specifications for user understanding and review), the system analyst sets out his answer to the problem at hand.

Program specifications should be created (by reference to the detailed system specification) to establish the purpose of each constituent program and to describe the processing logic used (usually with the aid of logic flowcharts).

Program coding represents the detailed set of instructions which will be used to process information within the computer. It should be written with reference to program specifications and reviewed to ensure that the installation's standards are adhered to (e.g. the inclusion of standard control procedures, such as verification of record counts and control totals, and descriptive information where required).

Test procedures should be used to verify the accuracy of the development phase before implementation. Standards must be established to determine the method of selecting the test data to be used, and should stipulate:

(*a*) the extent of user involvement in the creation and review of test data;
(*b*) the extent of test data used within the EDP department. Typically, the programmer may undertake his own initial testing of each program to satisfy himself that the logic used is correct (by a combination of desk checking and program testing). At this point, the analyst (i.e. an independent person) would perform system tests, e.g. processing test data through the full sequence of events;
(*c*) assigned responsibilities.

It is essential that *review procedures* be performed on the completion of each significant development phase. Thus,

(*a*) feasibility studies and system specifications should be reviewed by senior EDP and user management;
(*b*) program specifications and source listings should be reviewed by the systems analyst or if applicable, the senior programmer. In practice, formal

review of program coding is normally applicable to large installations only, although it represents an effective control to ensure that recognized techniques are used in problem solving;

(*c*) test results must be reviewed by user and EDP management and formal user approval must be obtained.

Additionally, the system of review should ensure that established timetables are maintained and that any delays are analysed for future reference and reflected in timetable revisions.

The extent to which auditors should be involved in the development of new systems is discussed in detail below. However, the general premise is that when the auditor seeks to place reliance on system controls, then his involvement should start before the programming phase is undertaken in order to ensure that the basic system design is not deficient for his purposes.

2. *Control over software maintenance*

Failure to control the software maintenance function undermines the effectiveness of those development procedures which should exist within the installation. Thus, for example, whilst test procedures for a given system may have been adequately performed, failure to subject amendments to similar procedures may result in the implementation of erroneous logic routines.

In addition to the procedures outlined, controls must be exercised as follows:

(*a*) Development routines must be isolated from operational programs and data files (where used in testing) to ensure that the 'production' system is not disrupted. This control normally involves establishing, for example, separate disc areas, and retaining programs and data files in accordance with test name conventions (e.g. prefixing all program names with 'TEST').

(*b*) Amendments should be authorized and sequentially controlled, e.g. by entering amendment details on pre-numbered documents. This procedure helps management to ensure that only authorized amendments are undertaken and to determine the progress made to date on each project.

The controls listed above monitor the development of 'authorized' system amendments. It is also essential to establish controls which prevent or detect the implementation of unauthorized amendments where such amendments by-pass the recognized procedures laid down with the installation. This area is dependent primarily on an effective segregation of duties between operations and development staff, on the procedures used to control the operation of the computer and on specific controls relating to program maintenance (see below).

Amendments to software packages acquired by the client are usually undertaken by the software house responsible for its development.

Therefore, whilst any amendments should be subject to internal test and review procedures by the client himself, it is important that the package is supported by a formal maintenance contract with such a software house.

3. *Implementation controls*
Conversion of data files

Data-file conversion may be undertaken by a program which forms part of the regular processing cycle (e.g. setting up records on a customer file by means of a maintenance program which can add, change or delete records) or via a special program (e.g. loading cumulative pay details when implementing a payroll system part way through a tax year).

Strict control must be exercised over this phase of development since conversion errors may have a serious impact on subsequent processing cycles. Thus, it is important to:

(*a*) Establish a timetable for data conversion and identify the exact point in time at which the converted data files will commence (e.g. a new tax year for a payroll system, or a given month-end for ledger systems). In doing so, due regard must be given to the additional work involved in this process, and, where necessary, provision made to employ additional resources;

(*b*) Reconcile the results of data conversion to the manual or previous computer system records. In broad terms, reconciliation of transaction files would normally be restricted to transaction totals (e.g. loading an open item ledger file would be controlled by agreeing the total value of transactions on an 'account by account' basis). However, significant master-files (e.g. selling-price information held on a stock file) should be checked on a record by record basis;

(*c*) Ensure, where data conversion is performed using special 'one-off' programs, that programs are developed in accordance with the controls set out above and contain validation routines to detect all input errors. This is particularly important if conversion can give rise to an error condition which is not envisaged in the main processing cycle, e.g. an open item ledger system, which also summarizes each account balance on a separate master-file, must contain a check to ensure that each account balance is equal to the sum of the open items on the transaction file. (Note that such conditions should also be reviewed to determine whether they should be incorporated into the main production system);

(*d*) Test the operational programs against the converted data files. Normally, this involves processing the new system in parallel with the old manual (or computer) system. Parallel running verifies that the new system is functioning properly, and may detect errors which had not been tested for during the earlier test phases. However, although it represents the safest option, full parallel running may prove impractical given data volumes or other circumstances. (In such cases, parallel running against a small section of the new system should be considered.) Where a new computer system represents a significant advance such that it is not possible to run in parallel, procedures should be used to pilot-test the new system in a controlled environment.

Implementation of operational programs

There should be formal procedures to monitor the transfer of programs into the operational libraries, i.e. transfers should only take place after the new system/programs have been authorized by both user and EDP management.

Approval should be evidenced (e.g. by authorization of an implementation checklist) and the implementation routines reviewed by management to ensure that they have been undertaken properly (e.g. by reviewing library contents or by controlling program generation numbers assigned by the system software).

Note that the transfer to production libraries will usually involve both source- and object-coded programs which must represent the same version of the program. The proper transfer of source code is essential since it may be used to recompile the object code of an 'operational' program and because the source version may be used for further program maintenance. Compilation procedures provide source-code listings which should therefore be reviewed to ensure that the appropriate version of the program has in fact been compiled and transferred.

Controls to ensure that only authorized (and approved) amendments are transferred into the production libraries of a typical batch-type mainframe should include authorization checks by operations staff over all amendments submitted for processing. In this instance, however, the classic problem is to ensure that amendments are not themselves changed after they have been authorized. In general, this may be achieved by physically restricting access to amendments by development staff after authorization, or, more normally by reviewing compilation listings. (It is also worth emphasizing that this problem is essentially one of fraud and deliberate intent. As such, the auditor should have regard to it although the detection or prevention of fraud is not the primary audit objective.)

Password procedures within the system software should be used to restrict access to production libraries in an installation with on-line terminals located in the user and EDP development departments.

Further controls over this area are referred to in the section dealing with computer operations (particularly the review of work performed and the isolation of development staff from the machine itself, i.e. to minimize 'hands on' testing by development staff).

Documentation of new and amended software

Adequate documentation is essential to minimize the risk of error during the subsequent operation, control and maintenance of a system. Additionally, it reduces the reliance which is otherwise placed on the continued employment of key personnel and provides a better understanding of the system's objectives and methodology. Accordingly, it is important that documentation is issued to assist the following functions:

(*a*) *System maintenance*
— Specifications/flowcharts
— File layouts
— Record of all amendments
— Test documentation
(*b*) *Program maintenance*
— Specifications/logic flowcharts
— Source listings
— Details of all codes/tables used
— Test documentation
(*c*) *Data preparation/control*
— Preparation instructions (for each type of input form)
— Authorization checks (by data control)
— Input/output reconciliations
— Output distribution
(*d*) *Computer operations*
— Standard run procedures (often in flowchart form and detailing the files used and the sequence in which jobs should be processed)
— Run parameters (e.g. month-end dates, payroll week numbers)
— Switch selection (to select 'optional' logic routines within a program, e.g. month-end statements)
— Message responses
— Halt and restart procedures, indicating which point the operator should return to (if at all) to restart the processing cycle
(*e*) *User operation and control*
— Instructions on the completion of forms
— Interpretation of output, including error messages and response
— Recommended user control procedures

Finally it should be emphasized that the development controls outlined above are applicable to all software used by the installation, i.e. both applications and the operating system and, since system software is usually beyond the experience of the user departments, the control process will be exercised primarily by EDP management itself.

Control over computer operations

This control relates to the physical operation of the computer and seeks to establish control over operator activities. Whilst it is true to say that many operational errors should be detected by subsequent user checks outside of the DP department (see below for the section on procedural controls), operator controls minimize the occurrence of such errors and ensure that the company's records are processed in a proper environment. In addition, they should prevent other errors which could pass undetected by users.

1. *Control and supervision of operator activities*
Job assembly procedures (which contain job control statements, parameter cards, run instructions, run dependencies and restart procedures) should be controlled by persons independent of the operating staff. This minimizes the risk of error during the assembly phase, and should be complemented by a review of the computer-log/job-control statements after processing has taken place.

Retrospective control over operator activities should involve a review by EDP management of the computer log which is produced by most operating systems. (This log normally identifies each job processed and each time the various computer files are accessed.) This review confirms not only the accuracy of operator actions, but also the authorization of processing (i.e. it should detect unauthorized jobs). In addition, it should bring to management's attention all abnormal processing errors (e.g. re-runs, hardware failures, etc.), including instances where operators have by-passed automatic software checks. However, review of the computer log is subject to a number of problems, which the auditor must take into account:

(*a*) Logs are usually voluminous documents, with the result that EDP management may be unable to review them in full. (One solution to this problem is to install software which will summarize machine activities.)

(*b*) In many cases, the printing of computer logs is optional or utilizes spooling files, which are in themselves open to amendment. As a result, there is no guarantee that management are in receipt of all logs unless they contain control information which would indicate missing sections (e.g. time details or the sequential numbering of log sheets by the operating system).

(*c*) An effective review usually involves a high degree of technical expertise which, in practical terms, may be restricted to operations management or include those personnel which the review is designed to control.

Thus whilst management review of such logs represents an effective control over operations, the effort it requires is such that many installations (particularly smaller ones) do not use it as a prime control.

In many cases, management rely on manual logs created by the operators themselves. Depending on the extent of these records, such logs can provide management with useful information to analyse 'abnormal' events, although they would not necessarily highlight the processing of unauthorized jobs (particularly where these are initiated by the operators themselves).

In larger installations, operations control may be achieved by the physical presence of more than one operator; thus, operators act as a check to prevent errors by other operating staff, and collusion would be required before deliberate manipulation of computer records could be undertaken. Where this form of control is relied upon, it is important to establish whether adequate provision has been made for holidays, shift working, rest periods and staff holidays. The employment of more than one operator also allows management to rotate processing duties so that no single operator is responsible for running the same application from cycle to cycle.

Finally, in assessing this area of control, the auditor should evaluate the software routines which can be used to ensure that the correct data files and programs are used in processing.

2. *Use of comprehensive operating instructions*
Standard instructions should be used to guide the operators through each job step and thus minimize the risk of error. As noted above, it is essential that such documentation be kept up-to-date (to reflect all subsequent development work), and reviewed by operations management to ensure its adequacy.

3. *Control to restrict use of the computer to authorized personnel only*
Whilst review of operating activities should detect the processing of unauthorized jobs and other operator errors, other controls should be employed to prevent such events from occurring in the first instance. Thus physical access to the computer area should be restricted to authorized personnel only (e.g. by installing mechanical locks or electronic card/key devices). In this event, it is clearly important to control the issue of the appropriate key/cards. This control also helps safeguard the computer from physical threats such as malicious damage, etc.

Physical restriction over access to the machine room is, however, undermined in installations where on-line terminals are located in other areas. Whilst it is normally impractical to suggest that these terminals be sited in secure areas specifically designed to house them, there are a number of methods which can be used to control their use:

(*a*) Physical on/off key devices may be fitted to each terminal. Alternatively, key board covers can be attached.

(*b*) Password procedures should be used to control access to the facilities available on the VDU. The password structure should reflect the logical segregation of duties within the company, i.e. passwords to sales ledger programs should be known to sales ledger personnel only. Additionally, 'sensitive' routines (e.g. resetting credit terms) should be protected by a second level of password to further restrict their use. Note that passwords should not be displayed on entry and should be changed on a frequent and random basis to limit knowledge thereof.

(*c*) Software routines should be used to restrict the capabilities of terminals (e.g. specific terminals may not be allowed to access payroll applications, even though the operator may have gained knowledge of the payroll passwords).

Particular attention should be paid to the ability of maintaining program libraries through terminals, since a lack of control in this area severely undermines the development and integrity controls discussed in the previous section.

Safeguarding the computer records

This control objective seeks to determine whether there are any procedures to ensure that computer-based files are maintained correctly and to highlight any attempts to manipulate these files or the production programs. Thus, when evaluating these controls, the auditor must have regard to the operational procedures discussed above, since these are complementary to the control objective.

1. *File labelling procedures*
Software routines should, where possible, verify file (internal) labels to ensure that the most recent version of the file is processed. Conversely, labelling techniques can be used to ensure that files are not accidentally overwritten before their usefulness has expired. Normally this is achieved by the use of retention dates, which warn operators that a file is about to be updated before the retention date has expired.

External labelling of 'portable' file devices (i.e. exchangeable disc packs and tape reels) should be used physically to identify each device and its contents. This minimizes the risk of the operator loading the wrong version of the file.

2. *Off-line storage*
Proper storage arrangements (e.g. tape and disc racks) help to minimize the risk of confusion or loss of file devices. Larger installations may segregate the custody of off-line file devices from the operating staff by creating a separate librarian function. The responsibilities of this function would include:

(*a*) authorization checks to ensure that files are only issued with the appropriate authorization;
(*b*) logging of all devices and contents;
(*c*) procedures to account for all files and to ensure that they are returned after use.

Where a separate librarian function is created, access to the library area should be restricted to authorized personnel only (i.e. the librarian and senior operations management), and provision made to ensure that the library is controlled at all times (e.g. through night-shift operations). Environmental storage conditions (temperature, humidity, etc.) should be suitable for device storage, thereby reducing the possibility of read/write errors and prolonging the usable life of a file device.

3. *Access to programs and data files*

Access to programs and data files can be controlled by a number of procedures, many of which have been discussed in earlier sections:

(*a*) Review of the computer log by EDP management acts as a detective control to highlight unauthorized access.

(*b*) Restricting the access to, and use of, on-line terminals prevents unauthorized personnel from manipulating computer-based information.

(*c*) Controlling any standard utility programs which the installation may possess, since these programs can be used to copy or edit computer files without leaving any hard-copy evidence (or audit trail). If used fraudulently, such activities may give rise to a breach of company security (there have been several cases of EDP staff selling copy master-files to competitors) or to the manipulation of clients' records.

Edit programs are particularly significant since they do not contain the strict controls normally found in specific applications programs and because they do not necessarily give a hard-copy audit trail of the amendments processed. Thus, for example, an edit utility may be used to amend an employee's rate of pay, which may pass undetected by the user section (particularly if control totals such as a hash total of all rates of pay used, are obtained from control records and not by adding each individual rate of pay held on file). Control over utilities should include a combination of:

— password protection;
— off-line storage of utilities;
— restricting the files which such utilities are allowed to access;
— management review of each occasion on which such utilities are used. (Details thereof will normally be contained within the main computer log, or, in some instances, may be given on logs specific to the utility in question.)

(*d*) Protecting program integrity, which is a significant problem when considering the protection of records, since a program is basically an interpretation of computer-based information. Thus, changing the logic routines of a production program would also change the way in which the financial records were maintained. Controls over the development of new programs and program amendments are discussed above, but it is important to emphasize the controls which should be used to ensure the integrity of program libraries:

— manual authorization of all program amendments (in a batch system) or password controls to restrict access to libraries through on-line terminals. Note that the issue of passwords itself should be subject to authorization controls.

— control of program version numbers (where given by the system software) to ensure that management is aware of all program amendments. This control is extremely effective where the system software cannot be used to amend the version numbers assigned.

— review of library contents (which are normally printed on a directory listing provided by the system software).

— review of program code on a periodic, 'surprise' basis. However, if this procedure is performed manually, it can be very time-consuming and is, in practical terms, restricted to source-code only. Alternatively, periodic comparison may be achieved by specific software routines which compare the operational version of a given program to a security copy of the same program maintained in the custody of, for example, the internal audit team.

4. *Procedures to control the data processed through the EDP department*
On-line and real-time systems by-pass the traditional data-control routines since data is entered directly from the user departments. Control in this situation therefore passes to the terminals themselves, and is discussed in the procedural controls outlined below. By contrast, in a typical mainframe batch-type system, users will create input forms, submit them to EDP for processing, and receive output listings from EDP after processing has been completed. Within the EDP department itself, data will pass through a series of processing steps including conversion, verification, job assembly, operation and distribution. In this environment, it is important that control procedures are used to check the data received for processing and to control its flow through the EDP department. To achieve these objectives, a separate data control section should be created, responsible for:

(*a*) checking the authorization of data received for processing (by reviewing input forms, or batch header slips for the appropriate signatures);

(*b*) ensuring, where possible, that all data have been received. For example, a user authorization form (instructing EDP to proceed with a processing run) may include a list of the batch numbers to be processed: by checking these numbers to the batches received, data control can ensure that there are no omissions;

(*c*) monitoring the data as it is processed through the department (using registers to log the receipt of data and the subsequent action taken);

(*d*) input/output reconciliations to identify any processing errors or omissions which may have occurred within the EDP department. Note that it is not data control's responsibility to identify and correct user errors, which must be returned to the originating department for investigation;

(*e*) control of the distribution of output reports (usually in accordance with predetermined distribution lists).

Verification of the conversion routines (i.e. the re-punching or re-typing of data by a second clerk) is an important control within any computer system since it can highlight punch (or key) errors made by a data preparation clerk. The technique can be used in on-line/real-time systems, or in the traditional batch-type installation where data are transferred to punched card or magnetic media (via key to disc machines).

It is important to emphasize that the procedure exercised by data control complement user controls, but do not replace them. The duties of data control are to vet input data received and to monitor the progress of such data within the EDP department. Ultimate control over the accuracy, completeness and validity of processing rests with the user departments who maintain and use the computerized records.

Physical procedures to ensure the continued existence of DP facilities

Physical protection of the computer facility is necessary to safeguard what is, in general terms, a very costly asset and because business concerns may be heavily reliant on their computer systems to maintain trading activity. Indeed, in extreme cases (where, for example, a company is dependent on strict cash-flow constraints) such failures can bring into question the viability of the company as a going concern.

1. *Protection of the computer installation*
Controls should be implemented to protect the installation from malicious damage and to minimize the damage caused by fire or other disaster. Such controls will include:

(*a*) *Restriction of access* to the computer room. This area should be locked at all times, and access to the appropriate keys or other means of access restricted to a minimum of personnel (e.g. operations and security staff).

(*b*) *Environmental controls* should be used to ensure that the operating environment is in accordance with the manufacturer's recommendations. This prolongs the life of the machine and minimizes the risk of machine malfunctions. Such controls normally include air-conditioning equipment, the use of temperature and humidity recorders (often attached to alarm devices) and dust detectors. Environmental controls should also include provision for regular hardware maintenance carried out on a preventative basis.

(*c*) *Fire prevention/detection measures* should include the installation of a detection system (e.g. smoke detectors) and an adequate system of fire fighting. (Many systems are based on inert gases.)

2. *Protection of data files and programs*
Back-up procedures must be established to recover from the loss of operational versions of data files and programs with the minimum disruption, i.e. by only having to recreate from a recent point in time.

Tape-based systems lend themselves readily to the solution of back-up security, since each file update will create another tape file, thereby allowing processing on the 'grandfather-father-son' basis. Disk-based systems must include specific copying routines, since files are not processed on the same generation basis as tapes (i.e. since file updates usually happen *in situ*, it is an additional job to create a copy of each file). Usually at least two sets of security copies should be maintained as a further precaution against losing the security copies themselves. In on-line/real-time systems, where update is a continuous process, copying will be undertaken on a periodic basis (e.g. at the end of each day) as well as after each update process.

Back-up copies of data files should extend to all master and important transaction files. Program files should be copied on a regular basis, particularly after any program amendments have been undertaken. Copies should be taken of catalogued job-control statements and the operating system.

Adequate arrangements must be made for the storage of security copies. The best practice uses fireproof media (e.g. safes, strongrooms) to store security copies maintained in or around the computer room, and a remote location (i.e. a separate building or bank vault) to provide additional protection against major disasters. Clearly, any remote location should be physically secure and environmentally suitable for the storage of magnetic media.

Back-up facilities should include hard-copy documentation relating to the operation, control and maintenance of the system. In particular, a set of system and programming documentation, and the operating instructions, should be stored in a remote location to facilitate the continued operation of the system.

Review of back-up procedures must be performed by management to ensure that they are adequate and that they are being followed by operations staff. Where back-up documentation is maintained, there should be a procedure to ensure that all amendments are properly reflected in the security copies.

3. *Provision for the use of alternative computer facilities*
Standby arrangements should be established with other compatible installations so that the business may continue its computer operations should its own machine be put out of action for a prolonged period of time. In general terms, this arrangement is usually reciprocal between two installations, although the more recent trend of larger installations is to establish a consortium (of say five or six companies) to fund the cost of a separate, 'fallow' installation. (Some installations purchase a second computer specifically to act as back-up.) Standby arrangements should be established on a

contractual basis, and include procedures whereby changes in standby configurations are notified to the parties involved. In general terms, it is essential that the standby installation is tested to ensure compatibility and to resolve any problems before the need to use the alternative site arises (e.g. periodically, and each time the configuration is changed).

In determining standby arrangements, due regard must be given to whether the alternative site has sufficient spare capacity to undertake the urgent processing needs of the business (e.g. weekly payroll, statements, etc.). Consideration must also be given to the unique problems of on-line and real-time systems. Such systems are not suited to the usual standby arrangements (which traditionally offer processing facilities in the evening or night-time periods), and many require the acquisition of a 'fallow' installation or services (see above).

When applicable, alternative manual procedures may be devised to record transactions during the period of machine failure.

4. *Insurance cover*
Provision should be made to protect the business from the costs of reconstructing its computer installation. These costs, which can be substantial, include:

(*a*) hardware replacement, including file devices such as disc packs;

(*b*) reconstruction of data, which involves recovering the computer files to the point in time at which the operational versions were lost. Reconstruction costs will vary enormously, depending on data volumes and on the adequacy of the back-up procedures used by the installation;

(*c*) additional cost of working, including the costs of alternative methods of data collection and the cost of using alternative computer facilities not owned by the business. The less tangible costs which result from the degradation of system performance should also be evaluated since these can have a significant impact on business performance and cash flow.

Employee fidelity cover should also be considered to minimize any loss through fraudulent activities of EDP and other staff.

Audit tests

It will, of course, be necessary for the auditor to carry out certain audit work, aimed at both verifying the information given to him, and also ascertaining that the various controls are operating as specified. The actual audit work to be carried out will depend upon the controls operating within the installation, and whether or not any major weaknesses in control are identified. The following tests give an indication of the sort of audit work which will need to be carried out. They will, of course, need to be adapted or extended according to the circumstances in any particular case.

Additionally, the auditor should remember that some of the controls he may test (particularly those dependent on observation) may not necessarily be operated by the client in his absence.

Many of the tests listed below involve a system of manual review and testing. However, other controls may only be tested with the aid of the computer itself (e.g. re-performing jobs to test for standard label checking or using audit software) which emphasizes the changing procedures the auditor must employ to achieve his objectives.

Segregation of duties

1. Review the functions of the EDP department to determine that they are effectively segregated from users who initiate and authorize transactions.
2. Review the organization of the DP department to determine that there is adequate division of duties within the DP function.

Software development controls

1. Review the standard procedures for system development to ensure that systems are developed in accordance with the installation's standards and with user requirements.
2. Examine feasibility studies and systems specifications for new systems for evidence of review and acceptance by DP and user management.
3. Examine the tests undertaken on new systems to determine that adequate testing has been carried out and that formal user approval has been obtained.
4. Examine systems and program documentation for evidence of review by senior DP staff and to ensure it is in accordance with installation standards.
5. Examine the documentation relating to program amendments and ensure that these have been properly authorized; check supporting documentation to ensure that all EDP aspects have been updated with the amendment details (including operating instructions/authorization).

Control on computer operations

1. Review job assembly documents for evidence that all jobs are authorized by a responsible official.
2. Examine the computer log for evidence that it has been reviewed by the operations manager or other designated official. Review a section of this log and obtain explanations for all entries. (Where applicable compare the computer log with other documentation including usage reports, operator logs and job schedules.)

N.B. As mentioned above, effective review of the console log usually requires considerable technical expertise which may not be available to the auditor.

3. Review a selected sample of operating instructions to ensure they accord with installation standards and are up-to-date. Ensure that they have been

authorized by the appropriate official.
4. Observe the measures used to restrict access to the machine room and determine the adequacy thereof.
5. Review the adequacy of those procedures used to control the use of computer terminals. Test these procedures (by attempting to gain access through terminals) to ensure that they are operating as specified.
6. Examine any error logs and:

(*a*) determine the reason therefor;
(*b*) ensure that each instance has been reviewed by senior operating staff (e.g. by reference to authorizing signatures) and actioned.

Safeguarding the computer records
1. Examine librarian procedures and ensure that:

(*a*) adequate records are maintained of all files. Verify the accuracy of these records by checking a sample of entries to the appropriate file devices;
(*b*) issues of files are supported by documents authorized by the appropriate official;
(*c*) physical access to the library is adequately restricted.

2. Assess the adequacy of the software checks available within the operating system. Determine whether these checks are used by the installation and test by:

(*a*) printing a sample of file labels and examining the contents thereof (e.g. for retention dates);
(*b*) re-performing jobs under controlled conditions to test for standard label checking and rejection of incorrect files.

3. Examine any logs which detail oçcasions on which operators have overriden software controls and ensure that these logs have been reviewed (and authorized) by operations management.
4. Assess the adequacy of program library controls and:

(*a*) test password controls by attempting to gain access without the use of recognized passwords. (Prior to this test, the auditor must obtain management approval and evaluate the potential effect the test may have on operational systems);
(*b*) test sample details of the directory listings to supporting program documentation (for program names, version numbers, etc.).

N.B. Audit software may be used to compare operational program code to security copies and highlight any discrepancies for investigation. Alternatively, program code can be compared on a manual basis (although this can be a time-consuming task), or may be tested by means of a test pack.

5. Review the controls used to restrict access to utilities and examine any records of usage for the appropriate authorization.
6. Examine data control procedures and test that:

(*a*) documents are properly authorized;
(*b*) where appropriate, control records are kept up to date and any discrepancies/omissions have been followed up.

Physical procedures to ensure the continued existence of DP facilities
1. Assess the adequacy of back-up procedures and:

(*a*) test a sample of the contents of back-up locations to the control registers;
(*b*) assess the adequacy of the back-up location;
(*c*) select a sample of file devices stored in the back-up location and arrange for disc-maps/file-labels to be printed. Ensure that file details correspond with the prescribed back-up procedures;
(*d*) select a sample of back-up documentation and confirm that it is up to date.

2. Observe the fire protection/detection and other environmental controls within the key areas (e.g. computer room, file library, etc.) and assess their adequacy.
3. Examine standby arrangements by reference to any contractual evidence and/or direct confirmation with the standby installation. Determine whether such arrangements have been used (either for production or test purposes) and examine the results of the exercise.
4. Examine insurance policies for adequate cover. Vouch payments of premiums on a sample basis.

Computer System Reviews

Having completed the review of the installation, and satisfied himself as to the adequacy of the organizational controls, the auditor will be in a position to review in detail the design and operation of individual systems. His approach to this task will be similar to that employed in any other system-based audit, namely:

(*a*) document the system;
(*b*) evaluate the controls operating over the system;
(*c*) design the audit programme, taking into account any system weaknesses identified in this review.

The auditor should seek to involve himself in the development process of each computer system which has a material impact on the accounting function prior to its implementation. His role is to ensure:

(*a*) that the system design is consistent with system objectives;

(*b*) that the system is being developed in accordance with recognized departmental standards, i.e. that EDP and user reviews, acceptance procedures and system documentation standards are being adhered to;

(*c*) that adequate system controls and procedures are provided for. These will include both program controls built into the system, e.g. validation procedures over input data, and user controls, e.g. establishment of control over input and balancing of output against the appropriate control totals;

(*d*) that a satisfactory audit trail exists, i.e. that it is possible to trace individual transactions and/or control totals through the system from initial input through intermediate processing stages to the final update and back again. Where a 'full' audit trail is impractical, the auditor should seek to ensure that provision is made for the printing of detailed reports when required.

The approach to this work will normally involve a review of the system and program specifications and discussions with EDP development and user department personnel. Additionally the auditor may develop 'test packs' himself to prove specific program controls within the system. These are discussed in more detail later in this chapter.

Clearly, if the auditor cannot satisfy himself on the above points, he should make representations to management to ensure that any weaknesses are corrected before the system becomes operational. It is invariably more difficult to make amendments once the system has gone 'live' than it is during system development. Accordingly, the auditor should evaluate the adequacy of any new computer system of financial significance before the system is implemented since it will be easier to incorporate any suggestions or requirements the auditor may have. Where this is not possible (e.g. the auditor is not informed of the development until the event), the auditor should still evaluate the system for control purposes; if this review highlights unacceptable weaknesses, the auditor should recommend system changes, or, where these are impractical, determine whether other compensating controls could be exercised by the users. Failing this, the auditor may need to abandon a systems-based approach and resort to substantive verification of the client's profit and loss account and balance sheet.

Particular problems apply to systems which are developed by outside software houses and these are discussed later in this chapter.

Documenting the system

The task of documenting a computer system is not dissimilar from that of documenting any other accounting system. The auditor should refer to the system and program specifications and to the user manual prepared by the analysts responsible for designing the system. These documents should provide the following information:

(*a*) System specification.
(*b*) Program specifications.
(*c*) User manual.

The standard of documentation available will clearly vary from installation to installation. Additionally, the auditor may have difficulties in gaining access to documentation where systems have been written by outside software houses or where the client has bought a package or uses a bureau system.

The information will need to be assembled in a manner which will facilitate an evaluation of the system on the 'key question' principle. Clearly, no hard-and-fast rules can be laid down, but it will normally be convenient to use the outline system flowchart as the principal record of the system, and to supplement this flowchart with the following three main schedules.

1. *Schedule of input types*
This can be drawn up in the form of a columnar schedule, and should record, in respect of each type of input document or magnetic file, the following information:

(*a*) the name and purpose of the document or file;
(*b*) the source of the file, or the person or department responsible for input document preparation and authorization;
(*c*) the volume and frequency of transactions;
(*d*) the principal fields of data used (e.g. in the case of a sales invoice, the sales amount, the VAT amount, the invoice number and the account number);
(*e*) the primary input program to the system and edit program, if this is a different program;
(*f*) details of the audit trail (i.e. the report where individual transactions and control totals next appear);
(*g*) the principal program and user controls over input, including controls over the resubmission of rejections.

It is useful to obtain specimen copies of input documents and details of the record layouts for magnetic files.

2. *Schedule of files*
Files may be categorized as either:

(*a*) Master files. These are files which permanently hold data and may be further subdivided between those which hold:
Standing data (e.g. a customer name and address file in a sales ledger

system, or a file of employee records in a payroll system); or
Balance data, which is updated at regular intervals (e.g. monthly sales ledger balances, or cumulative totals of sales);

(*b*) Transaction files. These are files which hold data temporarily during processing and which do not therefore retain data beyond the processing cycle (e.g. a sales ledger transaction file which accumulates during a month prior to a monthly update of sales ledger balances, after which it is erased).

The auditor should draw up a schedule, again in columnar form, recording the following details in respect of each file:

(*a*) the name and purpose of the file;
(*b*) a brief description of its contents;
(*c*) file organization, record type and length (i.e. details of the manner in which data are stored on the file);
(*d*) record layouts, including header and trailer records, highlighting important fields within each record (e.g. employee gross pay and tax deducted, in a payroll system).

File descriptions are important to the auditor, since by reviewing them, the auditor can identify potential control problems.

3. *Schedule of output reports and files*
This schedule should record, in respect of each output report or file, the following information:

(*a*) the name and a brief description of the output report or file;
(*b*) the name of the output system;
(*c*) the frequency and distribution of reports and the frequency and purpose of output files;
(*d*) the detailed records output and the sequence in which these records appear (e.g. customer code, customer name, sales invoice number and sales invoice amount by customer code);
(*e*) the totals output (e.g. total sales for each customer, plus grand total) and the method used for arriving at these totals (e.g. through accumulation or by using trailer records);
(*f*) details of the audit trail. This will be a record of the data to which either individual transactions or control totals reported can be reconciled and in many cases will provide a direct link with the information contained in the schedule of input types;
(*g*) the controls exercised by users over output reports.

Again it is useful to obtain example copies of output reports.

The outline system flowchart, together with the three main supporting schedules outlined above, should provide the auditor with the bulk of the information which he requires for his evaluation of the system. However, further information may also be required in certain cases where the system has special or unique characteristics (e.g. a formula for calculating average stock prices in a stock records system). Organizational controls which are particular to a system (e.g. details of password controls in a terminal-based on-line system) should also be recorded. Such characteristics clearly cannot be categorized, nor can standard methods of recording those characteristics be evolved. However, the auditor must satisfy himself that his notes record adequate details of these special features.

At this stage it is also appropriate to review the flowcharts relating to the work carried out in the user areas, both on input documents prior to submission for processing, and on output reports when they have been received after processing. This will then link with information recorded on the schedules of input types and output reports and so ensure that the general system review and the computer system review interface correctly and that the overall evaluation covers all procedures, whether manual, mechanized or computerized.

Evaluating the system

Having completed his documentation of the system, the auditor can undertake his evaluation of the internal controls operating within the system.

Usually, this evaluation involves an internal control questionnaire, which should seek to review the following key control areas:

(*a*) the authorization of data;
(*b*) the accuracy of input data;
(*c*) the completeness of input data;
(*d*) the correct maintenance and updating of master-files.

These four key areas are the fundamental controls which must be incorporated within any computer system. However, in undertaking his review, the auditor must have regard to the controls and weaknesses identified during his evaluation of the installation controls since these factors may have significant impact on the system in question. In particular, the auditor should review the development controls and the security and documentation controls as they are applied specifically to each system.

For the purpose of this chapter, the discussion of control techniques is based on the key areas of control listed above. However, since the techniques used will depend on the mode of processing, it will be necessary to distinguish between batch mode and on-line/real-time environments.

In broad terms, controls may be divided into two main types, these being (*a*) controls which would prevent the insertion of invalid data and (*b*) controls which would detect the existence of such data within the data system.

Before discussing the control techniques which may be used to achieve the objectives listed above, it is worth noting that there are a number of different questionnaires currently in use. In broad terms, these fall into two classifications:

1. The first type establishes the various control techniques under the four basic principles of authority, accuracy, completeness and correct file maintenance. Thus, the same questionnaire would be used to evaluate each type of system, e.g. payroll, sales ledger, etc. With this type of questionnaire, the auditor must interpret the results of his review to determine the audit implications thereof, e.g. failure to control the completeness of input data has different ramifications within different types of system.

2. The second type of questionnaire seeks to establish the same key control objectives as those used in the audit of manual systems (see chapter 4). Consequently, the questionnaire would vary according to each type of system, although the basic areas of control remain unaltered.

Controls to ensure that only authorized data are processed

1. *Segregation of duties*

Underlying this control objective must be a segregation of duties within the staff operating the system to reflect the basic division between:

(*a*) initiation and authorization;
(*b*) recording of transactions;
(*c*) custody of assets.

In this respect, users should be independent of the EDP department which, in turn, would be subject to its own internal segregation of duties. (This has been discussed under organizational controls.) Additionally, the function of maintaining standing data should be exercised by personnel independent of those responsible for raising transactions. This segregation helps to establish independent checks over the data processed, and minimizes the possibility of manipulating data fraudulently. For example, the authority to insert new employees within a payroll system should be exercised by officials independent of those responsible for submitting the actual hours worked.

Clearly the segregation of duties will determine the system of authorization and review of data.

2. *Authorization checks*

In a batch-mode system, input documents should be authorized by the appropriate officials and checked by a separate control section within the EDP department. Authorization procedures applied to batch header slips only may be adequate but, in such cases, batch totals must be sufficient to prevent any changes to the batch after its creation, e.g. by using document counts and value totals. Authorization checks performed by the data control section would involve lists of specimen signatures for comparison, although, in practice, this control is usually implemented in the larger installations only.

Where data are input directly to the computer from the user department (via terminals in an on-line/real-time environment), the manual authorization checks which would be exercised by a data-control section are by-passed and the control passes to the terminal itself, calling for special techniques to be used, as described previously.

Independent review of system output reports also constitutes an effective control which may highlight the presence of unauthorized transactions. Such output reports are produced by:

(*a*) the application which processes the data and would be reviewed by user personnel;

(*b*) system software listing terminal activities, which would be reviewed by EDP user staff.

Controls to ensure the accuracy of processing input data

1. *Control of data preparation and conversion/entry stages*

Input data should be submitted on pro-forma documents to minimize the risk of confusion and resultant error during the data-conversion phase. An inherent danger of this control is the possibility that transcription errors will occur. However, the use of pro-forma documents containing pre-printed data (e.g. a transaction code on a cash receipt form) should reduce the possibility of manual errors during data creation.

Programmed procedures, built into either the data-conversion routines or the main application programs (see below) should also be used to highlight and report input errors. Data-conversion routines may include automatic assignment of field values, format checking, comparison of control totals and check-digit validation. Additionally, data entry routines using screen-based terminals include an element of visual checking by the operator, and are normally based on the question and answer concept to guide the operator in the steps to be performed.

2. *The use of programmed procedures to prevent the processing of materially incorrect data*

The controls which can be coded into application programs are almost unlimited, but, in general terms, should include the following:

(*a*) range and format checks, i.e. range checks limit the acceptable range of values which may be input for any particular field (e.g. a discount field on a customer record may not exceed 10%). Format checks identify individual fields (e.g. as numeric, alphabetic) within each record;

(*b*) check-digit routines which may be applied to important master-file codes (e.g. a customer account number). Note that whilst check digits prevent transposition errors, they will not detect the incorrect use of a 'valid' check-digit code (i.e. posting invoices to a valid, but wrong, customer account);

(*c*) master-file compatibility checks. These involve matching input records to a master-file record. The purpose of this check for transaction data is to ensure that all such data can be recorded somewhere on the master-file, e.g. clock card input can be related to a valid employee record on the payroll master-file. With regard to the input of standing data amendments, this check should be designed to prevent the duplicate insertion, or overwriting, of master-file records, or the attempted amendment/deletion of a record which does not, in fact, exist on file. In broad terms, compatibility checks should be carried out as near to the input phase as possible;

(*d*) logical checks over the contents of each record and over the relationship of records. For example, if an invoice transaction contains gross, net and VAT values, the input program should check that the net and VAT values equal the gross figure. An example of the relationship of records is a sales order transaction which is checked against the customer master-file to determine whether the customer is allowed further orders against his account;

(*e*) comparison of control totals. In a batch-mode system, this would typically involve comparison of the batch header totals to the sum of the detailed records within the batch. In an on-line/real-time system, control totals should be applied at the document level, e.g. entry of a sales order transaction may involve a control total of the number of items ordered, which would be checked within the computer to the sum of the detailed order lines.

The methods which are used to handle errors highlighted by the built-in program controls will vary according to the type of system involved. In a batch system, such errors should be printed on a rejection report which should be returned for subsequent user review and action. In an on-line/real-time system, however, such errors would normally be displayed for immediate operator correction, i.e. further processing would not be allowed until the operator had corrected (or aborted) the transaction in question. Controls over the resubmission of corrected data are dealt with in the discussion of completeness controls (see below).

Program routines should also be used to control the maintenance of computer master and their associate files, and to provide users, where possible, with exception reports to highlight abnormal or exceptional transactions. Whilst other system reports will also contain such transactions, these may be lost in a mass of detail, and overlooked. Examples of exception reporting include gross/net pay values over/under predetermined values and a listing of all sales ledger customer accounts whose balances exceed their credit limits. Controls over master-file maintenance are dealt with below.

3. *User reconciliation of input to output*
It is essential that adequate totals are produced by each system and reconciled to input totals created by the user (or originating) department.

In a batch-mode system, these totals are commonly raised for each batch of input data. The manual totals raised for transaction batches will depend on the type of system involved, but the general principle is that they must be created over all fields of vulnerable or important data. For example, input batches in respect of a sales ledger system should record the value of documents processed, whilst an hourly payroll system would normally involve a total figure for the number of hours worked by employees. The total number of documents within each batch should also be controlled since this provides an additional check over the completeness of processing input data. Batches relating to standing data amendments may include a document count, and hash totals over all significant information. Examples of such information include rates of pay (for a payroll system), selling prices (for a sales order processing system), or depreciation rates (for a fixed asset system).

Output controls over transaction batches will normally be restricted to reconciliation of batch totals. However, it is standard practice to check significant standing data amendments (e.g. selling price changes) to original input documentation on a one for one basis, since the incorrect insertion of such data will corrupt all subsequent processing runs until discovered and corrected by users. Thus, the financial impact of processing a sales ledger invoice incorrectly is restricted to the value of the transaction in error. However, repeated use of the wrong selling price to generate invoice transactions has potentially a much greater effect on the business.

Reconciliation of input/output information must be undertaken by the originating user department, since they are ultimately responsible for the data within their system. Additional, independent checks should also be carried out by the data control section to resolve processing errors within the DP department and to notify users of error conditions.

On-line and real-time systems invalidate the use of batching techniques as a method of controlling the accuracy of data. As an alternative, document totals should be used to control the accuracy of each transaction processed. Additionally, retrospective user controls may be applied to transaction listings, for example, checking daily run totals to a history report of the input records submitted during the day. Other controls may include data entry validation where, for example, transactions are keyed in by one operator and subsequently (i.e. re-keyed) by a second operator before further processing is allowed.

It is important to emphasize that user controls should be applied to the system as a whole. Thus, it is insufficient merely to reconcile batch totals to input listings, since this control would not highlight subsequent processing errors (e.g. incorrect use of master-files or a failure in the update cycle). The overall reconciliation of processing results is dealt with in the section below on file maintenance.

Controls to ensure the completeness of processing input data

1. *User controls to ensure that all input documents are submitted for processing*

The control procedures which may be used to achieve this objective are dependent on the type of system involved (i.e. batch or real-time). However, the fundamental control problems of any system are to ensure that:

(*a*) input documents are raised in respect of each transaction undertaken by the company;

(*b*) all documents raised are subsequently processed by the system.

A number of techniques can be used manually to control completeness, the most common being to allocate each transaction a unique number, and to review the completeness of processing by accounting for all available numbers; for example, reviewing a sales ledger input listing to identify any omissions in the sequence of invoice numbers processed. This procedure generally involves document registers which should signify the numbers available and the stage of processing which each document has reached.

The allocation of sequence numbers should be at the earliest possible stage in order to minimize the risk of mislaying documents during their processing cycle. In this respect, the ideal situation is the use of pre-numbered documents, although this solution may be rendered unworkable through practical circumstances, e.g. where the same document type emanates from a number of different sources, as is often the case with stores requisitions in a stock-control system. Other control techniques involve periodic reconciliations of output totals to manual records or addlists created at the time of receiving the transactions in question (e.g. to an addlist of cash receipt transactions or to the cash book itself).

Batch-orientated systems normally include the assignment (by users) of unique batch numbers which in turn should be controlled in the same way as documents. In such cases, control over the completeness of processing input data should be exercised by monitoring the sequence of batch numbers used and by reconciling user batch totals to their corresponding computer figures (to ensure that each batch is processed completely). In practice, this control technique involves the maintenance of a batch register to record the details of each batch created (e.g. number, date and value) and to evidence its subsequent processing and reconciliation to output reports. Batch registers should also be used to highlight rejected information and to control the resubmission thereof. Note, however, that these controls do not actually ensure that each document is batched in the first instance (see above).

In systems where no input documents are raised, e.g. a telephone sales ordering system, a primary control over the completeness of input is the timescale involved between receipt of the data and its submission for processing. In such cases, where input documents cannot be checked in detail, it remains important to establish control totals over input data at the earliest possible stage (e.g. the listing of all orders processed) since these will allow users to control subsequent processing routines.

2. *Programmed routines to verify the completeness of input data*
Sequential control over input documents may be built into the application programs. Depending on how any omissions were handled, such routines may produce exception reports (highlighting missing numbers) or rejection reports, detailing those transactions rejected on the basis that they do not relate to the next available number.

Matching input data against a previously created computer file can highlight missing input records. An example of this may be an order processing system holding separate files for orders, despatches and invoices. After matching the order file to the despatch file, the system could print out details of all outstanding orders. Similarly, matching despatches against invoices would identify all uninvoiced despatches. Clearly, effective user controls are necessary to monitor the data printed out on these 'outstanding items' reports.

3. *Controls to ensure that all rejections are investigated and, where appropriate, resubmitted for processing*
All rejected data must be reported by the system for subsequent user review (either as part of the full input listing or as a separate report). Reports should contain adequate 'heading' and 'end of report' messages so that users can ensure that they have reviewed all rejected transactions. For example, each rejection report may be assigned a unique identification number by the system, whereby users could identify any reports not received. Alternatively, reports should indicate the extent of the data processed within each run, e.g. identification of all batch/document numbers processed.

Errors notified to users must be logged (for example, on an error or batch register), and the log used to ensure that all items are resubmitted.

It is essential that all error reports are controlled in this way. Thus, for example, a batched sales ledger system may contain two validation phases, the first checking for range and format and the second monitoring the update routines. In this instance, users must ensure they are in receipt of, and action, both sets of error reports.

The use of rejection reports in on-line/real-time systems is more limited because the data entry routines normally identify input errors as they occur, and demand prompt operator action, i.e. processing may not continue until the operator has corrected the error or aborted the transaction (because the cause of error may not be readily apparent). In the latter instance, it remains essential that such transactions are controlled either by logging routines or by completeness controls which seek to reconcile output listings/totals back to input records.

Where practical, records processed in a batch system should be rejected only after the whole record has been validated. In this way, multiple errors (e.g. in fields 1 and 6 of the record) can be brought to the user's attention and the record resubmitted in the next processing run. Failure to use this technique complicates error-correction routines since, in the example used, the record in error would be rejected a second time on account of the error in field 6. On-line/real-time systems lend themselves readily to comprehensive validations on input, since terminal entry programs usually have access to all relevant computer files and can thus perform all master-file compatibility checks at the time of entry.

Controls to ensure that computer files are maintained and updated correctly
The objectives of this key control area are to ensure that the correct computer files are used in processing and to verify that subsequent processing routines are performed accurately. Processing routines include the updating of master-files, all arithmetical calculations within the system (e.g. the calculation of gross pay from the insertion of the numbers of hours worked) and the internal generation of transactions.

1. *Controls over the use of the correct computer files*
Procedures should be built into the software to ensure that the most recent versions of master and transaction files are used for processing. Generally, this control is achieved by the use of internal ('header') labels which identify:

(*a*) file name;
(*b*) generation number;
(*c*) creation and retention dates;
(*d*) file sequence number (applicable to multi-volume files).

Additionally, trailer records may be used to accumulate the total number of records on file and/or hash totals of significant data fields (e.g. the value of sales ledger balances, or a hash total of all stock prices held on file). Such information would be used to verify the correct and complete reading/writing of files.

Label maintenance (and checking) is usually performed by routines within the operating system itself, which should, therefore, be reviewed during the evaluation of control. However, reliance on these standard routines must have regard to the fact that label checking may be by-passed by the operator or may not be used to the full extent (e.g. generation numbers and retention dates are usually optional features which need not be specified in the job control statements). Management control over these 'overrides' has been dealt with in the review of installation controls (see above). Label checks applied to file devices as a whole are also used to ensure that the correct tape reels or disc packs have been loaded. This control is commonly used in minicomputer installations where, for example, the set of 'live' disc packs is distinguished from the set of 'copy' packs, any attempt to update files resident on these copy packs being rejected by the system.

The software controls described above act as a preventative measure against loading the wrong files. It is, however, essential that any system provides users with the facility to control file maintenance on an independent basis. To this end, file control totals should be produced after each processing run in respect of all significant information, including:

(*a*) key fields of standing data (e.g. hourly rates of pay, depreciation rates, sales prices, etc.);
(*b*) balance of data of financial importance (e.g. the total value of sales ledger balances).

Where such totals are derived from trailer records (see above), provision must be made to prove this information on a periodic basis. For example, a monthly sales ledger system with a number of inter-month updates may utilize the trailer record totals to summarize the effect of each update process. However, at some time during the month, trailer totals should be proved by an independent program which totals, for example, the value of individual sales ledger balances and prints the results for user review. (Typically, this would be undertaken at the month-end, using, for example, the aged-debt analysis program.) Unless this task is performed, users may not detect errors which alter individual records on file whilst not affecting the overall figures shown on the trailer record (as may happen if edit utilities are used incorrectly).

Reconciliation of file totals from one run to the next ('run-to-run' controls) proves not only that the correct file has been used for processing, but also that the information within each computer file has not been corrupted for any reason. However, such assurances can only be given in respect of data which are actually totalled and controlled. Thus, controlling balance information within a sales ledger master-file would not detect the fact that the sales ledger file contains obsolete discount rates (updated onto a more recent version of that file).

The generation of file control totals for each processing run is particularly suitable to batch systems where data is accumulated and processed at specific times in the accounting period. However, real-time systems update master-files on a continuous basis (i.e. as and when data is input to the system) which renders it difficult to define specific update points. Thus, whilst it remains essential to generate the appropriate file totals, it requires an arbitrary decision to determine at which points in the accounting cycle these should be produced (e.g. each hour/day/week).

2. *Controls over the accuracy of fundamental calculations performed by the system*
Examples of fundamental calculations include multiplying hours worked by a rate of pay to arrive at a gross pay figure, or applying depreciation percentage rates to fixed asset values to obtain a depreciation charge. Basic casting routines (e.g. report totalling) are not classified as fundamental calculations.

Controls to prove the accuracy of calculations performed by the system should include a combination of the following procedures:

(*a*) printing the data used in the calculation, and checking file control totals thereof. Thus, in the gross-pay calculation above, the file control total would be expressed in terms of the rates of pay held on each employee's master-file record;

(*b*) regular user test checking of calculations performed to ensure the accuracy of the calculation routines;

(*c*) 'reasonableness' checking of results by users who are familiar with the 'norm' for that output;

(*d*) reconciliation of the results of calculations to the results of the previous run. This procedure can usually be exercised over a wages system when control totals are unlikely to vary greatly except for holiday pay. In other systems, however, where the results may fluctuate violently from run to run (e.g. a sales order processing system), these reconciliations are not feasible.

3. *Controls over data generated by the system*
Examples of generated transactions are the automatic production of a monthly payslip, or the printing of reminder letters for any customer whose aged balance exceeds a predetermined time limit. The important point is that no direct input is required for such transactions, and, therefore, they cannot be subject to the 'normal' input/output checks outlined above.

In broad terms, the techniques used to control generated transactions are similar to those outlined for fundamental calculations (see above).

4. *Reconciliation of update programs to input data*
Overall reconciliation of output reports to input data must be undertaken by the users to ensure that the update phase of processing has been performed correctly. Additionally, such reconciliations may also prove that:

(*a*) all data submitted by users have been processed (providing that users can ensure that all input data are taken into account, see above);

(*b*) only authorized data are processed by the system (providing the users can ensure that only authorized input data are taken into account — see above);

(*c*) balance data has been maintained correctly since the last processing run.

Reconciliations should involve agreement of output control totals for all significant transaction data to independently maintained records (e.g. the sales ledger control account in the nominal ledger) or to manual input registers created before processing is undertaken. Control over the updating of significant standing data amendments should involve one-for-one checking of input documents against master-file listings (e.g. a sales invoicing price list) or the reconciliation of movements in file control totals (e.g. a weekly payroll system may report a hash total of all rates of pay maintained on the payroll master-file; by reconciling any difference between the current week's rates to the value for the preceding week users would, subject to the possibility of compensating errors, confirm the accurate maintenance of individual rates of pay).

Independent user control over the update routines is complicated when the system involves a change of control field. For example, despatch notes would normally be submitted for invoicing in terms of the number of items despatched; and it is normal practice for users to control such information in the same way, e.g. by raising batch or document totals over the number of items involved. However, if the system control totals over the invoicing routines only report the sterling value of invoices produced, it is difficult for users to ensure that all items despatched have in fact been invoiced. To resolve this problem, invoicing totals should be extended to overlap the original input control field; thus, in the example above, invoice summaries should indicate the number of items invoiced as well as the total value invoiced.

Designing audit tests

Having documented the system and evaluated the controls operating therein, the auditor will be in a position to design his audit programme. It is important that any controls which are to be relied on are operational throughout the audit period and this must therefore be considered when designing the audit tests. It should be emphasized that the principles involved are identical to those in any other systems-based audit, namely that the auditor is seeking to assess and test the operation of the system, so that he can rely on the information produced thereby. If he can satisfy himself as to the reliability of the system, this does not, of course, obviate the necessity for balance-sheet verification work. Thus, even though the auditor may be satisfied as to the operation of the computer systems, it will still be necessary to verify, for example, purchase ledger balances against statements and stock ledger balances against physical stock counts.

The principles to be employed in designing computer system audit tests are again similar to those employed in designing audit tests in respect of manual or mechanized systems. If the answer to a key question enables the auditor to be satisfied that no fundamental internal control weakness exists, then he imposes a compliance test to establish that the system is operating satisfactorily. Alternatively, he may devise substantive tests to assess the significance of any weakness. If, at the conclusion of those tests, he is satisfied that no major error could occur, he reports the weakness to management, and continues with normal balance-sheet verification work. If he thinks that a major error could occur, he must then impose additional verification tests, or perhaps qualify the audit report.

It is not practical to specify a standard computer system audit programme which can be used in all cases where no major weakness has been identified. It is, however, possible to give an indication of the normal tests which would be included in a transactions audit programme where there is no loss of audit trail (i.e. input can be directly related to output, and vice versa). These tests would, of course, have to be supplemented or modified according to the particular circumstances encountered.

Specimen tests would be as follows:

Authorization controls

1. Check a sample of input to ensure that it has been authorized by an appropriate official. Where data are entered via on-line terminals, tests should be performed to determine the effectiveness of terminal controls (e.g. dummy passwords, etc.).

2. Where the system generates transactions or data ensure that these have been subsequently reviewed and authorized.

Controls over completeness and accuracy of processing

1. *Transaction data*

(*a*) Trace a sample of input to the update and other appropriate reports (and vice versa) for each type of transaction.

(*b*) Test check any fundamental calculations performed by the system.

(*c*) Agree a sample of batch totals to the reported batch totals. In the case of on-line systems this may involve document totals or daily transaction totals.

(*d*) Follow through the actions taken to correct any rejected transactions and ensure that their final treatment is correct.

2. *Standing data*

(*a*) Check a sample of master-file amendment details from the input forms to the amendment report.

(*b*) Reconcile the movements in any significant standing data control totals to the amendments, insertions and deletions processed in the period.

File maintenance

For a selected period, reconcile the movement in control totals over balance data by reference to the input transactions processed in the period. This should be done by reference to any input registers, batch slips or other independent controls over input.

In addition to the above testing, the auditor may wish to rely on specific program controls within the computer software. Where such reliance is placed, the auditor must adopt procedures which will verify the existence of these controls, for example, using test packs or software which compare the operational version of a given software routine to a second copy thereof. These techniques are discussed in more detail in the section on computer-assisted audit techniques.

The tests described deal with the basically simple situation where it is possible to link input directly with output by means of a clear audit trail. However, losses of, and change in, traditional audit trails are encountered increasingly in the more advanced computer applications, such as management by exception or many real-time systems. In such cases only the control totals are printed, together with certain exception reports such as overdue balances. There is, therefore, no output report against which the auditor can compare input or use to prove the control totals. A common-sense attitude should be adopted to losses of audit trail of this nature. The auditor must adapt his technique to suit the situation. A number of choices are open to him — including some of the more specialized techniques outlined in later paragraphs.

Techniques used in these circumstances include:

(*a*) arranging for special printouts of additional information for the auditor's use. This often involves an additional suite of programs which are activated at the auditor's request;

(*b*) testing on a total basis, ignoring individual items (e.g. comparing analyses in total only against budgets and previous periods, ignoring the individual items within the analysis which cannot be traced);

(*c*) use of a computer audit program directly to interrogate the magnetic file and output information specifically selected by the auditor;

(*d*) use of a 'test pack' to test the correct processing of data;

(*e*) relying on alternative tests (e.g. if the movement making up stock balances cannot be tested, but the balances are checked regularly against physical stock, the auditor could test the stocktaking procedures and examine the procedure for dealing with discrepancies);

(*f*) clerical recreation of records to prove otherwise unsupported computer totals.

Small Business Computers

As its name suggests, a small business computer (or 'mini', or 'micro') is a computer which is used to process comparatively low volumes of data using relatively straightforward business applications. However it is difficult to provide an exact technical definition since there is no broad agreement within the computer industry as to what is a 'mini' or 'micro', and because technological advances have blurred the distinction between 'minis' and mainframes in terms of memory size, access speeds, complexity of operation, and costs. It is perhaps more meaningful to discuss the characteristics of housing, software and staffing which generally apply to this type of machine and which have a direct impact on the audit approach thereto.

Whilst the following is aimed primarily at 'stand alone' small business installations with little or no in-house EDP expertise, it must be emphasized that minicomputers are used in many different business applications. Thus, they can be installed as front-end processors to a large mainframe computer or as part of a distributed network of computers servicing user requirements for separate geographical locations while maintaining accounting information for the business as a whole. In these cases, it is probable that the computer function will be supported by in-house EDP expertise, although it remains commonplace to use outside software houses for system development work. Where in-house EDP expertise is used, the controls over computer departments are similar to those in the section on installation controls.

Housing

The environmental requirements are probably the most tangible difference between 'minis' and mainframe. Typically, minicomputers are located in the accounts department or in the general office of a company; mainframes, however, are nearly always sited in separate offices. Mainframes also require special housing considerations which do not apply to minicomputers. Indeed, one of the great 'plus' factors of minicomputers is that the cost of installation, in terms of these special considerations, is almost nil, although in practical terms some means of controlling the operating environment (e.g. elementary air-conditioning units) should be established.

Software

All system and program development is normally undertaken by third-party software houses, who usually offer standard packages to satisfy customer requirements. Where the package does not meet these requirements, it is usual for the software house to amend the 'standard' package or, in extreme cases, to write bespoke software specific to the client. In any event, in-house software development is unusual in the 'mini' environment.

System software may offer fewer control procedures than mainframes, e.g. label checking. This is particularly true of some of the new low-cost microprocessors which were initially developed in a non-commercial environment.

Staffing

Mainframes are serviced by specialist staff employed by the company and usually grouped within a distinct department, i.e. the DP department. These specialists include operators, systems analysts and programmers, whose jobs and responsibilities do not extend outside the department. Minicomputers, however, are staffed by a minimum number of in-house personnel, mainly involved in operating the machine on a day-to-day basis. Such personnel may also perform book-keeping functions, and usually receive only a limited amount of EDP training.

The audit impact of small business machines

Given that the main audit objective is not affected by the introduction of computerized systems, the auditor need have regard only to the procedures which he uses to satisfy his audit opinion. In general terms, the approach he will adopt should be similar to that used in the audit of mainframe installations, described above. However, small business installations have their own unique problems which are inherent in the characteristics of such machines, and which must be taken into account by the auditor during his evaluation of internal control.

The major problems which the auditor will be faced with are in the area of installation controls:

Lack of an effective segregation of duties

This is a fundamental problem in most small business installations, and arises not only out of the small number of EDP staff employed but also from the integration of the EDP function within a larger unit, usually the accounts department. Specifically, problems may arise in terms of:

(*a*) The DP 'department' may be the responsibility of the chief accountant, who is also responsible for the authorization and custody of assets.

(*b*) There is no segregation between the functions of operations and control. Typically, the same clerk may be responsible for creating input documentation, operating the machine and controlling output results. Note, however, that one 'plus' factor of this type of installation is that the level of EDP knowledge within the user business is usually so restricted that the company itself cannot undertake program amendments. As such, there may be an effective segregation of duties between the development and operating/control disciplines.

Lack of control over software development and maintenance

Inexperience and the lack of EDP knowledge within senior management often leads to inadequate control over project development and maintenance. Specifically, this problem can give rise to:

(*a*) Inadequate definition of system objectives, including feasibility studies of cost effectiveness, system design and future growth capacities. As a result, the system may not correspond with user requirements, and indeed may not represent the 'optimum' solution to the problem. Additionally, system constraints (including maximum storage capacities and data entry times) must be assessed fully when selecting the appropriate systems, to avoid premature amendments/enhancements, in themselves often extremely expensive.

To overcome these problems, management must be fully involved in development work and ensure that all factors are identified and taken into account before selection is finalized. This, in turn, may involve the use of independent consultants, including early participation of the auditor himself. Additionally, management must ensure that it alone has the authority to approve systems before implementation is undertaken and the project completed.

(*b*) Development being usually undertaken wholly by an outside software house, which tends to reduce management's ability to control timetables (and often costs) and assess the adequacy of amendment procedures. As a result, projects can experience considerable delays, and implementation may occur without adequate testing of the final design (thus allowing program errors to pass undetected until after the system is operational).

To resolve this problem, management must define a timetable and insist on regular project meetings to review progress to date. Where possible, fixed-priced contracts should be negotiated to prevent the 'blank cheque' problem. Responsibilities must be defined exactly, so that each party (and member of staff) knows what is expected of him. It is also essential that their own staff be involved in system testing and that provision is made, where appropriate, for file conversion and a period of parallel running. It is worth noting that the general tendency is to minimize user involvement (particularly in system testing) and to avoid parallel runs on the basis that client staff cannot be spared from their operational duties within the business.

(*c*) Program maintenance difficulties, since this is again outside management's direct control, unless provision is made for maintenance support. To this end, management must ensure that a support contract is established with the software house responsible for system design. Whilst such contracts should guarantee support facilities, they are subject to:

(i) The financial viability of the software house. Clearly, support will not be guaranteed if the software house ceases to trade, and, to this end, management should build into the contract provisions which clarify ownership of, or rights to, the underlying system and programming documentation (including source code listings).

(ii) Unless amendments are undertaken by the software house or its recognized agent, there is a danger that the support service will be nullified, i.e. where an amendment is undertaken by, for example, the chief accountant (who may have an elementary knowledge of the programming language used), the software house may disclaim responsibility for support should a subsequent software error arise.

Finally, support arrangements should extend to all aspects of software, i.e. both applications and operating system.

(*d*) Inadequacies of system and programming documentation (including amendment procedures), since it is usually 'transparent' to management's main objectives, i.e. it often appears to have no immediate impact on the operation of the system. However, good documentation is essential for orderly development and maintenance and helps to reduce the otherwise total reliance which is placed on the software house. Thus, management should ensure that such documentation is kept up to date and is accurate, either by relying on their own review or, where appropriate, by using independent consultants/auditors.

(*e*) Inadequacies of procedures to control program amendments, and therefore to ensure the integrity of operational programs, in view of a lack of management control over the operation of the computer, and, in many cases, inadequate restrictions preventing access to the computer and to source program codings. This weakness is also compounded by the relative ease which some of the more popular languages (e.g. BASIC) can be learnt, and made available on the machine.

To overcome this problem, a number of controls can be introduced, including:

(i) password control to restrict use of the computer;

(ii) restricting access to programs, either through further password control or by removing the compiler off-line. (Note that interpretative languages, which maintain programs in source code and interpret them during execution time, do not use compilers, and so this control does not apply);

(iii) removal of source-code off-line. Many packages are only supplied with object code, which is difficult to change and so helps to prevent unauthorized amendments;

(iv) storage of programs in 'read-only memory' (ROM), which prevents any amendments to the programs stored therein. In these cases, amendments are undertaken by physically replacing the ROM unit (e.g. a chip) with one containing the amended program versions.

Other techniques for detecting unauthorized program amendments (for example, software to compare two versions of the same program) are not common to the small business machine. However, the most significant control to prevent unauthorized amendments is perhaps the system of user procedures which independently verify the results of each processing run.

Lack of control over the operation of the computer

Many of the traditional procedures which can be used to control the operation of mainframe installations are not feasible (or indeed practical) in the small business organization. Specifically:

(*a*) computer logs may not be produced, with the result that management cannot review machine activities or determine whether essential operations (e.g. back-up procedures) have been completed successfully.

(*b*) to resolve this problem, management should establish a system of manual recording for all salient machine activities and recognize the (emphasized) importance of other procedures such as password controls.

(*c*) there may be inadequate control to prevent unauthorized use of the computer. Specifically:

(i) the computer and its terminals may not be located in a protected area.

(ii) to overcome this problem, management should consider the use of physical on/off key devices attached to the computer itself and ensure that it is standard procedure to log-off terminals when not in use. File devices should be stored in secure areas (e.g. safes) when not in use. Where possible, the machine should be located in a lockable room, or, as a minimum, not sited in areas which experience large volumes of pedestrian traffic.

(iii) standard software routines may not be sufficient to restrict access to sensitive programs and utilities (particularly edit routines).

Management must consider security routines during machine selection and determine whether these could be enhanced, where necessary, by password controls within specific application programs. Utilities may be subject to similar password routines or controlled by off-line storage procedures.

(*d*) documentation for all operating and data entry routines may not be comprehensive nor supported by adequate staff training. As a result, operators may not understand the significance of processing errors, nor handle error situations correctly.

Management must ensure that such documentation is available before acceptance of the system, and that adequate provision is made with the software house for user understanding and training. Note that it is essential to establish back-up personnel for the DP supervisor and operators to cover in the event of sickness, holidays, etc.

Lack of control over computer data files

Standard software routines may not perform internal label checking, nor verify the reading or writing of data files through control (e.g. trailer) records. Additionally, the standard of program checks built into each 'standard' package varies considerably. As a result, incorrect files could be used in processing or errors may occur in handling input data and master-file records.

To resolve these problems, management should:

(*a*) recognize the importance of software controls during the selection process and insist that internal label checking and other controls are performed within the machine to minimize operator error;

(*b*) where the level of software controls is poor, greater reliance is placed on external labelling procedures, which must, therefore, be sufficient to clearly identify each 'portable' file device used in the installation. Where appropriate, logs should be used to monitor the contents of each device;

(*c*) enforce a system of independent user controls, to monitor the accuracy of each processing run.

Physical control over the computer facilities

Although the scale of operations is usually smaller in a minicomputer installation than in a traditional mainframe, many of the physical controls over the computer environment are no less important. Specifically:

(*a*) measures should be taken to protect the machine from unauthorized personnel.

(*b*) the environment of the computer area should be controlled to avoid extremes of temperature.

(*c*) security copies of data files and programs must be taken on a regular basis and stored in locations which are remote from the machine area. In this respect, software houses tend to act as a good back-up for system and application software, since they normally retain their own copies; however, special arrangements may be required if amendments have been undertaken which are unique to the business.

(*d*) hardware maintenance contracts should be established to facilitate recovery from machine failure.

(*e*) insurance cover should be arranged to minimize the cost to the business should its computer systems be disrupted for any reason.

In principle, there is no difference in the audit approach to small business systems *vis à vis* those run on mainframe installations. Thus, the auditor will seek to determine a system of internal control which will verify:

(*a*) the authorization of data;
(*b*) the accuracy of input data;
(*c*) the completeness of input data;
(*d*) the correct maintenance and updating of master-files.

However, the general tendency is for the auditor to place less reliance on the program controls within small business systems since the level of control over the computer is, in general terms, likely to be less effective. (Thus, for example, the auditor may not be able to rely on file maintenance controls, because software routines do not perform internal label checks.)

As is the case with installation controls, the fundamental problem of small business systems is the lack of an effective segregation of duties. Where this cannot be improved without an impractical increase in the number of staff employed by the client, the auditor must determine the degree to which management supervise and control output data.

On a practical level, the auditor may find that the necessary technical information is not available from the client. Therefore, it will be necessary for him to visit the software house responsible for the particular application, although many software houses are unwilling to divulge this information. In such cases, the auditor should inform management that he is unable to obtain the necessary information, and request that management attempt to do so directly. Alternatively, the auditor may choose to rely on his evaluation of the manual control procedures (to the exclusion of any computer-based controls), or, where these are insufficient, to abandon a systems-based approach to his audit and concentrate on substantive testing of the items shown in his client's account.

To summarize the main points which emerge from the above, it is essential that management be involved in all aspects of computer development, and control of subsequent operation. During the selection and development phases in particular, they may need to consult independent EDP specialists, including the auditor, who can provide valuable assistance in evaluating the standard of software controls. The fundamental weakness of any small installation is the lack of an effective segregation of duties which tends to weaken control over computer operations. Where this factor is combined with inadequate software controls within the machine, the auditor will normally place less reliance on installation procedures, and switch his attention to the independent system of user control and management review of the 'end result'. Should this area also prove inadequate, the auditor may need to abandon the system-based approach, and concentrate his effort on substantive testing of the client's assets and liabilities.

Computer Assisted Audit Techniques

Computer assisted audit techniques (CAATs) use the power of the computer itself to assist the auditor with his audit procedures. They have developed significantly with the growth of complex systems (not capable of audit verification through the traditional manual procedures) and with the philosophy that they can be used to replace manual procedures on other less sophisticated systems to improve both the quality and efficiency of the audit.

The use of CAATs extends to both audit tests on the system of internal control (including 'loss of audit trail' systems) and to verification of balance sheets and profit and loss accounts.

There are a number of CAATs available to the auditor of today, including:

1. Test data, which can involve the use of independent test packs or,

alternatively, data submitted through dummy branches, etc. (the integrated test facility).

2. Computer audit programs, i.e. programs written by the auditor himself to interrogate specified client files for selection, verification or simulation purposes. Such programs may be run in isolation or as part of the client's operational system.

3. Examination of program code, which may be performed manually or, more commonly, by audit software which compares operational code to secure versions of the same program.

4. Tracing, which is software used to identify the sequence in which program instructions are executed when processing transactions. By using this technique, the auditor can verify that processing is undertaken in the way specified.

5. Snapshot — a snapshot, or 'picture', of a computer memory taken during processing. By obtaining a series of these 'snapshots' the auditor can reconstruct the processing cycle and confirm its accuracy.

6. Mapping, which is a method of determining which statements have or have not been executed during program execution. Mapping can detect the existence of redundant code within, and evaluate the efficiency of, any given program.

It is not the intention of this chapter to discuss in detail each of the techniques listed above. Instead, the following sections explore those techniques which are commonly used by auditors, namely test packs and computer audit programs. Points relating to the examination of program code have been raised in earlier sections of this chapter, and, accordingly, are not repeated below.

Before discussing the detailed use of test data and computer audit programs, it is important to emphasize the fundamental difference between the two techniques. In broad terms, the computer audit program seeks to verify 'actual' client data (using programs written by the auditor himself) whilst the test data method attempts to test the client's programs with the auditor's own date. As such, the computer audit program generally has a more direct impact on the audit opinion, since it scans data which forms part of the client's accounts. Test data, however, seeks to test the client's controls and does not have a direct impact on the accounts; accordingly, its results (particularly those which emanate from processing conditions not normally associated with the client's method of operations) may have no direct significance on the audit opinion.

Test data (or test 'packs')

A test pack consists of selected data which are processed through the client's programs and the output compared to predetermined results. In this way, the auditor can establish that:

(*a*) the client's programs are functioning correctly (e.g. correct control totals are obtained, or depreciation rates are calculated accurately);
(*b*) the program controls are functioning as specified, i.e. they react properly to error conditions.

The method of selecting test data may involve preparation of the data by the auditor himself, which enables him to test those program controls he wishes to place reliance on. Alternatively, data may be selected from the client's own data, or by a combination of both client and test data.

The comparison of output results involves checking output reports to manual records independently prepared by the auditor.

In general terms, the advantages and disadvantages of using test packs may be defined as follows:

Advantages

(*a*) They provide an assurance that program checks are functioning properly and therefore can be relied upon.
(*b*) They can be used on a continuing basis (assuming that the system does not radically change).
(*c*) Once set up, running costs can be relatively cheap.
(*d*) It is relatively easy to add on more tests, or vary the testing to include different controls.

Disadvantages

(*a*) They require a detailed knowledge of how the system works.
(*b*) They may require special programs to set-up computer files or by-pass earlier processing steps which do not need to be tested.
(*c*) Initial set-up costs can be expensive.
(*d*) They may give rise to processing halts, with their attendant effects on the computer department operations.
(*e*) Processing time will be required to perform a test pack.

The considerations listed above are expressed in general terms, and their real impact will depend on whether the auditor uses test packs in isolation or whether he integrates the procedure within the client's operational system (known as the integrated test facility or ITF).

Isolated test packs usually involve processing test data through copy files, often using a copy of the operational program itself. The main problem with this approach is that by isolating his test from the production 'environment', the auditor cannot be sure that he is testing the operational version of his client's programs. Thus, it is easily possible for the computer department to process the test data using a modified version of the operational program. (To some extent, this assurance can be obtained by requesting copies on a surprise basis, or by comparing the program used to a secure copy of the operational version.)

ITF involves establishing a dummy set of records within the client's operational system/data files, and processing test data alongside actual data. This approach reduces the risk of not testing the operational version of the client's programs, since test and production runs are now combined. It also obviates the need for arranging special computer runs and facilitates testing on an on-going cycle-to-cycle basis. However, extreme care must be taken to isolate the test records within the production files and to adjust the 'operational' output results by the value of the test data. (In general terms, this would involve creating a separate 'unit' within the system, e.g. a division, company, department, etc.) The isolation of test data is perhaps the biggest disadvantage of using ITF, particularly in integrated and other complex systems where a single transaction can have an effect on several aspects of the system.

The procedure for the use of test packs would incorporate the following steps:

1. Review the system and be sure of what the system does.
2. Identify program checks and the functions to be tested.
3. Discuss the operation with the client.
4. Agree the format of input and output reports.
5. Prepare the data to be tested.
6. Manually predict the results of the exercise.
7. Attend the running of the program.
8. Evaluate the results.
9. Summarize the results.

Computer audit programs

Computer audit programs are those used by the auditor to:

(*a*) read computer-based files and extract specified information for subsequent audit work (e.g. to select from a disc file all personnel having a gross wage in excess of £100 per week, or to perform random selections);

(*b*) carry out audit work on the contents of the files (e.g. to add up balances, or to compare files against each other).

This type of program is often known as an 'enquiry' or 'interrogation' program. Such programs can be written by the auditor himself, either in any of the programming languages available (this requires a great deal of technical expertise), or using a standard 'information retrieval package'. On occasions, use can be made of interrogation programs already written by the client.

These programs can be used to assist in audit work as follows:

(*a*) To select representative types of transactions for audit tests; the selection basis will depend on the auditor, but may include, e.g. the use of random-number or stratification techniques.
(*b*) To scrutinize files and select exceptional items for examination; for example, interrogation of a customer file may be used to select all customers with excessive discount rates.
(*c*) To compare two files and select normal or exceptional changes.
(*d*) To stratify data as an aid to its investigation.
(*e*) To carry out certain detailed tests and calculations, thereby simulating client reports, for example, checking the arithmetic accuracy and principles of the client's stock obsolescence provision.

Advantages
(*a*) They can be used to examine data faster and more accurately than clerical audit tests.
(*b*) They may provide the only practical method of scrutinizing large amounts of data.
(*c*) They can continue to be used until the file layouts are changed.
(*d*) They can be made flexible by leaving the parameters (e.g. the amount above which all balances are to be printed out) to be set each time the program is used.
(*e*) Once set-up, the 'running' costs from year to year are relatively low, and offer considerable overall time-savings.

Disadvantages
(*a*) Technical skill and expense are required to develop a program which works. In particular, it is essential that adequate testing of such programs is performed, since errors may have a material impact on the audit procedures used and the conclusions drawn.
(*b*) Greater knowledge of the system is required than for conventional audit tests.
(*c*) The program needs to be changed to take account of any system amendments.
(*d*) Difficulties may be experienced in obtaining adequate computer time for testing. An alternative to using the client's installation is to arrange for machine time at an independent computer bureau, in which case, arrangements will have to be made with the client to procure copies of the files to be interrogated.

As with test packs, the benefits and drawbacks listed above are expressed in general terms, and their real impact will depend on how computer audit programs are used by the auditor. Again a division can be made between audit software which is used in 'isolation' and that which is used as an integral part of the client's system (known as systems control audit review file or SCARF).

Where the computer audit programs are run in isolation, i.e. on a 'once-off' per year basis, the auditor will be dependent for his results on the data files supplied by the computer department. Therefore, he is at risk that these files are modified in some way before copies are made available for his purposes. To minimize this risk, the auditor may request files on a 'surprise' basis, and should build into his own software sufficient control totals which enable him to agree to the client's own output reports. For example, when performing selection routines over a sales ledger file, the audit software should accumulate the total number of accounts and the total value of balances held on file; clearly any disagreement between these and the corresponding client totals should alert the auditor to further investigation.

The SCARF technique involves integrating an audit program within an operational system, so that each transaction processed through that system is analysed by the audit software and, where it satisfies certain parameters, is captured for subsequent audit review. (Note that the transaction is not otherwise affected and will continue to be processed through the system in the normal fashion.) The main advantage of this approach is that it can be used to review all transactions passing through the system during the audit period, and not simply those which are outstanding at the time when an 'isolated' audit program is run. As such, it also minimizes the auditor's dependence on the computer department for the files which he wishes to interrogate. Against this, the resident audit software risks manipulation by the client's own computer department, with the result that the auditor should employ additional procedures (such as program code comparison) to guarantee his audit objective.

The main problem with special complete audit programs is that a suitable period of time has to be allowed for program testing before a working version is developed and the required output produced. This observation, however, is not necessarily applicable to all specially written programs, especially those written in a very simple language, e.g. RPG II. With such programs, it is quite possible to write a simple interrogation and totalling program that will work and give correct results at the first attempt.

However, to combat this difficulty generalized audit packages are much more widely used in the complex type of file interrogation and system duplication exercises where a great deal of information in a standard format is required. The criteria for such a model audit packages are as follows:

(*a*) the ability to access any files, however organized and on whatever device from any computer;

(*b*) the ability to handle any form of data manipulation; this should include:

Arithmetic
Summarization and calculation
Logical
Selection
Error detection
Comparison
Categorization
Stratification and analysis
Sampling
Statistical routines
Sorting

(*c*) the availability of flexible output data with control reports and data reports in flexible format;

(*d*) the facility for production of other files for future reference or interface with the client's systems;

(*e*) it should be easy to use and run, and also be economical;

(*f*) the demands for computer time and assistance from client's staff should be minimal;

(*g*) the package should be reliable.

To summarize the main advantages of such a package, it can theoretically be used, with only minor alterations, at different installations and on different applications, accessing different types of files. In practice, however, this is not always the case, as packages are not always as adaptable as their creators claim. The final choice between the use of a special program or a generalized package will depend to a large extent upon the machine in use and the type of files to be interrogated.

Computer Bureaux

The same audit principles and procedures should be applied by the auditor where his client uses a computer service bureau (rather than an in-house computer). Thus, where the auditor seeks to place reliance on computer-based controls, he must review the installation and system controls operating both within the bureau and at his client.

Before discussing the audit points which are unique to bureaux organizations, it is important to remember that the auditor has no direct relationship with the bureau itself. As a result, it may be difficult for him to gain access to the bureau and evaluate their control procedures. Where access is refused, the auditor may have recourse to third-party audit reports, since the bureau may have other customers using the same systems or, indeed, may have been reviewed by its own auditors. Failing this, the auditor must rely on his review of the client's own control procedures, and where these are ineffective, resort to substantive test procedures. In any event, where the auditor is unable to review the bureau controls, he should report to management to this effect, and consider the audit implications of those areas which he has been unable to review.

Any evaluation of installation controls within a bureau should cover the principal areas of operations, system development and maintenance, safeguarding the client records and ensuring the continued existence of EDP facilities. Additional points to which the auditor should have regard include:

(*a*) *Financial stability of the bureau.* Clearly, EDP facilities will be disrupted should the bureau cease to trade. The auditor should therefore research the financial stability of the bureau and determine whether the client has made arrangements for alternative facilities (including manual systems).

(*b*) *Protection of client files.* The nature of any bureau is such that the accounting records for a number of clients are held within the same organization. It is essential therefore, that there are controls to ensure that the client's data are adequately separated from other bureau customers, and that it is properly protected. Such controls will include:

(i) Software procedures, such as client codes to identify the client's files. Where the client is linked to the bureau by on-line terminals, controls should be implemented to control the use thereof;
(ii) Physical measures to protect confidentiality of data, for example storage of data in protected areas not accessible by unauthorized personnel or visitors to the bureau.

(*c*) *Physical movement of data.* It is often appropriate to retain a copy on microfilm of documents sent to the bureau.

(*d*) *Contractual relationship.* A formal contract between the client and bureau is essential to define the respective responsibilities and liabilities of the two parties. *Inter alia* the contract should stipulate:

(i) Liability of the bureau for any loss incurred by the user as a result of processing errors or disclosure of confidential information within the bureau. (Current practice, however, tends to minimize the bureau's responsibility in this respect);
(ii) Processing schedules and charges;
(iii) Ownership of data files and file devices. Note that where these belong to the bureau, the user may incur heavy file set-up costs should he choose another form of computerization at a later date.

(*e*) *Segregation of duties.* The tendency of a bureau operation is to establish an effective segregation of duties between the user departments (i.e. the client) and the EDP function (i.e. the bureau). However, this division of responsibility is less effective in many time-sharing systems where the user is linked to the mainframe by terminal, and, indeed, can undertake program development and amendment work. In any event, there must be a clearly defined liaison between bureau and user, and it is normal for a senior member of the user's staff to be made responsible for this work. Within the bureau itself, the segregation of duties should be similar to any other mainframe computer installation, so as to facilitate the system of internal control.

The objectives of system controls remain as before, i.e. to ascertain the validity, accuracy and completeness of processing. Additional points specific to bureau-based systems include:

(*a*) *Definition of the responsibilities* (and therefore control procedures) of the bureau staff. As mentioned above, these should be defined on a contractual basis, and should extend to authorization checks and any balancing controls which would detect the bureau's own processing errors. It is essential that the client does not rely on these procedures to the extent that he discontinues his own system of control over data.

(*b*) *Carefully planned rejection procedures.* The bureau must provide sufficient documentation for the users to identify any errors. It remains the user's responsibility to ensure the prompt correction and resubmission of rejections to meet the bureau's processing schedules.

(*c*) *Output distribution controls.* In particular there should be procedures in the user company to ensure that all exception/error reports are received from the bureau.

(*d*) *The need for users to exercise effective control*, with input/output reconciliations and run-to-run controls. This is emphasized in the bureau environment, since user management has little influence over the bureau operations and control procedures.

Glossary of Technical Terms

1. Application program/system

A program (or suite of programs) which processes data for a particular business function (e.g. payroll, sales ledger and order processing). Contrast to operating system.

2. Audit trail

A visible means of tracing items of data from output back to original source data, and vice versa. Usually refers to hard copy (see below).

3. Back-up

Copies of data files and software taken for use should the original version be lost for any reason. This term can apply to copies of:

(*a*) master and transaction files of data held on computer media (e.g. disc);
(*b*) programs held either in magnetic-file form, punched-card or paper-tape form or written versions;
(*c*) documentation either of programs and/or systems details.

4. Batch processing

The submission and processing of batches of transactions to be dealt with in one computer run. Predetermined batch totals may be reconciled directly to output reports. This contrasts with transaction processing used by on-line and real-time systems (see below).

5. Check digit

An additional digit included in a code number which provides a means of checking for errors in that code.

6. Checkpoint

A system of recording the current processing position at a given point in time to facilitate restart in the event of a subsequent software failure. The program may be restarted from the last checkpoint rather than from the beginning of the processing.

7. Compatibility

The ability of a computer to handle the file devices and programs of another computer installation.

8. Compiler

A computer program which operates on a program written in a high-level language and converts it into a machine language program. (See Program)

9. Configuration

The collection of hardware making up the computer, including the way in which peripheral devices are connected.

10. Console

An electric typewriter or visual display unit which is on-line to the computer and which is used by the operator to communicate with the computer.

11. Console log

A record of messages and instructions to and from the operator which is printed directly on the console typewriter or, on some computers, from a spool file.

12. Data

The basic facts on which computer processes are performed. Information is data reported in some meaningful way.

13. Data-control section

The section within a DP department which receives data from users and monitors progress through the various stages of processing to the distribution of output reports.

14. Data preparation

The process of preparing and recording data on an input medium suitable for the computer such as punched cards, paper tape or floppy discs.

15. Desk checking

To check manually a program for accuracy and logic prior to its compilation or testing on the computer.

16. Directory

A listing of the contents of a program library or the files contained on a magnetic disc.

17. Disc (file)

A direct-access storage device in which data are recorded in a number of concentric circular tracks. Data are read from these tracks by means of moveable 'read/write' heads. Details of the files held on a disc can be examined using a disc map or volume table of contents (VTOC).

18. File

A collection of information (e.g. a series of related records stored in a specified sequence): files must be held on some form of storage device (e.g. tape reel or disc pack), known as a file device.

19. File labels

(*a*) External labels. Legible information (e.g. a written label on a reel of magnetic tape) to identify the device and its contents;

(*b*) Internal label. A block of data either at the beginning (Header label) or end (Trailer label) of a file (e.g. a magnetic tape), for identification purposes. Usually also contains control totals and other security information.

20. File layout

Written description of the manner and sequence in which data are stored on a magnetic file.

21. File library

The storage area for magnetic tapes, discs and punched-card files which are not actually being used on the computer.

22. Front-end processor

A small computer used to handle the input and carry out limited processing routines before transmission of the input to a larger computer system (to which it is linked).

23. Generation processing

The cyclical period during which a magnetic file containing records is not overwritten, so that records can be reconstructed in the event of loss of information on a subsequent run. If three generations are maintained, this is known as the 'grandfather-father-son' cycle (see also Back-up).

24. Halt re-start procedures

Written instructions to the computer operator as to the action to be taken in the event of a specified halt during a run.

25. Hands-on testing

Testing of programs on the computer by the programmer or analyst responsible for writing the program.

26. Hard copy

A printed record of computer-based information, e.g. an aged debt report or a program listing.

27. Hardware

Any electric, electronic or mechanical equipment in an EDP installation (compare Software).

28. Hash total

A control which is the sum of values in a specified field or record area of a file, where the sum has no particular significance other than for control purposes (e.g. a sum of clock numbers).

29. Implementation

The stage in system development when a system is first used to process live data.

30. Input/output controls

Controls reconciling input to output to establish the accuracy of processing.

31. Job assembly area

The physical area within the installation where input media, files and discs are collected together prior to the processing run.

32. Job scheduling

The drawing up of a schedule to determine the sequence of jobs to be processed on the computer, and the expected processing time.

33. Language (see Program)

34. Logic flowchart

Block diagram showing the sequence of operations within a computer program.

35. Multi-volume file

A computer file which spans more than one file device (e.g. tape reels).

36. On-line

Used to indicate that a device can communicate directly with the computer. Often used to describe data entry through a visual display unit.

37. Operating system

A special program provided by the computer manufacturer to manage the resources of the computer. Also includes service programs (e.g. program language compilers) and general-purpose utility programs (see below).

38. Parallel running

A method of systems testing in which the new system is run concurrently with the existing system using the same data, and comparing the results.

39. Peripheral equipment

Devices which are connected to and controlled by the central processing unit (e.g. line printers, card readers and visual display units).

40. Pilot testing

A method of testing a new system by controlling data from a selected section or division prior to full implementation of the system.

41. Program

A sequence of instructions for carrying out work on a computer. A program is usually written in a high-level language, a programming language which approaches normal English or mathematical notation (e.g. COBOL, FORTRAN, R.P.G.). The program is then translated into machine-readable form (machine language), using a compiler. The original program is known as the source program and the compiled version as the object program. In some languages the source program is interpreted at execution time and there is therefore no permanent copy of the object program.

42. Program listing

A listing of a program in the high-level language (source program).

43. Program library

A collection of programs on magnetic tape or disc. These may be classified as *production* (i.e. the operational programs) or *test* libraries.

44. Program maintenance

The making of minor amendments to programs.

45. Real-time system

An on-line system in which each transaction updates the relevant master file(s) as it is entered.

46. Record count

A control total produced by a computer program of the number of records processed during a given run.

47. Retention period

The period of time for which data on a magnetic file are to be protected from inadvertent erasure or overwriting (see also Generation processing).

48. Retrieval package

A general-purpose computer program designed to select, total and print specified information from a magnetic file.

49. Run-to-run control

Control procedures designed to ensure that the commencing position for one run is the terminating position of the previous run.

50. Software

The general description for all forms of program instructions as opposed to the computer hardware. This includes utilities, application programs and the computer operating system.

51. Spooling

The use of magnetic files to hold temporarily output details to slow devices such as line printers to relieve the constraints of output on a program's operation.

52. Suite

A collective term used to describe a set of related programs or routines.

53. System software

A term synonymous with the operating system (see above).

54. Test pack

A quantity of test data designed to test the accuracy of a computer program.

55. Transaction processing

The philosophy of processing transactions as and when they arise. This is applicable to on-line/real-time systems and contrasts with batch systems where data are accumulated before submission for processing.

56. Utility program

A general-purpose program usually supplied by the manufacturer for basic data-handling routines, e.g. copying, sorting and editing data.

57. Validation checks/validation program

Examination of data for correctness against certain criteria, such as upper and lower cash limits, the maximum number of items per account and compatibility with the master-file.

58. Write-permit ring

A device attached by the operator to a reel of magnetic tape when writing is to take place: its absence prevents writing on that particular tape.

7 The profit and loss account and balance sheet

In Chapter 2 attention was drawn to the need to plan the progress of an audit throughout the year, and to the opportunities for phasing various aspects of the work. For the most part, it has so far been the interim audit which has been receiving attention, the assessing and testing of internal control, and the checking of transactions. The other principal phase of an audit is the final audit, which primarily concentrates on the scrutiny of a company's balance sheet and profit and loss account to ensure that they show a true and fair view of the state of affairs at the balance sheet date and of the results for the period ended on that date. Before dealing with the factors involved in such final audit work, it may be helpful briefly to recapitulate the accounting considerations and conventions to be observed in the preparation of the profit and loss account and balance sheet.

Grouping Items in Final Accounts

The profit and loss account and balance sheet are summaries; that is to say, most of the individual items included therein are composed of a number of separate amounts, and it is the duty of the auditor to examine such details and to see that the summarizing and grouping of the items are done correctly. He must see that only transactions and items of a like nature are grouped together; that is, that the heading given fairly describes every component item: otherwise, incorrect classification may make the results shown by the accounts misleading.

Subject to the provisions of the Companies Acts (dealt with in the next chapter), the exact form of the final accounts, the headings under which the transactions should be classified, and the grouping and order of the items in the profit and loss account and balance sheet, are all matters of personal opinion and predilection, and such opinions can and do differ. The auditor is not concerned with these questions, provided that the accounts give a true and fair view of the state of affairs and of the results of operations for the period on which he reports. He must see that only items of a like nature are grouped together, that there is sufficient subdivision to make the accounts clear and intelligible, and that there is no suppression of material facts. Furthermore, the auditor must see that the accounts are drawn up in accordance with any Act of Parliament which applies to the concern in question, with Stock Exchange requirements, where relevant, and also in accordance with Statements of Standard Accounting Practice for application to all financial accounts intended to give a true and fair view of financial position and profit or loss.

Accounting Standard M2, 'Disclosure of Accounting Policies', *inter alia* defines and explains four basic accounting concepts — going concern, accruals, consistency and prudence — which are said to be so fundamental that it is not even necessary to mention that they have been assumed in the preparation of accounts. What follows in this and subsequent chapters, dealing with the preparation and the audit of profit and loss accounts and balance sheets, is on the footing of these broad basic assumptions. However, it behoves the auditor to make sure these assumptions are justified in the individual circumstances, and great care will be needed if there is any risk that any of these assumptions may not be valid, for the explanatory foreword to these Standards makes it clear that the onus is on the auditor. And further, in addition to these concepts, the Accounting Standard requires the accounts to contain a clear statement of the policies which have been adopted in their preparation.

The final accounts, then, are summaries built up from what may be thousands of constituent items. Their purpose is to disclose the combined effect of all the business transactions which have been carried out during the period of the accounts and the state of affairs at the end of the period. Only by going behind the accounts and examining the details can the nature and result of the various transactions be appreciated, and the accuracy of the summaries be verified. It is for this purpose, therefore, that the auditor is appointed, namely, that he may make such a detailed examination as will satisfy him as to whether or not the transactions are in order, and that the accounts are correct summaries, giving a true and fair view of the results of the operations of the period, and the financial position at the date of the balance sheet.

The Principles Governing the Preparation of Financial Statements

Profit and loss account

The *Royal Mail Steam Packet Company* case (1931) was the first one to raise the question of the auditor's responsibilities as regards the profit and loss account. Until this case, the view of the profession was that, as the auditor's report referred only to the balance sheet, he was merely concerned with ascertaining that the final balance shown by the profit and loss account did represent a surplus which was available for distribution, regardless of the sources from which that surplus had been built up. This case profoundly altered the views of accountants, and the lessons learnt from it are clearly reflected in the provisions of the Companies Act 1948. The basic principle now is that the profit and loss account should give a true and fair view of the normal earnings of the business during the period under review. Abnormal items brought to account, if material in amount, should be shown separately in the profit and loss account, so that the account may reveal a true and fair view of the trend of earnings from year to year. For this reason, therefore, if there have been brought to credit non-recurring items such as transfers from reserves created in past years, or, in the case of a holding company, if dividends have been declared by subsidiary companies out of profits earned in preceding years, or if the basic accounting policies have been altered, these facts should be made clear in order that a false view may not be given of the trend of earnings. The exact form and wording of the profit and loss account as submitted to the shareholders of a company has therefore become a matter of great importance, and the guiding principle should be that a misleading view of the normal earnings for the period must not be given to the proprietors of the concern. In this connection the reader should consult Accounting Standard M6, 'Extraordinary items and prior year adjustments'.

It is of the greatest importance that the annual accounts shall be prepared from year to year upon the basis of consistent accounting principles. Otherwise, if the basis is altered, the results shown by the accounts will not be truly comparable with those of preceding years. In these circumstances, a misleading view will be given of the trend of earnings. It is the duty of an auditor, not only to see that accounts are prepared upon correct accounting principles, but also to satisfy himself that those principles have been applied consistently from year to year. If, therefore, the basic principles have been altered and the amounts involved are material, the auditor will be obligated to make these facts clear in his report to the proprietors. These principles are clearly provided for in the Companies Acts, and again in Accounting Standard M2, 'Disclosure of accounting policies'. In American practice it is customary for the auditor to state in his audit report that the accounts have been prepared in accordance with generally accepted accounting principles consistently applied. Although not explicitly said here, it is certainly presumed in the absence of contrary indication.

It must, however, be understood that the detailed form of the profit and loss account as it would commonly be submitted to management differs from that on which the auditor reports. The Cohen Committee, in its report in 1945, expressed the view that the profit and loss account was more important than the balance sheet. In the case of companies, the Companies Act 1948 laid down particular of information which must be disclosed to shareholders in the profit and loss account. The Companies Act 1967 has extended the range of information to be given still further, but regrettably, the majority of published accounts continue to provide only the minimum information required by the Companies Acts.

Balance sheet

There is a considerable amount of misunderstanding as to what exactly a balance sheet is, and what it purports to show. It is, therefore, of the utmost importance that every auditor should understand the true meaning and purpose of a balance sheet.

Historically the form of a balance sheet was invariably to show on the left-hand side the shareholders' funds and the liabilities, and on the right-hand side the assets of the company. This form of 'horizontal balance sheet' may still commonly be found, but in the UK it is now widely regarded as old-fashioned.

A more contemporary look to a balance sheet, it is submitted, is achieved by adoption of the 'vertical' format. Whilst there are no hard and fast rules about the best form of presentation in this manner, perhaps the most usual is the division of the balance sheet into two sections, 'assets employed' and 'finance employed'.

Firstly there will be set out the net book values of the fixed assets of the company, and to these will be added the net current assets (i.e. current assets less current liabilities) to derive a total of 'assets employed'. Whilst the detail of all these assets and liabilities may be shown on the face of the balance sheet, again it is becoming more common now to relegate such explanatory detail into the notes to the accounts. In either event it is frequently the case that the order in which the constituent items making up the totals are set out, is related to their degree of liquidity; for instance, in the case of current assets, the order of presentation would often be stocks and work-in-progress, debtors, balances at bank.

Below the total of the assets employed, in a typical vertical layout, would be the section of the balance sheet explaining the sources of the 'finance employed'. Here would appear the total of shareholders' funds remaining in the company, both share capital subscribed and undistributed profits, as well as perhaps debentures and other long-term loans used to finance the running of the company's business.

In either event the balance sheet will be signed by two nominated directors of the company to indicate the responsibility of the Board for its preparation.

If properly prepared, a balance sheet should show a true and fair view of the state of the financial affairs of the concern, and in particular will show the nature of all the assets and liabilities. But it will often include other items as well, and, therefore, these latter should be clearly described so that the whole position may be clear. An auditor's duty is to satisfy himself that the balance sheet is properly drawn up upon correct and consistent accounting principles, and to report accordingly to those employing him.

The main objects with which a balance sheet is drawn up are to ascertain the financial position at a date, and whether the shareholders' equity is intact or not, and how such capital is invested. The shareholders' equity represents the excess of assets over liabilities, though, for this purpose, debit balances carried forward upon such accounts as preliminary expenses, advertising suspense, etc. are shown with the assets. If, therefore, the surplus of assets over liabilities has increased during a given period, this must mean that a profit has been made since the date of the last balance sheet; on the other hand, should the surplus be less, a loss must have been incurred. But, in comparing the opening and closing capital for this purpose, it must be seen whether any further capital has been subscribed. If so, in order to arrive at the profit or loss, the capital additions must be deducted from the closing capital, the resulting figure compared with the opening capital disclosing the profit or loss. A profit may be said to be an increase and a loss a decrease in the shareholders' equity in a company. A profit and loss account merely amplifies the information disclosed by the balance sheet, the former showing exactly how such profit or loss has arisen.

As the shareholders' equity represents the surplus of assets over liabilities, and as the increase or decrease of such surplus represents the profit or loss, it will be seen that the ascertainment of the profit or loss is absolutely dependent upon the amounts at which the various assets are stated in the balance sheet. It is possible, as a rule, to ascertain the amount of the liabilities exactly, except in the case of contingent liabilities, such as claims which are the subject of dispute, in which case the total liability under this head will have to be estimated: but, on the other hand, though the assets belonging to a business can easily be ascertained, it is difficult in many cases to arrive at the correct amount at which such assets should be stated in the balance sheet.

The Statement of Assets in a Balance Sheet

Under differing circumstances the various assets, etc. of a business may be stated in the balance sheet in different ways, as representing:

(*a*) the estimated amount which an asset would produce if sold or liquidated (known as the 'realizable value');

(*b*) the amount which, it is estimated, the asset would cost to replace (known as the 'replacement value' or 'current cost');

(*c*) the amount which an asset historically cost, when purchased or acquired, less the provisions made for depreciation since acquisition (known as 'written down' or 'going concern' value);

(*d*) the remaining balance of revenue expenditure which is being written off over a period of years (e.g. the balance appearing in the balance sheet as 'Deferred Revenue Expenditure' or 'Prepaid Expenses').

It will be seen later that all the above bases may be used in connection with the statement of the various classes of assets, etc. in balance sheets and that differing accounting conventions require such use of differing bases.

Moreover, the profits or losses of a continuing business are absolutely dependent upon the valuation of the assets of the business which it is impossible to fix with absolute precision, and whilst what follows is mainly concerned with a company's primarily historical accounts, we shall also be alluding to the preparation and audit of supplementary current-cost accounts in accordance with Statement of Standard Accounting Practice 16, 'Current Cost Accounting'. These facts must be realized and appreciated by accountants, who should make these root principles clear to their clients, whom they must not lead into the belief that absolute exactitude and certainty can be achieved in the periodical accounts of their business. Dealing with this point in a lecture many years ago, Mr George O. May, FCA, stated:

> 'Financial accounts must always be largely a matter of convention, judgement and opinion — not a matter of certainty. Whoever claims more for them is doing a disservice to the investor, the business man, and to the profession itself. Certainty would be very welcome in this field just as security in life would be, but it is unattainable and it is mischievous to encourage the belief that it has been or can be achieved.'
> (see *The Accountant,* April 1938, Vol. XCVIII, page 597.)

The truth of his remarks has been re-emphasized in recent years in the debate concerning a method of accounting for inflation, even if only in consequence of this multiplicity of available bases.

The Auditor's Position as Regards Financial Statements

The steps which an auditor should take, in order to satisfy himself regarding the financial statements, will be discussed in the course of the following chapters, but, before proceeding further, the limitations and the difficulties of an audit, especially with regard to the assets, should be clearly understood and appreciated. Accountants should not claim for an audited balance sheet absolute exactitude, but merely that it shows a fair estimate of the position of affairs, arrived at in accordance with the accepted conventions, and the truth of which has been checked and tested in every reasonable manner. On no account should the impression be given that an audit guarantees that the position shown is correct in every detail. The future may show that the most carefully prepared and audited balance sheet has, in the light of subsequent events, considerably misstated the real position of affairs. Great harm only can be done to the profession if accountants claim for an audited balance sheet virtues that it does not and cannot possibly possess.

Form of Balance Sheet and Profit and Loss Account

There is no standard form of balance sheet or profit and loss account, except in the cases of certain statutory and insurance companies. With the ordinary industrial and trading companies this matter is left in the hands of the directors, who are responsible for the form in which the information is presented, subject, however, to the provisions of the Companies Acts, which are dealt with in Chapter 8. The auditor has no power to alter the form of the director's balance sheet, although his advice is generally taken; but if, in his opinion, the form is such that the balance sheet is misleading and does not show a true and fair view of the company's financial position, then the auditor must report to this effect to the shareholders.

The balance sheet should be grouped in such a way that the chief aspects of the financial position are clearly revealed. It should be seen at a glance what proportion of the total capital available is invested in fixed assets, current assets and intangible items, and what is the working capital. The ratio of the total current liabilities and provisions to the total current assets should be seen readily, which is one of the key points in the reading of every balance sheet.

Generally speaking, the form in which accounts in this country were presented in the past was particularly uninformative. Great improvements have been effected in recent years. But there is still room for further improvements, and accountants should be constantly striving to make accounts as clear as possible and simple and easy for the layman to read and understand. However, the responsibility for this falls upon the directors of the company and not upon the auditor. The responsibilities of the auditor are to satisfy himself, so far as he reasonably can, that the various assets and liabilities of the business are fairly stated in the balance sheet, that accepted accounting principles have been adopted and that they have been consistently applied, and that the financial statements as a whole present a true and fair view.

Audit Review of Financial Statements

A critical review of financial statements is thus a vital step in obtaining audit evidence. 'The Auditors' Operational Standard' states that:

'The auditor should carry out such a review of the financial statements as is sufficient, in conjunction with the conclusions drawn from the audit evidence obtained, to give him a reasonable basis for his opinion on the financial statements.'

The Auditing Guideline 'Review of Financial Statements' states that the auditor is required to 'form his opinion on the enterprise's financial statements as a whole'. It recommends that 'he should carry out an overall review to determine whether in his opinion:

(*a*) the financial statements have been prepared using acceptable accounting policies which have been consistently applied and are appropriate to the enterprize's business;

(*b*) the results of operations, state of financial affairs and all other information included in the financial statements are compatible with each other and with the auditor's knowledge of the enterprise;

(*c*) there is adequate disclosure of all matters necessary for the financial statements to present a true and fair view and the information contained in the financial statements is appropriately classified and presented;

(*d*) the financial statements comply with all statutory requirements and those other regulations relevant to the constitution and activities of that enterprise; and ultimately whether:

(*e*) the conclusions drawn from the other tests which he has carried out together with those drawn from his overall review of the financial statements, enable him to form an opinion on the financial statements.'

In the light of the above, it may be advisable to employ a checklist in relation to the presentation and disclosure of financial statements, such as that set out below. It is introduced at this stage during our preliminary discussion of the profit and loss account and balance sheet, because of the importance of overall review to the conduct of the audit. In practice the completion of such a checklist would generally be one of the final stages in an audit, undertaken only in the light of the results of all the audit tests such as we describe in the following chapters.

Review of financial statements — presentation and disclosure

Client:		
Accounting date:		
	Initials	*Date*
Completed by:		
Reviewed by:		

	N/A	*Satis-factory*	*Refer to note*
1. Companies Acts checklist completed and reviewed (see chapter 8)?			
2. Items in the financial statements properly classified and grouped to avoid unnecessary detail?			
3. (*a*) Information essential to the true and fair view presented prominently (and not relegated to a note which may obscure its impact)?			
(*b*) Does balance sheet clearly show ability of company to meet current indebtedness?			
4. Chairman's Statement/Directors' Report reviewed for consistency with accounts?			
5. Accounts reviewed for consistency with any previously published forecast and (for listed companies) interim announcements?			
6. (*a*) Income from associated companies (SSAP 1) brought in (i) in the company's own accounts, on the basis of dividends received and receivable; (ii) in the group's accounts (or in the accounts of a company with no subsidiaries), on the basis of the group's share of the associates' profits/losses?			
(*b*) Investments in associated companies stated at cost (less any amounts written off) plus share of post-acquisition retained profits and reserves?			
7. (*a*) Full disclosure of any respects in which the assumptions on which the accounts are based do not conform with the fundamental concepts (SSAP 2) of (i) going concern (ii) accruals (iii) consistency (iv) prudence?			
(*b*) All significant accounting policies (SSAP 2): (i) clearly disclosed and explained;			

	N/A	*Satis-factory*	*Refer to note*
(ii) consistent with the previous year; (iii) prudent?			
8. (*a*) For listed companies, calculation of earnings per share (SSAP 3) based on consolidated results (after minority interests and preference dividends but before extraordinary items) divided by the number of shares in issue and ranking for dividend in respect of the period?			
(*b*) Any future obligations regarding share capital accounted for by calculating full diluted earnings per share?			
9. Government grants (SSAP 4) credited to revenue over the useful life of the asset by either (i) reducing the cost of the fixed assets; or (ii) setting up a deferred credit, a portion of which is transferred to revenue each year?			
10. (*a*) 'Extraordinary' items (SSAP 6) limited to those which derive from events or transactions outside the ordinary activities of the business and which are both material and non-recurring?			
(*b*) Prior-year adjustments (i) limited to items arising from the correction of fundamental errors or from changes in accounting policy; (ii) accounted for by restating prior year?			
(*c*) 'Exceptional' items limited to those which arise from ordinary activities of the business which are abnormal in their size and incidence?			
(*d*) Unrealized surpluses on revaluations of fixed assets credited direct to reserve?			
11. (*a*) Basis of valuation of stock and work-in-progress (SSAP 9) (other than long term contract work-in-progress) based on the lower of cost and net realizable value?			
(*b*) Value of long-term (more than 1 year) contract work-in-progress (i) based on cost-plus attributable profit and less foreseeable losses and progress payments received and receivable; (ii) provision made for excess where anticipated losses exceed cost less progress payments to date?			
12. (*a*) Depreciation (SSAP 12) provided on			

	N/A	*Satis-factory*	*Refer to note*
all fixed assets (including buildings) which have a finite useful life?			
(*b*) Where assets revalued, depreciation based on the revalued amount?			
13. (*a*) Expenditure on pure and applied research (other than on fixed assets) written-off as incurred?			
(*b*) Development expenditure (SSAP 13) (other than contract) (i) written-off as it is incurred; or (ii) only deferred if there is a clearly defined project for which the expenditure is separately identifiable and of which the feasibility and viability have been assessed with reasonable certainty?			
14. (*a*) Deferred taxation (SSAP 15) accounted for on all short-term timing differences.			
(*b*) For all other timing differences, deferred taxation not provided only on reasonable evidence that no liability will crystallize within 3 years?			
15. Current-cost accounts drawn up in accordance with SSAP 16?			
16. Where an accounting policy is not the subject of an SSAP, we are (and there is evidence that we are) satisfied that the adopted policy is appropriate to the circumstances of the business?			
17. Where a change of accounting policy has occurred:			
(*a*) adequate disclosure of the fact of the change and the reasons for it;			
(*b*) effect of the change properly disclosed and quantified (see 10(*b*) above);			
(*c*) are we satisfied that the new policy produces a fairer presentation of the results and financial position of the business?			
18. Significant post-balance-sheet events either adjusted for in the accounts or disclosed and explained as necessary?			
19. Nature (and, if practicable, an estimate of the amount) of any contingent loss fully disclosed?			
20. Disclosure of any long-term commitments (e.g. under leases) sufficient in circum-			

	N/A	Satis-factory	Refer to note
stances? 21. Borrowing powers not exceeded? 22. Adequate disclosure of all matters which require disclosure is as to make the accounts not misleading?			

Current-cost Accounts

We have referred already both to the historical-cost convention upon which this book concentrates and to Statement of Standard Accounting Practice No. 16 issued in March 1980. This latter envisages that in most instances a company's 'primary accounts' will continue to be prepared under the historical-cost convention, *inter alia* stating assets in a balance sheet in most cases at, or by reference to, their original cost. SSAP 16, however, is an attempt to switch the forms of accounts away from 'uncorrected' historic figures and to highlight how these are often misleading, as a result of inflationary distortions, when compared with accounts based upon current costs. Generally, current-cost accounts will be published — where relevant — as a form of supplementary accounts, but more courageous companies are giving these figures prominence and their chairmen are emphasizing their importance to the understanding of the 'real' results of trading.

SSAP 16 may create some problems for the auditor — and we shall hope to help him deal with these later — but in considering the format of accounts, some general guidance on this aspect of the Standard may help the reader. Basically the Standard deals with disclosure requirements, coupled with some explanation of the objectives and concepts associated with current-cost accounting. However, no detailed measurement rules are contained within the Standard, being relegated to 'guidelines', thereby allowing a degree of flexibility and encouraging companies to develop solutions appropriate to their individual circumstances. Thus the specified disclosure requirements are restricted to a current-cost profit and loss account and a current-cost balance sheet, together with explanatory notes explaining the bases and methods used in arriving at the principal differences by comparison with the historical-cost accounts.

These would include notes covering:

(*a*) the valuation of fixed assets, and the calculation of the depreciation adjustment;

(*b*) the valuation of stock and work-in-progress, and the calculation of the cost of sales adjustment;

(*c*) the calculation of the monetary working capital adjustment;

(*d*) the calculation of the gearing adjustment.

The first three adjustments above re-state the historical-cost profit in terms of current-cost operating profit — the surplus after allowing for the impact of price changes on the operating capability of the existing business. The last adjustment takes account of the impact on shareholders of the extent to which the net operating assets of the business are financed from other sources.

It is by these adjustments it is presently hoped that accountants will be able to develop a useful and practicable method of accounting in time of inflation, and thereby eventually satisfy the diverse requirements of management and other users of accounts. Unless they are able to implement a concept which expresses financial information in terms of valid values, they risk renewed criticism of being 'now't but scorers' — and not very helpful scorers at that.

8 The Companies Acts 1948 to 1981

The Companies Act 1948 represented a great advance in company legislation, particularly with regard to the accounts of companies. This was then supplemented by the Companies Act 1967. In 1962, Lord Jenkins' Company Law Committee reported (Cmmd. 1749) on the working of the Companies Act 1948, and on current trends in the drawing up of accounts. The Companies Act 1967 arose largely out of that Committee's recommendations and itself was referred to by the Government as a first step in the further development of company law. The 1976, 1980 and 1981 Acts provide further reinforcement in specific areas.

It is necessary that an auditor should be familiar with the greater part of the provisions of these Acts, but it is proposed here to deal only with those sections which are of particular importance to the auditor.

Keeping Accounting Records

Section 12 of the Companies Act 1976 provides that every company shall keep accounting records which 'should be sufficient to show and explain the company's transactions'. They must 'disclose with reasonable accuracy, at any time, the financial position of the company at that time' and enable the directors to produce statutory accounts. The accounting records must include, in particular, detailed records of the company's assets, liabilities, receipts and payments. Where the company's business involves dealing in goods, they shall also include details of stocks held at the financial year-end, stocktaking statements from which the stock figures are derived and statements of goods sold and purchased identifying the individual buyers (except in the case of retail sales) and sellers.

Accounting records should be preserved, in the case of a private company, for three years and, in the case of a public company, for six years from the date on which they are made.

Directors who fail to maintain adequate accounting records as described above are liable to a term of imprisonment not exceeding two years, or a fine, or both.

In the course of his audit, an auditor must form an opinion as to whether or not the terms of Section 12 have been complied with.

Profit and Loss Account and Balance Sheet

Section 1 of the Companies Act 1976 provides that the directors of every company shall prepare and lay before the company in general meeting a profit and loss account for each financial year of the company, together with a balance sheet made up to the end of that period. The accounts should also include reports of the auditors and directors under Sections 156(1) and 157(1), respectively, of the Companies Act 1948, and, in the case of a holding company, group accounts.

A copy of the complete accounts and reports must be sent to every member and debenture holder of the company not less than twenty-one days before the date of the relevant general meeting. Failure to do this may result in the company and every officer of the company who is in default being liable to a fine.

The length of a company's financial year (which may or may not be a calendar year) will be determined by reference to an accounting reference period.

Section 2 of the Companies Act 1976 provides that a company may register with the Registrar of Companies a date which is to be the end of its accounting reference period (its accounting reference date). If no such date is registered within six months of the company's incorporation, the accounting reference date will be 31 March. The accounting reference date of current and future reference periods can be altered under Section 3 if the company gives notice to the Registrar of Companies. The reference date of a past reference period can also be altered, but only so as to make the reference periods of holding and subsidiary companies co-terminus. In this case notice of the alteration must be given to the Registrar within the period allowed for laying and delivering the accounts of that financial year. No reference period may exceed eighteen months.

The period allowed under Section 6 after the end of an accounting reference period for laying and delivering accounts is, in the case of a public company, seven months and, in the case of a private company, ten months.

Three months' extension to these periods may be obtained by companies incorporated in Great Britain which have interests outside the United Kingdom, the Channel Islands and the Isle of Man, on giving notice to the Registrar of Companies.

Section 149 of the Companies Act 1948, Sections 3 to 12, together with the Second Schedule of the Act of 1967, and Section 1 of the 1976 Act, as amended by the Act of 1981, lay down the exact basis upon which both the profit and loss account and the balance sheet are to be prepared, and also the information which must be disclosed in those accounts.

Section 149 provides that every profit and loss account and balance sheet shall give a true and fair view of the profit or loss of, and the state of the affairs of, a company. Furthermore Section 149 provides that the requirements of the Eighth Schedule of the 1948 Act must be complied with. This Schedule was amended and re-written as the Second Schedule of the 1967 Act and further revised in the 1981 Act. The effect of this is to define clearly the information required to be disclosed in the annual accounts of companies.

The Eighth Schedule of the Companies Act 1948 as Revised by the 1981 Act and Schedules

Every accountant should be familiar with the whole of the provisions contained in the important Schedules to the Acts dealing with disclosure and presentation. These regulations represent the working rules which govern the preparation of the balance sheets and profit and loss accounts of companies. The terms of the Schedules are of particular concern to auditors who have to report on compliance therewith.

The Schedules deal with the general provisions governing the balance sheet and profit and loss account, and provide a choice of specified formats to be used. The Act of 1981 states that the directors of the company shall adopt the same format in preparing the accounts for subsequent financial years unless in their opinion there are special reasons for a change. If the format of the accounts is altered, then particulars of the change shall be disclosed and the reasons for the change shall be explained in a note to the accounts in which the new format is first adopted.

It also specifically enacts the accounting principles set out in SSAP 2, 'Disclosure of Accounting Policies', i.e. going concern, consistency, prudence and accruals. In addition historical cost accounting rules are set out, although provision is made for alternative rules to be adopted in relation to certain classes of assets.

The 1981 Act further governs notes to the accounts and requires disclosure of accounting policies used, and supplementary information to the balance sheet and profit and loss account.

The word 'material' occurs in various parts of the Schedule in relation to the disclosure of certain items. In these cases, it is a matter of professional judgement as to whether an item in a particular case can escape disclosure on accounts of its insignificant nature — bearing in mind that a true and fair view must always be shown. Some guidance on this question can be found in the Institute of Chartered Accountants in England and Wales Statement V.10 issued in 1968; and it emerges that materiality is a function not only of absolute and relative size, but also, bearing in mind the purpose of accounts and financial statements, of the likely effect on their users. In this context we would refer the reader to our discussion of this topic in Chapter 5.

Concessions for Small and Medium Companies

Small and medium-sized companies are relieved by the Companies Act 1981 of some of the objectives in relation to the delivering of accounts to the Registrar for filing purposes. However, the exemptions do not in any circumstances apply to:

(*a*) any public company or members (unless dormant) of a group of companies including such a company;
(*b*) any banking insurance of shipping company or members (unless dormant) of a group which includes such a company.

Small or medium-sized companies are those which, in both the financial year concerned and the preceding financial year, satisfy two of the prescribed limits as regards

(*a*) turnover;
(*b*) balance sheet totals;
(*c*) the number of employees during the year, averaged on a weekly basis.

A group of companies is treated as a single unit and its figures are aggregated in deciding whether the small or medium-sized conditions are met. If they are satisfied, then both the group accounts and the accounts of the holding company may take advantage of the relevant concession.

The concessions given in relation to accounts filed with the Registrar of Companies are as follow:

	Medium-sized	*Small*
(*a*) Balance sheet	Full	Abridged
(*b*) Profit and loss account	Abridged — details of turnover and gross profit margins omitted	Not required
(*c*) Notes to the accounts	Omit details re turnover	Limited need
(*d*) Directors' report	Full	Not required
(*e*) Auditors' report	Full and also a special report	Full and also a special report

It must be noted that the above concessions do not detract from the obligation to produce full accounts for the shareholders. In the special report accompanying abridged accounts, the auditor must state that the requirements for exemption are satisfied and he must reproduce the full text of his report on the full accounts.

The Directors' Report

Under the Companies Act 1948 only a minimum amount of information had to be given in the directors' report. The 1967 and 1981 Acts, however, greatly extended this and the requirements should be studied carefully.

As a result of the 1981 Act, it is now the duty of the auditors of the company to consider whether the information given in the directors' report relating to the financial year in question, is consistent with the accounts. If the auditors are of the opinion that the information given in the directors' report is not consistent with the accounts, then that fact should be stated in the auditors' report.

Companies' Accounts Checklist

From the foregoing brief review it may be seen that the disclosure requirements for limited companies under the Companies Acts are both complex and voluminous. This becomes even more so when there have to be applied the requirements of the Stock Exchange, contained in 'Admission of Securities to Listing', and of the Statements of Standard Accounting Practice. In the light of these requirements it is advisable to employ a checklist in relation to a company's accounts to ensure proper compliance with all these different requirements. An example of such a checklist with which one of the writers has been concerned has been published by the Institute of Chartered Accountants in England and Wales in the form of an 'Accountant's Digest', and it is our view that every audit file should contain such a checklist completed in respect of the accounts the audit of which is covered by that file.

Public and Private Companies

The Companies Act 1980 divides companies into 'public companies' and 'private companies'.

A public company is defined as one which:

(*a*) is limited by shares or by guarantee and has a share capital;
(*b*) in its memorandum, states that the company is to be a public company; and
(*c*) has complied with the provisions of the Companies Acts, concerning registration or re-registration as a public company.

Any company which does not fall within this definition is a 'private company'.

In order to qualify as a public company, as defined, a company must fulfil certain conditions:

(*a*) it must have not less than two members;
(*b*) the name must end with the words 'public limited company', or 'plc', and the word 'limited' must not precede the words 'public limited company';
(*c*) the memorandum must state that it is a public company;
(*d*) the authorized minimum share capital of a public company is £50 000.

A company registered as a public company on its original incorporation, must not do business until either:

(*a*) the Registrar of Companies has issued a certificate that the company is entitled to do business, or
(*b*) the company is re-registered as a private company.

Apart from special cases, a private company may be re-registered as a public company if:

(*a*) it has share capital; and
(*b*) a special resolution, that it should be so re-registered, is passed; and
(*c*) an application is delivered to the Registrar; and
(*d*) certain conditions are fulfilled, especially as to share capital.

The special resolution above must alter the company's memorandum so that it states that the company is to be a public company. The application must then be signed by a director or secretary of the company, and accompanied by various documents including the following:

(*a*) a printed copy of the altered memorandum and articles;
(*b*) a copy of a balance sheet prepared as at a date not more than seven months prior to the application for re-registration;
(*c*) the auditors' unqualified report;
(*d*) the auditors' written statement that, at the balance sheet date, in their opinion the relevant balance sheet showed that the amount of the company's net assets was not less than the total of its called-up share capital and undistributable reserves;
(*e*) a statutory declaration *inter alia* that there has been no change in the financial position of the company between the balance sheet date and the application for re-registration as a public company so as to result in the amount of the company's net assets becoming less than the total of its called-up share capital and undistributable reserves.

An auditors' unqualified report in relation to a company's balance sheet is defined in the following terms.

If the balance sheet was prepared in respect of an accounting reference period (the normal situation), it is a report made in the usual terms and stating, without material qualification, that:

(*a*) in the opinion of the auditor, the balance sheet has been properly prepared in accordance with the Companies Acts; and

(*b*) unless the report is made for a banking or other discount company taking the benefit of the CA48, Schedule 8, Part III, in the opinion of the auditor, the balance sheet gives a true and fair view of the state of the company's affairs at the balance sheet date.

Where the balance sheet does not relate to an accounting reference period, the report must state without material qualification that:

(*a*) in the opinion of the auditor, the balance sheet complies with the CA48, S149 and S155 (contents, form and signing of accounts); and

(*b*) unless the report is made for a banking or discount company taking the benefit of the CA48, Schedule 8, Part III, in the opinion of the auditor, the balance sheet gives a true and fair view of the state of the company's affairs at the balance sheet date.

A qualification is not regarded as being material if, but only if, the auditor states in writing that the thing giving rise to the qualification is not material in determining, at the balance sheet date, whether the amount of the company's 'net assets' was at least equal to the total of its 'called up share capital' and 'undistributable reserves'.

In principle, a private company cannot be re-registered as a public company unless certain conditions relating to its share capital are met at the time the special resolution to re-register is passed. These conditions include the requirement that the nominal value of the company's allotted share capital must be at least £50 000 and that each of its allotted shares must have been paid up at least to the extent of 25% of the nominal value of the shares.

Per contra, a public company is entitled, or may be required, in certain circumstances, to re-register as a private company.

This may be of particular importance in the circumstances that the Companies Act 1980 re-introduces for the first time since 1967 new requirements for public companies which are more stringent than those for private companies.

9 The audit of a company's profit and loss account and balance sheet

The principles of auditing apply to all audits, but the audit of companies incorporated under the Companies Acts, 1948–1981, forms a preponderantly large proportion of the audit practices of accountants and accordingly, as in previous chapters, has been used to illustrate these principles.

The approach used has been to work through the sections of the suggested current working paper file index set out in Chapter 2, pointing out particular principles and problems to be borne in mind in relation to each section, and providing under each an appropriate audit programme for substantive testing of items appearing in financial statements. The wide application of the principles associated with the audit of a profit and loss account and balance sheet allow for considerable standardization in such audit programmes. However, it cannot be over-emphasized that a good audit will always be dependent in part upon the individual flair of the auditor, and accordingly such programmes should never be allowed to become rigid and inflexible, but should rather be regarded as setting-down a minimum acceptable standard of audit practice. In addition, there remains the problem of determination of sample sizes appropriate to each of the audit procedures. In this connection, particular attention should be given to points brought forward from the interim audit and the previous year's final audit and to the balance sheet implications of the assessment of internal controls and the testing of transactions, which must be properly followed through.

Analytical Review

The purposes of a general analytical review within the overall review of financial statements is to examine critically the inter-relationship between items on balances contained within the financial statements to ensure that they are consistent with one another, with known trends and with the auditor's knowledge of the business. Its roles are emphasized by the Auditing Guideline 'Review of Financial Statements'.

Whilst an analytical review is not of itself a sufficient basis upon which to express an audit opinion, it can nevertheless provide additional assurance in areas where the result of other audit work has been inconclusive. Investigation of apparent inconsistencies revealed by analytical review may disclose errors, irregularities or omissions which would not have been disclosed by other audit procedures.

If the review is to be effective, it is essential that the auditor should have a sound background knowledge of the activities of the business and of the markets and environment in which it operates. This information should be on record in the permanent file which should be updated as necessary when each review takes place.

A review calls for the exercise of skill and judgement. Whilst the assembly of comparative figures, ratios, etc., may be delegated, it is essential that the conclusions derived from the review are subjected to overview by an experienced auditor.

The scope of the review will vary with the circumstances of each audit in order to concentrate the review effort in material and relevant areas. In general terms, however, an analytical review will comprise:

Comparison

- between specific items in the financial statements and corresponding amounts for the previous period;
- between budgets, management accounts and actual results;
- between monthly or periodic totals or ratios, to establish trends;
- between the performance of the business under review and similar businesses in the industry.

Review

- of the amounts contained in financial statements for their consistency with available non-financial data (e.g. sales, production and inventory quantities; employment statistics etc.);
- of inter-relationships between specific items in the financial statements (ratios).

Investigation

- of unusual or unexpected variances;
- of expected or anticipated variances which do not occur.

The precise scope and content of the analysis can only be determined when the auditor has established:

(*a*) the financial data, ratios, or other statistics which are of significance to the business, and

(*b*) the nature and relevance of other data which are available for the purposes of comparison.

The most important aspect of the review is the interpretation of its results and in particular the investigation of any unexpected variations or anticipated variations which fail to occur. The results of the review should be interpreted against the auditor's background knowledge of the business and its environment. Factors to be considered include:

— the rate of inflation;
— changes in buying and selling prices;
— seasonal factors affecting the pattern of trade;
— any planned expansion or contraction, or major contracts or customers gained or lost;
— changes in the level of activity in the industry and in the economy as a whole;
— technological advances, industrial disputes and government regulations affecting the business' operations.

The explanations obtained should be assessed in the light of the conclusions drawn from other areas of the audit work. Where the results of the review indicate the possibility of errors or misstatements in the financial statements, it will be necessary to consider the extent to which substantive testing must be increased in order to provide an acceptable level of audit assurance.

The following is a list of some of the amounts and ratios which it will often be appropriate to include in an analytical review. The list below would cover the main areas in relation to analysing the profit and loss account and balance sheet for most companies, but it is not intended to be exhaustive as it must always be capable of adaptation to individual circumstances.

1. Profit and loss account analysis

Turnover
Amount in £
% annual increase
Quantity/volume (if available)
% increase
Selling prices: % increase
Discounts as a % of sales
Returns/allowances as a % of sales
Cost of sales
Amount in £
% material content
% labour content
% overhead content
Gross profit
Amount in £
as % of sales
Expenses
Advertising (as % to sales)

Selling expenses (as % to sales)
Administrative expenses (£ amount)
Financial expenses (£ amount)

Payroll

Average number of employees
Aggregate remuneration
Average payroll cost per employee
Wage settlements made during period (% increase)

Plant

Repairs/maintenance (amount)
Depreciation charge for period (amount)

Interest

Total interest charge as % of total debt

Net profit

as % of:
sales
shareholders' funds
capital employed

2. Balance sheet analysis

Liquidity

Current ratio (current assets divided by current liabilities: shows ability of company to meet current debt)

Quick ratio (current monetary assets divided by current liabilities: shows immediate solvency of the business)

Capital structure

Borrowing ratio (fixed-interest loans divided by capital employed: measures proportion of capital employed raised by fixed-interest debt)

Gearing ratio (fixed-interest loans plus preference capital divided by capital employed: measures proportion of capital employed not financed by ordinary shares)

Interest cover (profit before interest and taxation divided by interest: indicates to lenders the security of interest payments)

Dividend cover (profit after interest and tax, divided by ordinary dividends: shows amount of profit cover for the ordinary shareholder's dividend)

Creditor/purchaser ratio (creditors divided by average purchases per day indicates amount of credit taken from suppliers)

Use of assets

Stock turnover (cost of sales divided by stocks: indicates number of times stock turned over in year)

Stock holding period (number of days in year divided by the result of above expresses average length of time stock is held)

Debtors-turnover (sales divided by debtors: expresses relationship between volume of business and outstanding debtors)

Debtors: average collection period (debtors divided by average sales per day: indicates effectiveness of the credit control of the company)

Minutes

It is important that an auditor should inspect, and make his own notes from, both the shareholders' and particularly the directors' minute books, for the minutes are the only authority for many of the transactions of a company. Apart from this, by reading the minutes, an auditor often becomes aware of important matters that are taking place, and which should be provided for in the accounts, such as pending litigation in connection with disputed claims. Nor should he overlook the information which is available in the agenda papers considered by the meeting which usually provide more detailed commentary on the decisions which are contained in the minutes.

Such minutes should also be examined beyond the date to which the financial statements are made up, right up to the time of signature of the audit report, for they will provide an essential pointer towards critical events which may have taken place subsequent to the year end, e.g. changes of policy, or decisions regarding capital investment; changes of product lines or markets served; major changes in staffing levels.

Suggested audit tests

Client:				Approved by:	
Audit programme: Minutes				Reviewed by:	
Accounting date:					
Audit tests	Details of tests	Errors, etc.	Audit sch.	*Work done by* Intls	Date
1. Obtain copies of, otherwise extract, relevant information from all minutes of: (*a*) shareholders' meetings; (*b*) directors' meetings; (*c*) any policy-making or financial committee meetings up to date of examination.					

Audit tests	Details of tests	Errors, etc.	Audit sch.	*Work done by* Intls	Date
2. Check that minutes are approved and signed by the chairman. 3. Check that recorded minutes indicate that a quorum was present. 4. Obtain confirmation that minutes are recorded for every board meeting and that none is missing. 5. Cross-reference minutes or notes to audit working papers. 6. Record any other items found during audit where approval should have been minuted. 7. Check to statutory books, e.g. directors' appointment.					

Conclusions	Yes/ No	Audit sch.	*Senior* Intls	Date
Are you satisfied that: (*a*) there are no significant matters omitted from the minutes which should have required board approval? (*b*) relevant matters recorded in the minutes have, where appropriate, been reflected in the accounts?				

Post-balance-sheet Events, Contingencies and Commitments

Financial statements are prepared at, and for a period up to, a specified date. The audit opinion on the truth and fairness of those statements is given with specific reference to that date. As a general principle, transactions and events occurring after that date will be accounted for in the financial statements for the subsequent period.

However, many of the figures appearing in financial statements are subject to estimation, and events may occur after the balance sheet date which provide additional evidence as to the reasonableness of the estimates made. These post-balance-sheet events may be seen to fall into two broad categories — adjusting events and non-adjusting events.

Adjusting events, which provide additional evidence of conditions which existed at the balance sheet date and affect the auditor's view of the estimates made for the purpose of preparing the financial statements, e.g. provision for stock and bad debts; amounts received or receivable in respect of insurance claims which were being negotiated at the balance sheet date.

Non-adjusting events, which deal with conditions which did not exist at the balance sheet date but arise subsequent to that date, but nevertheless may require disclosure of the events to be made in order to prevent the financial statements from being misleading, e.g. major changes in the composition of the company (for example, disposal of a subsidiary); financial consequences of losses of fixed assets and stock as a result of fire or flood.

Circumstances may also exist at the balance sheet date, the final outcome of which is dependent on the occurrence or non-occurrence of some uncertain future event. Thus there may be liabilities which may arise in the future but in respect of transactions effected in the past, such as bills under discount, pending litigation, guarantees, etc. Particular attention should be given in this context to any dealing on Stock Exchanges, commodity markets, or in foreign exchanges, where there may be an open forward position. The auditors should inquire into any such matters with a view to seeing that adequate provision is made in the accounts for these liabilities and/or that the position is made clear by means of notes upon the balance sheet. If a contingency could materially affect the financial position of the business, it should be disclosed.

The nature of the disclosure will depend on the information available at the time, and on what assessment can be made of the likely outcome. In making this assessment, information which becomes available after the balance sheet date will clearly be relevant.

Akin to this is also the requirement of the 1967 Act that there are to be disclosed in respect of contracts for capital expenditure, any such sums contracted for but not provided for in the accounts and, in addition, any further amounts authorized by the directors but not contracted for at the balance sheet date.

Whilst it is management's responsibility to have regard for events occurring after the balance sheet date, to evaluate their impact on the state of affairs at that date, and to make adjustments or disclosures as necessary, it is the auditor's duty to review the period immediately following the date of the balance sheet, to establish whether there have been any significant subsequent events which have not been adjusted for or disclosed, and to consider whether that non-adjustment or non-disclosure significantly impairs the truth and fairness of the financial statements which are being reported upon.

A checklist to assist with this review is attached to the end of this section. It describes the scope of the review, the areas of inquiry, and a list of the points which it will usually be appropriate to discuss and review with management. It is also designed to act as a checklist of the kind of subsequent events which might normally be expected to give rise to adjustments or to require disclosure.

When making the review, regard should be had for the concepts of both materiality and prudence. Whether they give rise to adjustments or merely require disclosure, subsequent events need only be recognized if their financial effect is material. Events which give rise to adjustments should normally be recognized only if they result in provision for losses; they should not usually be recognized if they would have the consequence of anticipating profit (notable exceptions would be subsequently declared dividends receivable and events which subsequently mitigate a loss which had been provided for in a previous period).

Events which do not give rise to adjustments should nevertheless be disclosed if they are of sufficient significance — whether favourable or unfavourable — to effect a shareholder's view of the value of his investment (or a creditor's view of the security for his credit). Information regarding post-balance-sheet events should normally be disclosed in the notes to the accounts, although a reference in the Directors' Report may sometimes be appropriate.

Events subsequent to the balance sheet date should be reviewed up to the date on which the financial statements are approved and the review should therefore be made as near as possible to the date on which the auditor's report is signed. The results of the review should be substantiated, where necessary, by drafting appropriate paragraphs into the letter of representation.

Where an event of excessive significance occurs after the signing of the audit report, the auditor must still consider what action should be taken to ensure that shareholders are fully appraised of the facts. Whilst this is an area of great difficulty, nevertheless the auditor's responsibilities remain and he must continue to be alert to them.

Suggested audit tests

Client:	Approved by:
Audit programme: Post-balance-sheet events, contingencies and commitments	Reviewed by:
Accounting date:	

Audit tests	Details of tests	Errors, etc.	Audit sch.	*Work done by* Intls	Date
1. Peruse: (*a*) Board minutes and any other sources of authorization; (*b*) outstanding purchase orders; (*c*) contracts and other relevant documentation, including progress reports from outside contractors for approved capital expenditure, and check to or prepare schedules thereof, differentiating between that which has and that which has not been contracted for, at the balance sheet date. Consider adequacy of amounts on long-term contracts, where final price is not fixed. 2. Complete the 'Review of post-balance events and contingencies' checklist.					

Conclusions	Yes/ No	Audit sch.	*Senior* Intls	Date
Are you satisfied that: (*a*) the amounts included in the accounts have been adjusted, where necessary, for any significant post-balance-sheet events? (*b*) other significant events, commitments and contingencies have been adequately disclosed?				

Checklist for review of post-balance-sheet events and contingencies

	Initials	*Date*
Completed by		
Reviewed by		

A. Review, for the period since the year-end:

Comments/ref. to further notes

- All books of prime entry, for individually material or unusual items.
- Nominal ledger balances, for material variations in individual balances.
- Operating results; investigate unusual variations.
- Statutory books and minutes.

B. Discuss with officers of the company the following matters relating to the period since the year-end:

Notes on discussion

1. Matters which, although not giving rise to adjustments, may require disclosure

- Destruction or expropriation of major assets.
- Acquisition or disposal of material assets or investments.
- Significant reversal of sales or profit trends.
- Reasons for any suspension or interruption of operations, or discontinued products.
- Loss of major customers or contracts; new contracts entered into.
- Forward dealing in materials or commodities; potential losses on forward contracts.
- Forward order position.
- Major exchange-rate movements.
- Imposition of exchange controls.
- Major changes in market price of investments.
- Acquisition, or withdrawal, of short-term borrowing facilities; cash-flow position.
- New issues of shares or acquisition of loan capital.
- Effect of any new legislation or government regulations.

	Notes on discussion
2. Matters which may give rise to adjustments (but only require disclosure if exceptional or extraordinary)	
● Subsequent evidence as to cost of acquisition, or proceeds of realization, of fixed assets or investments (contracted pre-balance-sheet date).	
● Subsequent evidence as to the value, at the B/S date, of fixed assets or investments.	
● Stock and work-in-progress: subsequent sale proceeds; evidence as to NRV at B/S date.	
● Long-term contracts; subsequent information affecting estimated final result.	
● Adequacy of bad debt provision; evidence as to collectability of debts.	
● Dividends payable/receivable declared after balance sheet date.	
● Taxation: changes affecting accounting period under review.	
● Subsequent information regarding any contingent liability (see below) which makes it reasonably certain that loss will arise.	

C. Ascertain from officers of the company whether there is any contingent liability regarding the following matters (whether arising prior or subsequent to the year-end)

	Notes on discussion
● Claims under costed contracts.	
● Claims for faulty goods, or for failure to implement guarantees or warranties.	
● Claims for damages.	
● Claims for breach of contract.	
● Claims under guarantees given by the company on behalf of others.	
● Discounted bills receivable.	
● Taxes in dispute: Inland Revenue enquiries.	
● Assets pledged as security for any liability.	
● Purchase commitments in excess of normal requirements or at prices in excess of prevailing market rates.	
● Commitments to sell products forward at prices below prevailing selling prices.	
● Commitments or options given or taken by the company for the purchase, sale, or repurchase of any securities.	

	Initials	Date
Completed by		
Reviewed by		

- Options on the company's own capital; bonus or profit-sharing arrangements.
- Defaults or breaches of covenant — relating to principal interest funding, or redemption provisions — under any loan or credit agreement or share issue.
- Any other commitments, contracts or leases which might adversely affect the company.
- Any other liabilities in dispute, pending law suits, proceedings or unsettled litigation.

Notes on discussion

Share Capital and Statutory Books

Memorandum of association

Every company limited by shares must have a memorandum of association, stating:

(*a*) the name of the company;
(*b*) whether the situation of the registered office of the company will be in England or Scotland;
(*c*) the objects of the company;
(*d*) that the liability of the members is limited;
(*e*) the amount of share capital with which the company proposes to be registered, and the division thereof into shares of a fixed amount.

The most important of these from an auditor's point of view is the 'objects' clause which must set out exactly the purposes for which the company is formed, and the nature of the business which it is intended to carry on. A company has no power to enter into any transaction which does not come within the terms of its objects clause and, whilst this clause is usually made as wide as possible, an auditor should check that the company has not broken the provisions thereof and entered into *ultra vires* transactions.

The terms of the memorandum can, however, be altered by complying with the provisions of the 1948 Act whereby a company may by special resolution alter the provisions of the objects clause of its memorandum of association.

The memorandum of association may be said to govern the external affairs of a company, and every clause is of interest and importance to all persons entering into business relations with a company.

Articles of association

A company need not have a special set of articles, and the Companies Act 1948, First Schedule, contains a model set of articles known as Table A, which governs all companies for which special articles have not been drawn up. Upon formation a company may exclude the whole or parts of the provisions of Table A, and substitute therefor its own specially drawn articles. An auditor must check whether Table A, or parts thereof, have been thus excluded, for he must be familiar with the exact regulations which govern the particular company.

The articles of association govern the internal affairs of the company, and an auditor must check that the terms thereof are complied with. The articles can be altered at any time by a special resolution of the shareholders. The following are examples of matters which may be covered by the terms of the articles:

The rights of shareholders *inter se.*
Calls on shares.
The forfeiture of shares on account of the non-payment of calls.
Alterations of capital.
The appointment of a managing director.
The appointment of directors.
The powers and duties of directors.
The declaration of dividends.
The accounts and audit.
The borrowing powers.
The payments of underwriting commissions, and commissions on placing shares.
The payment of interest out of capital during construction.
Transfer of shares, etc.
The holding of general meetings.

Share capital

The share capital of a company is often divided into preference and ordinary shares, and the rights of the respective shareholders are governed by the terms of the articles. The preference shares, as a rule, are entitled to a fixed dividend out of the profits, the surplus profits after the payment of the dividend on the preference shares belonging to the ordinary shareholders. It depends upon the terms of the articles whether the preference shares also carry a preferential right as regards capital; that is to say, whether, in the event of liquidation, the preference shareholders are entitled to the return of their capital before there is any return on the ordinary shares. The articles must expressly provide that the preference shares are to be preferential as to capital, otherwise they rank *pro rata* with the ordinary shares in this respect. The preference shareholders' rights to dividend may be either cumulative or non-cumulative; if cumulative, it means that in the event of there not being sufficient profits in any year to pay the preference dividend, such arrears have to be made up in any future years when the profits are sufficient, and thus there can be no dividend paid upon the ordinary until all such arrears upon the preference shares have been paid. If non-cumulative, the preference shareholders are entitled to a fixed dividend out of the profits of each year, and if such profits are insufficient, then there is no right to make up shortages out of the surplus profits of future years. All preference shares are cumulative, unless the articles specially provide that they shall be non-cumulative. In some cases the preference shareholders participate in any surplus profits, after, as a rule, a certain rate of dividend has been paid upon the ordinary shares. Such shares are known as participating preference shares.

Particular points to bear in mind in connection with the issue of shares are:

Prohibition of provision of financial assistance by a company for purchase of its own shares

By the terms of Section 54 of the Companies Act 1948, and Section 35 of the Companies Act 1980, a company is prohibited from directly or indirectly assisting any person financially, either by means of loans or otherwise, in the purchase of shares in the company or in its holding company, except in connection with the purchase of shares by or for the benefit of employees.

Issue of shares at a premium

Section 56 of the Companies Act 1948 provides that, where a company issues shares at a premium, the amount of such premium shall be credited to an account to be called 'the share premium account'. However, the Companies Act 1981 provides some relief from the requirements of Section 56 including the need to establish a non-distributable share premium account in cases of:

(*a*) merger by the formation of a new holding company;
(*b*) takeover by a new holding company;
(*c*) group reconstructions;
(*d*) share for share acquisitions prior to February 4 1981.

In the balance sheet, the balance upon the share premium account must be shown as a capital reserve, and can be used only as follows:

(*a*) by way of an issue of fully paid up 'bonus' shares;
(*b*) by way of writing off preliminary expenses;

(*c*) by way of writing off the expenses of an issue of shares or debentures, including commissions paid or discounts allowed on any issue of shares or debentures;

(*d*) by way of providing for a premium payable on redemption of redeemable preference shares or any debentures.

Where shares were issued at a premium before 1 July 1948, then, if ascertainable, the amount of such premium must be dealt with in accordance with the terms of Section 56.

Issue of shares at a discount

In accordance with the terms of Section 57 of the Companies Act 1948, a company may issue at a discount shares of a class already issued, under the following conditions:

(*a*) The issue must be authorized by resolution in general meeting and sanctioned by the Court.

(*b*) The resolution must specify the maximum rate of discount at which shares are to be issued.

(*c*) Not less than one year must, at the date of issue, have elapsed since the date on which the company was entitled to commence business.

(*d*) Shares to be issued at a discount must be issued within one month after the date on which the issue is sanctioned by the Court or within such extended time as the Court may allow.

Where a company has issued shares at a discount it will be compelled to show the amount of the discount separately on every subsequent balance sheet until the whole of the discount has been written off.

Redeemable preference shares

In accordance with the terms of Section 58 of the Companies Act 1948, a company, if authorized by its articles, may issue redeemable preference shares, such shares to be shown separately on every balance sheet, with particulars of the earliest date on which they are liable to be redeemed. No such shares shall be redeemed unless they are fully paid, and they must be redeemed out of the profits of the company which would otherwise be available for dividend or out of the proceeds of a fresh issue of shares made for the purposes of redemption. If redemption takes place out of profits, then an amount equal to the nominal amount of the shares redeemed shall be transferred out of profits to a capital redemption reserve fund; in the balance sheet this balance must be shown as a capital reserve. For the purposes of reduction of share capital, this fund will be treated as part of the paid-up share capital of the company. In other words, this fund will not be available for payment of dividends. It may, however, be applied in paying up unissued shares of the company to be issued as fully paid 'bonus' shares.

The auditor should always be watchful for compliance with these provisions as their significance is not always appreciated by company directors.

Statutory books

Every company registered under the Companies Acts must keep the following books:

Register of Members (Sections 110, 111 and 112, Companies Act 1948), in which must be entered the names and addresses of all the members of the company, the shares held by each, the distinguishing numbers (if any), and the amount paid or agreed to be considered as paid on such shares; also the dates at which each person was entered in the register, and the date at which any person ceased to be a member.

The register of members is open to the inspection of any member without charge, and to the inspection of any other person on payment of a fee (Section 113).

Minute Book (Section 145, Companies Act 1948), in which must be entered minutes of all proceedings at every meeting of the shareholders and directors or managers of the company.

Register of Directors and Secretaries (Section 200, Companies Act 1948). Every company shall keep at its registered office a register of its directors and secretaries, containing particulars in the case of each individual director as to his present forenames and surname, any former forenames or surname, his address, nationality, his business occupation, if any, particulars of any other directorships held by him and in certain cases the date of his birth; in the case of a corporation, its corporate name and registered or principal office. A copy of such register has to be sent to the Registrar of Companies.

The register is open to the inspection of any member of the company, without charge, and to any other person on payment of a fee. Particulars of the secretary or secretaries are also required.

Register of Directors' Shareholdings, etc. (Sections 27 to 32, Companies Act 1967). Every company shall keep a register containing particulars, as regards each director of the company, of any interest in shares in or debentures of the company held by or for any director and his wife and children, including shares or debentures of any subsidiary company or in the holding company. This provision covers shares and debentures held in a director's own name or held in trust for him, or of which he has any right to become the holder. The register shall also show the date of, and price or other consideration for, the transaction.

This register is open to any person. Each director must notify the company of his interest (and that of his family) within fourteen days of his appointment or of any change in the holding.

Register of Debenture Holders (Sections 86 and 87, Companies Act 1948). Every company shall keep a register, giving particulars as regards all debenture holders. Particulars of the place where the register is kept must be sent to the Registrar of Companies.

The register is open to inspection by any debenture holder or shareholder without fee and by any other person on payment of a fee.

Register of Charges (Section 104, Companies Act 1948). In this register must be entered particulars of every mortgage or charge specifically affecting the property of the company, giving in each case a short description of the property charged, the amount of the charge, and, except in the case of securities to bearer, the names of the persons entitled thereto.

The register is open to the inspection of any creditor or member of the company, without fee, and to any other person on payment of a fee.

Directors' Service Contracts (Section 26, Companies Act 1967). Although a register for these need not be kept, copies of directors' service contracts must be kept available for inspection by members. If there is no written agreement, the statement supplied under the Contracts of Employment Act 1963 should provide the information to be made available. Contracts with less than twelve months to run or those which can be terminated within the next twelve months need not be available.

Interests in Quoted Companies (Section 26, Companies Act 1976). Persons holding 5% or more of the nominal voting capital of a quoted company must notify the company of their interest. This information must be kept up to date and must be recorded in a register by the company. This is available for inspection by any person.

Annual return

Section 124 of the Companies Act 1948 provides that every company shall once at least in every year make a return containing a list of all persons who, on the fourteenth day after the company's annual general meeting for the year, are members of the company, and of all persons who have ceased to be members since the date of the last return, or, in the case of the first return, of the incorporation of the company. This return contains various particulars as regards the share capital of the company, the amount called up and paid up on the shares, the total amount of calls unpaid, and various other particulars.

This annual return must include a written copy, certified by a director and by the secretary of the company to be a true copy, of the last audited balance sheet, including every document required by law to be annexed thereto, together with a copy of the auditor's report. These provisions are contained in Section 127 of the Companies Act 1948, and, since the abolition of the exempt private company, apply to all limited companies.

Suggested audit tests

Client:				Approved by:	
Audit programme: Share capital and statutory books				Reviewed by:	
Accounting date:					
Audit tests	Details of tests	Errors, etc.	Audit sch.	*Work done by* Intls	Date
1. Extract balances in registers and agree to issued share capital, debenture stock, etc. 2. Confirm total issued share capital, debenture stock, etc. from Memorandum and Articles of Association and minutes. 3. Check entries made in register of directors' shareholdings, with share registers noting holding at beginning and end of period. 4. Check completion of previous annual return. 5. Test share and debenture stock transfers, etc. during year and minutes authorizing new certificates, and sealing thereof. 6. Test payment of dividends, interest, etc. and agree amount outstanding at end of accounting period. Obtain bank certificate to cover bank balances. Reconcile outstanding and unclaimed dividends and interest. 7. Where there are independent registrars obtain certificates to cover items 1 and 6 and carry out any further work necessary in the circumstances.					

8. Examine permanent file for Memorandum and Articles of Assocation and notes of amendments thereon to start of accounting period. Update file with any amendments in year and note changes in audit file. 9. Ascertain borrowing powers and note any apparent excess borrowings. 10. Examine and note entries in register of charges. 11. Vouch issue of shares, debentures, etc. with: (*a*) minutes; (*b*) issue documents; (*c*) funds or other consideration received. 12. Examine: (*a*) register of directors; (*b*) register of secretaries; (*c*) register of substantial shareholdings. Note entries in register ensuring that all the statutory requirements have been complied with and, where relevant, those of Stock Exchange.					

Conclusions	Yes/ No	Audit sch.	*Senior* Intls	Date
Are you satisfied that: (*a*) the statutory records meet the requirements of the Companies Acts? (*b*) there are no respects in which the company has been in breach of its Memorandum and Articles of Association?				

Reserves

Regarding the use of the word 'reserve', this term was at one time applied both to appropriations of profits which were free for distribution, and to provisions for specific requirements, such as depreciation, bad debts and other contingencies, which represented charges against earnings.

The Companies Act 1967, clarified this matter in Part IV of the Second Schedule, as follows:

Provisions represent amounts charged against earnings for depreciation, renewals and diminution in value of assets; or amounts 'retained by way of providing for any known liability of which the amount cannot be determined with substantial accuracy'. 'Provisions' are therefore, charges against earnings and must have passed through the profit and loss account. In the balance sheet, any part of the provisions which are in the nature of liabilities will be shown under the heading of 'Current liabilities', any other parts which represent the diminution in the value of an asset, such as provisions for depreciation, are usually deducted from the appropriate assets.

Capital Reserves represent amounts such as premiums on an issue of shares and similar items, which may be regarded as not being free for distribution.

Revenue Reserves represent all amounts of accumulated profits which are regarded as being free for distribution (the Companies Act 1967 does not distinguish between capital and revenue reserves (as the 1948 Act did), although many companies continue to use the division).

As regards reserves, the auditor's responsibility is to satisfy himself that the regulations of the company have been complied with and that the state of affairs is made clear in the financial statements submitted to the shareholders. For this purpose, therefore, he must be fully conversant with the principles and the legislative background concerning the availability of profits represented by reserves for distribution to shareholders.

The Companies Act 1980 provides for statutory restrictions on the distribution of profits and assets of a company. The general provisions are divided between companies generally (i.e. other than investment companies and insurance companies), investment companies and insurance companies.

In this section we are concerned only with the provisions regarding companies generally, in which context two basic restrictions have been imposed upon company distributions:

(*a*) No company may make a distribution except out of profits available for distribution (S39(1)).

(*b*) No public company may make a distribution except out of assets available for distribution (S40(1)).

Both restrictions refer to a 'distribution' which, in principle, means every description of distribution of a company's assets — whether in cash or otherwise except in circumstances such as an issue of shares as fully or partly paid bonus shares.

In connection with the first restriction that a distribution may only be made out of profits available for distribution, 'profits' means revenue and capital profits of any description made at any time (S45(3)). A company's profit available for distribution are thus its net realized profits, i.e.

(*a*) its accumulated realized profits — so far as not previously utilized by distribution or capitalization, less

(*b*) its accumulated realized losses — so far as not previously written-off in a reduction or reorganization of capital duly made.

Thus, unrealized profits are not available for distribution.

It should be appreciated, however, that, whilst distributions are only permitted to be made out of profits available for distribution, the Companies Act 1980 does not affect any other restrictions on making distributions which may be laid down, for instance, by any provision of the company's memorandum or articles.

In connection with the second restriction that a distribution may only be made out of assets available for distribution, the rules concerning the assets available for distribution mean that they equal the amount of net assets less the total of called-up share capital and undistributable reserves (S40 (1)).

The undistributable reserves of a company with which we are left are therefore:

(*a*) the share premium account;
(*b*) the capital-redemption reserve fund;
(*c*) the amount by which

(i) the company's accumulated unrealized profits, so far as not previously utilized by any capitalization (except a transfer of any profits of the company to its capital-redemption reserve fund), exceed
(ii) its accumulated unrealized losses, so far as not previously written-off in a reduction or reorganization of capital duty made, and

(*d*) any other reserve which the company is prohibited from distributing
(i) by any enactment, other than one contained in the Companies Act 1980, S39 to 45, or
(ii) by its memorandum or articles.

Taxation

Provision should be made for all taxation payable, and, as regards the profit and loss account, corporation tax should be provided out of the profit shown and stated separately. Such corporation tax provided is normally payable between nine and twenty months after the balance sheet date and the amount should therefore be shown as a separate item in the 'Current

Suggested audit tests

Client:					Approved by:
Audit programme: Reserves					Reviewed by:
Accounting date:					

Audit tests	Details of tests	Errors, etc.	Audit sch.	*Work done by* Intls	Date
1. Vouch and record in audit files all movements in reserves. 2. Maintain continuous record of: (*a*) share premium account; (*b*) reserves not available for distribution. Differentiate reserves representing unrealized capital surpluses. 3. Ensure that no amounts are taken direct to reserves which should properly have been dealt with through the profit and loss account (See SSAP 6).					

Conclusions	Yes/ No	Audit sch.	*Senior* Intls	Date
Are you satisfied that reserves fairly reflect amounts attributable to ordinary shareholders and that there are adequate records of those which are available for distribution and those which are not?				

liabilities' section of the balance sheet, with the due-date noted. Any corporation tax recoverable should generally be shown separately in 'Current assets'.

Where assets have been sold and the profits have become subject to corporation tax, the tax should be provided from the sale proceeds before any surplus is transferred to a capital reserve. Similarly, where the assets have been revalued, but not sold, and a surplus has been shown which would be the subject of tax on an actual sale, provisions out of the capital reserve created may be made — or at least the contingent liability to tax should otherwise be noted.

In addition to the situation where an asset has been revalued, other examples of 'timing differences' can arise where items of income and expenditure are included in tax computations in periods different from those in which they are included in financial accounts.

SSAP 15, 'Accounting for Deferred Taxation' (issued in October 1978) provided significant changes to the methods of accounting for deferred taxation previously adopted in the UK. The position now, following the availability of accelerated tax allowances, particularly on capital investment and on increased stock levels, is:

(*a*) deferred taxation should be accounted for on all short-term timing differences, and

(*b*) deferred taxation should be accounted for on all other originating timing differences except those which can be demonstrated with reasonable probability to continue in the future.

SSAP 15 goes on to identify the circumstances in which it will be reasonable to assume that timing differences will continue in the future. These circumstances are where the company is a going concern, where the directors are able to foresee on reasonable evidence that the timing differences will not be reversed for at least three years, and where there is no indication that after three years the situation is likely to change. If such timing differences are foreseen as continuing, then full provision for all tax so deferred is no longer required.

The financial statements should disclose the potential deferred tax on all timing differences by way of a note to show the main categories of timing differences and, for each category, how much has actually been provided within the accounts.

If full deferred tax has not been provided within the accounts, the auditor must ensure that the directors have justified this treatment. The types of evidence which the auditor should seek might include:

(*a*) information regarding the trend of past capital expenditure and stock levels, including past levels of success in forecasting;

(*b*) forecasts of future capital expenditure and stock levels, together with cash-flow projections and profit forecasts. These should be for at least three years ahead;

(*c*) directors' minutes authorizing policy changes, capital expenditure plans, etc.

(*d*) any special features relating to the industry, i.e. raw material shortages;

(*e*) letters of representation.

SSAP 15 requires that the position should be reviewed annually as circumstances are always likely to change, and each type of timing difference should be examined separately on each occasion.

A company which is not able to provide this type of information may find it difficult to demonstrate that full provision for deferred tax is not required. If the auditor is not satisfied that the directors have supported their accounting policy with reasonable evidence, he will no doubt recommend full provision for deferred tax within the accounts. Should the directors be unwilling to do so, the auditor will have to consider whether or not to make some reference to this difficult aspect in his audit report.

In all cases it is the duty of the auditor to see that provision for tax is adequate, so that a 'true and fair view' is shown. Often, the auditors themselves prepare the tax computations, although this is not part of the auditor's duty as such. Where they do not, the computations should be inspected to ensure that the provisions are fair estimates of the liability.

Suggested audit tests

Client: Approved by:

Audit programme: Taxation Reviewed by:

Accounting date:

Audit tests	Details of tests	Errors, etc.	Audit sch.	*Work done by* Intls	Date
1. Examine taxation files and note main points on correspondence with Inland Revenue. Obtain copy of last agreed computation or note areas of open points. Review outstanding tax provisions in last period's accounts.					
2. Review or prepare schedule of movements on taxation accounts during the year.					
3. Inspect forms CT61 and CT62 and reconcile with position as shown in the accounts.					
4. Prepare or review computation of provision for taxation based on the profits/					

losses for the year under review. 5. Prepare or review computations of tax equalization reserves/deferred taxation in respect of taxation deferred or paid in advance by reason of: (*a*) capital allowances; (*b*) interest payable or receivable; (*c*) royalties payable or receivable; (*d*) ACT on dividends; (*e*) other items. Check that treatment is in accordance with the declared accounting policies. 6. Consider implication of 'closed company' status under the requirements of the Income and Corporation Taxes Act 1970 and prepare or review shortfall computations. 7. Submit all relevant schedules and accounts to the Tax Department of the firm for checking, clearance and confirmation that the provisions as stated in the accounts are adequate, or 8. If the firm is not responsible for the client's taxation matters, obtain confirmation of above aspects by inclusion in the letter of representation or by reference to other professional advisers.					

Debentures and Loans

Upon any issue of debentures or loans, the auditor should see that the articles give the directors power to borrow money in this way, and he should examine the directors' minute exercising that power. The actual debenture or trust deed should be examined in order that the exact terms of the issue may be ascertained. It must further be seen that any charge given upon the assets of the company is entered in the register of charges, in accordance with Section 104 of the Companies Act 1948, and that the necessary particulars are filed with the Registrar of Companies.

The entries in the accounting records should also be checked, and if debentures or loans are issued at a discount, the full nominal amount must be credited to the liability account, as that is the actual amount of the liability which will have to be repaid, with the amount of the discount being debited to a separate account. If this discount is written-off to profit and loss account over a period of years, the amount carried forward should be shown as a separate item in the balance sheet to comply with the terms of Para. 3(d), Second Schedule, Part 1, the Companies Act, 1967. It is prudent for the discount to be written-off to revenue as soon as possible, but, subject to the provisions of the articles of the particular company, in a going concern an auditor could raise no objection if the discount were to be written-off over the period of the debentures or loan.

If debentures or loans are issued at a premium, the nominal amount again must be credited to the liability account, and the amount of the premium itself must be credited to a premium account.

If debentures or loans are issued at par but are repayable at the end of a period at a premium, then they should appear on the balance sheet at the nominal amount, with a note that they are repayable at a certain date at a premium. The premium is in the nature of a payment of deferred interest, which should be provided for out of revenue over the period of the debentures or loans, as otherwise the whole amount of the premium will have to be charged to the profit and loss account of the year in which they are redeemed. If a sinking fund is being created to provide for the redemption then it should include the premium too.

Debentures may be issued to creditors of a company, perhaps most commonly to secure bank loans and overdrafts. In such a case, in the balance sheet the bank would be shown as a creditor in the sum of the loan and overdraft balance, and against this item would appear a note indicating that the bank held a debenture as collateral security. No interest is paid on the debenture as such, but if the company defaulted then the bank could take up its security.

An auditor should see the loan agreement (if any) and the directors' minute issuing these debentures for this purpose, and he must see that the position is shown correctly in the balance sheet. He should ascertain that these debentures have been entered in the register of charges, and enquire as to whether the necessary particulars have been filed with the Registrar of Companies under Section 96 of the Companies Act 1948.

He must, furthermore, consider whether the balance sheet presentation of such items is such as to show a true and fair view of the ability of the company to meet its current debt. Whilst information concerning repayment dates attaching to bank loans and overdrafts is often relegated to a note to the accounts, best practice demands that sums repayable within 12 months should be aggregated with other current liabilities. It is submitted that not to adopt this form of presentation could be construed as misleading in some circumstances, notwithstanding that the matter is not covered by statutory requirement.

Suggested audit tests

Client:	Approved by:
Audit programme: Debentures, secured loans and unsecured loan stock	Reviewed by:
Accounting date:	

Audit tests	Details of tests	Errors, etc.	Audit sch.	*Work done by* Intls	Date
1. Examine Deeds of Trust, if any, and note whether the rules stated therein are being adhered to, with particular reference to: (*a*) borrowing limits; (*b*) redemption reserves; (*c*) restrictions on dealing with assets. 2. Check issues and redemptions of loan stock and the payment of interest thereon to minutes and ensure that they are in accordance with the terms of issue. 3. Examine and note entries in register of charges relating to assets on which the debentures and loans have been secured, noting the type of charge operative (e.g. fixed, floating). 4. In respect of any other secured loans or unsecured loan stock: (*a*) inquire into the reasons therefor; (*b*) peruse documentation;					

Audit tests	Details of tests	Errors, etc.	Audit sch.	*Work done by* Intls	Date
(*c*) note terms and conditions; (*d*) check authorization; (*e*) obtain certificate at year-end confirming balance outstanding (principle and interest), interest paid during year, security, if any, and that borrower is not in default. 5. Ascertain that total borrowings, including any authorized but not being used, are within the limits imposed by the Articles of Association.					

Conclusions	Yes/ No	Audit sch.	*Senior* Intls	Date
Are you satisfied that: (*a*) the company is not in default of the terms of any loan agreement? (*b*) the amounts, terms, security, etc. for loans are properly reflected in the financial statements? (*c*) the company has not exceeded its borrowing powers? (*d*) adequate evidence is available on the file to support these conclusions?				

Creditors' and Accrued Expenses

Profits can easily be inflated by the suppression of invoices for either services or goods. In this latter area, therefore, at the end of the period, the auditor should pay particular attention to the cut-off of goods inwards and should trace into the accounting records a few of the deliveries received both before and after the year-end to ensure they are properly reflected in the correct accounting period to the timing of receipt. To help cover the former, the invoice file for the ensuing period should be inspected, and the dates of the invoices therein examined, to see whether any of these should be charged to the period under audit.

In order that the auditor may be satisfied that all creditors' invoices have been recognized and included he should consider whether he should arrange for the direct circularization of suppliers requesting them to furnish direct to the auditor a statement showing the balance due at a given date, or if nothing is owing, a notification to that effect. This is not regarded as an essential substantive test in every circumstance. Frequently, it may be acceptable to rely upon the company's internal controls. However, in situations where the final audit is to take place shortly after the balance sheet date, and where, therefore, the opportunity for substantiation by reference to subsequent documentation is restricted, the procedure should certainly be considered and is often to be recommended. In many smaller trading companies it is often possible by virtue of only a small number of circularization letters to obtain independent evidence of a significant proportion of the total balance shown as due to creditors.

The most common form of circularization letter is set out below.

(Address)

Creditor's name and address — Date:

Dear Sirs

In order to facilitate the preparation of audited accounts, we would appreciate your completing the confirmation below of the balance due to you by this company at .... and sending it together with a duplicate of your monthly statement direct to our auditors, Messrs .... at your earliest opportunity. A stamped addressed envelope is enclosed.

The above statement is in addition to your usual monthly statement, which should be sent to us in the ordinary way.

Yours faithfully

Serial No ....

We confirm that the balance due to us at .... was £....

Date — Signature..........

Title or position........ — Company..........

The statements received back should be compared with the ledger accounts and if all agree, it is good supportive evidence that the individual creditor's books agree with the books of the auditor's clients, and, therefore, that, as regards these accounts at any rate, no invoices have been omitted.

Of course, in some cases such statements may not agree, as goods may have been debited by the creditors in a different period of account from that in which they have been received and credited in the client's books. In such cases the auditor should carefully trace such goods through the goods-inwards system — confirming the dates — for consistency as regards treatment in his client's books.

It may be found that certain accounts are in dispute, and, therefore, the statements disagree — in these circumstances most careful inquiries should be made to see that adequate provision is made in the accounts for all estimated liabilities. If claims have been made by creditors which have not been agreed to or provided for in the accounts, the auditor may have to insist, if the amounts involved are large, on such claims at least being referred to in the balance sheet by way of a note; otherwise he may have to refer to the matter in his audit report. In the case of claims which are the subject of a pending lawsuit, the auditor should see that ample provision is made in the accounts for any likely liability under this head, including the legal charges. If he is not satisfied with the provision made, the matter will be one with which it may be necessary for him to deal in his report.

Any debit balances on the purchase ledgers should be carefully examined, to ascertain whether they are bona fide amounts owing; for example, for returns, allowances, etc. If any of such debit balances are of long standing, the auditor should go into them with a responsible official, and see that adequate provision is made for any possible bad or doubtful debts.

With regard to provision for outstanding liabilities, all the main expense accounts should be inspected to see that the various charges for the period have been included — these will consist, for example, of rent and rates; light, heat and power; repairs and maintenance; wages and salaries; professional fees, advertising expenses, and many other items of expense. The auditor may be able to trace outstanding amounts by an examination of the invoices debited during the period, noting the dates up to which such invoices run, and making inquiries where such dates fall short of the end of the financial period. An examination of the entries for the succeeding period often discloses items for which no provision has been made. In some cases, the amounts will have to be estimated.

Suggested audit tests

Client:		Approved by:
Audit programme:	Creditors' and accrued expenses	Reviewed by:
Accounting date:		

Review the related sections of the interim working papers and briefly summarize (e.g. 'Good', 'Medium', 'Poor') the degree of reliance that can be placed on internal accounting controls in this area. On the basis of this assessment determine the required scope and extent of year-end substantive work: indicate the sample sizes in the relevant column below and amend, delete, or add to the suggested substantive tests as necessary.

Remarks	Intls	Date

Audit tests	Details of tests	Errors, etc.	Audit sch.	*Work done by* Intls	Date
1. Test extraction and casts of purchases and agree list of balances at balance sheet date with the control account. 2. Test individual personal accounts and reconciliations with suppliers' statements, noting agreement of goods and cash. 3. Test ageing of accounts payable and inquire into: (*a*) old outstanding balances; (*b*) the reason why they have not been settled; (*c*) debit balances, and the reasons therefor.					

Audit tests	Details of tests	Errors, etc.	Audit sch.	*Work done by* Intls	Date
4. Consider creditors' circularization if not carried out during the interim audit. 5. Examine invoices received after date to ensure that all liabilities as at the balance sheet date have been brought into account. 6. Test that all liabilities in respect of goods to which title had passed at the balance sheet date have been included in the accounts, and correlate with stock records and cut-off procedures, including stocks held by third parties. 7. Examine provisions for accrued expenses. Check that they are complete and reasonable; compare with previous year. Test calculations and confirm with independent sources, when available. 8. Check that debit balances on purchases ledger are included in debtors, and credit balances on sales ledger are included in creditors, or are set-off where appropriate.					

Conclusions	Yes/No	Audit sch.	*Senior* Intls	Date
Are you satisfied that: (*a*) liabilities are fairly stated, and complete? (*b*) the basis of accounting is acceptable and consistent with previous practice? (*c*) adequate evidence is available on the file to support these conclusions?				

Fixed Assets and Depreciation

The primary thrust of the audit in the area of fixed assets is aimed at ensuring that:

(*a*) all items included within fixed assets do physically exist;
(*b*) the company has good title to all such assets;
(*c*) all capital items have been recognized as such and included in fixed assets;
(*d*) no expenditure more properly regarded as of a revenue nature has been capitalized;
(*e*) the costs of fixed assets are being written off over appropriate time periods;
(*f*) appropriate recognition is given to current values of fixed assets.

Plant and machinery

The verification of plant and machinery by the auditor is a matter of some difficulty. It is frequently impossible to substantiate this item with the degree of certainty possible with some other assets. However, there should be a plant register, or detailed back-up schedules of plant and machinery, identifying the specific items making up the balance in the financial statements, and this should be called for by the auditor. He should reconcile these records with the information supplied on his previous audit and the capital transactions for the period under audit which he will have already checked. He should select a few items at random and physically inspect them.

In the case of plant abroad or at sites in this country the auditor should require a detailed confirmation of the plant held, and whether it is working efficiently, and this should be compared with the plant register or schedule of plant. Where a considerable amount of plant is located at sites, the auditor should verify a proportion of the plant by physical inspection.

The auditor should discuss the whole question of depreciation fully with the management, and thus endeavour to ascertain the basis upon which they have founded their estimates and provisions, and whether they have acted upon proper advice. It is impossible for an auditor to estimate the working life of plant. All he can do is to make inquiry and satisfy himself whether or not this most important question appears to have been properly faced and considered; that correct principles have been acted upon and consistently adhered to; and that the provision made in the accounts appears to be reasonable and sufficient.

If plant registers are kept, these in course of time will reveal the actual experience of the working lives of the various types of plant. Such registers, therefore, are of the utmost value to the auditor in satisfying himself whether the provision for depreciation is adequate or not.

Freehold and leasehold land and buildings

As regards the verification of freehold property, the auditor must inspect the title deeds and see that they appear to be in order and refer to the particular property. He should inspect the abstract of title which gives the dates and parties to the various conveyances, seeing that such conveyances are there, and that the last conveyance is into the name of his clients. An auditor cannot guarantee that the title is good. All he can do is to see that the deeds are in his client's possession and appear to be in order. If in doubt on any points, he should refer to his client's solicitors.

Leasehold property will be verified by an inspection of the lease, the terms of which should be noted.

If freehold or leasehold property has been mortgaged, the title deeds or lease will be in the possession of the mortgagees or their solicitors, and, in this case, the auditor should apply direct to them for a certificate that they hold the deeds of the particular property as security for the advance. In other circumstances the client's own solicitors may hold such documents for safekeeping and again direct confirmation should always be obtained and any differences by comparison with the previous year be followed up.

The main object of providing for depreciation

SSAP 12, 'Accounting for depreciation', published in 1978 states:

> 'Depreciation is a measure of the wearing out, consumption or other loss of value of a fixed asset which can arise from use, effluxion of time and obsolescence through technological and market changes. Depreciation should be allocated to accounting periods so as to charge a fair proportion to each accounting period during the expected useful life of the asset. Depreciation includes amortization of fixed assets whose useful life is predetermined (e.g. leases) and depletion of wasting assets (e.g. mines).'

In all cases, therefore, where one of the direct results of earning revenue is gradually to consume fixed assets of a wasting nature, the depreciation of such assets must be provided for out of revenue. For the cost of such assets is, in fact, a direct revenue charge; but it is one which, in most cases, has to be spread over a period of years, as the benefits arising therefrom are not all exhausted in the one year, as is the case with the majority of the revenue charges, such as rent, rates, salaries, etc. The only fixed assets in respect of which no depreciation needs to be provided, following SSAP 12, are land and, in certain circumstances, investment properties.

Various methods are used in practice for writing off depreciation. The most common are:

Fixed instalment or straight-line system
Under this system a fixed instalment, calculated at the time of the original purchase of the asset, is written off each year.

Reducing instalment system

Under this system a fixed percentage is written off each year, calculated upon the reducing balance brought down upon the asset account.

Whichever method is used, it will be important for the auditor to substantiate the arithmetical accuracy of the calculations involved and to review the reasonableness of the rates used in the light of experience of asset lives.

Goodwill

Goodwill should not appear as an asset in a balance sheet, except in the case of purchase, when it should appear at cost. If the price paid for goodwill has not been fixed specifically in the contract of sale, the amount will be the difference between the total purchase price and the other assets at agreed valuations, less any liabilities taken over from the vendors. Goodwill must, in accordance with the Companies Act 1967, 2nd Schedule, Part 1, Paragraph 8(1) and (2), be separately stated in a balance sheet. But this asset may be aggregated with patents and trade marks, and thus these three assets may appear in the balance sheet as one item.

Questions are often raised as to whether depreciation should be charged against this asset; although this is undoubtedly a very wise financial policy, it is not compulsory, either from a legal or from an accounting point of view.

The figure at which goodwill appears in a balance sheet does not purport to show its present value, but merely the amount which has been expended in its acquisition, or, in other words, the amount of capital which has been invested in this particular asset.

The present saleable value of the goodwill of a business must depend entirely upon the financial position of the concern at date and its present earning capacity and future prospects. A purchaser would not be influenced in the least by the value placed upon this asset in the balance sheet.

In theory, goodwill represents the sum paid for anticipated future super profits, and therefore some authorities contend that the cost should be written off against the future super profits earned. Certainly goodwill is an intangible asset. It is, therefore, sound financial policy to write the cost down out of available profits or reserves, and in this way ensure that the whole of the capital of the business is represented by tangible assets. But this is a matter of financial policy, and, therefore, in the case of a company, is a matter for the directors to decide. An auditor cannot interfere, though he may give advice if asked to do so.

The auditor should see exactly how the balance upon the goodwill account is made up, and that it does represent the actual cost only, no improper items having been debited thereto. He should see that it is separately stated in the balance sheet and described as being 'at cost'. He cannot insist upon this asset being written down out of profits, unless, in the case of a company, the articles specially provide to this effect, but, on the other hand, goodwill should on no account be written up.

Suggested audit tests

Client:	Approved by:
Audit programme: Fixed assets and depreciation	Reviewed by:
Accounting date:	

Review the related sections of the interim working papers and briefly summarize (e.g. 'Good', 'Medium', 'Poor') the degree of reliance that can be placed on internal accounting controls in this area. On the basis of this assessment determine the required scope and extent of year-end substantive work: indicate the sample sizes in the relevant column below and amend, delete, or add to the suggested substantive tests as necessary.

Remarks	Intls	Date

Audit tests	Details of tests	Errors, etc.	Audit sch.	*Work done by* Intls	Date
1. Obtain and vouch schedules of additions and disposals during the period. Check calculation of cost of any asset created by the client.					
2. Depreciation:					
(*a*) Ensure that depreciation is charged on all assets with a finite useful life;					
(*b*) Check depreciation calculations, noting consistency of rates of depreciation used.					
3. Check calculation of profit or loss on disposals.					
4. Confirm reconciliation between plant registers and nominal ledger. Review plant registers for obsolete items.					
5. Valuation:					
(*a*) Check whether there is any significant difference between the market and balance sheet values of land and buildings.					

(*b*) Obtain copies of any valuations during the period. 6. Agree schedules to balance sheet and recorded accounting policies. Check notes concerning any assets revalued in the year. 7. Confirm existence of and title to all fixed assets (by direct confirmation from third parties, if required): (*a*) properties — inspect title deeds, leases, etc. ensuring that *all* properties are covered; (*b*) plant, equipment etc. — confirm client's own inspection procedures and test to plant registers; (*c*) motor vehicles — inspect registration records; (*d*) other material fixed assets — detail method of verification.				

Conclusions	Yes/ No	Audit sch.	*Senior* Intls	Date
Are you satisfied that: (*a*) fixed assets are fairly stated? (*b*) the depreciation rates used reflect a reasonable assessment of the remaining useful life of the assets concerned? (*c*) adequate evidence is available on the file to support these conclusions?				

Investments

At the date of each balance sheet, a schedule should be prepared for the auditor, giving particulars of each quoted investment, the cost thereof and valuation at the balance sheet date based upon current market prices.

Unquoted investments should appear upon a separate list, and should be shown in the balance sheet at cost or at a valuation made by the directors.

The auditor should refer to copies of the financial statements of the companies concerned so that he may form an opinion as to the reasonableness of the valuations proposed.

In the case of holding companies, the investments in subsidiaries are held for trade purposes. The question of the valuation of such shares is dealt with in chapter 10.

If the market values either individually or in total are less than the cost price of investments, the question arises as to whether or not provision should be made for this diminution in value. Any such provision should be separately stated in the profit and loss account, and shown in the balance sheet as a deduction from the total cost of the investments. The question whether, in the case of a company, it is legally necessary to provide for such a diminution in value is a difficult one, but there can be no question that this is a very wise course to adopt. Furthermore there is divergence of thought as to whether investments should be written down to the market value on an individual basis, or whether the best method is to deal with the investments as a whole and to make a provision to cover any estimated diminution in value to the date of the balance sheet. If no such provision is made then in such circumstances the investments are required to be shown in the balance sheet with a note against the item as to the aggregate market value at the balance sheet date.

In all cases the basis of the valuation should be stated upon the balance sheet, that is, whether the valuation is 'at cost', 'market value', or 'at cost less a stated provision', and, where the market value is given of an unquoted investment, the fact that this is a 'directors'' valuation.

So far as the auditor is concerned, he should check the comprehensiveness of the list of investments and check the valuations, seeing whether or not an adequate provision has been made against possible losses upon realization. If no such provision is made, he should see that a note as to the market value appears upon the balance sheet. The debentures or share certificates must be inspected too, and it should be noted that they are made out in the name of the auditor's clients or their nominees — in the latter case, a certificate should be obtained from the nominees that they hold for the auditor's clients, and that they have no charge upon such investments.

Further, it is recommended that, where the market value noted on the balance sheet exceeds the book value of investments, an estimate of what the tax liability would have been had the investments been sold at their market value, should also be given. Obviously, the true worth of a company could be materially effected by the payment of such a tax, and unless the potential liability is shown it could be said that the balance sheet does not show a true and fair view. The auditor should therefore see that, where this aspect is material in an appreciation of the accounts, the information is given.

Suggested audit tests

Client:	Approved by:
Audit programme: Investments	Reviewed by:
Accounting date:	

Review the related sections of the interim working papers and briefly summarize (e.g. 'Good', 'Medium', 'Poor') the degree of reliance that can be placed on internal accounting controls in this area. On the basis of this assessment determine the required scope and extent of year-end substantive work: indicate the sample sizes in the relevant column below and amend, delete, or add to the suggested substantive tests as necessary.

Remarks	Intls	Date

Audit tests	Details of tests	Errors, etc.	Audit sch.	*Work done by* Intls	Date
1. Obtain a schedule of investments at the balance sheet date showing: (*a*) subsidiary and fellow subsidiary companies; (*b*) associated companies; (*c*) listed investments; (*d*) unlisted investments and (i) test with detailed investment records; (ii) cast; (iii) prove total with nominal ledger.					
2. Check calculation of gains and losses on disposal and confirm taxation position thereon.					
3. Verify existence and title to all investments by physical inspection or by direct confirmation from third parties, including scrip due to and by the market.					
4. Check consistent valuation of investments:					

Audit tests	Details of tests	Errors, etc.	Audit sch.	*Work done by* Intls	Date
(*a*) for listed companies — with Stock Exchange official lists or other evidence if necessary; (*b*) for unlisted companies — bases used, including directors' valuations, and from available evidence from audited accounts, etc.; (*c*) for subsidiary or associated companies — examine audited accounts and consider underlying asset values, etc. in relation to both valuation and book value of the investments. 5. In respect of investments held by directors or nominees on behalf of the company, ensure that they are all covered by signed blank transfers and letters of trust. 6. Check whether, in respect of the investment portfolio, there may be contingent liabilities requiring disclosure in respect of uncalled capital, etc.					

Conclusions	Yes/ No	Audit sch.	*Senior* Intls	Date
Are you satisfied that: (*a*) investments are fairly stated? (*b*) the basis of valuation is consistent and adequately disclosed? (*c*) there is adequate evidence on file to support these conclusions?				

Inter-company Balances

Whilst the question of consolidated financial statements is dealt with in chapter 10, consideration must be given during the audit of the accounts of individual companies within groups, to inter-company debts, especially where the interests of creditors or minority shareholders in the lending company are involved.

Apart from trading transactions, it is common practice within groups for one company's surplus funds to be applied for use elsewhere in the group, often on a very informal basis. The auditor should consider recommending that all such financing should be arranged only on an arm's-length basis as regards security, etc., particularly if there are any doubts as to the solvency of the companies in question.

Suggested audit tests

Client: Audit programme: Inter-company balances Accounting date:				Approved by: Reviewed by:	
Audit tests	Details of tests	Errors, etc.	Audit sch.	*Work done by* Intls	Date
1. Agree balances on loan and current accounts with those in the books of group or associated companies, and obtain written confirmation from group and associated companies not audited by the firm. 2. Ensure that any items in reconciliation between inter-company accounts are entered in the books within the financial year. 3. Ensure that inter-company profits on sales or transfers of stocks or fixed assets have been segregated for adjustment in the consolidated accounts. 4. Consider whether amounts due to the company are adequately covered					

Audit tests	Details of tests	Errors, etc.	Audit sch.	*Work done by* Intls	Date
by net asset backing, making provision for any loss arising, or adjustment thereto, where necessary. 5. Consider the possibilities of further inter-company indebtedness arising under inter-company guarantees, and the need to make provision, or other form of disclosure.					

Conclusions	Yes/ No	Audit sch.	*Senior* Intls	Date
Are you satisfied that inter-company balances are: (*a*) properly segregated in the accounts? (*b*) classified consistently in the other group companies' accounts? (*c*) stated at amounts which are not distorted by 'window dressing'?				

Stock and Work-in-progress

Audit considerations within this area particularly must be seen against the accounting principles involved and the necessity for the valuation of stocks and work-in-progress. This arises because almost invariably certain goods are purchased or manufactured during one accounting period and sold in another. The purpose of the profit and loss account generally is to show the profit arising upon the sale of goods during the accounting period within which they are sold. If, therefore, some of the goods sold were purchased or manufactured in a preceding period, then the unsold goods in hand at the end of the first period should be charged on to the succeeding period. Against that principle, however, is that in certain circumstances which are dealt with later, stocks are commonly, for balance sheet purposes, valued below cost. The effect of this is to charge to the profit and loss account, for the period during which the goods were puchased or manufactured, an estimated loss, representing the difference between the cost of the goods and the lower figure at which they have been valued.

The basic principles of valuation (other than long-term contracts)

The accepted slogan of the accountancy profession for many years was that the basis of stock valuation should be 'the lower of cost or realizable value', but, unfortunately, there was no uniform definition of either 'cost' or 'realizable value'. The issuance in May 1975, by the English Institute, of SSAP 9 has done much to clarify this point, by defining both 'cost' and 'net realizable value'.

The meaning of cost

'Cost' is made up of:

(*a*) the price of goods purchased for resale or for the manufacture or assembly of finished goods;
(*b*) expenses directly incurred in handling or altering these goods;
(*c*) overheads carried forward in stock instead of being charged against current revenue.

As regards (*a*) there are different methods of assessing direct cost as follows:

(i) to value each item or batch on hand at the actual cost of the consignment of which it formed a part (known as 'unit cost');
(ii) to assume that the quantity held in stock represents the latest purchases and to value at these prices (known as 'first in, first out', or 'FIFO');
(iii) to value at the average cost during the year, i.e. the value of the opening stock plus the year's purchases, deducting consumption at the average price (known as 'average cost');
(iv) to value stock upon the basis of current selling prices, deducting therefrom the estimated cost of selling and distribution, plus the normal margin of profit (known as 'adjusted selling price').

The Statement of Standard Accounting Practice now effectively precludes other methods of valuation which tend to produce results significantly differing from actual cost e.g. 'last in, first out', or 'base stock method'.

The direct cost figure would in all cases be increased by any direct expenses such as freight, duty, landing, dock and reasonable warehouse charges, etc., and on the other hand all trade discounts and allowances should be deducted.

In the case of work-in-progress and finished stock, it is necessary to consider what addition should be made in respect of overheads. Several alternative methods are used to determine this addition. If, for example, the overheads are calculated as a percentage on direct labour, this percentage will fluctuate with the rise and fall in the volume of production and the question arises as to what percentage should be applied. In practice the following alternatives are used:

(*a*) the percentage for the last quarter or month of the accounting year;
(*b*) the percentage actually applied at the time the goods were manufactured;
(*c*) the average percentage for the year;
(*d*) a standard percentage based on the normal volume of production.

Whichever method is adopted, it must be designed to reflect overhead costs attributable to the stage of conversion.

No one method is universally applicable, nor is it possible to be dogmatic as to the method which must be used; it will depend entirely on the circumstances of the case. In the *Duple Motor Bodies* case (1961) the Courts refused to commit themselves to any particular method, and Lord Reid said:

> 'We have been invited to decide between these methods as a broad matter of principle, but that is very difficult. If the accountancy profession cannot do that I do not see how I can. The real question is what method best fitted the circumstances of a particular business.'

It is suggested that standard cost is a sound basis to adopt. Overheads (which would include all costs of the works production facilities used in converting the raw material into finished products, but which would not generally include selling and distribution expenses) should be added, at the current expenditure rates, and based upon a normal level of activity, taking one year with another.

By adopting a standard cost valuation, the value of any unit of stock at the beginning and end of the year would be varied as changes took place in the costs of raw materials, in direct labour, or in production overheads. Under this basis of valuation each year would bear the full cost of idle capacity, which it is submitted it correctly should do.

The meaning of net realizable value

Net realizable value may be considered as the net amount which would be realized if the particular goods held were sold at the prices ruling at the date of the balance sheet, after deduction of estimated further manufacturing costs and selling and distribution charges. Its use will be appropriate as a basis of stock valuation in situations where net realizable value is likely to be less than cost.

'Net realizable value' is interpreted to mean the net realizable value of the goods in the form in which they will in fact be sold, which in the case of a manufacturer is normally in the form of the manufactured goods. Thus in the case of stores and raw materials the bases would be, not their saleable value as stores and raw materials, but as component parts of the manufactured goods, except perhaps in circumstances such as obsolescence of products.

It is an accepted principle that the valuation of assets for balance sheet purposes is upon the 'going concern' basis. Therefore, in the case of a manufacturer, all classes of the inventory, i.e. stores, raw materials, process and finished goods, represent merely stages in the process of manufacture, and all are held with a view to the production and sale of the finished products in which the particular concern deals. In the case of a tyre manufacturer, for example, rubber is held with a view to conversion into and sale as tyres, and as a rule only in the event of liquidation would the rubber be sold in its crude form. It is submitted, therefore, that it is the net realizable value of the finished product which should be measured against the cost value of all classes of inventories in assessing the balance sheet valuations.

The auditor's duties as regards stocks

The auditor's position as regard stocks is one of very great difficulty, for the amounts involved are often very considerable and materially affect both the profit and loss account and the balance sheet; and falsification of accounts is frequently effected by means of stock manipulations. It is not, however, considered to be appropriate normally for the auditor himself to take or value the stock, but he should observe such counts and list all aspects of valuation most thoroughly as he is bound to rely very largely upon the internal audit tests in this connection.

The principal errors which have to be guarded against, all of which may be purposely or unintentionally committed, are as follows:

(*a*) the inclusion of stock which in fact does not exist;
(*b*) the omission or suppression of some of the stock sheets;
(*c*) the inclusion of goods in stock, the invoices for which have not been passed through the purchases;
(*d*) the inclusion of goods in stock which have already been sold and entered as sales, prior to the date of the balance sheet;
(*e*) the omission of stock in the hands of third parties;
(*f*) incorrect additions and calculations;
(*g*) incorrect prices and valuations;
(*h*) the valuation of stock upon the basis of incorrect principles;
(*i*) the omission to provide for diminution in value in the case of damaged, obsolete or excess stock.

If proper stock records and controls have been maintained, these will be of great assistance to the auditor for the purpose of checking the stock, and any large differences between the quantities shown by the stock books and the stocktaking sheets should be most carefully investigated.

At a physical stock check the auditor must see that the counting, inspection, recording, pricing, etc. are all properly carried out and checked. Thus he satisfies himself that the agreed procedures and checks are in fact carried out. At the same time the auditor, so far as he reasonably can, verifies by supervising physical tests of a proportion of the stock. If these tests are applied other than on the balance sheet date, care must be taken to adjust for intermediate movements of items. In cases where perpetual stock records are maintained and physical tests are carried out during the course of the year, then a full stocktaking is commonly dispensed with at the end of the accounting period. In this case the auditor would attend when the intermediate tests are being carried out and would apply the same procedures. Set out below is a specimen questionnaire dealing with the relevant aspects of an auditor's observation of physical stocktaking procedures.

The American case of *McKesson & Robbins* (1939), described in chapter 14, which uncovered a very serious fraud, turned a spotlight on audit procedures regarding stocks. American auditors thereafter took the lead in instituting attendance at stocktaking as a regular audit practice, and now this has become common in the UK. In July 1968, the English Institute issued recommendation U9 advising regular attendance, and this should now be regarded as an essential feature of an audit.

Physical stocktaking observation questionnaire

	Answer	Intls
1. Organization and control		
1.1 Name and position of official with overall responsibility for stock and work-in-progress.		
1.2 Are there written instructions covering the organization of the physical count, evaluation of stock, etc. issued by the company or group? (Copy to be attached.)		
1.3 Are there proper written instructions setting out the responsibilities of all persons taking part in the stocktaking? (Copy to be attached.) Have these instructions been fully explained to stocktaking personnel before they commence the count?		
1.4 Was a copy of the stocktaking instructions submitted to us sufficiently in advance for our comments?		
1.5 Do the instructions cover all locations and departments and stocks in the hands of third parties?		
1.6 Do the instructions provide for the segregation of goods belonging to third parties?		
1.7 Are there adequate procedures for controlling movements during stocktaking?		
1.8 Do procedures ensure all records accounted for? (Stock tags, tickets, rough sheets, summaries, etc.)		
1.9 Do the procedures control the transcription of the rough stock records into final stock sheet form?		
1.10 Do procedures include an independent check by the client's staff of:		

	Answer	Intls
(*a*) description; (*b*) quantities; (*c*) prices; (*d*) extensions? 1.11 Where there are stocks which require specialist knowledge to identify, verify or measure (e.g. chemicals, oil, etc.) is a competent official to be available for this purpose? 1.12 Is the physical count to be noted in the stock records? 1.13 Where maximum or minimum stock levels are specified, is the procedure for reviewing the levels regularly observed and is effective action taken? 1.14 Where there are maximum or minimum times for holding stock lines (e.g. perishable goods, seasonable stock lines, goods requiring maturing, etc.) do the procedures ensure that old or immature stocks are identified? 1.15 Is a significant proportion of the stock in non-standard (and therefore less saleable) sizes and quantities? 1.16 Does any of the stock and work-in-progress include development expenditure, or new products which are not yet being distributed, and are these adequately identified? 1.17 Do procedures ensure that all information required for accounting purposes is available regarding damaged, defective and slow moving stock? 1.18 Are stocks which are held subject to any reservation of title (Romalpa clauses); (*a*) adequately identified and segregated; (*b*) separately valued? 1.19 Are sundry stocks (e.g. loose tools, consumable stores) counted: if not, on what basis are they to be included in the accounts? 1.20 Where stock is taken other than at the year-end, how is the year-end cut-off point established for: (*a*) goods-inwards; (*b*) goods transferred between locations and departments; (*c*) goods-outwards? *2. Counting procedures* 2.1 Date of stocktake. 2.2 Method of stocktaking (continuous or complete physical count).		

	Answer	Intls
2.3 Value of stock under observation at previous year-end (or approximate current-year values, if available).		
2.4 Name and position of official responsible for stocktaking.		
2.5 Is the section/location arranged in a manner suitable for counting, measuring, etc. and generally in good order?		
2.6 Is each section/location subdivided so that each area is easier to count?		
2.7 What is the method of identifying items?		
2.8 How is the quantity/volume established? (Counted, weighed, measured, estimated.)		
2.9 Do the stocktaking or other records of work-in-progress include the degree of completion to be properly assessed and valued?		
2.10 Are damaged or defective goods identified during stocktaking?		
Is such stock segregated?		
2.11 Is slow moving or obsolete stock identified during stocktaking?		
Is such stock segregated?		
2.12 How is the information recorded:		
(*a*) identification of items;		
(*b*) quantity/volume;		
(*c*) damaged or defective goods;		
(*d*) slow moving or obsolete stock?		
Are descriptions pre-printed or are there stock lists? Are standard units prescribed for measurement of all stock items?		
2.13 Are any of the items owned by third parties? If so:		
(*a*) how is this shown?		
(*b*) are separate stock records kept?		
(*c*) is there a stocktake of these items which is agreed to the records?		
2.14 How is the issue and return of the recording media controlled? Are the documents pre-numbered?		
2.15 Where items are stored in more than one area, what is the procedure for collating information to agree the total stock?		
2.16 If the staff who are taking stock are collating the information themselves, do they provide sufficient detail so that the totals can be checked?		
2.17 Is the stock counted or checked by staff who are not responsible for the custody of the stock?		

	Answer	Intls
2.18 Is there a separate check count by another person or team? How is this evidenced? Is it made without reference to the first count result? How are discrepancies resolved?		
2.19 When goods have been counted/check-counted how are they marked to avoid duplicated counts?		
2.20 After the location/department has been counted is the section inspected to ensure that all items are marked as having been taken into stock?		
2.21 Do the counters and checkers sign or initial for work done on stock tickets, stock sheets and stock records?		
2.22 Make a number of test counts (paying particular attention to high-value items) and unless our counts can be checked with the client's counts on the spot, record them in sufficient detail to enable them to be checked to the final stock sheets (insert here reference to detailed working paper).		
2.23 'Cut-off'		
(*a*) What is used as the 'cut-off' point or points for each department for:		
(i) input from stores;		
(ii) input from production/other departments;		
(iii) input from outside suppliers;		
(iv) output to stores;		
(v) output to work-in-progress/other departments;		
(vi) output to goods-outwards/customers?		
(In all cases specify documentation and give details of the last document number processed before stock-taking.)		
(*b*) What procedure is used for partly finished goods or goods partly processed?		
(*c*) How are movements of stock or materials during the stocktaking controlled to ensure that the same stocks are not counted twice or omitted?		
(*d*) Provide schedules/notes of the following:		
(i) goods in dispatch not taken into stock;		
(ii) goods-received awaiting inspection not taken into stock;		
(iii) goods moved between areas during stocktaking;		
(iv) goods returned from customers awaiting inspection, not taken into stock.		
Continuous stocktaking		
3.1 To whom are stocktaking personnel responsible?		

	Answer	Intls
3.2 Do the stocktaking personnel render formal reports and are these promptly cleared by the responsible official?		
3.3 Are the stocktaking personnel independent of those responsible for stock, for stock records, and for stock custody?		
3.4 On what basis are items selected for count?		
3.5 How often (on average) is each item counted?		
3.6 What is the procedure for an authorization of adjustments to the stock records after counts have been made?		
3.7 Are the continuous stock records reconciled with the financial stock records?		
3.8 Is slow moving and obsolete stock identified during the counts and appropriately recorded?		
4. Conclusions		
4.1 Were the client's prescribed stocktaking procedures effective in providing complete data for a physical stock valuation?		
4.2 Were they properly carried out?		
4.3 Record on a separate sheet any recommendations for improving the client's stocking, stock recording or stock custody arrangements.		

Before commencing the actual checking of valuation the auditor should carefully inquire into the whole system of entering, pricing and checking stock, and find out the exact basis upon which it has been valued. As stated above it is very important to ascertain that the basis of valuation at the beginning and end of the year is consistent. As many persons as possible should be engaged upon the work and each step should be independently checked. Further, responsible officials should supervise the work, as juniors often have quite erroneous ideas concerning the principles governing stock valuation. Each person who takes part should initial the sheets he has entered up or checked so that progress on the task may be controlled.

In the case of a manufacturing business especially, the auditor should make most careful inquiries as to valuation of work-in-progress and finished stocks as the whole system employed for dealing with this, in many cases, is most complicated. In some factories, goods may pass through twenty or more distinct stages of manufacture before they are completed, and in each stage, wages, materials and expenses are being incurred. Therefore there will be goods at every stage, and the cost in each stage will be different. Unless a standard cost system is in operation it is very difficult correctly and accurately to value partly manufactured stock. The only means of checking which an auditor has is the comparison of the stock valuations with the cost records. Unless these cost records are properly integrated as part of the accounting system, and are therefore capable of proper audit check, the auditor is necessarily to a considerable extent in the hands of management, as there are practically no independent checks possible, except the comparison of the gross profit percentages shown by the accounts of other years. These are not conclusive, but may lead the auditor to the general conclusion that the stock valuations are unsatisfactory.

However, there are a growing number of businesses which have adopted modern forms of internal management accounting. If properly set up, they provide the auditor with a most important means of check on the value of the stock, and he should make most careful inquiry into any major differences. This may necessitate his doing a certain amount of routine checking and testing of the whole of the internal management accounts. The programme of work which follows may be of assistance in indicating the general scope of such work.

The valuation of special classes of stock

Forward contracts for the supply of raw materials

It is common practice for manufacturers to place forward contracts in order to ensure supplies of raw materials, and if, in such circumstances, the replacement price of such materials at the date of the balance sheet is below the contract price, the question arises whether any provision should be made for this 'loss' in the accounts for the past year. Practice differs. Some companies invariably provide for such differences at the date of the balance sheet and others do not. In cases where the forward contracts for raw materials have been placed to cover sales contracts, the prices for which have been fixed, and upon which, taking the raw materials at the contract prices, a margin of profit will be shown, there does not appear to be any reason, except cautious finance, why provision should be made in the preceding year's accounts for a fall in the market price of raw materials. The raw material contracts in these cases have been placed in order to ensure the margin of profit upon the forward contracts for the sale of the manufactured products. In cases where such forward contracts for raw materials have been placed but are not in respect of specific sales contracts, then it is obviously prudent that provision should be made so that, in effect, these raw materials are written down to a price at which the coming year can manufacture and sell without loss.

It would seem that the same basic principle applies, namely that the governing factor is the net realizable value of the finished products which will be manufactured from these raw materials. Nevertheless, circumstances may be encountered which require special consideration.

A manufacturer, for example, under the impression that his raw material market is likely to harden against him in the near future, buys heavily and finds himself at the close of his financial year with raw material stocks and forward contracts sufficient to cover his normal production for one and a half years as against the usual three to four months requirements which experience has hitherto proved expedient. At the date of the balance sheet it appears that his estimate of the market movements has been completely wrong. For the market value of these raw materials has dropped and appears likely to fall much further. At the date of the balance sheet the selling prices of the finished products have not yet been affected by the fall in the price of the raw material, and there is therefore a margin of profit on the basis of the actual cost of the raw material.

In these circumstances, obviously a very serious situation has arisen. Owing to the departure from the normal buying policy the holding of an abnormally large stock of raw materials, together with the heavy forward contracts, exposes an abnormally large area of vulnerability in that it is impossible to prognosticate what the selling conditions of the finished products will be a year and a half ahead. A comparatively long time, therefore, must elapse before either the wisdom or imprudence of the policy of heavy buying of raw materials is capable of demonstration, and considerable risks are involved.

It might, by some, be considered satisfactory to value the raw-material stocks and the forward contracts on the basis of the replacement prices at the date of the balance sheet. But in the circumstances described above where there is one and a half year's cover it is impossible to estimate the selling prices of the finished product, and there is the risk that raw material and selling prices may fall considerably lower. Therefore the valuation of the raw-material stocks and the treatment of the forward contracts become, it is submitted, a matter of judgement. In such circumstances, upon the principle of sound financial policy, and after weighing up all the circumstances of the case, drastic treatment may well prove to be the wise course.

Such treatment does not in any way impair the validity of the basic principles which have here been advocated, for it will be appreciated that, as the circumstances postulated are quite exceptional to the business, they require special treatment in the accounts.

It is clear that, if there is evidence of forward contracts, the auditor should carefully examine the whole position. If the total amount of these contracts is normal, and there is nothing to indicate losses upon them, then there would appear to be no reason why special mention of these forward contracts should be made in the balance sheet of a company. But, if the amounts involved are abnormal and obviously a speculative situation exists which may result in serious losses, then these facts should be made clear in the balance sheet.

Uncompleted contracts

In the balance sheet uncompleted contracts should be shown as a separate item, and any cash received on account thereof should be shown as a deduction.

For balance sheet purposes, the general rule is that uncompleted contracts, other than long-term contracts, should be stated at cost — that is, wages, materials, direct charges and a reasonable sum of overheads to cover the various indirect charges of the business, such as supervision, depreciation of plant and machinery, indirect wages, etc. A percentage is also sometimes added to cover administration expenses, such as directors' fees, staff salaries, office rents and rates. In this way, the actual cost of the work to date is carried forward to the succeeding period, and no profit is taken credit for in respect thereof. If, however, it is anticipated that eventually a loss will be incurred upon any contract, then provision should be made for this contingency.

In the case of a long-term contract, defined as one relating to a single entity where the time taken is such that a substantial proportion of the contract work will extend for a period exceeding one year, then the element of profit earned at the balance sheet date should be added to its cost. Thus the carrying value in accounts will be cost plus attributable profit, less any foreseeable losses. In taking up profit in this way, SSAP 9 warns against the difficulties of contract assessment prior to completion and provides for attributable profit to be reflected only where a contract's outcome can be assessed with reasonable certainty. For this reason warning is given to exercise prudence with regard to estimated sums receivable from approved contract variations, and to take account of receipts in respect of claims 'only when negotiations have reached an advanced stage and there is evidence in writing of the acceptability of the claim in principle and an indication of the magnitude of the sum involved'.

This practice with regard to long-term contracts is common in the case of large contractors, where the individual contracts often extend over periods of several years. If, therefore, credit were taken for the profits only when the contracts were completed, the results shown by the profit and loss account would vary very considerably from year to year. In one year a number of profitable contracts might be completed, with the result that the profit and loss account would show a large profit. In another year, though there might be several large and profitable contracts running, yet very few might have been completed during the period, and, therefore, owing to the profit and loss account having to bear considerable standing charges, the accounts might show a loss. Therefore, to even the results from year to year, profits are spread over the contract. But, where this is done, very great care must be exercised in estimating such profit, and ample provisions must be made for contingencies.

A contract may be progressing normally, and present figures indicate that a considerable profit will be earned, but some unforeseen contingency may arise, such as a strike, failure of part of the work, rise in the price of raw materials, failure to complete in the contract time thereby incurring heavy penalties, and many other such circumstances, which may result in the contract eventually showing a considerable loss.

Profits should be anticipated only when the contract is so far advanced that the cost to complete can fairly be estimated, and the probable eventual profit be arrived at. Therefore, all contracts which are in an early stage should be invariably valued at cost. When the results of the contract can be reasonably estimated, a heavy provision should be deducted for contingencies. For example, the proportion of the final profit, according to the proportion of work completed to date, should be calculated, and it is suggested that perhaps about one-third of such profit should be set aside, the remaining two-thirds only being taken credit for.

The auditor should go into the whole question of uncompleted contracts most carefully, comparing the balance sheet figures with the cost records. Proper cost records are essential to afford a very valuable check upon the valuation of the uncompleted contracts, and in addition the auditor should insist upon full particulars being supplied of any quantity surveyors' reports on all uncompleted contracts. He will need evidence showing exactly how the results have been arrived at, and these he should check as far as possible with whatever evidence there is available.

The auditor is bound to be very much in the hands of the management when dealing with this asset, but he should endeavour to check and test the figures as far as he reasonably can. For this purpose an audit programme specific to this difficult area is suggested as a guideline, and this is set out at the conclusion to this section. In practice, in a contracting concern of any size, its completion might be conveniently phased as between the interim audit of transactions and the final audit of the financial statements in the same manner as we have previously described in relation to other audit areas.

Suggested audit tests

Client:	Approved by:
Audit programme: Stock and work-in-progress	Reviewed by:
Accounting date:	

Review the related sections of the interim working papers (together with the physical stocktaking report) and briefly summarize (e.g. 'Good', 'Medium', 'Poor') the degree of reliance that can be placed on internal accounting controls in this area. On the basis of this assessment determine the required scope and extent of year-end substantive work: indicate the sample sizes in the relevant column below and amend, delete, or add to the suggested substantive tests as necessary.

Remarks	Intls	Date

Audit tests	Details of tests	Errors, etc.	Audit sch.	*Work done by* Intls	Date
1. Consider whether stocks are valued: (*a*) on an appropriate basis; (*b*) in accordance with disclosed accounting policies; (*c*) on a basis consistent with the previous year. 2. Where work-in-progress has not been subject to physical stocktaking, inspect to obtain evidence of existence and stage of completion. 3. Test that stocks have been valued correctly by reference to cost records, purchase invoices and other source data. Verify that all costs have been independently checked and approved by a responsible official. 4. Test extensions and casts of stock sheets and summaries and verify that all					

Audit tests	Details of tests	Errors, etc.	Audit sch.	*Work done by* Intls	Date
sheets have been independently checked.					
5. Check year-end cut-off with: (*a*) dispatch notes, sales records, etc.; (*b*) goods-received notes, purchase invoices, etc.					
6. Check proper accounting for progress payments and pro-forma invoices.					
7. Test that adequate provisions have been made in order to show stocks in the accounts at the lower of cost and net realizable value by testing that: (*a*) stocks of finished products are not excessive and that they are not stated in excess of net realizable value; (*b*) work-in-progress is current and that provision has been made for any losses expected or future costs which will not be recoverable; (*c*) stocks of raw materials are not obsolete or surplus to foreseeable production requirements; (*d*) there are no major forward commitments against which provisions should be made.					
8. Explain significant variations between year-end stock levels.					
9. Arrange for direct confirmation of stock held by third parties or arrange own inspection or count where necessary.					

10. Check total valuation of stock and work-in-progress to nominal ledger and accounts. 11. Where applicable, examine reconciliation between stocks valued as per physical count and book stocks for management purposes, and inquire into material differences.					

Conclusions	Yes/ No	Audit sch.	*Senior* Intls	Date
Are you satisfied that: (*a*) stocks and work-in-progress are fairly stated? (*b*) the basis of accounting is both acceptable (SSAP 9) and consistent with previous practice? (*c*) adequate evidence is available on the file to support these conclusions?				

Contracting — Suggested audit tests

Client:			Audit test approved by:		
Audit programme: Contracting			Work done approved by:		
Accounting date:					
Audit tests	Details of tests	Errors, etc.	Audit sch.	*Work done by* Intls	Date
1. Generally review system for obtaining contracts in relation to the following: (*a*) procedures for preparing quotations, including detailed description of method of estimating; (*b*) treatment of inflation					

Audit tests	Details of tests	Errors, etc.	Audit sch.	Work done by Intls	Date
during the contract, i.e. escalation clauses, etc.; (*c*) general method of financing, including progress payments; (*d*) penalty terms and conditions; (*e*) maintenance terms and conditions of release; (*f*) specific warranties and indemnities; (*g*) procedures for authorizing contract price adjustments and variation orders.					
2. Check a sample of contracts to ensure: (*a*) systems and methods outlined by management (in 1 above) have been applied; (*b*) any limits of authority operating have been adhered to.					
3. For a sample of transactions, check from source documents to contract ledger, and vice versa, to ensure costs have been allocated to the correct contract.					
4. Check that the overhead allocation is consistent with company policy and is costed to the correct contract.					
5. Agree contract ledger control account.					
6. Check a sample of cost transfers to source documentation to ensure properly authorized.					
7. Review periodic valuation procedures as carried out by clients' staff or by third-party surveyors or					

engineers, paying particular attention to: (*a*) stage of contract completion; (*b*) whether any broad estimation (as opposed to precise measurement) is involved in valuations; (*c*) the recording of work carried out against variation orders; (*d*) the recording of rectification work to be carried out; (*e*) measurement of materials on site.					
8. Enquire into system for controlling contract costs, paying particular attention to: (*a*) the frequency and method of comparison of actual costs to date with estimated costs; (*b*) how and when 'costs to complete' forecasts are prepared and reviewed with contract values, etc.; (*c*) the procedures in relation to variation orders and contract price adjustments; (*d*) the procedures for charging plant to contracts; (*e*) the procedures for dealing with sub-contracts.					
9. For a selection of contracts, note the payment terms and ensure that monies have been received accordingly.					
10. Review procedures for chasing overdue amounts and ascertain the reasons for any currently overdue amounts.					

Audit tests	Details of tests	Errors, etc.	Audit sch.	*Work done by* Intls	Date
11. Check postings from progress-payment applications (or other posting document) to ensure that retentions held and monies received have been posted to the correct contract records.					
Completed contracts					
12. Obtain schedule of all contracts completed during the year, with the following information recorded: (*a*) contract price; (*b*) final account value; (*c*) amount invoiced; (*d*) retentions; (*e*) disputed items; (*f*) outstanding costs (including maintenance and claims by subcontractors); (*g*) costs/profit per estimate; (*h*) actual costs incurred; (*i*) profit/loss obtained.					
13. Review all major profits/losses on contracts during year and ensure that these are in accordance with budgets/estimates/previous-year work-in-progress calculations.					
14. Agree total costs at 12(*h*) to general contract ledger.					
15. (*a*) Review contract correspondence files and site problems which may give dence of any technical problems which may give rise to rectification costs within the contract maintenance period, or claims by subcontractors,					

and for claims under specific warranty or indemnity clauses.

(*b*) Review contingency provisions for contracts within the maintenance period, and establish that they have been reasonably assessed.

(*c*) Review all contracts where the maintenance period has expired, inspect final acceptance certificate, and ensure that all monies due have been received, including the retention.

16. Discuss with company's surveyors or engineers any material claims for additional payments and peruse relevant correspondence. If it is the company's policy to take credit for claims before they are agreed, ensure that the amounts taken into accounts are conservative and that the policy has been consistently applied.

17. Review schedule of contract costs written off during the year for which there is no corresponding income, and confirm that this represents justifiable maintenance expenditure.

Contract work-in-progress

18. Review accounting policies to be adopted in the preparation of the accounts. In particular the following should be clearly defined:

(*a*) the exact definition of cost including treatment and allocation of overheads;

(*b*) the policy regarding profit taking on long-term contracts;

Audit tests	Details of tests	Errors, etc.	Audit sch.	*Work done by* Intls	Date
(*c*) the policy regarding profit taking on other contracts and compliance generally with SSAP 9; (*d*) the calculation and provision for anticipated future losses; (*e*) the accounting treatment of part deliveries; (*f*) the definition of the point of contract completion; (*g*) policy regarding accounting for claims for additional payment against clients (other than agreed claims). 19. Obtain/prepare schedule(s) of contracts-in-progress at the balance sheet date with the following information recorded: (*a*) contract price; (*b*) progress claims made to date; (*c*) progress claims paid to date; (*d*) amounts invoiced and profit taken; (*e*) retentions; (*f*) disputed items; (*g*) variation orders agreed; (*h*) variation orders not agreed; (*i*) costs to date per estimate; (*j*) costs to date per actual cost records; (*k*) estimated costs to complete; (*l*) anticipated final account (when contract nearing practical completion).					

20. In respect of all major contracts and a selection of minor contracts: (*a*) Compare details in contract documents with details in schedule (19 above). (*b*) Compare progress claims with contract terms and investigate non-compliance. (*c*) Examine external payment documentation (i.e. architects'/engineers' certificates, remittance advices) and agree valuations to date noting any discrepancy/contra claims with amounts invoiced. (*d*) Discuss and check build up of cost to complete and test as appropriate. Ensure that full provision has been made for all foreseeable future losses. (*e*) Obtain satisfactory explanations for all unusual items (e.g. unpaid progress claims, loss to date with overall anticipated profit). (*f*) Inspect build up of values taken in variation orders and ensure that they are within the terms of the contract and authorized by the client. (*g*) Agree total costs at 19(*j*) to general contract ledger. (*h*) Verify that all costs incurred prior to the balance sheet date (e.g. subcontractors' invoices, maintenance provisions, etc.) have been properly accounted for. (*i*) Ensure that allocated overheads are correctly treated.					

Audit tests	Details of tests	Errors, etc.	Audit sch.	*Work done by* Intls	Date
(*j*) Verify that profit taken on long-term contracts is in relation to profit earned, is in accordance with the client's accounting policy, and is consistent with prior years.					
21. Obtain copies of management minutes and ensure that all reported delays and problems on contracts have been accounted for in costs to complete; discuss and review all claims received to ensure that adequate provisions have been made.					
22. Scrutinize debtors ledger for evidence of overdue progress claims or retentions which may indicate that provisions for rectification or remedial work are necessary.					
23. Confirm that the contracts have been treated in accordance with the accounting policies, etc. outlined in 18 above.					
24. Prepare a memorandum summarizing contract policies and procedures, including comments on the effectiveness of the client's contract reviews, the scope of the audit tests, and the results of the audit work, together with explanations of any unusual items.					

Debtors and Prepayments

The most effective audit procedure with regard to trade debtors is for the auditor to verify the whole or a proportion of the debtors by direct application. This test acts as a check upon the sales as entered in the sales day book, and also the cash and other credits to the accounts of debtors.

There are two methods of obtaining direct confirmation of debtors' balances, 'positive' and 'negative'; they may, of course, be used in combination. By the positive method the customer is requested to reply directly to the auditor either to agree the balance or disagree; by the negative method he is asked to reply only if he does not agree the balance. The positive method is of greater value and — wherever practicable — this method should be used.

Subject to the state of internal control, there is no reason why the circularization should necessarily take place at the year-end. This could be done two or three months prior to the end of the year under audit review.

The client's support must be obtained before the circularization, and the request to the debtor should come from the client on client's notepaper with his signature. Each follow-up request should be authorized and issued by the client giving him no grounds to complain that the circularization has impaired customer relationships.

Care must be taken in the selection of debtor accounts to be circulated. The number will depend on the total number of debtors' accounts, the relation of their value to other assets and the level of internal control. Selection of accounts, stratified where necessary according to special circumstances, should be on a random basis but the selection should include balances which are nil, in credit, old and large, also debit balances on bought ledger. The list should be given to the client so that the requests can be completed with details of names and addresses and balances outstanding. When the selected statements have been checked, mailing must be carried out by the auditor and not entrusted to the clients. Details of debtors circularized should be entered on a control list. On receipt of replies—(i) Enter particulars on control list; (ii) Ensure that the reply appears to be authentic; (iii) Where the balance is disagreed, investigate and reconcile the difference.

Where no reply is received after the final request—(i) Confirm that the debtor exists by reference to directories, trade journals, correspondence, etc; (ii) Vouch the open items with orders, dispatch notes, copy invoices and signed delivery notes; (iii) Ascertain subsequent cash receipts and to what extent these clear specific invoices and test cash receipts with cash book, bank statement and customers' remittance advices.

Where a debtor replies that his accounting system does not enable any particular balance to be verified, copies of selected invoices making up the balance should be sent by the auditor to the debtor concerned, specifically requesting confirmation of these items.

When the circularization is complete a summary must be prepared showing the percentages of debtors circularized by number and value, and the percentages of the response obtained to the total circularization by number and value.

Suitable forms of letter are shown on pages 290 and 291.

Debtors' confirmation (positive)

Small & Steady Components Ltd

(Address)
Debtor's name and address Date

Dear Sirs

In accordance with the request of our auditors, Messrs.................., we ask that you kindly confirm to them direct your indebtedness to us at........which, according to our records, amounted to £........as shown by the enclosed Statement.

If the above amount is in agreement with your records, please sign in the space provided below and return this letter direct to our auditors in the enclosed stamped addressed envelope.

If the amount is not in agreement with your records, please notify our auditors direct of the amount shown by your records, and if possible, detail o the reverse of this letter full particulars of the difference.

Yours faithfully

Serial No..........

The amount shown above is in agreement with our records as at..........

Account no .... Signature ....

Date .... Company ....

Title or position ....

When examining the sales ledger accounts, the auditor should investigate any accounts which appear to him to be doubtful, such as those:

(*a*) where cash payments are irregular, or where small payments are made on account;

(*b*) where the balance on the account is increasing and is becoming substantially overdue;

(*c*) where cheques or bills have been dishonoured, and, therefore, have been debited to the account;

(*d*) where bills are constantly being renewed;

(*e*) where items have been owing for a time considerably beyond the period of credit which is customary in the particular trade;

(*f*) where notes appear upon the account, such as 'account stopped', 'in

Debtors' confirmation (negative)

Small & Steady Components Ltd

(Address)

Debtor's name and address Date

Dear Sirs

We enclose a statement of your account up to.........

If you do not agree the balance shown on the enclosed statement, we shall be obliged if you will show below the balance appearing in your books and return this letter direct to our auditors, Messrs..................together with, if possible, particulars of the difference.

Yours faithfully

Serial no..........

The balance shown in our books at ....is £..........

Account no .... Signature ....

Date .... Company ....

Title or position ....

solicitor's hands', 'in bankruptcy', or 'in liquidation', 'disappeared and address unknown', etc.

All queried accounts, or such of them as do not appear upon the list of bad and doubtful debts supplied to the auditor, should be gone into with a responsible official, and explanations sought from him. A good plan as each debt is discussed with the responsible official is for it to be agreed as 'good', 'bad', or 'doubtful' and, if doubtful, for his estimate as to the amount which probably will be received to be noted. Provisions for bad and doubtful debts are calculated sometimes by way of a percentage on the total book debts or upon the turnover for the period. However, this method is not by itself sufficient, and if it is adopted the auditor should proceed as explained above, to satisfy himself that the provision is a sufficient one on a specific basis.

The only way in which a reliable opinion can be formed as to the sufficiency of a provision for bad and doubtful debts is by examining the various debtors' accounts on an individual basis and inquiring into the circumstances of all doubtful looking accounts.

If, after completing his investigation under this head, the auditor is of the opinion that the provision is not sufficient, he should put his views before the directors and hear what they have to say upon the point. If, thereafter, he is still of the same opinion, and, nevertheless, the directors refuse to alter the accounts, he should then point out in his audit report that, in his view, the provision is inadequate.

It is increasingly common for firms to factor their debts, that is to sell them to a specialist who, on payment of a special premium, will bear all or part of the costs of bad debts. In addition credit insurance policies are available which enable firms to insure against bad debts. In such cases the detailed investigations of the auditor can be somewhat reduced.

Loans

In the case of advances upon mortgage, the mortgage and title deeds will be inspected, and it should be seen that the interest has been paid to date. If, as is generally the case, a valuation of the property was made at the time of the advance, such valuation should be inspected to see that the loan appears to be sufficiently secured.

With other loans, the auditor should inspect the written acknowledgement of the debt and any security which may have been lodged, such as a share certificate and blank transfer completed by the borrower. The auditor should also see that the interest is regularly paid, and that a sufficient provision is made for possible bad debts.

Particular attention should be paid in this general area to the position concerning balances on accounts with directors of the company. There has been a general prohibition on loans to directors since the Companies Act 1948 (Section 190), but this has been extended by the Companies Act 1980 to include similar transactions with a director's spouse and minor children in any case where a company is a public company or is in a group of which a public company is a member. The Companies Act 1980 has also introduced more comprehensive new disclosure requirements concerning loans to directors. A problem will arise in some instances where an account with a director is described as a 'current account' and the auditor must satisfy himself that this is a fair description and that the account is regularly cleared within the credit terms allowed by the Act. In other circumstances, it is submitted, such balances are more akin to loans. There are some exemptions from the general prohibition against loans and the auditor should first check whether any such loans do fall within these exceptions. In any case he should ensure compliance with all disclosure requirements and, if any irregular loans are material in relation to the accounts, however properly disclosed, he should consider drawing attention to them in his report.

Payments in advance or prepaid expenses

Under this head will be included rents, rates, insurance, advertising, subscriptions, etc., paid for periods which extend beyond the end of the financial year of the particular concern. The auditor should examine the nominal accounts and the relevant demand notes and receipts, seeing that a correct calculation has been made of the proportion unexpired at the date of the balance sheet. However, this may be more difficult in the case of any deferred revenue expenditure to be spread over a period of years, e.g. research and development expenditure. The auditor should carefully investigate the whole of the circumstances in order to satisfy himself that the carrying forward of part of this expenditure is fully justified, and that the accounting policy proposed is not so imprudent as to prejudice the true and fair view of the financial statements.

Suggested audit tests

Client:	Approved by:
Audit programme: Debtors and prepayments	Reviewed by:
Accounting date:	

Review the related sections of the interim working papers and briefly summarize (e.g. 'Good', 'Medium', 'Poor') the degree of reliance that can be placed on internal accounting controls in this area. On the basis of this assessment determine the required scope and extent of year-end substantive work: indicate the sample sizes in the relevant column below and amend, delete, or add to the suggested substantive tests as necessary.

Remarks	Intls	Date

Audit tests	Details of tests	Errors, etc.	Audit sch.	*Work done by* Intls	Date
1. Test extraction and casts of balances in the sales ledger and agree the total of balances at balance sheet date with the control account. 2. Select individual accounts from the list of balances, and: (*a*) Test that balance at accounting date represents specific invoices.					

Audit tests	Details of tests	Errors, etc.	Audit sch.	*Work done by* Intls	Date
(*b*) Test validity of outstanding invoices by comparing with orders, dispatch documents, copy invoices and subsequent payments substantiated by independent means. (*c*) Peruse entire account and investigate any entries arising from unusual sources. 3. Where direct, positive confirmation procedures are applied: (*a*) Investigate any differences arising from replies received. (*b*) Where the debtor has not replied, apply procedures for verification as above. 4. Where the detailed verification is carried out other than at the balance sheet date, establish that intervening control account movements are reasonable, and obtain at the accounting date an aged list of balances which agrees with the nominal ledger control account. 5. Examine the sales day book prior to the year-end to ensure items have not been inserted to inflate sales. 6. Examine after-date credits for items relating to the period under review. 7. Test year-end cut-off from dispatch records, etc. to ensure that movement of goods has been synchronized with the recording of sales and credits.					

8. Verify adequacy of provision for doubtful debts: (*a*) Examine ageing analysis with information regarding overdue accounts. (*b*) Test to ensure ageing analysis correctly prepared. (*c*) Check cover provided by credit insurers. (*d*) In respect of factored debts, check whether any loss contingency arises under recourse. 9. Obtain details of other amounts receivable at the balance sheet date, agree these to the nominal ledger and test that they can be collected in full, using direct confirmations where appropriate. 10. Test the basis and accuracy of amounts calculated to be prepayments: compare with previous year. 11. Consider deferred revenue expenditure to ascertain if reasonable and in accordance with established accounting policy. 12. Examine sales/debtor ratios to check if client's policy on credit control is operating satisfactorily. 13. Bills receivable: (*a*) Inspect bills held at balance sheet date. (*b*) Obtain confirmation of bills held by agents for collection. (*c*) Verify that bills which have matured subsequent to balance sheet date were met on the due date.					

Audit tests	Details of tests	Errors, etc.	Audit sch.	*Work done by* *Intls*	*Date*
(*d*) Check that no bills which have been discounted have been dishonoured.					

Conclusions	Yes/ No	Audit sch.	*Senior* Intls	Date
Are you satisfied that: (*a*) debtors and prepayments are fairly stated? (*b*) the bases of accounting (e.g. prepayments and bad-debt provisions) are both acceptable and consistent with previous practice? (*c*) adequate evidence is available on the file to support these conclusions?				

Bank and Cash Balances

Bank balances

Certificates should be obtained by the auditor direct from all bankers, verifying the balances according to the banks' books at the close of business upon the date of the balance sheet. A suitable form of letter of enquiry to elicit the information required by the auditor is set out opposite. Specific authority will be required from the client to his banker to enable this information to be released.

In normal circumstances the bank's reply to this letter will be merely to confirm the balance according to the bank statements already sent to the client and which will already have been agreed to the cash book by means of a 'bank reconciliation'. This reconciliation statement must be checked by the auditor and all reconciling items traced through, e.g. to ensure they are reflected on subsequent bank statements within a normal timescale.

When applying to the bank for this verification statement, the auditor should ask for particulars of all balances standing in the name of his client. There have been cases in which there were banking accounts in existence which were not disclosed to the auditor. The auditor should, at the same time, also ask for particulars of any bills or securities, etc. held by the bank on behalf of his clients. Difficulty may arise over getting UK banks to provide confirmation of client balances held by their overseas branches.

Cash in hand

Whilst this is rarely material to a balance sheet, the auditor during the year should check and vouch the petty cash book and count the cash, comparing it with the balances shown by the book to ensure that it is all properly accounted for and being subjected to adequate controls.

To the Client's Banker

Dear Sir

(Name of client)

For the purposes of our work in connection with the accounts of the above, will you kindly supply us with the following information relating thereto at the close of business on ....:

(*a*) Balances on current, deposit and other accounts with you.
(*b*) Balances of any overdraft, loan and other advances made by you.
(*c*) Bills held for collection.
(*d*) Liabilities of our client under:
  (i) acceptances undertaken on their behalf;
  (ii) guarantees;
  (iii) exchange contracts;
  (iv) bills of exchange discounted with you.

(*e*) Securities or other documents of title in your possession, stating whether held:
  (i) for safe custody only;
  (ii) as security for advances or otherwise.

(*f*) Any other obligations and outstanding matters
  (i) between our client and yourselves, or
  (ii) between our client and third parties of which you are aware.

(*g*) All interest and charges accrued due but not charged to our client's accounts.

Will you also kindly indicate:

(*h*) Any other accounts maintained with you by our client during the year ended on the above-mentioned date but closed before that date.
(*i*) The names of other parties concerned where any items arising under the foregoing headings are on joint account.
(*j*) Which, if any, of the matters mentioned in this request are not applicable.

Yours faithfully

Suggested audit tests

Client:	Approved by:
Audit programme: Bank and cash balances (including bank overdrafts)	Reviewed by:
Accounting date:	

Review the related sections of the interim working papers and briefly summarize (e.g. 'Good', 'Medium', 'Poor') the degree of reliance that can be placed on internal accounting controls in this area. On the basis of this assessment determine the required scope and extent of year-end substantive work: indicate the sample sizes in the relevant column below and amend, delete, or add to the suggested substantive tests as necessary.

Remarks	Intls	Date

Audit tests	Details of tests	Errors, etc.	Audit sch.	*Work done by* Intls	Date
1. Obtain a copy of the reconciliation of all bank accounts at the balance sheet date, check the casts and agree with the nominal ledger and bank confirmations.					
2. Obtain bank statements for the period subsequent to the verification date and trace through all the items outstanding on the reconciliations, noting items still uncleared at the time of the audit.					
3. Obtain direct confirmation of all bank balances at the balance sheet date (standard bank letter).					
4. Obtain a schedule of all cash holdings, etc. and agree with nominal ledger.					
5. Scrutinize receipts and payments for 10 days following balance sheet date; check validity and timing of any material exceptional items.					

6. Count and record all material cash holdings, etc. in the presence of the cashier or float custodian and reconcile with the year-end balance.					

Conclusions	Yes/ No	Audit sch.	*Senior* Intls	Date
Are you satisfied that: (*a*) cash and bank balances are fairly stated (without any overt 'window dressing')? (*b*) adequate evidence is available on the file to support these conclusions?				

Profit and Loss Account Review

It has been explained that it is part of the auditor's function to express an opinion on whether the accounts give a true and fair view of the company's results for the period ended at the balance sheet date. Although this opinion is only given on the published profit and loss account, with the specified minimum information to be contained therein prescribed by the Companies Acts 1948 and 1967, yet at the same time the relevant audit procedures enabling this opinion to be given must embrace the careful scrutiny of the detailed trading and profit and loss accounts.

Whilst the first inclination of many businessmen and lay shareholders is to turn to the profit and loss account initially as an aid to their understanding of the accounts, this is not generally the case as regards auditors whose procedures perhaps tend to concentrate on balance sheet verification. The auditor must at all times guard against becoming so involved in this aspect that he loses sight of the importance of an appreciation of the profit and loss account; hence our earlier emphasis on an analytical review of financial statements, whereby the auditor is able to stand back from these balance sheet audit routines and assess the information he is given with critical objectivity.

The range of checks described is diverse and their detail will, of course, depend both on the type of company and the precise accounting and other financial management information produced. In general terms, however, it is submitted that these should embrace an understanding of the main items in the trading and profit and loss account, together with documentary evidence of the audit work undertaken to test management's explanations of any unusual features therein by comparison with the previous period and the forecast out-turn for the period under review; general scrutiny of the management accounts and their underlying trends, budgets, sources and applications of funds, and cash-flow forecasts; appropriate ratio analysis and comparisons both internally and with comparable companies within the same industry group. And again, as with the transactions audit and the balance sheet audit, so with the profit and loss account review and the balance sheet audit, the auditor must appreciate the dependence of the one upon the other and recognize the balance sheet implications of the points which come to his attention.

Suggested audit tests

Client:	Approved by:
Audit programme: Profit and loss account	Reviewed by:
Accounting date:	

Review the interim audit papers and briefly summarize the degree of reliance that can be placed on internal accounting controls in so far as the amount and classification of income and expense items is concerned.

Scrutinize the analytical review and profit and loss account analysis.

Remarks	Intls	Date

Audit tests	Details of tests	Errors, etc.	Audit sch.	*Work done by* Intls	Date
1. Prepare analyses of amounts required for tax or statutory audit purposes. 2. Scrutinize the income and expense accounts for material items of an extraordinary or exceptional nature. 3. Ascertain where there have been changes in the bases of accounting which have led to a material increase or decrease in the recorded result.					

Conclusions	Yes/ No	Audit sch.	*Senior* Intls	Date
Are you satisfied that the profit or loss for the period is fairly stated and that any exceptional and/or extraordinary items are adequately segregated so as to provide a fair year-by-year comparison of the operating results of the business?				

Letters of Representation

Whilst the auditor must make every endeavour to verify the information supplied to him in support of the accounts he has been auditing, nevertheless some matters reflected can only remain questions of judgement and opinion. Accordingly it is advisable to obtain from the directors at the conclusion of the audit and prior to signature of the auditor's report, a letter confirming certain amounts appearing in the accounts. Such a 'letter of representation' therefore constitutes a formal record of representation made by management to the auditor in the course of the audit. It serves as a reminder to management of the representations made and acknowledges management's responsibility for them.

A letter of representation necessarily deals mainly with matters of policy, opinion and judgement. It is convenient to marshal the items in the letter of representation under accounts headings but matters of fact will not normally be included as they are capable of verification by independent evidence. A letter of representation may also cover matters of information which are not supported or fully supported by independent evidence. Much of the content of a letter of representation will normally consist of negative assurances, e.g. that, save as disclosed in the accounts, the company has not given any charge on any of its assets, etc.

As a company's accounts and accounting records are the collective responsibility of the Board of Directors, it is highly desirable that the letter of representation should be approved formally by the Board when they approve and authorize signature of the accounts.

The letter of representation does not in any way diminish the auditor's responsibility. Where the matters represented are capable of verification or testing, the letter does not obviate the appropriate audit procedures. Nor does it enable the auditor to substitute the judgements of the company's officials for his own. The representations made are merely further links in the chain of evidence on which the auditor bases his opinion.

The attached skeleton may serve as a useful guide as to the matters to be covered; in many cases additions will be necessary to meet the special circumstances of individual businesses:

Dear Sirs

We confirm the following information given to you in connection with your audit of the company's accounts for the year ended ....and the requirements of the Companies Acts 1948 to 1981,

(The wording should be suitably amended where the representations cover a group of companies.)

1. Assets

A. General

The assets shown in the company's balance sheet dated ....belonged to the company and were free from any charge except as follows: (Note that the client is not asked to confirm the existence of charge(s) since that can be independently verified. The client is asked to confirm that all charges have been disclosed.)

B. Land, buildings, plant, etc.

The net book amounts at which the freehold and leasehold land and buildings, plant, equipment and motor vehicles are shown in the balance sheet are arrived at:

(i) after taking into account all capital expenditure on additions thereto, but no expenditure properly chargeable to revenue;

(ii) after eliminating the cost and accumulated depreciation relating to items sold or scrapped;

(iii) after providing for amortization and/or depreciation on bases and at rates calculated to reduce the net book value of each asset to its estimated residual value by the end of its probable useful life in the company's business.

C. Contracts for capital expenditure

At the balance sheet date:

(i) Capital expenditure approved by the Board and contracted for amounted to approximately £

(ii) Capital expenditure approved by the Board but not contracted for amounted to approximately £

(iii) The figures for capital expenditure approved at the balance sheet date ((i) and (ii) above), included £ expenditure which is not scheduled to take place during (the succeeding accounting period).

D. Investments (other than investments in subsidiary companies)

The company does not hold (*a*) shares in any other company which exceed in nominal value one-tenth of the nominal value of the issued shares of the appropriate class in that other company, nor (*b*) which represent more than one-tenth (in terms of book values) of the company's gross assets, except for:

(In the case of listed companies, this paragraph requires amendment to cover the Stock Exchange requirements.)

E. Stocks

(i) The company's stocks (and work-in-progress) appearing in the balance sheet, having in total a value of £ were verified at the annual stocktaking carried out by the company's employees under the supervision of its officials on ....(or are in accordance with the balances on stock records, the accuracy of which was verified by a continuous stocktaking which covered all items at least once during the year). The stocktaking(s) (were) made by actual count, weight, or measurement, or, in cases where this was not practicable, the quantities were carefully estimated by responsible officials of the company.

(ii) The stocks (and work-in-progress) have been valued at cost, or in cases where the net realizable value/replacement price is less than cost, at their estimated net realizable value/replacement price. The general basis on which cost is determined is ....(first in/first out: average cost. etc.). The basis of valuation is the same as that used at the end of the previous financial year/period. The stocks in the balance sheet comprise the whole of the company's stocks (and work-in-progress) wherever situated (and stocks held on behalf of other parties have been excluded).

(iii) Full provision has been made in respect of all defective, obsolete or slow-moving stocks (and work-in-progress).

(iv) All executed sale orders (and completed contract work) have been invoiced to customers, and stocks relevant thereto have been excluded from the above stocks (and work-in-progress).

(v) Long-term contract work-in-progress is stated at cost plus attributable profit, less the full amount of foreseeable losses, less progress payments received and receivable. Attributable profits and foreseeable losses have been computed with due regard to estimated costs and direct expenses to completion of the contracts, including the effects of inflation except in so far as there are countervailing price adjustment clauses in the contracts.

F. Other current assets

On realization in the ordinary course of the company's business, the other current assets in the balance sheet are expected to produce at least the amounts at which they are stated. In particular, in our opinion, adequate provision has been made against all amounts owing to the company which are known or may be expected to be irrecoverable.

(Where the collectability of a particular debt or debts of significant amount has been under discussion between auditors and management, it is desirable here to give particulars of the specific debts and the amounts considered by management to be recoverable.)

2. Liabilities

G. General

All liabilities at the balance sheet date have been taken up in the books of account, including the liability for all purchases to which title had passed prior to that date, and for all items included in stocks.

H. Taxation

(i) The amounts included in the balance sheet are adequate to cover all unpaid taxation liabilities agreed or estimated, arising in respect of profits earned, chargeable gains realized, interest paid and distributions made prior to or on the balance sheet date and in respect of distributions for the period ending on that date proposed for subsequent payment.

(ii) Full provision has been made for any material amount of interest payable on overdue tax accrued at the balance sheet date.

(iii) In the case of unrealized gains on revalued assets and chargeable gains on which rollover relief has been claimed, the estimated tax payable has been provided or noted as a contingent liability.

I. Contingent liabilities

There is no pending litigation (in the hands of the company's solicitors or otherwise) and there were no contingent liabilities of a material amount, for which provision has not been made in the accounts, except as set out below:

(On all major assignments the client should be asked to request the company's solicitors for details of any claims or litigation and an estimate of the possible settlement and costs. If the solicitors are unable or unwilling to express an opinion, the client should do so. Any such matters would be referred to specifically in the letter of representation.)

J. Provision for losses

Provisions have been made in the accounts for all losses of a material amount which have resulted from, or may be expected to result from, legal action or otherwise, or from events which had occurred by the balance sheet date, including losses resulting from forward purchase and/or sale contracts.

3. General matters

K. Commitments

(i) There were no purchase commitments in excess of normal requirements or at prices in excess of the prevailing market prices, nor agreements to repurchase items previously sold.

(ii) There were no commitments for purchase or sale of investments or repurchase of any investments, nor any options given by the company, including options on the company's share capital, nor any bonus or profit-sharing arrangements.

(iii) There were no other material commitments save those relating to contracts for capital expenditure and save for commitments under leases and hire contracts.

L.

There were no defaults in payment of principal or interest or sinking fund or redemption provisions with respect to any issue of share or loan capital, or any breach of covenant of an agreement.

M. Profit and loss account
Except as disclosed in the accounts, the results for the year were not materially affected by:

(i) transactions of a sort not usually undertaken by the company;
(ii) circumstances of an exceptional or non-recurrent nature;
(iii) charges or credits relating to prior years;
(iv) any change in accounting policies.

N. Events subsequent to the date of the balance sheet
Since the date of the balance sheet no events have occurred which, though properly excluded from the accounts, are of such importance that they need to be disclosed to shareholders through some other medium.

O. Directors' interests
We confirm that all the directors have made proper disclosure of any interests in transactions with the company of themselves, their spouses and infant children or of related trusts or companies and that full disclosure of any significant transactions within this category has been made.

P. Working capital
We are of the opinion that the company has adequate working capital to cover its foreseeable commitments for the next twelve months and we are not aware of any reason why significant overdraft facilities should not continue to be available.

....
Chairman/Managing Director/Finance Director

....
Chief Accountant

Auditing Current-cost Accounts

This subject must be seen in context and, although current-cost accounts present in some respects a considerable challenge to the auditor, it must be understood that the majority of his work will not be affected. Most of the accounting procedures themselves will not be affected by a changed accounting convention, and thus the audit functions in these respects will remain unchanged. Similarly, in auditing the balance sheet, most of the considerations which apply to the foregoing audit of the historical-cost figures remain relevant. However, there are additional aspects which must be subject to scrutiny if the auditor is to express an opinion on the current-cost information.

In undertaking his work, the auditor will again have regard to the form of opinion which he hopes will ensue therefrom. In some cases this may take the form of a 'true and fair view' opinion; more commonly it will be a statement that supplementary current-cost statements 'have been properly prepared in accordance with the policies and procedures set out to give the current-cost information required by Statement of Standard Accounting Practice No.16'. It is with the above in mind that the following audit tests are put forward.

Suggested audit tests

Client: Approved by:

Audit programme: Current-cost accounts Reviewed by:

Accounting date:

Note: Reference should be made to SSAP 16 and the guidance notes issued by the ASC. Before commencing audit work establish with client whether audit report will be 'true and fair' or 'properly prepared in accordance with . . .'. This may influence the volume of checking required. Concentrate on those areas which may have a material bearing on the current-cost accounts.

Audit tests	Details of tests	Errors, etc.	Audit sch.	*Work done by* Intls	Date
Indices and arithmetic 1. Review and record indices used in calculation of depreciation adjustment, cost of sales adjustment (COSA) and monetary working capital adjustment (MWCA), and ensure that: (*a*) they are appropriate to the nature of business; (*b*) they have been correctly extracted. 2. Where 'in-house' indices are used, check underlying calculations. Ensure method used is appropriate to the business.					

3. Where current indices are not available, establish that any estimates made are fair and reasonable.					
4. Carry out extensive checks to arithmetic.					
Fixed assets and additional depreciation charge					
5. Confirm that *all* fixed assets in use are brought into the balance sheet (including assets written off in historical-cost (HC) accounts).					
6. Where indices are used to calculate net current replacement cost and current-cost (CC) depreciation charge, check underlying calculations. Confirm calculation of backlog depreciation. Ensure that revaluation surplus (net of backlog depreciation) is taken to credit of current-cost reserve.					
7. Review asset lives and depreciation rates used and establish that they are appropriate for current-cost accounting (CCA) purposes. Has proper consideration been given to 'future economic lives of assets'?					
8. Obtain copy of any professional valuations used to restate assets. In case of property, ensure that valuation is on basis of open market value for existing use. (If net building replacement cost exceeds existing use value, depreciation should be calculated on full existing use value.)					
9. Where adjustments are made to valuations produced in earlier years,					

Audit tests	Details of tests	Errors, etc.	Audit sch.	*Work done by* Intls	Date
review for reasonableness in light of general market conditions. 10. Is there any evidence of substantial technological change, so that use of indices is not appropriate? 11. Consider need for revaluation of balance sheet values to the recoverable amount to take account of permanent diminution of value. *Stocks and cost of sales adjustment (COSA)* 12. Check calculation of COSA, ensuring that indices applied to opening and closing stocks relate to the average date of acquiring those stocks. 13. Review valuation of closing stocks for CC balance sheet purposes. Compare with HC valuation to ensure that items stated at their recoverable amounts (net realizable value) have been treated consistently. 14. Where special items of stock (e.g. long-term contracts) are treated as monetary working capital, ensure that they are included in the calculation of the MWCA. 15. Review treatment of progress payments, which should be related to stock on a contract-by-contract basis. (Ensure that the excess of any progress payment over its related stock value is treated as a liability for MWCA purposes.)					

Monetary working capital adjustment (MWCA)					
16. Review MWCA calculation in light of CCA rationale. Ensure that the calculation only includes those items used in day-to-day operations (including VAT and the fluctuating part of bank balances and overdrafts).					
17. Review basis of selection of intervals over which calculations have been made. Where trade is subject to seasonal fluctuations, ensure that methods used to calculate COSA and MWCA are compatible.					
18. Where monetary working capital is a net liability, and that liability exceeds the value of stock, ensure that the excess is *excluded* from the MWCA calculation and *included* in the gearing adjustment. (In these circumstances MWCA would cancel out COSA.)					
Gearing adjustment					
19. Review basis on which average net borrowing and net operating assets during the period have been calculated. (Net operating assets should normally include share capital, reserves (including revaluation surpluses and current-cost reserve), proposed dividends, and minority interests. Deferred taxation (calculated in accordance with SSAP 15) should be included as a liability.)					
Note: If monetary assets (other than included in MWCA) included in calcula-					

Audit tests	Details of tests	Errors, etc.	Audit sch.	Work done by Intls	Date
tion exceed monetary liabilities (other than included in MWCA) no gearing adjustment is made.					
20. Confirm that gearing adjustment is also applied to the CC adjustment relating to significant disposals of fixed assets.					
21. Are there assets surplus to operating requirements and in excess of borrowing? If so, do the accounts show the change in effective purchasing power of this surplus?					
22. Where HC accounts include surpluses on property revaluations, gearing adjustment may be applied to too low a figure of supplementary depreciation. If this distortion is material, ensure that appropriate adjustment is either made or noted in the CC accounts.					
Other matters					
23. Review *inter alia* the following matters to ensure that their treatment accords with CCA rationale:					
(*a*) elimination of intra-group profits (as restated on a CC basis);					
(*b*) interests in and share of profits/losses of associated companies;					
(*c*) the restatement of any purchased goodwill retained in HC consolidated accounts. (*Note:* Where goodwill is carried at an amount established prior to introduction of					

SSAP 14, it should be reduced to the extent that it represents revaluation surpluses relating to assets held at the date of acquisition); (*d*) differences arising on exchange translation; (*e*) valuation of interests in wasting assets and intangible assets. 24. Confirm the taxation (and deferred taxation) charge and the dividends payable are consistent with HC accounts. 25. Review presentation of CC accounts and notes in the light of the recommendations that they should: (*a*) be informative; (*b*) contain sufficient information to explain the basis on which they have been prepared; (*c*) contain a reconciliation between HC and CC operating profit (including extraction of interest from HC accounts); (*d*) contain an analysis of current-cost reserve and indicate amounts realized and unrealized at balance sheet date; (*e*) contain the current-cost earnings per share based on the CC profit attributable to equity shareholdings before extraordinary items, and that this basis is explained in the notes; (*f*) contain comparative figures. Where these figures are adjusted to a common price basis with the period's results, check					

Audit tests	Details of tests	Errors, etc.	Audit sch.	*Work done by* Intls	Date
calculations and confirm explanatory note. Where 5/10 year statements are provided, check calculation of common price basis. 26. Is the audit report appropriate to the work carried out? *Additional work* *Overview* Partner to review the CC statement as a whole to confirm reasonableness from own knowledge of client, comparison with previous year's figures, bearing in mind rate of inflation, and from level of adjustments made by other companies in the same trade.					

Conclusions	Yes/ No	Reason/ Comments	Audit sch.	*Work done by* Intls	Date
Are you satisfied that: (*a*) the current-cost accounts are drawn up in accordance with SSAP 16, and, together with the notes, provide a true and fair view/are properly prepared to give the current-cost information required by the Standard? (*b*) there is adequate evidence on file to support this conclusion?					

10 Auditing consolidated financial statements

One of the most marked developments in industry and commerce has been that of the holding company, which is an organization comprising a parent company which holds a controlling interest in one or more subsidiary companies and in some cases sub-subsidiary companies.

Section 154 of the Companies Act 1948 provides that a company shall be a subsidiary of another if any one of three sets of circumstances applies. For example, company S is a subsidiary of company H if:

(*a*) company H holds more than 50% of the equity share capital of company S;

(*b*) company H has the ability to control the composition of the Board of Directors of company S;

(*c*) company S is a subsidiary of a third company which is itself a subsidiary of company H.

For this purpose the term 'equity share capital' includes all capital except capital which causes a fixed right in both profits and capital.

The Act provides that for the purpose of determining whether company S is a subsidiary of company H, shares held in company S by existing subsidiaries of company H shall be counted as if they were in fact held by company H.

Form of Organization

A holding company may control a large group of companies. There are many such organizations today of an international character and comprising a large number of companies all over the world.

From the commercial point of view there are many advantages in this type of organization, and it is a natural development of which experience has proved the benefits.

On the other hand, as is generally the case, there are weaknesses and one of the great difficulties is that this type of organization raises accounting problems of considerable complexity, in particular as regards the form of presentation of the holding company's accounts.

This form of organization was capable of being improperly used as a cloak to hide from shareholders the true position of the combine in which they were interested and there were grave abuses and spectacular crashes which shook public confidence.

In consequence a growing practice developed for holding companies to present, with the legal accounts of the holding company, consolidated balance sheets and profit and loss accounts. Then this practice of certain companies became legally enforceable upon all such companies as a result of the Companies Act 1948.

The Companies Acts 1967 and 1976, and Statement of Standard Accounting Practice 14, published in 1975, then extended the information which must be given by parent companies and subsidiaries.

However, the holding company itself and each of the subsidiary and sub-subsidiary companies remain separate legal entities and, in order to comply with the legal requirements, each of these companies must prepare its own accounts and submit them in the ordinary way to its shareholders in general meeting: and as each company within a group is a separate legal entity, auditors must be appointed to audit the accounts of each.

In addition to the subsidiary relationship, mention should also be made of 'associated' companies, where one company holds as a long term investment a significant part of another's equity voting rights, and participates in its financial and commercial decision-making processes. Accounting Standard M1 effectively lays down that where such a relationship exists then the investing company should 'consolidate' into its accounts its share of the associate's net assets and profits or losses for the year.

Requirements of the Companies Acts 1948 and 1967, and of Statement of Standard Accounting Practice 14

These deal *inter alia* with accounting requirements pertaining to this form of organization and certain sections are thus of the utmost importance to auditors of consolidated accounts.

Section 150 imposes upon a holding company the obligation to lay group accounts 'before the company in general meeting when the company's own balance sheet and profit and loss account are so laid'. However, subsection (2) provides for the following exceptions to the foregoing rule:

(*a*) group accounts are not required where a company is itself 'the wholly owned subsidiary of another body corporate incorporated in Great Britain'. (Section 150(2) (*a*), Companies Act 1948)

The object of this exception is to save unnecessary work, as the main holding company will be required to prepare group accounts embracing this particular subsidiary company and all of its subsidiary companies.

(*b*) group accounts need not include a subsidiary, if the holding company's directors 'are of the opinion that:

(i) it is impracticable, or would be of no real value to members of the company, in view of the insignificant amounts involved, or would involve expense or delay out of proportion to the value to the members of the company; or

(ii) the result would be misleading or harmful to the business of the company or any of its subsidiaries; or

(iii) the business of the holding company and that of the subsidiary are so different that they cannot reasonably be treated as a single undertaking; and, if the directors are of such opinion about each of the company's subsidiaries, group accounts shall not be required'. (Section 150(2) (*b*), Companies Act 1948)

The approval of the Department of Trade is required in the cases of exceptions (ii) and (iii).

Paragraph 21, *SSAP* 14 requires a subsidiary to be excluded from consolidation if:

(i) its activities are so dissimilar from those of other companies in the group that it would be misleading to consolidate it. Information would be better provided in the form of separate financial statements.

(ii) Although the holding company owns more than half of the equity capital of the subsidiary, either the holding company

(*a*) does not own more than half of the voting capital, or

(*b*) has restrictions placed on its ability to appoint the majority of the board of directors.

(iii) The subsidiary operates under severe long-term restrictions which significantly impair the holding company's control over the subsidiary's assets or operations.

(iv) Control is intended to be temporary.

If a subsidiary is excluded from the group accounts for any of the above reasons, paragraph 20, SSAP 14 requires the auditor to decide whether the resultant financial statements give a true and fair position of the whole group.

Section 151 makes it clear that the term 'group accounts' comprises a consolidated profit and loss account and a consolidated balance sheet. But subsection (2) provides that the same or equivalent information can be presented in some other form, 'if the directors are of opinion' that thus the position of affairs would be more readily appreciated by members of the company. The subsection makes clear that the alternative forms of presentation include (1) two or more separate group consolidations, (2) separate accounts for each subsidiary, (3) explanatory statements, regarding the subsidiaries, in the holding company's accounts 'or any combination of those forms'. Subsection (3) provides that 'the group accounts may be wholly or partly incorporated in the company's own balance sheet and profit and loss account'.

An example of (1) above would be a group with diversified activities consisting of manufacturing subsidiaries and insurance subsidiaries. There could be effectively two separate consolidated balance sheets consisting of:

(i) The holding company and the manufacturing subsidiaries. This balance sheet shows an item, net tangible assets: insurance subsidiaries.
(ii) The insurance subsidiaries showing the various assets and liabilities making up those net tangible assets.

It will be noted that the directors of a company have several alternatives available. Although it is for the directors to make these decisions, the auditor is generally asked to advise. Paragraph 15, SSAP 14 requires that group accounts should take the form of a single set of consolidated financial statements. Clearly the overriding requirement is to give a true and fair view of the affairs of the group.

Section 152 rules that the group accounts of a holding company 'shall give a true and fair view of the state of affairs and profit or loss of the company and the subsidiaries dealt with thereby as a whole, so far as concerns members of the company'.

Section 153 provides that 'a holding company's directors shall secure that except where in their opinion there are good reasons against it, the financial year of each of its subsidiaries shall coincide with the company's own financial year'. If the financial year of a subsidiary does not coincide with that of the holding company, then the accounts of that subsidiary for its financial year ending last before that of the holding company, shall be included in the group accounts; unless the Department of Trade otherwise directs. (Section 152(2), Companies Act 1948)

The following reasons can be put forward to justify including results of subsidiaries made up to non co-terminus year-ends:

(*a*) To avoid undue delay in the preparation of group accounts.
(*b*) Local legislation requiring accounts of particular subsidiaries to be made up to different dates.
(*c*) The subsidiary using an accounting date based in the natural trading cycle.
(*d*) The existence of a substantial minority interest making it difficult to change the accounting date.

Two possibilities arise:

(*a*) Use of interim accounts, provided the auditor is satisfied as to their reliability. For example, if the group makes its accounts up to 31 December each year but one subsidiary makes its accounts up to 30 September, then the consolidated financial statements could include:

(i) 1 January to 30 September based on audited accounts.
(ii) 1 October to 31 December based on interim accounts. The auditor would need to review these interim accounts to the extent necessary to ensure they were suitable for inclusion in the group accounts.

The group balance sheet would include the interim balance sheet of the company at 31 December.

(*b*) If it is not practical to prepare interim accounts, the group accounts will include a consolidation of subsidiaries made up to different accounting dates.

Paragraph 18 *SSAP* 14 requires 'appropriate adjustments for any abnormal transactions in the intervening period'.

Thus it would be necessary to adjust for, *inter alia,* sale or purchase of major assets, sale or discontinuance of a significant part of the business of the subsidiary, or major trading losses accruing in the intervening period.

Paragraph 18 above requires that the following information should also be disclosed for each principal subsidiary with a different accounting date:

(*a*) its name
(*b*) its accounting date
(*c*) the reason for using a different accounting date

In the United States of America the SEC disallows consolidation of accounts which differ by more than 93 days in their closing dates.

Section 3 *(Companies Act* 1967) requires the holding company to disclose the names of all subsidiary companies. It requires separately the names of sub-subsidiaries. In each case the country of incorporation must be given, the class of shares held and the proportion held of the nominal value of the issued shares of each class. Where the subsidiaries are incorporated or are trading abroad the Department of Trade may grant exemption from these requirements if their disclosure would be considered harmful. Further, if there are a very large number of subsidiaries and the directors consider that the required statement would be of excessive length, they need only give such details of the principal subsidiaries — that is those which contribute significantly to the group by way of turnover, profits, losses or assets.

Section 5 requires subsidiary companies to disclose the name of the company regarded by the directors as the ultimate holding company and its country of incorporation. The Department of Trade may grant exemption if the subsidiary trades abroad and disclosure would be harmful. (Companies Act 1967)

The requirements of Part I of the Second Schedule of the Companies Act 1967 apply generally to all company accounts, but Part II applies specifically to holding and subsidiary companies.

Paragraph 15(2) provides that in the legal balance sheet of a holding company there must be stated, separated from all other items, the aggregate amount of the share investments in subsidiary companies and also the aggregate amounts of all loans, current and other accounts owing by and to subsidiaries.

Paragraph 15(3) provides that, if subsidiaries hold shares or debentures in the holding company, the description and amount of such shares and debentures held by the subsidiaries must be shown by way of note on the legal balance sheet of the holding company or in a statement or report annexed thereto.

If group accounts are not submitted, then, in accordance with Section 15(4), a special statement must be annexed to the legal balance sheet of the holding company. In this statement there must be given the reasons why group accounts are not submitted, and also particulars of the aggregate amount, so far as it concerns members of the holding company, of the revenue profits less revenue losses of the subsidiaries for the year (*a*)not dealt with and (*b*) dealt with in the accounts of the holding company.

Paragraph 15(4) (d) provides that, in cases where group accounts are not submitted, the statement submitted to members must include particulars of any qualifications in the reports of the auditors of subsidiaries. Particulars must likewise be given of 'any note or saving contained in' the accounts of a subsidiary, and which otherwise would have been referred to by the auditors by way of a qualification in their report. It is not necessary to refer to such a qualification or note, in so far as the particular matter has been provided for in the holding company's accounts.

Problems Associated with the Preparation and Audit of Consolidated Accounts

Obviously, as is the case with every undertaking, in order to obtain a clear view of the financial position and progress of a holding company it is necessary to see on the one hand the earnings and on the other hand the financial position of the group of companies as a whole. If this information is available it is possible to judge whether the aggregate earnings represent a reasonable return upon the total capital invested in the group, and to follow the trend of this relationship from year to year. This is the paramount factor and the crux of the whole problem, and is the reason why the Companies Act 1948 provided for the submission of group accounts or statements, in the case of all holding companies.

In such consolidated accounts or statements, as regards both earnings and assets and liabilities, it is important to appreciate that they are statements prepared for the benefit of the shareholders of the holding company. These statements are built up from the profit and loss accounts and balance sheets of all of the companies within the group, and they are not therefore the accounts of one business undertaking.

In preparing these statements also it must be borne in mind that the adjustments have to be made in the case of all of these consolidated statements for the interest of outside shareholders. The holding company is entitled to a proportion only of the aggregate earnings and of the surplus of assets over liabilities of the subsidiaries. That proportion is governed by the holding company's share of the equity of the respective companies.

In addition, of course, all items representing inter-company indebtedness should cancel out. In those cases in which the financial years of the parent and subsidiaries do not coincide an adjustment has, of course, to be made.

Details of some of the difficulties which arise in the preparation and audit of such accounts are given below.

Uniformity of information

In order to facilitate the preparation of group accounts, arrangements should be made for the accounts of all subsidiaries to be prepared upon the basis of a standard form of presentation. In the case of foreign subsidiaries this is not always possible as regards the official accounts, which may have to comply with local laws and practices. But in such circumstances it is possible to arrange for special accounts to be prepared in the standard form, such accounts, duly audited, being submitted to the holding company, together with any necessary supporting information and particulars.

It is recommended that such a standard form of accounts should be supported by schedules covering the following information:

Balance sheet

(*a*) Movements in capital.
(*b*) Detailed movements in reserves.
(*c*) Summarized particulars of loan capital and other loans (other than dealt with in (*g*) below), including particulars of interest payable, security, if any, and repayment terms.
(*d*) Summarized details of trade and other creditors (distinguishing unusual items).
(*e*) Summarized details of amount owing to or by the holding company.
(*f*) Summarized details of amount owing to or by other group companies.
(*g*) Details of bank loans and advances (including security given where appropriate).
(*h*) Movements on taxation account (and a brief summary of outstanding matters of significance).
(*i*) Details of movements on material provisions.
(*j*) Details of movements on:
    (i) deferred taxation account
    (ii) other deferred liabilities

(*k*) Movements on freehold premises.
(*l*) Movements on leasehold premises over 50 years.
(*m*) Movements on leasehold premises under 50 years.
(*n*) Movements on plant, machinery and furniture.
(*o*) Movements on motor vehicles.
} and on depreciation accounts, stating basis and rates

(*p*) Movements on quoted investments (with market valuation).
(*q*) Movements on unquoted investments (with directors' valuation).
(*r*) Movements on investments in subsidiary companies.
(*s*) Summarized details of hire-purchase and other long-term debtors.
(*t*) Summarized details of debtors and payments in advance (distinguishing unusual items) and bad-debt, discount, etc., provisions.
(*u*) Particulars of contingent liabilities.
(*v*) Particulars of future capital expenditure:
 (i) contracted for but not provided for
 (ii) authorized by the directors but not contracted for
(*w*) Particulars of events occurring after the balance sheet date which are of significant importance to shareholders, but not dealt with in the accounts.

Profit and loss account

(*aa*) Summarized details of exceptional and/or extraordinary items.
(*bb*) Summarized details of profits and/or losses relating to previous years.
(*cc*) Emoluments paid to holding company directors.
(*dd*) Brief particulars of items supplied by other group companies included in stock.
(*ee*) Turnover (showing intra-group turnover separately).
(*ff*) Estimated computation of profits for taxation purposes and amounts transferred to and from deferred taxation accounts.
(*gg*) Particulars of: (i) transactions during the year of a sort not usually undertaken by the company or of an exceptional or non-recurring nature; (ii) any change in the basis of accounting; including a note of the extent to which profits have been affected by either of the above if not apparent from the accounts.

Note: Where the group instructions are not adequate in any particular, the group auditors may consider it appropriate to add additional questions to their questionnaire (see below); e.g. in the case of stock the auditors might add questions to determine the precise basis of valuation of all stocks and work-in-progress and to verify that a consistent basis is used throughout the group.

The holding company may find it convenient also to obtain through the medium of these schedules the following information required for the directors' report:

Average number of employees and payroll information.
Political and charitable donations.
Export sales included in turnover and intra-group turnover.

Multiplicity of auditors

As a general rule direct contact, as between the auditors of the holding company and the auditors of subsidiaries, is most helpful. One means of achieving this is where it is recognized that, although it is not legally necessary, there may be advantages in one firm of auditors acting for the whole of the companies within the group, as in this way the auditors may acquire direct knowledge of the whole of the ramifications of the group and may, therefore, be in a better position to trace through all inter-company transactions and ascertain that uniform principles have been applied. There have been cases where unscrupulous directors have been able to cover up improper manipulations which would not have been possible had one firm audited the accounts of all the companies within the group.

It is not, however, always possible nor always desirable to arrange for one firm to audit the accounts of all the subsidiaries, especially in the case of a holding company with subsidiaries in many different countries. If the auditors of the holding company do not audit the accounts of all the subsidiary and sub-subsidiary companies, then they should examine the audited accounts of each subsidiary and sub-subsidiary company, and in cases where these are submitted in an abridged form they should also have access to the detailed accounts. In addition, information and explanations from the directors and auditors of the subsidiaries should be obtained in connection with any questions upon which the auditors of the holding company are not clear, or upon which they require further data in order to be able to report on the consolidated accounts, which it is their responsibility to do.

Pre-acquisition profits

At the time when the shares in a subsidiary are acquired by the holding company there may be in existence undistributed profits in the accounts of that subsidiary. In arriving at the sum paid for the shares, the undistributed profits will have been taken into account in arriving at the purchase price of such shares.

If in a subsequent year the whole or part of such undistributed profits is distributed as dividend, then in these circumstances, on receipt of the dividend from the subsidiary by the holding company, the proportion (if any) representing profits which were undistributed at the time of acquisition of the shares should be deducted from the cost of the investment, thus reducing its value in the holding company's balance sheet (Second Schedule, Part II, Paragraph 15(5)).

Inter-company transactions

Inevitably in the case of a group of companies there are inter-company transactions, and, for example, company A may sell goods to company B. If at the date of the balance sheet company B has part of these goods in stock, they will be valued in the ordinary way at cost, if the realizable value has been maintained. This cost price will include the profit in the price which was charged by company A.

Companies A and B are separate legal entities and notwithstanding the legal position that A could sue B for the price charged, the fact remains that, from the point of view of the group as a whole, such a sale is a mere internal transaction; therefore unless and until the goods in question are sold to customers outside the group, no true profit can be said to have been realized.

A similar point arises if one company does work of a capital nature for another within the group, such as a sale of plant. The selling company may properly charge a price which includes a reasonable profit and the purchasing company will capitalize this item at the invoice price. In the accounts of the holding company credit should not be taken for this profit which lies in the accounts of the supplying company, because this again merely represents what is in effect an internal or inter-company adjustment. Therefore an adjustment for inter-company profits should be made and, in general, this provision should be made in the accounts of the holding company, because in the case of subsidiaries the position may be complicated by reason of the interest of minority shareholders in the subsidiary.

Balance sheet presentation

As regards the form of presentation of the balance sheets of the subsidiaries, no special points arise, except that the aggregate amounts of all indebtedness to and from the holding company and all fellow subsidiary companies, must be separately stated in the balance sheet of a subsidiary 'distinguishing in each case between indebtedness in respect of debentures and otherwise' (Second Schedule, Part II, Paragraph 16). But very important questions arise in connection with the balance sheet of the holding company.

Investments in subsidiaries

The auditor of a holding company must satisfy himself that the investments in and advances to subsidiaries have been stated in the holding company's balance sheet in accordance with correct principles.

Thus, Paragraph 15(2) of the Second Schedule provides that the aggregate amount of assets consisting of shares in, or amount owing (whether on account of a loan or otherwise) from, the company's subsidiaries, distinguishing shares from indebtedness, shall be set out in the balance sheet separately from all the other assets of the company. A practice which is commonly adopted to meet this requirement is to group together, under one suitable heading such as 'interests in subsidiaries', the separate totals of shares in subsidiaries and either:

(*a*) the aggregate amount of indebtedness of subsidiaries, whether on loan accounts or otherwise; or
(*b*) the separate aggregates of:
(i) long-term loans and advances to subsidiaries whether secured or otherwise;
(ii) other amounts owing by subsidiaries such as short-term advances and current accounts.

It may, however, be considered that in order to show a true and fair view the amounts owing from subsidiaries on current-account and short-term advances should be grouped with current assets. For the purpose of such grouping it is essential to include only amounts which can properly be described as current assets, namely, current accounts which are regularly paid and temporary advances to be repaid shortly. In practice, it will often be found that part of the amount described as owing on current account could in fact be more properly described as being a long-term advance and would therefore be unsuitable for grouping with current assets. If all amounts which may properly be described as current assets were eliminated from the aggregate of interests in subsidiaries, the residue (consisting of shares, debentures and other long-term loans and advances) would fall to be classified as fixed assets. Where it is the practice of the holding company to take into account dividends proposed to be paid by subsidiaries it will not be appropriate to include such dividends under current assets unless they are intended to be paid in cash or discharged through a genuine current account.

The provision of the Second Schedule in relation to interests in subsidiaries would appear to permit either:

(*a*) one aggregate (with appropriate subdivision such as that indicated above) to be stated in the balance sheet under a suitable heading shown as an intermediate group between fixed and current assets; or
(*b*) two aggregates (with appropriate subdivision) to be stated in the balance sheet, one grouped with fixed assets and the other grouped with current assets;

according to which method appears to satisfy the overriding requirement of Section 149 to show a true and fair view. Method (*a*), whereby all interests in subsidiaries are grouped together, is usually to be preferred. It is rarely possible to make the complete segregation of the current asset element which is essential for method (*b*).

Losses of subsidiaries

The auditor must ascertain exactly how the profits and losses of subsidiary companies have been dealt with in the accounts of the holding company and of the subsidiaries. In particular, he must ascertain whether or not the holding company has provided for its appropriate proportion of the losses sustained by a subsidiary company or companies. Under the Act it is not compulsory for the holding company to provide for its proportion of the losses of subsidiaries, but the overall position must be shown in a consolidated profit and loss account or in a supporting statement.

To take a simple illustration of a holding company with one 100% subsidiary only which was formed some years ago. Let it be assumed that the subsidiary has been consistently profitable, has paid regular dividends to the holding company, and that after payment of such dividends the subsidiary had a balance to the credit of its profit and loss account at the end of its previous financial year of, say, £7000. The holding company has not taken this balance of undistributed profit into its accounts and the investment in the subsidiary stands in the holding company's books at the original cost. If during the current financial year a loss of, say, £3000 is sustained by the subsidiary, thereby reducing its carry-forward to £4000, it would not be obligatory upon the holding company to provide for the loss of £3000 in its accounts, as no depreciation has taken place in the holding company's asset since acquisition, for the simple reason that the investment which stands in the holding company's books at cost is, notwithstanding this loss, worth £4000 more than its book value.

However, in the case of a subsidiary which over a series of years has made heavy losses, it is possible that these losses in the aggregate may amount to more than the issued share capital of that subsidiary. The finance of the subsidiary would then probably be provided by means of advances from the holding company once the whole of the share capital has been exhausted. In subsequent years the holding company should provide for 100% of the losses. Any outside shareholders cannot lose more than the whole of their interest in the company. When, therefore, the whole of their share capital and reserves has been lost the whole of the further losses are, in effect, encroaching on the holding company's advances.

Audit qualifications

It has been noted that, in cases where group accounts have not been submitted, the statement submitted to members must include particulars of any qualifications in the reports of the auditors of subsidiaries. The auditor of a holding company should, therefore, examine carefully both the accounts and the auditor's reports in respect of each subsidiary and make certain that these requirements are carried out.

In complying with this requirement it is felt that Paragraph 15(4) (*d*) is intended to embrace only those qualifications in which attention is directed, *inter alia,* to an overstatement in the value of an asset, the understatement of a liability, or the omission to indicate the existence of a contingent liability. In brief, the question for determination appears to be whether the qualification or note is manifestly intended to convey to the members that the financial position of the company is or may be worse than the figures in the balance sheet indicate. The governing factor is as to whether the matter in question 'is material from the point of view' of the members of the holding company.

Relying on the Work of Other Auditors

It has already been mentioned that the circumstances of a group and those of its auditors sometimes demand that the auditors of the holding company (the primary auditors) are charged by law with reporting upon consolidated accounts even though they have not themselves audited the accounts of some or all of the subsidiary companies.

The responsibility of the primary auditors for the report on the consolidated accounts is emphasized by The Institute of Chartered Accountants in England and Wales in their statement U21, 'Group accounts — reliance on other auditors', published in 1976, which says:

> 'The primary auditors are fully responsible for their opinion on the group accounts and need not for this reason refer in their report to the fact that the accounts of some subsidiary or associated companies have been audited by other firms. Such a reference may be misleading as it may be taken to imply a limitation of the scope of the primary auditors' opinion. This in no way takes away from the secondary auditors their responsibility for the audit of their client companies' accounts.
>
> It is considered, however, that the shareholders of the primary company are entitled to know that the accounts of some of the companies in the group have been audited by other auditors and the materiality of those companies to the group.'

The statement may suggest that this information should be disclosed by way of a note — possibly being incorporated in the schedule of principal subsidiary and associated companies.

The primary auditors have never had under law a right of access to the accounting records of subsidiary companies of which they are not the auditors and, on being required to express an opinion on the consolidated accounts, they are forced to assess the competence of other auditors. Section 18 of the Companies Act 1976 strengthened the position of the primary auditors by giving legal backing to their requirements for information and explanations about the subsidiary companies' accounts.

Clearly, in order to form an opinion on the consolidated accounts as a whole, the primary auditors must be satisfied as to the adequacy of the scope and standard of the audit work carried out in respect of the accounts of subsidiary and associated companies which they have not themselves audited.

In addition, information must be made available about the application of accounting policies throughout the group and about any other matters relevant specifically to the consolidated accounts. Statement U21, in recommending consultation between the auditors, says:

> 'In all material cases the primary auditors will need to consult the auditors of other group companies so that they may be familiar with the auditing procedures and standards applied by the auditors of the other subsidiary and associated companies (the secondary auditors). However, they should not contact the secondary auditors until they have received proper authority by means of arrangements made through the respective boards. In conducting these consultations the primary auditors would normally use one or more of the following procedures:
>
> (*a*) requests for written explanations of the secondary auditors' procedures and findings, and of the secondary company's accounting policies, supplemented as necessary by:
>
> (*b*) oral explanations;
>
> (*c*) examination of audit files, working papers and any relevant management letters . . .
>
> . . . If the primary auditors are not satisfied as a result of the above review, or if they need to obtain independent confirmation of additional accounting information required specifically for the group accounts, they should arrange for additional audit tests to be conducted, either directly by the secondary auditors on their behalf, or co-jointly with them. Only in exceptional circumstances are primary auditors likely to need to conduct their own tests independently of the secondary auditors.'

When drafting their audit report, the primary auditors should consider, in addition to possible qualifications which they may wish to make in respect of companies they have themselves audited, the following matters:

(*a*) whether any of the secondary auditors' reports contain qualifications which are material to the group as a whole and which should therefore be incorporated in the primary auditors' report;

(*b*) whether they have been able to satisfy themselves as to the scope and quality of the audits of all the secondary companies and as to the adequacy of the information and explanations which they have received from the secondary companies and their auditors;

(*c*) whether adequate disclosure has been made in the accounts as to which companies have been audited by auditors other than the primary auditors. Where no such disclosure is to be made, the primary auditors may refer to this in their report, but must not thereby give the impression of abrogating their responsibilities in respect of the accounts as a whole.

Section 18 of the Companies Act 1976 has given the auditors of the holding company important additional rights in relation to information about subsidiaries.

Where a parent company has a subsidiary, then if the subsidiary is a body corporate incorporated in Great Britain, the subsidiary and its auditors have a duty to give the auditors of the parent company such information and explanations as the parent company's auditors require for the purpose of their duties as auditors of the parent company.

If the subsidiary is not a body corporate incorporated in Great Britain and the parent company's auditors require it, the parent company must take all reasonable steps as are open to it to obtain from the subsidiary the above information and explanations. It should be noted that the foregoing does not apply to associated companies or their directors.

Since it is now customary for the holding company auditors to have direct communication with other auditors involved in the group, it is advisable that the necessary contacts be established as early as possible to enable adequate planning of requirements. To this end many holding company auditors have devised questionnaires to be completed and returned by the auditors of the subsidiary at the completion of their audit, in which respect the following may serve as a specimen:

Specimen Consolidated Questionnaire

	Yes/No
General	
1. Have the auditors examined the internal controls and accounting procedures during the year?	
2. If material weaknesses were revealed was the attention of the management drawn to these with recommendations:	
(*a*) in writing? or	
(*b*) verbally?	
3. Are steps being taken to rectify these weaknesses?	
4. Have the group instructions with regard to the preparation of schedules and accounts been carried out?	
5. Did the auditors obtain a letter of representation from the managing director/branch manager confirming the amounts shown in the accounts for fixed assets, debtors, stock and creditors, etc.?	
Fixed assets	
6. Is a register or registers of the following fixed assets maintained:	
(*a*) land and buildings;	
(*b*) plant;	

	Yes/No
(*c*) motor vehicles;	
(*d*) patents and trade marks;	
(*e*) other fixed assets?	
7. Are the registers reconciled annually with the financial accounts?	
8. Are the registers periodically checked and agreed with the actual physical fixed assets where appropriate?	
9. If the documents of title to land and buildings and other appropriate documents are held in the company's offices is a proper control exercised?	
10. If the documents of title indicated above are not held in the company's offices are they held by proper custodians?	
11. Have particulars of transfers of fixed assets from or to group companies been notified to the holding company together with the accumulated depreciation thereon?	
12. Where assets have been purchased under hire-purchase or instalment purchase agreements are the entries dealt with correctly in the books?	
13. In the case of land and buildings (and other assets where appropriate) have all documents of title at the balance sheet date been inspected by the auditors or have certificates from the custodian where appropriate been obtained direct?	
14. Have additions to fixed assets been tested with appropriate invoices and authorizations or with cost accounts where the asset has been constructed by the client company?	
15. In the auditor's opinion is the depreciation not excessive but appropriate to write down the cost of the assets over the estimated normal working life?	
16. Are the auditors satisfied that all assets sold or scrapped have been taken out of the asset account at their original cost and that the accumulated depreciation has been dealt with in the case of sales and scrappings?	
17. Is the basis of depreciation consistent with that of previous years?	
Investments	
18. If the documents of title are held in the company's offices is a proper control exercised?	
19. If the documents of title are not held in the company's offices are they held by proper custodians?	
20. Was the company's title to the investments at the balance sheet date confirmed either by direct inspection by the auditors or by certificates from custodians or bank nominees obtained direct?	
21. Where the investments are held in the name of the nominees has satisfactory evidence of the company's title been produced to the auditors?	
22. Have the documents of title been reconciled in detail with the	

	Yes/No
holdings shown in the accounts?	
23. In the case of those investments, which were not quoted, were the most recent balance sheets examined and the equity compared with the cost or book value as shown in the company's books?	
24. Have the auditors verified that all income which should have been received from the investments has been so received?	
25. Have the auditors ascertained that all rights and bonuses emanating from the investments have been accounted for?	
Stocks and work-in-progress	
26. Are there control accounts for all stocks both as to quantities and values in detailed records?	
27. Are the stocks under the control of a store-keeper or store-keepers, outside the control of the accounts department?	
28. Are the stocks periodically checked by some official other than the store-keeper and the results independently checked with the stock records?	
29. Are the stock records adjusted periodically to conform with the physical count?	
30. Are the amounts written-off authorized by a responsible official?	
31. Is there proper control exercised in respect of stocks passing between different factories and depots of the company where no sales invoices are made out?	
32. Was a physical count of all stocks and work-in-progress made at balance sheet date?	
33. If a physical count was not made at balance sheet date, was a physical count made of all stocks and work-in-progress at another specified date?	
34. If there is a perpetual inventory system, does it provide for all stocks to be physically checked at least once a year?	
35. Did the company issue adequate written stocktaking instructions for those engaged in taking stock and were the instructions properly carried out?	
36. Did the stocktaking procedures ensure a proper cut-off?	
37. In the opinion of the auditors are the records of stock reliable and adequate?	
38. Did the auditors observe the physical stocktaking and make independent test counts of quantities?	
39. Did the auditors observe the physical stocktaking outside by third parties and make independent test counts?	
40. Are the auditors satisfied that stocks of free-issue materials, consignment stock, and other stocks, held by the company as agents or bailee have been:	
(*a*) properly controlled and accounted for;	
(*b*) excluded from the company's own stocks?	

	Yes/No
41. Are the auditors satisfied that the group instructions, with regard to the valuation of work-in-progress and stocks, have been correctly carried out?	
42. Are the auditors satisfied that adequate provisions have been made for all slow moving and obsolete stock items?	
43. Are the auditors satisfied that the basis of valuation of both stocks and work-in-progress is consistent with the method adopted for the previous year?	
Other current assets	
44. Was an independent confirmation of debts obtained by a circularization or test circularization of debtors under the supervision of the auditors?	
45. Were satisfactory explanations received for all differences disclosed by the circularization?	
46. Were all debtor balances reviewed by the auditors with regard to collectability and the adequacy of the bad- and doubtful-debts provision?	
47. Were the auditors satisfied with regard to the adequacy of the bad- and doubtful-debts provision?	
48. Was the division of debtors as between current and long-term (over a year) reviewed by the auditors?	
49. Were bills receivable, drafts and any other evidence of indebtedness inspected by the auditors or independently confirmed by bank certificates?	
50. Were independent confirmations of bank balances obtained direct from the bank by the auditors?	
51. Does the auditor's letter requesting confirmation of the bank balances addressed to banks ask for information on all accounts operated by or in the name of the company and cover guarantees, open foreign exchange contracts, bills discounted and held for collection, etc.?	
52. Was all the company's cash counted by the auditors and agreed? If not, were suitable verifications obtained from higher executives?	
Intra-group balances	
53. Are reconciliations of group and associated company balances made regularly with statements from those companies?	
54. At balance sheet date have all inter-company balances within the group been confirmed and agreed, by statements from the group companies concerned or from their auditors?	
55. Where the company's stocks include goods supplied by other group companies have details of the amounts concerned been notified to the holding company for consolidation purposes?	
Long- and medium-term loans	
56. Are the following particulars of amounts due by the company shown on the face of the accounts or by way of note:	

	Yes/no
(*a*) whether secured wholly or in part; (*b*) the amount outstanding; (*c*) repayment dates; (*d*) premiums on repayment; (*e*) rates of interest?	
57. Were the amounts outstanding at the date of the balance sheet verified by the auditors by independent confirmation and certificates?	
58. Are the borrowings within the limits given by the Memorandum of Association, other regulations for the company, or instruments securing borrowings?	
59. Are the borrowings arranged only on the authority of the directors?	
Liabilities and provisions	
60. Were the books and, where appropriate, files of uncleared invoices, examined after date by the auditors to ensure that all liabilities, etc. had been taken up?	
61. In the opinion of the auditors were the amounts set aside as provisions adequate for their purpose, and not excessive?	
62. Where appropriate were liabilities and provisions independently confirmed?	
63. Were enquiries made by the auditors of officials and the company's solicitors as to pending litigation and of any other matters which could give rise to a claim, and as to the likely amounts involved?	
64. Were the auditors satisfied with regard to the provision for contingencies?	
Taxation on profits	
65. Is the provision for the current year prepared on a basis which takes account of the most recent legislation and of any agreement reached on prior years' assessments?	
66. Are there any material matters in dispute with the taxation authorities?	
67. Is adequate provision made for items in dispute and for any other unsettled tax point?	
68. Are the auditors satisfied that the taxation provisions in the accounts are adequate but not materially excessive to cover all estimated taxation payable on profits and chargeable gains earned and accrued at the date of the balance sheet?	
69. Did the auditors examine correspondence with the taxation authorities and vouch payments with assessment notices, demand notes and receipts where appropriate, etc.?	

It is recommended that the questionnaire should be sent by the holding company to the subsidiary company who in turn would send it to the subsidiary company auditors, and that the covering letter from the holding company should ask the subsidiary company board to give authority for the group auditors and subsidiary's auditors to communicate directly on matters concerning the group accounts and audits.

It is also recommended that the questionnaires should be dispatched so that they are in the hands of the subsidiary company auditors before the audit work for the year is commenced so that their audit programmes can be reviewed before the commencement of the audits.

Specimen Audit Programme

Client:

Audit programme: Consolidated financial statements — Approved by:

Accounting date: — Reviewed by:

Audit tests	Details of tests	*Work performed by* Intls	Date
1. Review the accounting and consolidation instructions issued to group companies with particular reference to the adherence to group accounting and consolidation policies. 2. Arrange, as necessary, for group audit questionnaires to be sent to other firms of auditors. Review the completed questionnaires with the subsidiary companies' accounts, with the holding company officials and the other firm of auditors, where possible, noting points of importance and indicating action taken. 3. Where accounts of subsidiary companies are received or are prepared in standard format for consolidation purposes: (*a*) check all consolidation adjustments; (*b*) check against the statutory accounts of the subsidiary companies (including notes, auditors' and directors' reports); (*c*) ensure that all items are correctly classified and relevant matters noted; (*d*) check casts. 4. In respect of foreign subsidiaries, check: (*a*) exchange rates used at accounting date from external sources; (*b*) basis of conversion of foreign currencies and consistency with declared accounting policies of the group;			

(*c*) calculations of conversions and differences arising thereon.

5. Where the accounts of subsidiary companies are not to be consolidated:

(*a*) ascertain the reason therefor;

(*b*) ensure that the alternative treatment proposed is permissible under the Companies Acts;

(*c*) examine any necessary Department of Trade approval;

(*d*) ensure adequate disclosure regarding statutory requirements in the notes on the holding company accounts.

6. Examine agreement of inter-company balances and ensure that all differences are adequately explained and adjusted.

7. Prepare or review working papers covering each item in the group accounts including the following information:

(*a*) details of consolidated reserves and reconciliation of movements thereon;

(*b*) details of outside interests in subsidiaries and a reconciliation of the movements thereon;

(*c*) details of borrowings;

(*d*) reconciliation of movements of fixed assets including transfers between group companies, eliminating inter-company profits/losses, where necessary, and group depreciation;

(*e*) the elimination of inter-group balances including inter-company dividends;

(*f*) bases of valuation of stocks and work-in-progress and the elimination of unrealized inter-company profits included therein;

(*g*) major variations of other assets and liabilities;

(*h*) analysis of group investments held as fixed assets, including valuations or calculations of the group's share of undistributed profits, where applicable, under statutory or other requirements;

(*i*) the terms of purchase and calculation of pre-acquisition profits/losses of new subsidiaries or increases/decreases in investment in existing subsidiaries;

(*j*) details of computation of reserve/goodwill arising on consolidation and a

Audit tests	Details of tests	*Work performed by* Intls	Date
reconciliation of the movements between the beginning and end of the year; (*k*) reconciliation of group trading profits with the results of individual companies; (*l*) details of turnover including the elimination of inter-group sales; (*m*) details of abnormal group profits or losses, including exceptional or extraordinary items and their presentation in the accounts; (*n*) overall reconciliation of group taxation charge; (*o*) summary of group taxation provisions showing estimated margins available to the group; (*p*) movements and make up of group tax equalization reserve or deferred taxation; (*q*) profits of the year applicable to outside interests; (*r*) detailed summaries of information required under the Companies Acts 1948 to 1981, e.g. director emoluments, audit fees. 8. Where subsidiaries have year-ends which are not co-terminus with that of the parent company: (*a*) examine subsequent interim financial statements up to or beyond the date of the parent company's accounts and consider provision for losses in that period; (*b*) consider any abnormal fluctuations in the pattern of trading; (*c*) examine movements on inter-company accounts in that period; (*d*) consider note to holding company balance sheet. 9. Where the company is itself a subsidiary company: (*a*) check that the parent company's consolidation and accounting policies have been adhered to; (*b*) complete (i) group audit questionnaire, and (ii) standard accounts for consolidation purposes, where required.			

10. Ensure that group accounts are prepared, generally, in accordance with: (*a*) The Companies Acts; (*b*) Statements of Standard Accounting Practice, as issued by the Institute; (*c*) Stock Exchange requirements (refer to check list) and conform with the above in respect of disclosure in the accounts.			

11 Audit quality control

One of the reasons for introducing Auditing Standards was to let it be seen by the public at large that auditors work to generally accepted standards of performance. In view of the criticisms of auditing in recent years and with increasing exposure to professional negligence, in a climate of improving standards the question of audit quality control is becoming a matter of primary importance. Each reporting partner is not only personally responsible for maintaining his own standards of work but in a practising firm he will be equally concerned as to the quality of work performed by all other reporting partners within that firm. Thus the auditor will wish to set up procedures to enable him to monitor and maintain the overall quality of work carried out within his firm.

There are many elements to the quality control of audit work. A major part of it relates to the various procedures which a firm adopts to control an audit whilst it is in progress. These have been dealt with in some detail in previous chapters and here we need to say no more than that the quality of an audit will depend largely on such matters as the care with which staff are allocated to jobs — so that the technical difficulty of the assignment is matched by the competence and experience of the staff responsible for it — and the supervision they are given during the course of their work.

Audit quality has its roots in the total organization of the firm. It begins with the quality of staff recruitment, and continues through the provision of training programmes — both for students and for partners, managers and qualified staff.

It is enhanced by adequate technical support. It will be documented by guidance manuals, working papers, checklists, and it will be generally put into practice through the implementation of detailed procedures such as those we have set out in the foregoing chapters.

Only when a firm has thus developed its own 'standards' will it have the yardstick against which to compare actual performance. This control — or comparison — of audit quality may take a variety of forms but an important distinction is whether it occurs 'live', i.e. before the audit is completed, or whether it takes place after the audit has been signed off.

Audit Review Panel

The essence of 'live' quality control is consultation. Any one reporting partner will have in mind that a professional decision taken by him individually commits the whole of his firm and all his partners within it. Appropriate consultation must take place on an informal day-to-day basis — whatever the size of the office. In addition, for all but the smallest practices, the process of consultation can be formalized into a 'review panel' procedure.

The purpose of the review panel is that reporting partners who encounter points of major difficulty on important assignments can have rapid access to advice. Review panels will act on an *ad hoc* basis and must be so constituted that they can be convened quickly. Panel membership will therefore be flexible, but if they are to operate efficiently — and consistently — it will be better for a firm to lay down certain rules of procedure. The substance of these rules will depend largely on the size of the practice in question but they would normally be expected to cover such matters as:

the procedures for convening a panel;
the minimum number of partners of which a panel should be comprised;
arrangements for minuting and filing panel decisions;
a list of the matters for which a reference to the panel is required.

These might include matters where conflicts of interest could arise; proposed qualifications in audit reports; prospectuses, profit forecasts or any other document to be signed by the firm and published (other than reports on annual financial statements); or any other matters on which the reporting partner wants a second opinion.

In addition to giving the reporting partner the comfort of a second professional opinion, a further benefit of review panel decisions is that they can provide a source of reference whenever similar problems arise in the future.

'Second Partner'

A further means of formalizing the consultation process is to allocate a 'second partner' to each audit assignment. The second partner might be responsible for carrying out a comprehensive review of all the files (before completion of the audit report by the reporting partner primarily responsible for the assignment). Here there is the difficulty, however, that for all but the largest jobs, a comprehensive second partner review will usually be impracticable and uneconomic. Alternatively the second partner might merely be identified as the primary source of consultation whenever the reporting partner encounters a major problem. Whichever is the case, it is essential that the second partner's responsibilities in connection with the assignment should be well-defined and that, whatever the extent of his review, it be documented.

To work effectively, the second partner should be fully acquainted with the client, his business, and the nature of the audit. It may be best if, occasionally, the reporting partner and the second partner alternate responsibilities.

'Hot Reviews'

An alternative 'live' quality control procedure — and one which is likely to be more economically viable for the medium-sized or small audit — is to appoint a manager or senior staff member with responsibility for carrying out 'hot reviews'. The reviewer must, of course be otherwise independent of the job. All files would be submitted to him for examination before final review by the reporting partner. Here again, the reviewer's duties must be clearly defined, but he would normally be responsible for ensuring, *inter alia*:

that the audit files conform generally to the firm's standards;

that all relevant third party confirmations and a letter of representation have been obtained;

that the accounts comply with statutory or other requirements, including acceptable accounting policies;

that all final points for review have been drawn together for consideration by the reporting partner;

that an appropriate management letter has been drafted;

that all systems documentation has been reviewed and updated;

that the audit programme has been signed off and completed.

If the reviewer finds the files to be deficient in any of these respects, he should refer them back to the manager or other staff member responsible for the job before they are submitted to the reporting partner.

Post-audit Reviews

As to the post-audit quality control, its scope and nature will be tailored to suit the requirements of the particular practice. However, the objectives of post-audit reviews will generally be:

(*a*) to ensure that the standards laid down by the firm are being applied;

(*b*) to determine whether the scope and results of the audit work are properly documented, and adequate to support the audit opinion;

(*c*) to establish areas of weakness in the firm's procedures, and, where identified, to have new procedures implemented;

(*d*) to provide an independent review of files and, by discussing them with reporting partners and staff responsible, to assist them in improving their audit performance and to give full exposure to problem areas.

Of course only a small proportion of a firm's work can be reviewed each year. However, as far as possible, the programme should ensure that all partners are brought within its scope and that as many partners as possible become involved in the review process. In a multi-office practice, the reviews will, as far as is practicable, be carried out by partners from another office. In a single office practice it may sometimes be desirable to collaborate with other local practitioners in establishing this form of audit quality control.

The jobs would normally be selected by random sample, possibly stratified to ensure the inclusion of jobs at all fee levels.

The extent of post-audit review will be for each firm to decide. It should normally be carried out in some depth and the use of a checklist will encourage a consistent approach to the work. However, as is the case with all checklists, it should be made clear that the checklist only prescribes the minimum framework for the review. More important is that the reviewing partner should use his judgement in deciding what additional fields to cover in his review and which aspects of the files might require his more detailed attention.

A vital aspect of a post-audit review is the communication of its results. These must, of course, be fully discussed with the partner whose work has been subject to review and it is important here that the review should be seen to have been carried out in a constructive manner. The primary purpose of a quality control review is that its results can be used to the benefit of future performance. It is equally important therefore that, at the end of a series of reviews, the results of each review should be drawn together into a general summary. It may well then be prudent to destroy the results of the individual reviews. The summary should highlight areas of weakness within the firm and, if used properly, will provide both a valuable pointer as to which aspects of the firm's procedures require clarification or improvement and, similarly, an influence on the future course of a firm's in-house training programme at all levels.

12 Audit committees

Historical Background

Before considering the role of audit committees in modern business management, it is salutary to remind ourselves that the very first auditing of joint stock companies was undertaken by committees of shareholders who checked the accounts of the company on behalf of their fellow shareholders. Then gradually these audit committees of 'amateurs' were replaced by 'professionals' who did the work on behalf of the shareholders — as they still do in the UK. It is interesting, however, that in the USA, where there is no statutory audit, the auditor works not on behalf of the shareholders but on behalf of the Board.

Likewise the directors of the original joint stock companies in the UK were themselves a committee of members who directed the company for their fellow shareholders — whereas today it is often not even necessary for a director to be a shareholder at all, and most of them are full-time executive managers of the company.

Currently this whole relationship between the company, its shareholders, its executive and non-executive directors, and the auditor is the subject of public discussion and practical development within business. In this climate of change there has developed an important role for the independent non-executive outside director, who may, or may not, be a shareholder, and one of whose important tasks is seen as being that of ensuring that the shareholders' interests are adequately taken into account in the policy debates and decisions of the board. Whilst, of course, all members of a unitary board share the responsibility equally, and no doubt have the same loyalties to the company, nevertheless the full-time executive director does have additional responsibilities which can, and do, colour his viewpoint. For example, he has a direct responsibility for the workforce, whose interests do not always coincide with those of the shareholders. A strong desire on the part of the executive to maintain harmony in industrial relations can militate against the shareholders' interests, on whose behalf the independent outside director may consider himself as holding a watching brief. Similarly, the current responsibilities of the full-time executive director tend to focus his attention on the present and the short-term, so the view has developed that the independent outside director has a useful monitoring role to perform on behalf of the general long-term interests of the company, its shareholders, and those who work for it.

Development

Against this background, the audit committee can be seen as a practical mechanism for enabling the independent outside directors to fulfil their role effectively, although it was originally conceived as having a somewhat narrower role. Audit committees were first publicly endorsed in 1940 in the aftermath of the McKesson & Robbins scandal in the USA, to which reference is made in Chapter 14, when both the Securities and Exchange Commission (SEC) and the New York Stock Exchange (NYSE) advocated the creation of audit committees.

It took some twenty years for much development to take place, and it was not until 1976 that the NYSE introduced a requirement for audit committees into its listing agreement. Likewise the SEC has stepped up its campaign to get audit committees introduced in all listed companies; and in some cases, as a result of enforcement proceedings, has obliged individual corporations to establish audit committees with specific duties. The result of these pressures has been that the audit committee, composed of outside directors, has become established as a normal part of the structure of corporations in the USA.

Similar developments took place in Canada, where the Business Corporations Act of 1975, and the provincial company laws, require that corporations offering securities to the public must have an audit committee of not less than three directors. Some provinces stipulate that the majority of the audit committee must be outside directors.

In the UK, development of the idea has been much slower, and has sometimes been resisted by different parties on what appear to be 'idealogical' grounds. Sight seems to have been lost of the fact that it can be developed as a useful adjunct to good company management. It can also serve to plug an odd gap in UK Company Law — namely, that the shareholder, who legally appoints the auditor and to whom the auditor officially reports, has no right of communication with the auditor, other than to receive his report. An audit committee of outside directors, with the shareholders' interest in the forefront of their minds, can have effective communication with the auditor to discuss and probe the detailed matters which are of concern to the shareholders, and which the shareholders might have themselves wished to discuss with the auditor were they permitted to do so.

Nevertheless, development will depend, in practice, on factors which are peculiar to each individual company. In any event, for the small company, an audit committee might be an organizational sledgehammer — even if the company did have any independent outside directors, which is normally not the case. In the medium- and large-sized companies, actual development will vary from company to company according to:

the character and personality of the chairman of the board of directors;
the attitude of the managing director, or chief executive;
the personalities and experience of the outside directors on the board;
the history and character of the company itself, and its management.

Object of Committees

Against this background, the development of audit committees should be seen as having the object of developing auditing in the broadest sense — as compared with the external audit which has the relatively 'narrow' objective of enabling the auditor to express an opinion on the accounts. In this broad sense, the Auditing Practices Committee of the Consultative Committee of Accountancy Bodies (CCAB) has published a booklet on Auditing Committees written by Richard Buckley (1979) in which the view is expressed that audit committees can

(*a*) help directors to fulfil their responsibilities;
(*b*) strengthen the role of non-executive directors;
(*c*) strengthen the objectivity and credibility of financial reporting;
(*d*) strengthen the independence of the audit function;
(*e*) improve the quality of the audit and accounting functions;
(*f*) improve communication between directors, auditors, and management.

In addition, if the directors and management wish to do so, the audit committee can be developed as a useful mechanism by which the board can monitor the running of the business. Of course, both the chairman of the board, and the chief executive of the company have important and direct responsibilities in this area, which are in no way diminished by the role of the audit committee. But the fact remains that the board carries ultimate responsibility, which its audit committee can assist it to discharge, without impinging on the responsibilities of its chairman, or of the chief executive, any more than does the board in the normal execution of its duties. Indeed some chief executives have found in practice that the audit committee can provide them with valuable support and reassurance.

Purely from a management point of view, then, the audit committee can be given the objective of helping the board by carrying out what is, in effect, a management audit, in order:

(*a*) to see whether board policies, in the different areas of management, appear to be properly implemented in practice;

(*b*) to appraise the company's style of management, and of business conduct, particularly in sensitive areas:

(*c*) to assess the strengths and weaknesses of the organization, and the manner in which it is reacting to the opportunities and pressures which surround it;

(*d*) to see how management performance is evaluated at different levels, and to assess whether management succession is being adequately provided to meet the board's plans for the future.

If the audit committee is seen as a means of helping the board of directors to discharge its responsibilities more effectively, then it follows that the audit committee should not generally take decisions. It should report to the board, with recommendations where appropriate, and leave decisions to be taken by the board and the management structure below it.

Such a view of audit committees was endorsed by Mr Gordon Richardson, the Governor of the Bank of England, in a speech to the Institute of Directors in November 1978, in which he spoke of the experience of the Bank of England that

> 'in a number of problem cases with which the Bank had been involved, the likelihood of troubles being identified in good time might have been increased had an audit committee been in existence to help outside directors perform their function.'

He went on to express the view that the inclusion of outside directors in company boards was highly desirable to ensure:

(i) that management's plans were subjected to independent scrutiny;
(ii) that management succession was less incestuous;
(iii) that management was seen to be accountable.

Setting Up the Audit Committee

As indicated above, the audit committee would normally be a non-executive subcommittee of the board, working with the full authority of the latter. Its composition will depend on the circumstances of the particular company, and preferably should consist entirely of independent outside directors. However, in many companies this may not be practicable, but even then a majority of members should be non-executive directors. When executive directors are appointed to the committee, it is preferable that they be independent of any responsibility for financial management within the company. This latter requirement is particularly important as regards the chairman of the audit committee, upon whom will probably depend the success, or otherwise, of the committee.

It must inevitably take time for a newly appointed committee to develop its own skill and experience, and indeed to define more precisely the job which it is trying to do. It is, therefore, important to achieve a reasonable continuity of experience amongst the committee members, whilst balancing this against the desirability of achieving some rotation of membership in order to strengthen the independence of the committee. Each company will have to solve this problem in its own way.

In setting up an audit committee and establishing the basis on which it operates, the company must seek to ensure that

(*a*) the audit committee is seen to have the full authority and backing of the board;

(*b*) the committee is seen to be independent, both in the make-up of its membership, and in actual practice; and in particular that it is not under the influence of the chief executive;

(*c*) the committee has clear terms of reference, and all levels of management understand what the board expects it to do; and in particular that the committee does not create conflict by encroaching on the executive responsibility and authority of management at any level;

(*d*) the committee establishes a clear working relationship with financial management, the internal auditor, and the external auditor.

The precise means of achieving these ends must depend on the circumstances of each individual company, but the first step would normally be a Resolution of the Board, which formally establishes the audit committee. An example of such a Resolution is given below.

Board resolution

Audit Committee

1. After consideration of Board paper No. ....., dated.........., the Board *agreed* to establish a permanent non-executive sub-committee of the Board to be called the Audit Committee.
2. It was *agreed* that the Chairman of that Committee shall be one of the outside directors of the Company and shall for a period of five years but shall be eligible for reappointment. The Committee shall have four other members, of whom at least two shall be outside directors of the Company. Initially, one of the ordinary members shall retire each year in succession, but shall be eligible for reappointment. Thereafter, each ordinary member shall retire after three years.
3. The following are hereby *appointed* to the Audit Committee:

Mr	Chairman
Mr ....,	to retire in 19....
etc. ....,	to retire in 19....

4. It was *agreed* that the terms of reference of the Audit Committee should be as follows:

(*a*) To make recommendations to the Board concerning the

appointment and remuneration of the external auditors of the Group and of each of its subsidiary and associated companies;

(*b*) To review with the external auditor his terms of engagement and his proposed plan for the annual audit, and discuss with him any significant problems which he can foresee, or to which the Committee may wish to draw his attention, and to consider whether the auditor's terms of reference should be extended in any respect beyond the field of his statutory audit;

(*c*) In consultation with the chief internal auditor, the finance director of the Group, and the external auditor, to review the scope and effectiveness of internal audit procedures, to review the reports and findings of the internal audit department and, where considered appropriate by the Committee, to make recommendations;

(*d*) To keep under review the Group's systems of accounting, and internal control, and the system of reporting to management and to the boards of directors of the subsidiary companies, and of the Group;

(*e*) To review the auditor's evaluation of the system of internal control and accounting;

(*f*) To review with the auditor the results of his audit and discuss with him any matters which he may wish to raise, or on which the Committee may require further information or explanation either from the auditor or from management; also to review the letter of representation, and any other certificates or matters of confirmation provided by the Group to the auditor in connection with the annual accounts;

(*g*) To review the interim and annual financial statements before their submission to the Board for approval;

(*h*) To review the share registers in respect of dealings in the shares of the Group by employees, officers and directors of subsidiary or associated companies and of the Group;

(*i*) To meet either at the request of the external or internal auditor, or on the Committee's own initiative, to consider any matter which either the auditor, or the Committee, believes should be brought to the attention of the directors or shareholders;

(*j*) To review the procedures adopted throughout the Group for implementing the policies of the Board, to assess whether there are any weaknesses in those procedures, and, where considered appropriate by the Committee, to make recommendations;

(*k*) To monitor the Group's business conduct generally and particularly in sensitive areas; to appraise whether the style of management in different parts of the Group is best suited to achieve the objectives of the Board; and where appropriate, to make recommendations;

(*l*) To assess the strengths and weaknesses of the organization; and

assess whether it is reacting successfully to the opportunities and pressures which surround it;
(*m*) To see how management performance is evaluated at different levels; and to assess whether management succession is being adequately provided to meet the Board's plans for the future;
(*n*) To make recommendations to the Board regarding any change in these terms of reference which the Committee considers desirable.

5. Within the Group the Audit Committee has the authority of the Group Board to call for any documents, or other evidence, which it may require, and for explanations from any employees, officers or directors of the Group and of any of its subsidiaries, or associated companies.
6. The Audit Committee should report to the Group Board either formally in writing, or verbally, as it considers appropriate on the matters within its terms of reference at least once a year, but more frequently if it so wishes. It shall report to the Group Board on any specific matters referred to it by the Board for investigation and report.
7. The Audit Committee has the authority of the Group Board to incur reasonable expenses in carrying out its responsibilities including the out-of-pocket, hotel and travelling expenses of its members. It is also authorized to incur fees for the services of outside professional advisers or consultants up to an initial budget of £ . The members of the Audit Committee shall be entitled to a *per diem* fee of £ pro rata for the work undertaken. The total of its annual expenditure shall be included in its annual report to the Group Board.
8. It was *agreed* that the Group Managing Director will circulate a memorandum to all Heads of Departments at Group Headquarters and to all Managing Directors of Subsidiary and Associated Companies explaining the setting up of this Committee, together with a copy of its Terms of Reference.

The Committee's style of operating will depend critically upon the individuals concerned, but it is essential that it establish a spirit of mutual co-operation and trust with all parts of the organization. This is particularly important as regards the chairman of the board and the chief executive of the company, on whose executive responsibility and authority the audit committee must not trespass in any way. However, it has been found in practice that an audit committee can relieve the chief executive of what might be termed the approbrium of simply checking up on line management, and he can largely leave to the committee the task of monitoring the whole system of internal control.

From the point of view of the external auditor it, of course, provides a channel of communication with the board, though only his report can provide a channel of communication to the shareholders. If the external auditor finds himself faced with a difficult, or delicate, situation, particularly if it involves the chief executive or other senior directors or managers, then the audit committee can be most valuable to him. It is for this reason that clause 4(i) above of the terms of reference gives the auditor the right to approach the chairman of the audit committee to request a meeting with the committee.

As regards the internal auditor much will depend on the particular circumstances as to how his relationship with the audit committee is built up. Much will depend on the internal audit department's size, the scope of its responsibility and authority, and its established reporting procedures. However, since the audit committee should have a strong non-executive bias, it would be entirely wrong for the internal audit department to be put directly under the control of the audit committee. Nevertheless, clause 4(i) of the above terms of reference gives the internal auditor the same right of direct access to the audit committee as it gives to the external auditor. In practice, this should help to strengthen the position of the internal auditor, and provide an effective channel of communication between the internal auditor, the board, and the external auditor.

Method of Operation

It will be found in practice that the timing of meetings of the audit committee needs to be scheduled well in advance in order to fit in with what is normally a very tight timetable for the production of the company's interim and final accounts. Likewise the audit committee may want to plan meetings with different departments and subsidiary companies, so that over a period of years it covers the whole of the area included in its terms of reference.

It will almost certainly find it useful to keep minutes of its meetings, but this may present problems if its terms of reference include matters such as clause 4(*j*) above. Discussion between the audit committee and senior directors and managers may be inhibited if it takes place in the knowledge that the matters raised will be minuted and those minutes circulated. There is also the problem of finding an individual of sufficient seniority and confidentiality to do the minute-taking.

The committee will have to decide on the extent to which its minutes are circulated beyond its own membership. It may well decide that some, or all, minutes should go to:

members of the main board;

the external auditor;

the internal auditor;

where appropriate, the heads of main departments such as the finance department;

where appropriate, the managing directors of subsidiary companies or associated companies.

However, internal distribution of the committee's minutes below the level of the main board should be made through the chief executive.

Above all, minutes are useful in order to ensure that there is a proper follow-up of the matters on which the audit committee decides that action is needed. Although the committee has no executive authority itself, it will probably find it sufficient if a copy of the appropriate minute is sent as a recommendation to the managing director, or chief executive. More important matters may have to go as a recommendation to the board of directors. Subsequent meetings of the audit committee will need to follow up whether, or not, the recommended action was taken. If there is not adequate explanation as to why no action has been taken, then the audit committee will have to take the matter up with the chief executive or the chairman of the board.

Audit Committee Questionnaire

As the audit committee tackles its job, it will help to focus the thrust of its inquiries if it prepares in advance of each meeting a list of questions which it proposes to discuss. It may circulate these questions only to its own members, or it may decide to send some of them in advance to those concerned, so as to give time for the information to be prepared, and so as to avoid meetings of the audit committee taking on too much of the air of an inquisition.

Likewise the preparation of a set of detailed questions can help the audit committee to ensure that, over a period of time, it covers the whole of the ground in its terms of reference; for the committee would not attempt to cover the whole of an extensive questionnaire in the course of each year's work.

Section 1

Questions for discussion with management before the year's audit starts

1.1 Is there any reason for making any change of auditor, either for the Group as a whole, or for any of the subsidiary or associated companies?

1.2 Are any problems expected regarding the fees likely to be charged by the external auditors?

1.3 Are there any points which need to be raised with the auditor before he starts the audit of this year's accounts?

Section 2

Questions for discussion with the external auditor before the year's audit starts

2.1 With reference to his original letter of engagement, does the auditor see the need for any change in the terms of his engagement?

2.2 What is the auditor's time budget for the audit work to be undertaken in the coming year?

2.3 What are the rates to be charged for the different grades of staff and what is the budget of fees to be charged for auditing the year's accounts?

2.4 What other services does the auditor perform for the Group, and how are these charged and to whom?

2.5 Does the auditor perform any personal services for any of the people employed in the Group, and are any of the audit personnel employed on such work?

2.6 Does the auditor do audit, tax, or accountancy work for any other activities, or funds, related to the Group, such as sports or social clubs?

2.7 What degree of continuity from previous years will there be in the audit staff?

2.8 Who is the second audit partner concerned with the audit and what role is it proposed he play during the forthcoming assignment?

2.9 What is the scope of the audit in terms of UK subsidiary companies and locations visited? What is omitted and why? Are any other firms of independent auditors involved, and if so, how?

2.10 What arrangements are being made to audit the overseas subsidiaries? Is another firm of overseas auditors involved? If so, what are the terms of relationship with those other auditors? How frequent, and in what form, is the contact with the other auditors? To what extent does the auditor review the work performed by the other auditors?

2.11 Are any changes expected in:

(*a*) the levels of materiality used during the audit;
(*b*) The emphasis of the audit;
(*c*) the timing of the different parts of the audit?

2.12 Is the scope of the audit likely to be affected by changes in:

(*a*) accounting standards;
(*b*) generally accepted accounting principles;
(*c*) auditing standards;
(*d*) reporting requirements instituted by regulatory authorities such as the Stock Exchange, EEC, etc.?

2.13 Can the auditor foresee any particular developments either within the business, or outside it, which are likely to cause the auditor problems in the future?

2.14 Are any prospective changes of personnel within the Group likely to cause the auditor problems, or on the contrary, facilitate his task?

2.15 Are there any significant problems which the auditor can foresee arising in the near future? Or in the distant future?

2.16 What is the basic approach to the proposed audit, and is it to be systems oriented or by detailed testing of transactions?

2.17 Has the auditor staff with the necessary training and experience to audit the computer operations?

2.18 What is the proposed timing of the audit, and if verification steps are carried out prior to the year-end, how does the auditor propose to cover transactions between the verification date and the year-end?

2.19 Is there any work which could be undertaken by the internal audit or other staff of the Group which would simplify the auditor's task, and reduce the time spent by him and his staff on the audit?

Section 3

Questions for discussion with the external auditor after the interim audit

3.1 What is the level of experience of the staff who have been employed on the audit, and will there be any changes at the time of the year-end audit?

3.2 To what extent was the work of the internal auditors integrated with the work of the external auditor? Is there any scope for further integration? Is the auditor satisfied with the level of experience, skills, and general effectiveness of the internal auditors?

3.3 Does the auditor have any comments to make on:
(*a*) the quality of the internal accounting records;
(*b*) internal accounting policies;
(*c*) the timeliness, relevance and completeness of the accounting information provided to management for the running of the business?

3.4 Are there any areas where the auditor considers that the advantages of better internal control would be sufficient to warrant the cost of additional controls?

3.5 Are there any changes of any other kind within the Group which the auditor would advocate?

3.6 Did the auditor encounter any problems in connection with computer systems?

3.7 Is the auditor satisfied that the computer equipment, programs and data are:
(*a*) adequately controlled to prevent improper use;
(*b*) secured against fire risk;
(*c*) duplicated, or otherwise protected, against risk of accidental loss or damage?

3.8 Are there any matters of internal control which the auditor raised in his management letters in the course of past years' audits, which have not been dealt with?

Section 4

Questions for discussion with management at the time of the interim audit

4.1 What steps has management taken to correct deficiencies in internal control
(*a*) brought to their notice by the auditor;
(*b*) of which they became aware, independently of the auditor?

4.2 What points have been raised by the auditor in his management letter, and what has management done about them?

4.3 Does management consider that physical security of plant, premises and other assets is adequate?

4.4 What steps are taken to control personal transactions going through the books, such as private purchases at trade prices?

4.5 Are there any grounds for thinking that any significant amount of business is being done in any part of the Group with, or through, the relative of an employee of the Group?

4.6 Are there any unusual features in the half-yearly statement being submitted to the board for subsequent distribution to shareholders; and how do these results compare with the monthly management accounts to the same date?

4.7 Is there any reason to doubt the value of stock and work-in-progress at the date of the half-yearly statement?

4.8 Are there any other special provisions or reserves which ought to be made at the date of the half-yearly statement?

4.9 Are the subsequent half-year's results expected to differ very markedly from those now being published?

Section 5

Questions for discussion with management when appropriate

Audit

5.1 Are there any matters which might require special investigation by the auditor, beyond the field of his statutory audit, in particular any potentially sensitive subjects such as:

(*a*) conflicts of interest;
(*b*) incompetent or inadequately trained staff in any departments;
(*c*) inaccurate budgeting, or estimating;
(*d*) inadequate security of assets;
(*e*) potential areas of defalcation, or fraud;
(*f*) transactions of dubious legality (including bribery);
(*g*) any other matters of concern to management although not directly related to the audit function?

Board policies

5.2 What steps are taken by subsidiary company directors to disseminate, and ensure compliance with, resolutions of the Group, or subsidiary company, Board?

Reporting procedures

5.3 Does management have any comments to make on the timeliness, relevance and completeness of reports to:

(*a*) members of management;
(*b*) directors of subsidiary companies;
(*c*) the Group Board?

Operating procedures

5.4 What operating procedures have been reviewed by management with a view to making them more effective and less expensive?

Environmental pollution

5.5 Do any of our activities pollute the environment in any way? If so, what would be the cost of eliminating the pollution?

Products

5.6 What products or services have been studied by management with a view to reducing their cost and increasing their profit?

5.7 What steps are subsidiary companies taking regarding the development of:

(*a*) new products;
(*b*) new markets for old products?
(*c*) and what are our competitors doing in these fields?

5.8 Do any of our products involve a significant product risk? If so, what would insurance cover cost?

Cash, etc.

5.9 What explanation is there for any major divergence during the year between the actual bank (+ cash) balance and the projected cash flow for the year?

5.10 Who 'authorizes transfers between current account and deposit account or short-term investments? In what is he authorized to invest funds? Have any losses (or profits) been made on any such investments?

5.11 Are any such deposits, or investments, pledged or encumbered in any way? Who holds the certificates?

5.12 Who is authorized to accept Bills of Exchange? To what amount? On the other hand, do we ever draw Bills of Exchange on customers? Have any been dishonoured?

5.13 Have we ever cashed a cheque for an employee, and had it 'bounce'? Or been asked for loans by any employees? Did we make any such loans? Have they been repaid?

5.14 How much actual cash do we have on different premises? Do we really need to?

5.15 How are foreign exchange transactions handled, and are there any forward dealings? What is our open position?

Sales

5.16 Who fixes selling prices, and how? How often do we get it wrong? How do we take account of inflation?

5.17 How are estimates prepared for contracts, and who is authorized to fix the price at which a tender is submitted?

5.18 If we win the contract, do the works check the budgeted cost against the estimate? What mistakes has this brought to light recently? What about subsequent actual costs?

5.19 If delivery is a long time ahead, who takes what steps to cover us against rising costs of bought in materials and components and wages?

5.20 A contract having been taken at an agreed price, the customer may subsequently agree additions, or modifications, to the original contract. How do we ensure that this gets properly recorded, and that cash payments therefor do not get misappropriated?

Debtors

5.21 Have any sales invoices been factored, or pledged in any way? If so why?

5.22 How are credit levels fixed for different customers? How often are they breached and what was done about it?

5.23 Do we have any special arrangements for providing finance for stocks of our goods in the hands of customers? If so, are we entirely satisfied that each customer can meet his commitments? Does title to such goods remain ours until sold by the customer?

5.24 How are debts 'aged', reviewed, chased and recovered?
5.25 What large debts have been written-off recently? Are any substantial current debts probably uncollectable? What is the trend of our bad-debt experience over recent years?
5.26 Are any debts outstanding from directors or employees of the Group?

Purchases

5.27 How are levels of authority fixed as to who can commit the Group, for purchases or services, up to what amount? When did somebody last exceed their authorization limit, and what was done about it?
5.28 How do we control modifications to contracts which we have put out to suppliers to ensure that payment is not made for goods or services which we have not received?
5.29 Can any forward commitments be entered into? Are there any?
5.30 What regulations are there about suppliers and others sending presents to purchase officers and other employees? When did it last happen and what was done about it? How do we know that it is not still happening?
5.31 Where repeat orders are regularly needed for goods or services are purchase orders correctly issued each time?
5.32 Are procedures for obtaining competitive tenders for purchases properly carried out?

Creditors

5.33 Do we pay all our creditors promptly, and how promptly? If not, who authorizes the delay, and why?
5.34 Are there any disputes, or pending writs, in respect of amounts we owe to suppliers or others? What are the largest amounts which have recently been in dispute, and how were the disputes settled?

Stocks and work-in-progress

5.35 What different treatment is given to high-value and low-value items?
5.36 Is the physical security of high-value items adequate? What have we recently lost?
5.37 Have we undertaken strategic stock-piling of any materials? If so, what material, why, how many months' usage, and of what total value?
5.38 How do we control stock and plant out on sites? What have we recently lost? What about loose tools in the works?
5.39 How much slow moving and obsolete stock have we as a proportion of the total stock of each class?
5.40 Of what important items have we recently run out of stock? If none, are we holding unnecessarily large stocks?
5.41 How are stock levels, and re-order quantities, fixed? How and when were they last reviewed? With what result?
5.42 How do we control the disposal of unwanted stock, scrap, etc.? How did the price we got for it compare with the book write-off?

Guarantees and insurance

5.43 What guarantees have been given within the Group, and what is the potential liability thereunder?

5.44 Does the Group itself carry any part of any insured risk? If so, what is the potential liability? Have we ECGD cover on all our exports?

5.45 What insurance cover is maintained, of what risks, and is it reviewed regularly to ensure adequacy in times of inflation, and in the light of changes in trading patterns?

Assets

5.46 What asset registers are maintained, and by whom? How is the physical existence of the asset checked against the register? When did we last find that we had lost an asset? What? Could it happen again? What about office equipment, typewriters, pocket calculators?

5.47 For whom do we provide cars? Who authorizes each purchase? Do we provide anything else, or any other perks, or benefits?

5.48 Do we lease any cars, or plant, or other equipment? How are these identified on the asset registers? Do we capitalize the lease commitment, or else how do we account for these items? Do the asset and capitalized liability on the lease both appear in the accounts?

5.49 How do we capitalize plant made in our own works? Do we take out any patents on this?

5.50 Do we take out patents on designs from our own Design Office? Should we capitalize the value of any such patents?

5.51 How do we account for trade marks, goodwill or other intangible assets?

5.52 What idle, and unused, plant or equipment have we got? Or empty buildings or land? How is this acounted for? What are we going to do about it? Will there be any losses to write off? Or profits to be made or realization?

5.53 How do we decide when plant is obsolete? What new technology are we investigating? Shall we be ready to install new technology before the current methods become obsolete? Can our projected cash flow support the investment?

5.54 Is any property mortgaged or pledged in any way as security for loans or other commitments?

5.55 Have our insurers placed any special limits or conditions on the insurance cover of any buildings, plant or equipment?

Personnel

5.56 How do our rates of pay compare with those in the area? Can we recruit the skilled employees we need? And the right type of youngsters?

5.57 How do we identify 'high fliers' and what steps do we take to train them and give them opportunities to rise?

5.58 What senior, skilled, or key personnel have we had to dismiss recently, and why, and who authorized it?

5.59 Who has recently left of their own accord—and we wished they had not? How could we prevent this happening again?

5.60 How do we assess management performance at different levels and what mistakes have we made in promotions? Can we correct them?

5.61 Are we satisfied that, in the light of inflation, we have fulfilled all our moral obligations to all our pensioners, their widows and families? If not, what might the liability be?

5.62 Have any recommendations been made regarding health and safety at any of our places of work by Factory Inspectors, Trades Union Safety Representatives, Fire Officers, Police Authorities, Health or Medical Authorities, which we have not yet put into effect? What might the cost be?

Share transactions

5.63 Have any material dealings in the shares of the Group been undertaken by the relatives of, or the individuals themselves, who are:
(*a*) employees;
(*b*) officers;
(*c*) directors;
of a subsidiary company or of the Group?

5.64 Has any such person requested permission to deal in the shares of the Group and been refused such permission?

5.65 Does the auditor, or any member of his staff, hold any shares in the Group?

5.66 Do any important competitors, suppliers or customers, hold shares in the Group?

5.67 Have any shareholders substantially increased their holdings during the year?

Section 6

Questions for discussion with management before the accounts are finalized

6.1 Is management reasonably satisfied that:
(*a*) the auditor and his staff carried out their work satisfactorily;
(*b*) covered all aspects adequately?

6.2 What has the auditor required in the way of:
(*a*) letters of representation;
(*b*) other certificates?
In what respects do these differ from those required in previous years? Did management have any doubt, or reservations, about any of the figures provided? How were those doubts resolved?

6.3 Are any subsidiary companies not consolidated? Why not?

6.4 Did any unusual, and significant event occur during the year such as:
(*a*) the acquisition of a new business;
(*b*) the commissioning of new plant;
(*c*) the purchase, or erection, of new buildings;
(*d*) the leasing of substantial assets;
(*e*) the disposal of significant segments of the business?
If so, how were these transactions treated in the financial statements? And, how does it affect comparability with last year's figures?

6.5 Has any new capital been raised, or substantial borrowing undertaken? If so, is it correctly shown? And, does it affect comparability with last year's figures?

6.6 What have been the limits on overdrafts or other forms of fluctuating borrowings, and have these limits ever been breached during the year? Or substantially changed? If so, why?

6.7 Are there any unusual items in the financial statements such as:
(*a*) prior period adjustments;
(*b*) extraordinary items;
(*c*) transfers direct to, or from, reserves;
(*d*) capital profits, or losses, or special write-offs;
(*e*) transfers between subsidiary companies?
If so, what accounting treatment has been given them? And, what alternative treatments were there?

6.8 Has adequate provision been made for contingencies? Do the financial statements adequately disclose other unusual uncertainties?

6.9 Has the Group or any subsidiary company entered into contracts or agreements involving long-term or unusual commitments, which have not been disclosed in the financial statements?

6.10 Were there any items which were on the threshold of materiality which it was decided not to disclose separately in the financial statements? If so, what were they? And, what would the separate disclosure have been?

6.11 Are the financial statements significantly affected by transactions which were not at arm's length? If so, what was the impact of such transactions on the statements?

6.12 To what extent do the financial statements take account of post-balance-sheet events? Are there any omissions in this respect?

6.13 How does the total of debtors and amounts due to the Group compare with the previous years, and with the current level of trading?

6.14 Is management satisfied about the cut-off procedure at the year-end in connection with goods and services and current liabilities? When did the procedure last go wrong?

6.15 How did the physical stocktake compare with the book figure? How did the year-end stock adjustment compare with previous years?

6.16 What is the basis of year-end stock valuation; and who fixes, and how, the cost or realizable value?

6.17 How does the Group depreciation policy compare with the actual physical life of the assets? How do we treat assets which have been written-off but are still in use—in the annual accounts; in costs and in the management accounts? What are we doing about inflation accounting?

6.18 What items are in dispute with the Inland Revenue in connection with our tax assessments? Is there any likelihood of a material increase, or reduction, in our liability?

6.19 How much of the deferred tax liability is likely to be paid in cash in the near future? If a slump, or strike, or other calamity caused a material fall in our sales, and also a material reduction in the level of our stock and work-in-progress, might we have to pay tax deferred by stock appreciation relief?

6.20 Have we met all our obligations to our debenture holders or other providers of long-term loans? Will any of these fall due for repayment in the near future?

6.21 How does the trend of sales of different products and services compare with previous years, and with what was budgeted? How is the difference explained, and can we separately identify the separate effects of price changes and volume changes?

6.22 Do we have any overseas contracts running in countries with a high political risk? Or countries where exchange control regulations are liable to change?

6.23 Have we any major disputes with customers over which we may incur a material liability?

6.24 How do we cover ourselves against fluctuations in exchange rates? Both for sales, and also any purchases abroad? What is the extent of our exposure?

6.25 Do we have personnel, or investments, in countries where there is a danger of expropriation, or loss? If so, what is our potential write off, and what might be the cost of our responsibilities to our personnel?

6.26 Does the Source and Application of Funds Statement include any significant transactions which have been netted one against another? Are all non-recurring, or unusual, items fully disclosed?

6.27 What undisclosed provisions were brought forward from last year's trading and how were these disposed of? What undisclosed provisions are we making in these financial statements?

6.28 In the case of our long-term trade investments, what do we assess to be their current value in the light of earnings and asset values, as compared with their book value?

6.29 Are any of our quoted investments not readily marketable?

6.30 Is there any doubt as to whether any of our associated companies, or trading partners, will have the liquid funds to pay us on the due dates what they owe us under loan or trading agreements?

6.31 Are there any restrictions on what can be distributed, or remitted, in the way of profits by any of our subsidiary or associated companies in the UK or overseas?

6.32 In view of the impact of inflation on the cash resources of the Group should any restriction be imposed on the amount of dividend distribution, either by the Group or any of its subsidiaries?

6.33 Are there any legal actions pending either in the UK or overseas in which substantial claims might be made against us? If the claim has to be noted on the accounts as a contingent liability, how can this be done without prejudicing our position in the courts?

Section 7

Questions for discussion with the external auditor after the year-end audit, but before the accounts are finalized

7.1 What is the wording which the auditor proposes for his report, and what is the significance of any deviation from the normal form, or from the wording used in previous years?

7.2 Are there any particular problems which the auditor encounters now, which he used not to encounter?

7.3 Has the auditor identified any matters which in his view merit special investigtion either by management or by the internal auditor, or by the external auditor himself outside the field of his statutory audit?

7.4 Did the auditor receive full co-operation from all personnel in the Group?

7.5 Was there any attempt, either overt or covert, to restrict the scope of the auditor's work in any way?

7.6 To what extent has the auditor had to rely on the professional opinion of experts, with regard to such matters as:
(*a*) the valuation of properties;
(*b*) the valuation of plant and machinery;
(*c*) the valuation of stocks, or work-in-progress;
(*d*) actuarial valuations of pension, or other funds or liabilities?

7.7 Was the auditor satisfied with regard to the working of cut-off procedures in connection with:
(*a*) services and supplies;
(*b*) goods-inwards, stocks, and current liabilities;
(*c*) finished stocks, goods-outwards, and debtors?

7.8 Were there any differences of opinion with management relating to judgement items such as:
(*a*) depreciation;
(*b*) slow moving, or obsolete, stock;
(*c*) bad, or doubtful, debts;
(*d*) warranty provisions;
(*e*) contract terms?
How were such differences resolved?

7.9 What audit steps were taken regarding any significant transactions out of the ordinary course of business, such as:
(*a*) investment in new plant;
(*b*) new business activities?

7.10 Have any of the Group's funds been placed under the personal control, or discretionary use, of any director or employee of the Group?

7.11 To what extent has the auditor tested different ratios disclosed by the financial statements, and do any of these disclose significant fluctuations?

7.12 To what extent has the auditor tested the financial statements against the management accounts, and did this disclose any significant differences?

7.13 Are there any covenants, or requirements, of trust deeds, bankers, or other lenders which must be met in the preparation of these financial statements, and which do not appear to have been met, or which need to be disclosed?

7.14 Have there been any changes in the accounting principles used during the year, or changes in the method of applying those principles? If so, why? What has been the effect? Does the auditor agree that, in the circumstances, the changes are:
(*a*) appropriate;
(*b*) preferable to what was done before?

7.15 Did the auditor have any significant disagreements with management as to:
(*a*) accounting policies;
(*b*) disclosures in financial statements?

7.16 To what extent do the accounting principles used now by the Group conform with those currently being developed for *future* use:
(*a*) in business generally;
(*b*) in this industry in particular?

7.17 How do these financial statements compare with those of companies in similar situations and industries as to:
(*a*) extent, and
(*b*) method of disclosure?

7.18 Do the statements fail in any way to meet statutory requirements? To what extent do the statements fail to conform to the best professional standards of disclosure?

7.19 Should there be incorporated now in these financial statements any changes pending, or in prospect, in statutory, contractual, or professional requirements, or standards, which might affect future disclosure?

Of course, it is not envisaged that every audit committee would discuss all the above questions every year. Some committees will in any case have more restricted terms of reference, whilst others may be given a wider field to cover. Nor are the questions necessarily exhaustive. In particular circumstances there will be important matters to consider which are not included above. The above questions are set out as an indication of the sort of ground which an audit committee ought to cover. Some questions it will discuss every year. Other parts of the questionnaire it will aim to cover bit by bit as the years go by.

Problems

Any innovation is bound to run into objections and problems. It has been suggested that an audit committee might create divisions within a board and conflicts with the executive management of the company. Of course it could, but there is no reason why it should. Any board can create subcommittees for any purpose without causing itself problems, so long as the subcommittee remains clearly subordinate to its board. There is, therefore, no reason why an audit committee should create problems if its members behave sensibly, and remember the collective responsibility of the whole board.

It is for this same reason that it is considered that an audit committee must not report directly to the shareholders, as some people advocate that it should. Were it to do so, it must automatically tend to create divisions within a board. An audit committee which reported to the shareholders would take on the nature of a supervisory body, along the lines of the two-tier board practised in some countries. The collective responsibility of the board is better preserved by keeping the audit committee strictly as a non-executive subcommittee of that board.

In the same vein, there is no reason for a non-executive audit committee to create conflicts with executive management. All the questions suggested for discussion above are ones about which any board of directors is entitled to obtain reassurance. In this case it is envisaged that the audit committee will satisfy itself about these matters on behalf of the whole board. Having more time to do so, the audit committee is more likely to arrive at a sensible conclusion than would a full board of directors with all the other day-to-day matters which must occupy the time of its meetings.

However, it is important that the audit committee avoids springing surprises on executive management, as for example could happen if the auditor raised with the committee a matter which he had not discussed with management. Only if the matter were one of supreme personal sensitivity should this ever happen, if management are not to feel that the auditor is going 'behind their backs'. For the same reason, the committee will probably invite the relevant members of management to attend those parts of their meetings at which the managers' responsibilities are being discussed. Or, if they do not attend the meetings, arrange through the chief executive that they receive the relevant extracts of the minutes.

Advantages

The advantages obtained from setting up an audit committee will depend on how the whole operation is undertaken, from setting it up, to selecting its members, to it doing its job. Experience demonstrates that it can be a useful instrument in helping a board to see that the company is run in the way in which the board are seeking to run it.

It can assist the board, particularly the independent non-executive outside directors, to achieve a much better understanding of the company's affairs. Indeed it could prove to be one of the best ways of increasing the usefulness and effectiveness of outside directors within a business. Discussion of the sort of questions outlined above is bound to improve their knowledge and understanding of the way the company operates, and its problems and opportunities. But, of course, it requires time — time of the outside director to attend the discussions of the committee.

Perhaps of more importance is the opportunity it provides for the directors on the committee to meet and get to know the subsidiary company directors and line managers at lower levels within the organization, in the course of discussing the questions outlined above. As time goes by this could be of great help to the committee members when assessing proposals to the main board for promotion to senior management, or to subsidiary company boards, or even to the Group board.

On the other side, practice shows that the discussions of the audit committee with directors and managers of subsidiary companies or departments can be very beneficial to the morale of the whole organization. Admittedly, junior managers may find it a gruelling test of their knowledge of their own business; but at the same time they find it encouraging that senior directors of the Group are prepared to spend time to discuss in detail the operations of the subsidiary companies and departments for which the junior managers are responsible.

13 Special audits

The principles of auditing demonstrated in the earlier chapters should ensure no difficulty in managing audits of varying types of conern.

However, certain types of special audit do require specialized knowledge and, in some cases, familiarity with statutes and regulations other than the Companies Acts. It is essential that such knowledge be assimilated prior to starting the assignment. The effectiveness of the work programme will be dependent upon it and no auditor will ever be able to plead ignorance as a justifiable excuse for any shortcomings in his work.

In addition, the auditor has a special role to play in connection with prospectuses and profit forecasts, which is described below.

Share transfers

An auditor must audit the share books upon an issue of shares, and when calls are made, in order that he may satisfy himself that the whole of the money due has been accounted for. In subsequent years, it is not part of his duty to carry out a transfer audit. All that is necessary is that the balances upon the share ledger should be checked onto a list of balances to see that the total thereof agrees with the total issued capital. However, auditors are often instructed to carry out transfer audits, but this is a matter of special arrangement. The procedure at a transfer audit should be as follows:

(*a*) Check transfers with the transfer register, making certain that transfers have been properly signed and stamped, and check the distinctive numbers of the shares into the register. Thereafter, cancel the transfer with the auditor's audit stamp. If the shares have been converted into stock, there will, of course, not be any distinctive numbers to check.

(*b*) Verify a proportion of the signatures of transferors with shareholders' previous transfers, application letters, or dividend instructions.

(*c*) Check old certificates with transfers, and thereafter cancel the certificates.

(*d*) Check entries in the transfer register to the credit of the transferor's account in share ledger, seeing that he has the shares and checking the distinctive numbers.

(*e*) Check entries in the transfer register to debit of the transferee's account in share ledger.

(*f*) Check and initial new certificates, and if the transferor has not sold the whole of his shares, check and initial balance certificates issued to him.

(*g*) At subsequent audits, see the directors' minute passing the transfers previously checked.

(*h*) Count the number of transfers, and see that the whole of the transfer fees have been accounted for.

Special audits under other statutes

The following is a list of other concerns, which will be dealt with less frequently by most auditors, and for which the auditor will need to refer to other statutes and regulations.

Banks.
Building societies.
Charities.
Churches.
Friendly societies, etc.
Insurance companies.
Underwriting Syndicates at Lloyds
Local authorities.
Nationalized industries.
Solicitors.
Trustee Savings Banks.
Stockbrokers, and stock jobbers.
Trusts.

In all such special cases, the auditor must be absolutely sure that he is not only fully conversant with the statutes and regulations concerned, but also fully understands the peculiarities and technicalities of the operations being accounted for. If he is not confident of his own mastery of the subject, he would be wise not to undertake the audit, and instead pass the work to a professional colleague who has practical experience of that particular field.

Prospectus for a capital issue

When a limited company raises capital by means of a public issue of shares or debentures, a prospectus, containing the information specified in Part I, Fourth Schedule, Companies Act 1948, must be compiled by the directors. In addition, both the auditors of the company and any other independent accountants (normally known as the 'reporting accountants') must submit reports giving the information required by Part II of the Fourth Schedule. Where a private company becomes a public company without a public issue, a statement in lieu of a prospectus must be filed with the Registrar of Companies and reporting accountants must report in similar terms.

As far as the work of the reporting accountants is concerned this is, of course, undertaken in the knowledge that audits under the Companies Acts have already taken place, normally without qualification. The accounts of the company should therefore comply with the requirements of the Companies Acts and, to a large extent, the figures from these accounts which it is necessary to publish, will therefore be readily available. The reporting accountants themselves, however, will need to ensure the correctness of the figures used and will need to see the company's records and the auditors' working papers. Other aspects besides these are relevant and require careful consideration, especially the adequacy of the information regarding the ascertainment of stocks and work-in-progress and the consistency in the bases of their valuation, the reasonableness of provisions for depreciation and amortization, the adequacy of the provision for deferred taxation, and the extent to which the accounts have been drawn up in accordance with the standard accounting practices of the accountancy bodies.

Often, as a result of the investigation and in order to show a true picture, adjustments are made to the figures shown in the audited annual accounts. In this event Part III of the Fourth Schedule requires that the report shall indicate that such adjustments have been made. Recommendation N16 of the English Institute, 'Accountants' reports for prospectuses: adjustments and other matters', issued in 1953, explains:

> 'The accountants' report is necessarily confined to past results and does not purport to deal with future prospects. The intending investor is concerned with the future and he will regard the accountants' report, showing the trend of past results, as being submitted to assist him in forming his own assessment of the prospects. It may therefore be necessary, in order that the trend of past profits may be fairly presented having regard to the purposes of the prospectus, either to make appropriate comments thereon or to adjust the figures.
>
> The circumstances in which adjustments to the figures of profits or losses are usually required fall generally under the following headings:
>
> (*a*) where there are material facts which should have been taken into account in preparing the profit and loss accounts for the various years covered by the report if those facts had been known at the time when the accounts were prepared;
>
> (*b*) where there have been material sources of revenue or categories of expenditure which are expected not to recur;
>
> (*c*) where during the period covered by the report there has been a material change in the accounting principles applied or where accepted accounting principles have not been applied.'

And in Recommendation S18 issued in 1972, dealing with the absence of detailed stock records:

> 'It is difficult to give generalized advice to members, but it is considered that a serious deficiency in information casting doubt on the results of any of the last three years to be covered, in particular where the trend of profit might be materially distorted, would be grounds for the reporting accountants declining to allow their name to be associated with the prospectus.

'Similar considerations will apply to auditors appointed during or after the period concerned since they are, in relation to years prior to their appointment, in the same position as reporting accountants, with the exception that they cannot decline to report since they are required to do so by the Companies Act 1948. In such cases their qualification should give appropriate emphasis to the reasons for it and may even include a disclaimer of opinion.

'Where the reporting accountants or the present auditors are qualifying their reports on these grounds, confirmation should still be sought from the auditors acting for periods for which records are no longer available that they examined those records during their audit of the accounts of the years in question and were satisfied at that time that the stocks were properly and consistently ascertained and valued. It will generally be appropriate to refer to these assurances in the reservation.'

Profit forecasts

Over recent years auditors have become increasingly involved in profit forecast reports and this represents a unique departure for the profession. Hitherto reporting accountants had been concerned solely with certifying historical reports which could therefore, in the majority of instances, amount entirely to statements of fact. However much profit forecasts rely on the historical performance pattern, the forecasts must finally be based on commercial assumptions and the reporting accountant must therefore use his utmost skill in considering these. It must be emphasized that the actual forecasts are the responsibility of the directors only and that the auditors' duty is to verify the accounting bases and calculations.

Profit forecast reports can be required in varying instances. They may be required as part of a general investigation into the purchase of a business, or as part of a prospectus for a public issue of shares. Issued in 1978 mainly in connection with the latter, Statement S23 of the Institute of Chartered Accountants in England and Wales gives valuable guidance. In particular:

'Review of a profit forecast

In carrying out their review, the main matters to which the reporting accountants will direct their attention are as follows:

(*a*) the nature and background of the company's business;
(*b*) the accounting practices normally followed by the company;
(*c*) the assumptions on which the forecasts are based;
(*d*) the procedures followed by the company for preparing forecasts.

The nature and background of the company's business

The reporting accountants will wish to review the company's general management and recent history, with reference to such matters as the general nature of its activities and its main products, markets, customers, suppliers, divisions, locations, labour force and trend of results.

The accounting policies normally followed by the company
The reporting accountants will wish to establish which accounting policies have been adopted by the company in published financial statements so as to ensure that they are acceptable and have been consistently supplied in the preparation of interim accounts and the profit forecast.

The assumptions on which forecasts are based
It is the responsibility of the reporting accountants to determine that the profit forecast is consistent with and has been properly complied on the footing of the given assumptions . . . the reporting accountants have no specific responsibilities for and are not required by the regulations to report on the assumptions. However, in the course of their work on the accounting policies and calculations, they will need to consider the assumptions on which the profit forecast has been based. They should not allow an assumption to be published which appears to them to be unrealistic (or one to be omitted which appears to them to be important) without commenting on it in their report.

The procedures followed by the company for preparing the profit forecast
In carrying out their examination of the accounting policies and calculations for the profit forecast, and of the procedures followed by the company for its preparation the main points which the reporting accountants will wish to consider include the following:

(*a*) whether the profit forecast under review is based on forecasts regularly prepared for the purpose of management, or whether it has been separately and specially prepared for the immediate purpose;

(*b*) where profit forecasts are regularly prepared for management purposes the degree of accuracy and reliability previously achieved, and the frequency and thoroughness with which estimates are revised;

(*c*) whether the profit forecast under review represent the management's best estimate of results which they reasonably believe can and will be achieved as distinct from targets which the management has set as desirable;

(*d*) the extent to which profit forecast results for expired periods are supported by reliable interim accounts;

(*e*) the details of the procedures followed to generate the profit forecast and the extent to which it is built up from detailed profit forecasts of activity and cash flow;

(*f*) the extent to which profits are derived from activities having a proved and consistent trend and those of a more irregular, volatile or unproved nature;

(*g*) how the profit forecast takes account of any material extraordinary items and prior year adjustments, their nature, and how they are presented;

(*h*) whether adequate provision is made for foreseeable losses and contingencies and how the profit forecast takes account of factors which may cause it to be subject to a high degree of risk, or which may invalidate the assumptions;

(*i*) whether working capital appears adequate for requirements; normally this would require the availability of properly prepared cash-flow forecasts; and where short-term or long-term finance is to be relied on, whether the necessary arrangements have been made and confirmed;

(*j*) the arithmetical accuracy of the profit forecast and the supporting information and whether forecast balance sheets and sources and applications of funds statements have been prepared — these help to highlight arithmetical inaccuracies and inconsistent assumptions.

The accountants' report

The accountants' report will be addressed to the directors and will normally include statements dealing with the following matters, so far as appropriate:

(*a*) specific identification of the profit forecast and documents to which the report refers;

(*b*) the fact that the directors are solely responsible for the profit forecast;

(*c*) the fact that the reporting accountants have examined the accounting policies and calculations used in arriving at the profit forecast;

(*d*) if, as will frequently be the case, the reporting accountants have not carried out an audit of results for expired periods, a statement to that effect;

(*e*) whether in the opinion of the reporting accountants the profit forecast so far has been properly compiled on the footing of the assumptions made by the board of directors, as set out in the document, and is presented on a basis consistent with the accounting policies normally adopted by the company.

The report should be qualified if, *inter alia*, the reporting accountants:

(*a*) have reason for material reservation about the accounting policies or calculations for the profit forecast;

(*b*) have reason to consider the accounting policies and calculations to be inconsistent with the stated assumptions;

(*c*) have not obtained all the information they consider necessary (for example the fact that they were unable to review the profit forecasts of material subsidiary or associated companies or because of unduly restrictive time limits).

If any of the assumptions which are to be published appear to them to be unrealistic, or if any assumption is to be omitted which appears to them to be important, they should include an appropriate comment in their report.

Specimen report

An accountants' report might, in appropriate circumstances, where there are no grounds for qualifications, read as follows:

"To the directors of X Limited
We have reviewed the accounting policies and calculations for the profit forecasts of X Limited (for which the directors are solely responsible) for the periods . . . set out on pages . . . of this circular. The forecasts include results shown by unaudited interim accounts for the period . . . In our opinion the forecasts, so far as the accounting policies and calculations are concerned, have been properly compiled on the footing of the assumptions made by the Board set out on page . . . of this circular and are presented on a basis consistent with the accounting practices normally adopted by the company." '

The following questionnaire may be a useful *aide-memoire* to auditors dealing with a profit forecast:

Preparation

(1) Obtain written instructions from the client for the review of the profit forecast. Where this is not practicable, it is suggested that a letter recapitulating the verbal instructions received from the client should be sent by the reporting accountant.

(2) Obtain a statement of assumptions used in the forecast.

(3) Ensure that all personnel working on the profit forecast review are instructed:

(*a*) to list all documents and bases on which they are prepared, and to ensure that copies of all important documents are obtained and filed;

(*b*) that in all cases where information is obtained verbally from any official, indication is given in the relevant part of the review of the name and position of the official and the date the information was given.

Nature and background of the company's business

(4) Attach brief notes of the history of the company.

(5) Attach notes of the general nature of the company's activities.

(6) Attach notes with regard to the following:

(*a*) the main products;
(*b*) the main markets;
(*c*) the principal customers;
(*d*) the principal suppliers;
(*e*) the production capacity of the factories (where relevant in relation to forecast turnover);
(*f*) the labour force (where relevant in relation to forecast turnover);
(*g*) the organization of the Company;
(*h*) the office and factory locations;
(*i*) the trend of results over a period of years and explanation of any fluctuations or special factors affecting the results.

Note: In connection with (*a*) to (*d*), the intention is that areas of the Company's business which are of particular importance to the results of the Company can be readily identified.

The accounting procedures normally followed by the company and followed in the forecasts

(7) Obtain from the company a statement of the accounting procedures normally adopted.

(8) Where not otherwise included, make notes on:

(*a*) the methods followed, and the nature of overheads included in determining the amount to be carried forward for stock and work-in-progress, and the identification, judgement and accounting treatment of obsolete and slow-moving items;
(*b*) the bases adopted for recognizing profits and providing for losses on long-term contracts;
(*c*) the bases for calculating depreciation charges;
(*d*) the accounting treatment of research and development expenditure;
(*e*) the accounting treatment, and adequacy of disclosure, of exceptional items;
(*f*) the accounting treatment of taxation, and government grants.

(9) Examine specifically, note and comment on the bases used in the forecast as follows:

(*a*) the method of arriving at turnover and verification carried out;
(*b*) the gross margins on products and the methods used in their determination;

(*c*) give consideration to reliability of (*a*) and (*b*) by comparison with previous years' figures, interim or management accounts, etc.;
(*d*) the method of valuing stock and the method and dates on which physical stock was last taken;
(*e*) consider the impact of obsolete and slow-moving stocks on all the forecasts.

(10) Identify any unduly conservative or optimistic principles where the effect has been to depress materially or inflate disclosed profits.
(11) Ensure that the arithmetic is checked for the forecast, together with any supporting documents.
(12) Examine, generally, accounting procedures adopted and note any which:

(*a*) have not been applied consistently during the forecast period/periods under review;
(*b*) are not normally acceptable;
(*c*) are known to differ from those adopted by the other party to the takeover or merger.

Note: In the case of a merger it may be essential that there should be no significant differences in procedures between the parties arriving at their respective forecast profits and to ensure that the published documents disclose the effect of any change in principle during the periods under review, and, where known, any principles which might be changed on completion of the takeover or merger so as to materially affect the results subsequently disclosed.

(*d*) consider the impact of unrealized profit on intra-group stock on profits reported for the purposes of the forecast, and ensure that this has been dealt with where appropriate;
(*e*) examine the bases adopted for assessing profit and for losses on long-term contract and ensure that bases are consistent with those previously used;
(*f*) depreciation:

(i) examine bases for calculation of depreciation charges and ensure that bases are consistent with those previously used;
(ii) examine treatment of surpluses or deficits arising on revaluation or disposals of assets and possible effects on depreciation charges;

(*g*) obtain a schedule showing main items of interest receivable and payable and examine and indicate *all* items relating to group companies. Consider effect of new borrowings in current year;
(*h*) where appropriate consider:

(i) how items of a revenue nature actually arising in a period but reasonably attributable to the year as a whole have been dealt with, e.g. advertising expenditure;
(ii) how income and expenditure of a substantially seasonal nature has been dealt with;

(*i*) where appropriate:

(i) consider and note exchange rates used;
(ii) consider effect of overseas Exchange Control restrictions on remittances of profits.

(*j*) confirm that consideration has been given to bad debts and provision made. Note any large items for which no provision has been made but which might be described as doubtful;

(*k*) taxation:

(i) examine basis of provision;
(ii) ensure that any necessary adjustments are made if alterations are effected to income or expenditure figures during the course of the review;
(iii) in the case of United Kingdom companies, compare written-down values with net book values of appropriate fixed assets and comment on deferred tax implications.

Note: Forecasts are normally of profits before taxation. However, it is necessary to examine the recent taxation history in order to ascertain whether there are special features of the taxation position relevant to the validity of the forecast as a guide to distributable profits.

(*l*) examine all prior-year adjustments and exceptional items (whether or not dealt with in the profit and loss account);

(*m*) consider the effect on forecasts of any acquisition or disposals of investments in companies or trades. Note treatment of pre-acquisition profits and consider whether apportionment should be on a time basis or any other basis (e.g. seasonal factors);

(*n*) inquire as to the last date of agreement of intra-group balances;

(*o*) inquire as to unprovided contingencies, e.g. open positions on forward dealings in foreign exchange or commodities, forward option dealings in securities, guarantees, litigation and other claims, including taxation, and note all significant items;

(*p*) scrutinize minutes for any matters which might affect forecasts;

(*q*) in the case of United Kingdom companies, accounting treatment of investment or other government grants and ensure that method is consistent with that previously used;

(*r*) if a forecast balance sheet has been prepared as at the end of the review period, compare with the last audited balance sheet and the last balance sheet prepared from the books of account, note significant differences and consider effect on profits forecast;

(*s*) note and consider effect on forecasts of any other matters not specifically dealt with above.

The assumptions on which the forecasts are based

(13) Note assumptions made (including commercial assumptions) and determine whether the forecasts have been properly compiled on the footing of the assumptions. Ensure that (where appropriate) they have been correctly applied to accounting bases and calculations.

Note: Assumptions made by the board might include that:

(*a*) profit margins generally during the remainder of the financial year will continue at the levels shown by the latest management accounts;

(*b*) there will be no changes in rates of exchange during the remainder of the year;

(*c*) there will be no significant change in interest rates during the remainder of the year;

(*d*) the results will not be materially affected by industrial disturbances or by supply interruptions attributable to other causes;

(*e*) there will be no significant variation in taxes and duties wherever imposed;

(*f*) there will be no change in the basis of accounting hitherto applied in the company and its subsidiaries for a company subject to a takeover;

(*g*) there are no other unforeseen factors which might affect the turnover profits and assets of companies in the group.

(14) Consider what other assumptions of significance *have been made in fact* for the purpose of the forecasts but not included above.

(15) If further assumptions noted have a material affect on the figures, ensure that these are included in the board's assumptions.

Procedures followed by the company for preparing forecasts

(16) Are profit forecasts under review based on forecasts regularly prepared for the purpose of management, or have they been specifically prepared for the immediate purpose? Are these forecasts best current estimates as opposed to desirable targets?

(17) Obtain from the company:

(*a*) a manual of accounting procedures or, where one is not in use, a description of the methods used in preparing its financial and management accounts;

(*b*) a reconciliation of the last published audited accounts with the management accounts covering the same period of trading;

(*c*) the working papers supporting those accounts.

(18) Compare the forecast with any earlier forecast made in respect of the same period and obtain explanations for any material change.

(19) Compare the results shown by the most recent management accounts with the forecast (if any) originally made for that period and obtain explanations for any material difference:

(*a*) In order that an examination may be made of the trend of past results and of the company's success in predicting those results, obtain from the company a comparison of the detailed results and forecasts for the past three completed years;

(*b*) If practical, where the level of activity fluctuates, whether for seasonal or other reasons, the examination should be extended to past periods equivalent to the completed part of the current year;

(*c*) The details required will depend on the size of the company or group under review but will normally include, at least on a test basis, a review of the main items of income and expenditure.

(20) Where the forecast results differed materially in the past from the actual results achieved inquire whether any alterations have been made to the forecasting procedures which should help to reduce any differences which might arise on the forecast profits for the period under review.

(21) Specific note should be made where the achievement of the forecast is subject to a high degree of risk. Examples of such situations are:

(*a*) businesses where sales levels are difficult to predict;
(*b*) long-term contracts at fixed prices;
(*c*) new or unproven products or processes.

(22) Inquire as to the adequacy of working capital and obtain from the company:

(*a*) a cash-flow forecast for a period not less than that covered by the profit forecast or, if different, the period covered by the directors' comments on working capital. (*Note:* It is desirable that the review should extend beyond the period reported on so as to ensure that account is taken of any relatively large payments, e.g. taxation falling due soon after the date specified.) The statement should be prepared on a monthly or quarterly basis so that seasonal fluctuations are shown.

(*b*) a forecast balance sheet as at the end of the review period and at any interim periods if available.

The cash-flow forecast and projected balance sheet should be carefully examined to establish whether:

(*a*) the cash forecasts are reconciled with profit forecasts regularly prepared for management purposes;
(*b*) the cash-flow forecast for the period is reconciled with the profit forecast and closing balance sheet;
(*c*) compare cash-flow forecasts made in the past, if available, with the ultimate out-turn indicate weaknesses in the forecasting procedure;
(*d*) the forecasts prepared by subsidiaries are based on the same assumptions as those on which the results forecast are based.

Final points on the forecast

(23) Procure and file copies of up-to-date *written* assurances from management:

(*a*) that the figures contained in actual and forecast accounts are based on the same accounting principles as those applied in the audited annual accounts of the previous year;
(*b*) that all items of an exceptional or non-recurring nature (actual or expected) have been disclosed either in the actual or forecast accounts or by report and comment thereon (including such items as material contingent liabilities and capital losses or profits not normally dealt with in the profit and loss account);
(*c*) that management is at the present time aware of no reason why the estimated results (state amounts) are unlikely to be achieved.

(24) Check that the forecasts of trading subsidiaries or branches which have been the subject of detailed examination have been correctly included in the consolidated forecast.
(25) Test the arithmetical accuracy of the consolidation working papers.
(26) Consider whether any adjustment to the forecast is necessary on account of the reviews made and reported on by other firms.
(27) Ensure that detailed examination has been made, and letters of representation received, in respect of all companies, branches or divisions which contribute materially to the forecast.
(28) Ensure that the results have been adjected for intra-group transactions and unrealized profits.
(29) Ensure that the forecast together with the assumptions upon which it is based is formally adopted by the board of directors who should also take sole responsibility for it.

Other investigations

Auditors are often asked to act also as accountants and report on special situations for clients. Again, this is done outside the Companies Acts and the basis and scope of the investigation must therefore be made quite clear.

Investigations can be in connection with a proposed purchase of a business, suspected fraud, on behalf of an incoming partner or of a bank advancing credit, or in a number of other situations. The way in which the work is approached will therefore be influenced by the purpose to which the report will be put. The investigating accountant must plan his programme to this end after becoming familiar with the business concerned and will often have to fit this into a required time schedule. There will not, therefore, be time to waste on irrelevancies and the accountant must use his experience in pinpointing the essential issues and concentrating on those.

It is not proposed to describe in detail the nature of investigations of the types mentioned; a separate volume could be devoted to this. However, an experienced auditor, who has mastered the principles dealt with in this book, should have no difficulty in applying his knowledge to such new and challenging situations.

Readers are advised to study Statement S13, issued by the English Institute in 1968, as this sets out useful principles to be observed in the preparation of special reports.

14 The legal position of auditors

The Auditor's Responsibility to Shareholders

The subject of the exact legal position of auditors is one of considerable complexity and difficulty. The various Acts of Parliament dealing with the appointment of auditors do not define in any detail the auditor's responsibilities and liabilities. There are several important cases dealing with the subject which indicate the legal view, but it cannot be said that finality has been reached, for auditing standards are constantly improving, bringing a continual extension to an auditor's responsibilities. For example, it is now acknowledged that the profession was for far too long mesmerized by the case of *Kingston Cotton Mill Co.* (1896), and that, if a similar case were to arise today, the Courts, while taking into consideration that decision, would certainly have regard to the auditing standards of today rather than those of the last century. Indeed, in *re Thomas Gerrard & Son Ltd.* (1967), the judgement given specifically referred to the more exacting standards of care and skill being required now. Similarly it may be likely that an auditor's responsibilities in this country regarding inventories would not be held to be less than those required in the United States of America, and for that reason the American case of *McKesson & Robbins* (1939), on which American practice in this respect is based, has been included in the leading cases which follow.

Again, on the whole, the Companies Act 1948 is silent as to the exact responsibilities of auditors in connection with the audit of the accounts of companies. The Companies Act 1967, though, contains a somewhat more positive emphasis in requiring, under Section 14(4), the auditors 'to carry out such investigations as will enable them to form an opinion' on the adequacy of the books of account and their agreement with the balance sheet and profit and loss account. Whilst previously the auditors had to 'report' on those matters and, although their basic duties have not been enlarged and only a negative reference is now necessary in the auditors' report, still the new Act writes in these duties in a more deliberate manner. It would appear that, as the agent of the shareholders, an auditor must exercise reasonable care and skill in carrying out his duties, and that, if he fails and his clients suffer damage through his neglect or default, he is liable to them in damages. What is reasonable care and skill depends upon the whole of the circumstances of the particular case. But it must be pointed out that it is here that the whole difficulty of this question arises, for the circumstances of individual audits vary enormously, and, notwithstanding the promulgation of Statements of Auditing Standards, the auditor must decide for himself in each case what steps are necessary, and, for this purpose, an auditor must be possessed of considerable skill, knowledge and judgement.

The Auditor's Responsibility to Third Parties

For many years it was thought that in the absence of fraud, an auditor was not liable to third parties who suffered damage, even though he had been negligent. However, this view was upset as a result of the House of Lords decision in *Hedley Byrne & Co. Ltd* v. *Heller & Partners Ltd* (1963). This case extended the duty of care when the House of Lords held that there may be liability for financial loss arising from negligent mis-statements.

Such liability had previously been possible in respect of physical loss or damage, but before *Hedley Byrne* the rule was that in the absence of fiduciary or contractual relationship, and except where physical loss was sustained, there was no general duty to refrain from making careless mis-statements. This was emphasized in 1951 by the Court of Appeal in *Candler* v. *Crane Christmas & Co.*

The facts of *Hedley Byrne* were that the appellants asked their bank to ascertain from the respondents the financial position of Easipower Ltd. The respondents replied, 'without liability', that they considered Easipower to be a respectably constituted company considered good for its ordinary business engagements. Relying on this reply Hedley Bryne allowed Easipower credit of £17 000 before the latter company went into liquidation. In an action for negligence when replying to the inquiry, it was held (House of Lords) that, because of the respondents' disclaimer, they were not liable, but without the disclaimer a duty of care would have existed without a contractual relationship. During his judgement Lord Morris said:

> 'I consider . . . that if someone possessed of a special skill undertakes, quite irrespective of contract, to apply that skill for the assistance of another person who relies on such skill, a duty of care will arise. . . . Furthermore if, in a sphere in which a person is so placed that others could reasonably rely on his judgment or his skill or on his ability to make careful inquiry, a person who takes it on himself to give information or advice to, or allows his information or advice to be passed on to, another person who, as he knows or should know, will place reliance on it, then a duty of care will arise.'

Following this case, the English Institute issued Statement V8 in 1965 on 'Accountants' liability to third parties', which concluded:

'The *Hedley Byrne* decision has modified the liability of accountants for professional negligence in an important, but limited, respect. It has not introduced a new concept of negligence: for an action in damages under the *Hedley Byrne* principle to succeed, negligence must first be shown. But accountants may now be held in law to owe a duty of care to persons other than those with whom they are in a contractual or fiduciary relationship and may be liable for neglect of that duty if, but only if, they know or ought to know that a financial report, account or statement prepared by them has been prepared for a specific purpose or transaction, will be shown to a particular person or class of persons, and may be relied on by that person or class of persons in the particular connection.

Accountants have always recognized that they have a responsibility to third parties in these circumstances, even if it was hitherto considered to be unenforceable in law, and it is recognized best practice that, in the interests of all concerned, the extent to which the accountant accepts responsibility should be made clear beyond possibility of misunderstanding. The *Hedley Byrne* decision underlines the importance of observing best practice; and Counsel has further advised that where an accountant specifically restricts the scope of his report or expresses appropriate reservations in a note attached to and referred to in the financial statements he has prepared or the report which he has made thereon, this can constitute a disclaimer which will be effective against any action for negligence brought against him by third parties.'

Auditing Case Law

There are many very important decisions relating to the subject of an auditor's duties and liabilities, but there is only space here to consider the leading cases. The conclusions to be drawn therefrom will be summarized at the end of the chapter.

Leeds Estate Building and Investment Co. *v*. Shepherd (1887). In this case it was held that it was not sufficient for an auditor merely to compare the balance sheet with the books of account, thus verifying its arithmetical accuracy, but that he had also to satisfy himself that the balance sheet was a 'true and accurate representation of the company's affairs'. In this case the terms of the Articles had not been carried out, and it was held that 'it was no excuse that the auditor had not seen the Articles when he knew of their existence'. As a result of the auditor's neglect, dividends, directors' fees and bonuses were improperly paid, and he was, therefore, held liable for damages.

In Re London and General Bank (1885). In this case it was held that where an auditor did not report to the shareholders that the balance sheet was incorrectly drawn, knowing it to be the case, he was guilty of a misfeasance. In this case the company had advanced considerable sums to customers, but the corresponding securities held were wholly insufficient. The company had, however, taken credit for the interest accrued due upon such loans, whereas the interest was never, in fact, paid. One of the principal reasons for the failure of the bank was the heavy loss in respect of these loans, and, had proper provisions been made for bad debts, no profits would have been shown available for dividend. The auditor apparently was aware of the real state of affairs, and reported fully to the directors, who, however, refused to alter the accounts. In his report to the shareholders, the auditor made no mention of the lack of security, etc., but merely stated 'The value of the assets as shown by the balance sheet is dependent upon realization'. The auditor was found guilty of a misfeasance, and was held jointly and severally liable with the directors in respect of two dividends declared, amounting to some £14 000, on the ground that he ought to have reported the true facts to the shareholders. The words contained in his report to them were quite meaningless, and, therefore, he had failed in his duty, as a result of which failure the company had paid these dividends out of capital. Part of the judgement reads as follows:

> 'It is no part of an auditor's duty to give advice either to directors or shareholders as to what they ought to do. An auditor has nothing to do with the prudence or imprudence of making loans with or without security. It is nothing to him whether the business of a company is being conducted prudently or imprudently, profitably or unprofitably; it is nothing to him whether dividends are properly or improperly declared, provided he discharges his own duty to the shareholders. His business is to ascertain and state the true financial position of the company at the time of the audit, and his duty is confined to that. But then comes the question: How is he to ascertain such position? The answer is: By examining the books of the company. But he does not discharge his duty by doing this without inquiring and without taking any trouble to see that the books of the company themselves show the company's true position. He must take reasonable care to ascertain that they do. Unless he does this, his duty will be worse than a farce . . . An auditor, however, is not bound to do more than exercise reasonable care and skill in making inquiries and investigations. He is not an insurer; he does not guarantee that the books do correctly show the true position of the company's affairs; he does not guarantee that his balance sheet is accurate according to the books of the company. If he did, he would be responsible for an error on his part, even if he were himself deceived, without any want of reasonable care on his part — say, by the fraudulent concealment of a book from him. His obligation is not so onerous as this.

Such I take to be the duty of the auditor; he must be honest — that is, he must not certify what he does not believe to be true, and he must take reasonable care and skill before he believes that what he certifies is true.

What is reasonable care in any particular case must depend upon the circumstances of that case. Where there is nothing to excite suspicion, very little inquiry will be reasonable and sufficient; and, in practice I believe, businessmen select a few cases haphazardly, see that they are right, and assume that others like them are correct also. When suspicion is aroused, more care is obviously necessary, but still an auditor is not bound to exercise more than reasonable care and skill even in a case of suspicion; and he is perfectly justified in acting on the opinion of an expert where special knowledge is required . . .

A person whose duty it is to convey information to others does not discharge that duty by simply giving them so much information as is calculated to induce them, or some of them, to ask for more. Information and means of information are by no means equivalent terms . . . An auditor who gives shareholders means of information, instead of information in respect of a company's financial position, does so at his peril, and runs the very serious risk of being held, judicially, to have failed to discharge his duty.'

In Re Kingston Cotton Mill Co. (1896). In this case the accounts had been falsified to a very considerable extent by the managing director, by means of extensive over-valuations of the stock. The stock had been certified by the managing director, and it was held on appeal that the auditor was entitled to accept such certificates, and that he was not liable in respect of the dividends which had been paid out of capital as a result of the manipulation of the stock.

The Judge referred to the circumstances which led to the auditors being deceived and came to the conclusion that they were not wanting in skill, care or caution in accepting the figures of the manager, and he concluded as follows:

'The duties of auditors must not be rendered too onerous. Their work is responsible and laborious, and the remuneration moderate. I should be sorry to see the liability of auditors extended any further than in *re The London and General Bank* . . . Auditors must not be made liable for not tracking out ingenious and carefully laid schemes of frauds, when there is nothing to arouse their suspicion and when those frauds are perpetrated by tried servants of the company and are undetected for years by the directors. So to hold would make the position of an auditor intolerable.'

In this case, therefore, an auditor was entitled to rely upon the certificate of a responsible official as regards the stock-in-trade. But, an auditor today would be running considerable risks if he acted too literally upon this decision, which is an old one. Opinions and practice have changed greatly since this case was decided. If the auditor were to accept, say, the manager's certificate, without in any way checking or testing the stock, although every other item in the balance sheet may be tested and checked in every way, it means that the official responsible for the valuation of the stock could make the accounts show whatever results he pleased, by manipulating the valuation. The auditor would be in no position to express an opinion as to whether, or not, the accounts showed a true and fair view of the company's affairs. In order, therefore, that the audit may be of some real value, the auditor must test the stock as far as is reasonably possible. Where there are goods in course of manufacture, it may be difficult for an auditor to satisfy himself completely as regards this asset. However, he can, and there is no doubt he should, make inquiries and use reasonable tests, so that he can show, in the event of his being challenged, that he used every reasonable precaution in order to satisfy himself as to the correctness of this important item in the accounts. Thus a too literal construction should no longer be placed upon the ruling in this case.

Irish Woollen Co. Ltd *v.* Tyson and Others (1900). In this case the auditor was held liable for damages where the accounts had been falsified by the suppression of invoices, it being held that had he used reasonable care and skill, he should have discovered the fraud. Part of the judgement reads as follows:

> 'For these reasons I am of the opinion that if due care and skill had been exercised, the carrying over and the suppression of invoices would have been discovered, and the auditor is liable for any damage the company has sustained from the understatement of liabilities in the balance sheet due to this cause since 4 January 1892. I consider that not only are Mr Kevans and his assistants not free from blame for this, but also for the mechanical way the audit was carried out.'

The London Oil Storage Co. Ltd *v.* Seear Hasluch & Co. (1904). In this case the auditors were held liable for damages on the grounds that they had failed to verify the existence of the petty cash in hand, which according to the books amounted to £760, whereas, in fact, there was only £30, the difference representing the secretary's misappropriations.

In this case it was clearly established that the directors had been negligent in their control of the affairs of the company. No doubt for this reason the damages were limited to the nominal sum of £5·25. The fact remains, however, that the auditors were held to have been guilty of a breach of duty. In this case the Lord Chief Justice stated:

> 'I entirely agree with the view of the law as explained . . . that the auditor cannot shelter himself for any breach of duty under the neglect of the directors; he is there to do his duty to the company; the only point on which the conduct of the directors may become material is upon the

subordinate question as to whether there is anything to arouse the suspicion of the auditor, and whether or not the loss has really been occasioned by the auditor's conduct . . . The auditor most undoubtedly does undertake very considerable responsibilities and is liable for the proper discharge of his duties, and if by the neglect of his duty or by want of reasonable care, he neglects his duty, and damage is caused to the company as such, he is responsible for that damage . . . The conduct of the directors is no answer to any breach of duty by the defendant, but it is a circumstance you must take into consideration, because if you are of opinion that the loss was occasioned by a man stealing the money in consequence of there being a want of proper control over him, then the fact of there being a breach of duty by the auditor is what we lawyers call a *causa causans* which contributed to, but would not be the cause of, the loss.'

Arthur E. Green & Co. *v.* **The Central Advance and Discount Corporation Ltd (1920).** In this case the auditors were charged with negligence, on the grounds that the profits of the company were considerably overstated, owing to the provision for bad debts being insufficient, and also on the grounds that the item 'securities' included leases which had lapsed. The book debts included a great number of very old debts, many of which were statute-barred, but the auditors relied upon the manager's estimate of the provision for bad debts. Upon the death of the manager the new manager investigated the position and bad debts to the amount of £13 000 were written-off. The company claimed damages against the auditors upon the grounds that commissions had been paid to the managers to the extent of £950 on the overstated profits. This case was decided in favour of the company and judgement was held for £614. The Judge remarked as follows:

'He desired to say, with regard to the cases that had been cited to him, that there did not seem to be any reported cases in which the exact duties of auditors, with regard to dealing with book debts, were laid down. He thought it must rest upon the general principles of the law on professional negligence. One had to fall back upon the words of the statute. If there were circumstances which seemed to call for inquiry, the auditor must make the proper inquiry, and if he did not take the proper steps to have the matter sifted, he did not fulfil the duty he owed to the company as one of its officers. He (the Judge) regretted very much that Mr Green's firm, possibly owing to the masterful nature of Mr Foot (the late manager), fell short of that standard, but he could not help arriving at that conclusion, and he therefore found as he had stated.'

In Re City Equitable Fire Insurance Co. Ltd (1924). This case is of great interest to all auditors, and is worthy of close study.

Extensive frauds had been perpetrated by the chairman of the company, and the Official Receiver took action against several of the directors and the auditors.

As regards the auditors, the charges were that they were guilty of negligence in respect of the audit by them of the balance sheets of the company for the years ending 28 February 1919, 1920 and 1921. The charges of negligence and breach of duty came under three heads:

(1) That the debt due to the company from Ellis & Co., the stockbrokers of the company — Mr Bevan, the chairman, being a partner in that firm — and the debt due from Mr Mansell the general manager, were misdescribed by being included under 'loans at call or short notice' or 'loans', or, in the case of part of Ellis & Co.'s debt, under the heading of 'cash at bank and in hand'. Further, that the auditors failed to disclose to the shareholders the existence of these debts.

(2) Their failure to detect the fact that much larger sums were in the hands of Ellis & Co. at the date of each balance sheet than were so included.

(3) Their failure to detect and report to the shareholders the fact that a number of the company's securities which were in the custody of Ellis & Co. were being pledged by that firm to its customers.

Generally speaking, the Judge found that the auditors had displayed great skill, care and industry.

As regards the first charge, the position was that the balances owing to the company from Ellis & Co., in 1919, amounted, according to the books, to £51 423 and rose in 1921 to £423 650. The amount due from Mansell was £6225 in 1919 and in 1921 had increased to £96 233. In the 1919 balance sheet these sums were included under the heading of 'loans at call or short notice', and in the 1921 balance sheet £350 000 owing by Ellis & Co., and the £96 233 owing by Mansell, were included under the heading 'loans', and £73 650 owing by Ellis & Co., on investment account, was included as 'cash at bank and in hand'.

His Lordship held that it was not the duty of the auditors specifically to draw the attention of the directors and the shareholders to these debts. Even if these items were incorrectly described in the balance sheet — and in the case of the debt of £73 650 classified as 'cash at bank and in hand', the Judge held that this was a misdescription — any such misdescription did not involve damage to the company.

The auditor, however, must not include at its face value a debt that is not a good one; but in this case the credit of Ellis & Co. at that time was good, and, further, the company held collateral security. As regards the debt due from Mansell, at that time there was no reason to suppose that this was not a good debt. In this case, however, the auditors were informed that security had been given and Bevan certified that he held that security. As regards the acceptance of this certificate by the auditors, the Judge held, as will be seen later, that they should have called for the production of these securities.

As regards the second and third charges, these involved 'window dressing' operations carried out by Bevan each year, the charge being that the auditors should have detected these and thus have discovered the extensive frauds.

The 'window dressing' operations were carried out each year by a pretended purchase of Treasury Bonds just before the date of the balance sheet, followed by a pretended sale just after that date. In this way, at the date of the balance sheet, the debt due from Ellis & Co. was materially reduced, and the gilt-edged securities shown in the balance sheet increased.

These operations were effected by Ellis & Co. giving an order on their own behalf to another firm of brokers for the purchase of the bonds; at the same time they arranged for the brokers to advance to Ellis & Co. the sum involved, the bonds being given as security for the loan. A few days afterwards Ellis & Co. gave an order for the sale of the bonds, when the loan would be repaid.

Upon the purchase of the bonds, Ellis & Co. debited the company, and in the books of the company the corresponding entries were made.

Part of the charge was that the auditors should have noticed from year to year that the bonds purchased just before the date of the previous balance sheet were sold immediately afterwards in the succeeding financial year, when it would have been obvious that these were 'window dressing' operations. This part of the charge failed.

The second part of the charge was that the auditors should have called for the production of the Treasury Bonds shown by the company's books to be held at the date of the balance sheet; in fact, the auditors accepted certificates from year to year from Ellis & Co. that they held these bonds for the company. His Lordship held that the auditors should have called for these securities and that they were not entitled to accept the certificate of the company's stockbrokers. If the auditors had called for these securities the fraud must have been revealed, as Ellis & Co. could not have produced the bonds, as they were charged to the brokers against the loan by them to Ellis & Co. It was held, therefore, that in this direction the auditors were guilty of a breach of duty and of negligence, and they would have been held liable for damages, except for the fact that one of the company's articles of association provided that the directors, auditors and officers of the company should be held indemnified by the company, except in the case of wilful negligence. His Lordship held, therefore, that as the negligence of the auditors did not amount to wilful negligence, they were protected by the article and therefore escaped liability. Auditors can no longer be protected by a similar article. (See Companies Act 1948, Section 205)

In the course of the evidence it was established that in cases where the securities of a client were held by a bank of standing, it was the custom for auditors to accept the certificate of the bank as verification of such securities. His Lordship referred to this custom and questioned its soundness. This point, however, was not decided in this case, but his Lordship appeared to be of the opinion that in all cases an auditor should personally inspect all securities, wherever or by whomsoever held.

Royal Mail Steam Packet C. Case (Rex *v*. Kylsant) (1931). In this case the chairman of the company, Lord Kylsant, was charged under the Larcency Act 1861 in respect of the company's accounts for 1926 and 1927 on the grounds that he knew them to be false and that the annual reports concealed from the shareholders the true position of the company with intention to deceive. The auditor, Mr Morland, was charged with aiding and abetting Lord Kylsant to commit the offence.

The circumstances of the case were that the company had made substantial profits during the 1914–1918 War and up to 1921; thereafter the company's earnings had fallen off considerably. During the years 1921 to 1927 the profit and loss accounts were credited with special items amounting to approximately £5 000 000 which represented excess profits duty recoveries, obsolescence and deferred repairs allowances, excess taxation provisions and bonuses from subsidiaries paid out of past profits. As a result of crediting these items the company was able to pay its debenture interest and dividends on its ordinary and preference shares. In the accounts of the company the balance available was described as:

> 'Balance for the year, including dividends on shares in allied and other companies, adjustment of taxation reserves less depreciation of fleet.'

The main point at issue was whether there was an intent to deceive shareholders by failing to give a clear and specific indication in the accounts of the amounts of the special credits and whether the words 'adjustment of taxation reserves' was a sufficient indication. In the event, both Lord Kylsant and Mr Morland were found not guilty, but Lord Kylsant was found guilty of a further charge relating to a prospectus.

This case, which is now of historical interest only, had a profound effect at the time, as the public conscience was greatly shocked and the lessons learnt from it did much to shape the Companies Act 1948.

Armitage *v*. Brewer & Knott (1932). In this case damages were claimed against the auditors in consequence of frauds committed by an employee, and judgement for £1259 was given against the auditors. This case is worthy of detailed study. The frauds were perpetrated by a Miss Harwood, who had complete charge of the books, and the payment of wages; there was no system of internal check. The main point of the case was whether or not the auditors had exercised reasonable care and skill.

Part of His Lordship's summing up reads:

> 'However much it might be wrapped up, the defendants' case came to this, that systematic fraud for two and a half years by one person could

not be detected by the exercise of reasonable care on the part of the accountants. His Lordship did not like to use strong language, but that appeared to him to be bordering closely on nonsense. On the evidence it was an allegation which did not bear a moment's examination.'

In fact, another firm of professional accountants had been called in to investigate the frauds, and Miss Harwood was prosecuted at the Central Criminal Court and pleaded guilty. The importance of an auditor following up small discrepancies is clearly brought out in this case. His Lordship stated:

'It was doubtless true that to detect required minute examination of a large number of documents, but that was exactly what the defendants undertook to do . . . As to the suggestion that some things were too trivial to notice, audits differed greatly as to scope and special instructions. A 6s. 1d. had been altered to 16s. 1d. That was passed in what purported to be a meticulous examination. The most casual inspection would detect the discrepancy on the voucher; both figures were there. His Lordship was struck by the audacity with which many of these frauds were committed. It looked as though Miss Harwood had found that she had nothing very formidable to fear in the way of audit. It was the duty of the auditor to bring that 10s — which was indicative not only of fraud but of forgery — at once to the notice of the principal. That one piece of paper raised a grave suspicion. It was of critical importance. It was by little things like that the forgeries and frauds were found out.'

The main part of the fraud arose in connection with the falsification of wages sheets and it was clear that had these wages sheets been examined thoroughly the fraud must have been disclosed. His Lordship stated: 'It was no use looking at such documents as were found here unless one did it with scrupulous accuracy'. And, further, that: 'When there was something to make one uneasy His Lordship thought that defendants should have been doubly vigilant'. And also that 'it was clear that a good many documents were suspicious on their face and called for inquiry'.

This case brings out clearly the vital importance of the exercise of vigilance and care in the vouching of documents.

In Re S. P. Catterson & Sons Ltd (1937). In this case the liquidator of the company brought a summons against the auditor under Section 276 of the Companies Act 1929 (Section 333 of the Companies Act 1948).

The facts of the case were that in the showroom of the company the system was that upon cash sales being effected a cash invoice was made out in an invoice book, these invoices being serially numbered. One copy of the invoice was receipted and handed to the customer and the counterfoil remained in the invoice book. Subsequently from the counterfoils the cash sales were entered in a daily cash sales book, the serial numbers being recorded and the total cash was handed to the manager who was one of the directors of the company.

From time to time sales were effected on short credit terms when the same invoice book was used and the system was that in those cases where credit had been given the counterfoils were turned up or 'dog-eared'. When the customer paid, the system was that the counterfoils should be turned down. The utilization of this same cash invoice book for both cash and credit transactions at once destroyed the system as the regular consecutive numbering of the counterfoils being accounted for in cash was broken. The clerk in charge of the showroom effected the defalcation by misappropriating cash paid by short credit customers and, therefore, on receipt of the cash did not turn down the counterfoils. In this connection His Lordship stated: 'Now the evidence to my mind is clear that that system of using the invoice book for ready money transactions as well as for short credit transactions had been going on for years, and it is equally clear to me that that system and the so-called system of keeping a record of the transactions done on credit by turning up the invoice was also known to the directors and had been known to them for years'.

The auditors pointed out to the directors that the system was not a satisfactory one and they recommended improvements, but these recommendations were disregarded.

His Lordship stated: 'It is clear that the unsatisfactory system employed in the showroom was clear to the mind of the auditor and that it was called by him to the attention of the directors, and that notwithstanding that fact they preferred, for some reason or another, to continue the system as it was. I am not prepared to hold in those circumstances and on those facts that there was any duty upon the auditors to insist upon that system being changed. It is not their business to tell the directors how to carry on and conduct their accounting system; they make their recommendations and, if they are not acceded to, the responsibility is not the auditor's responsibility, but it is the responsibility of the directors.'

In reviewing the responsibility of the auditors generally, His Lordship stated: 'The first fact which seems often to be lost sight of is that the primary responsibility for the accounts of a company is with those who are in control of the company, that is to say, the directors, and in the case of the directors of this company, they were not a satisfactory team'.

His Lordship stated that 'I have no doubts as to where the primary responsibility for finding out the defalcation of this man Spicer lies. It lies upon the shoulders of the man whose duty it was as a director of this company to collect from Spicer the cash that he received. If that man had done his duty in any degree at all the frauds could not have been perpetrated in the way in which they were perpetrated'; and he concluded by stating that, in his opinion, the auditor was an honest man trying to do his duty and that in view of all the facts of the case and the audit notes, the applicant had 'quite failed to satisfy me in respect of the matters charged that there was any negligence. The result is that the application fails and must be dismissed.'

McKesson & Robbins Case (1939). This American case arose out of the operation at the Bridgeport offices of McKesson & Robbins Inc. of a wholly fictitious foreign crude drug business shown in the books of the Connecticut division of the corporation and McKesson & Robbins Ltd (Canada), one of its subsidiaries.

To accomplish the deception, purchases were pretended to have been made by the McKesson companies from five Canadian vendors who were purported to retain the goods at their warehouses. Sales were pretended to have been made on McKesson's account by W. W. Smith & Co. Inc., and the goods shipped directly by the latter from Canadian warehouses to the customers. Payments for goods purchased and collections from customers were pretended to have been made by the Montreal banking firm of Manning & Co. Invoices, advices and other documents prepared on printed forms in the names of these firms were used to give an appearance of reality to these transactions.

The foreign firms to whom the goods were supposed to have been sold were real but had done no business of the type indicated with McKesson. W. W. Smith & Co. Inc., Manning & Co. and the five Canadian vendors were either entirely fictitious or merely blinds used to support the fictitious transactions.

The fraud was engineered by Frank Coster, president of the corporation; George Dietrich, assistant treasurer; Robert Dietrich, head of the shipping, receiving and warehousing department at Bridgeport; and George Venard, who managed the offices, mailing addresses, bank accounts and other activities of the dummy concerns with whom the McKesson companies supposedly did business. In reality these four men were brothers whose real name was Musica.

In 1937, the last year for which a financial statement was issued to stockholders before discovery of the fraud, fictitious sales exceeded \$18 000 000, and included in the balance sheet at 31 December 1937 were fictitious assets amounting to some \$19 000 000. These consisted of inventories (approximately \$10 000 000), accounts receivable (approximately \$9 000 000) and bank balance (approximately \$75 000). At the time of the exposure of the fraud in December 1938, these fictitious assets had increased to approximately \$21 000 000.

In a summary of its findings and conclusions on the case, published in 1941, the American Securities and Exchange Commission stated that:

'*Investigations of new clients*

The facts of this case suggest that for new and unknown clients some independent investigation should be made of the company and of its principal officers prior to undertaking the work. Such an inquiry should provide a valuable background for interpreting conditions revealed during the audit or, in extreme cases, might lead to a refusal of the engagement.

Review of the client's system of internal check and control

We are convinced by the record that the review of the system of internal check and control at the Bridgeport offices was carried out in an unsatisfactory manner. The testimony of the experts leads us to the further conclusion that this vital and basic problem of all audits for the purpose of certifying financial statements has been treated in entirely too casual a manner by many accountants. Since in examinations of financial statements of corporations whose securities are publicly owned the procedures of testing and sampling are employed in most cases, it appears to us that the necessity for a comprehensive knowledge of the client's system of internal check and control cannot be over-emphasized.

Cash

The record is clear that the cash work performed on this engagement by Price, Waterhouse & Co. conformed in scope to the then generally accepted standards of the profession. It is unusually clear to us that prior to this case many independent public accountants depended entirely too much upon the verification of cash as the basis for the whole auditing programme and hence as underlying proof of the authenticity of all transactions. Where, as here, during the final three years of the audit, physical contact with the operations of a major portion of the business was limited to examinations of supposed documentary evidence of transactions carried on completely off-stage through agents unknown to the auditors save in connection with the one engagement, it appears to us that the reliability of these agents must be established by completely independent methods. Confirmation of the bank balance under these circumstances was proven in this case to be an inadequate basis for concluding that all the transactions were authentic.

Accounts receivable

Viewed as a whole the audit programme for accounts receivable as used by Price, Waterhouse & Co. conformed to then generally accepted procedures for an examination of financial statements although confirmation of the accounts was not included in the programme. The facts of this case, however, demonstrate the utility of circularization and the wisdom of the profession in subsequently adopting confirmation of accounts and notes receivable as a required procedure ". . . wherever practicable and reasonable, and where the aggregate amount of notes and accounts receivable represents a significant proportion of the current assets or of the total assets of a concern . . ."

Inter-company accounts

The record indicates that it is not enough for auditors to reconcile inter-company balances and that valuable insight into the company's manner of doing business may be gained by a review of the transactions passed through such accounts durby a review of the transactions passed through such accounts during the year. Best practice we believe requires the latter procedure. In this case the recommended procedure, although employed to some extent, was not applied in a thorough-going and penetrating manner.

Inventories

Price, Waterhouse & Co.'s audit programme for the verification of inventories was essentially that which was prescribed by generally accepted auditing practice for the period. However, we find that a substantial difference of opinion existed among accountants during this time as to the extent of the auditors' duties and responsibilities in connection with physical verification of quantities, quality and condition. Price, Waterhouse & Co., in common with a substantial portion of the profession, took the position that the verification of quantities, quality and condition of inventories should be confined to the records. There was, however, a substantial body of equally authoritative opinion which supported the view, which we endorse, that auditors should gain physical contact with the inventory by test counts, by observation of the inventory taking, or by a combination of these methods. Meticulous verification of the inventory was not needed in this case to discover the fraud. We are not satisfied, therefore, that even under Price, Waterhouse & Co.'s view other accountants would condone their failure to make inquiries of the employees who actually took the inventory and to determine by inspection whether there was an inventory as represented by the client. We commend the action of the profession in subsequently adopting as normal, procedures requiring physical contact with clients' inventories.

Other balance sheet accounts

(*a*) The testimony in respect to the auditing of plant accounts suggests that some accountants, including Price, Waterhouse & Co., could, with advantage, devote more attention to physical inspection than has been general practice with them in the past.

(*b*) The work in respect to liabilities was in accord with generally accepted practice, but suggests that desirability of independent inquiry when large purchases are made from a very few otherwise unknown suppliers.

(*c*) The record demonstrates the necessity of a thorough understanding of the client's tax situation, which apparently was not obtained by Price, Waterhouse & Co., in regard to the application of Canadian law.

Profit and loss accounts
We are of the opinion that such analyses of profit and loss accounts as were made were applied to improper combinations of departments, with the result that significant relationships were concealed. It is our conclusion that the independent accountant is derelict in his duty if he does not insist upon having proper analyses available for his review. It is our opinion that best practice supports this view.'

This case brought about the same revolution in American audit practice as did the *Royal Mail* case in the form of English published accounts. However, the profession in this country for far too long ignored the *McKesson & Robbins* case and was far too slow in assimilating the best of American audit practice.

In Fomento (Sterling Area) Ltd *v.* **Selsdon Fountain Pen Company Ltd (1958)** the old auditing adage was again quoted: 'the auditor was a watchdog, not a bloodhound; his duty was not detection but verification. But gagging the dog and locking him in his kennel at the bottom of the garden is not the best way to let him keep watch.'

This case, in fact, provided a good illustration of the manner in which the Courts expect an auditor to pursue his enquiries beyond merely taking someone's word as to the facts, and in turn to derive acceptable audit evidence.

A chartered accountant carried out an inquiry for clients, the appellants, to ascertain royalties payable to the clients by a company, the respondents, under a document called a 'deed of terms'. By this agreement, and a sub-licence, the respondents were licensed to make and sell ball-point pens and refills which were protected by letters patent in favour of the licensors, the appellants. The respondents produced to the accountant documents giving details of transactions in ball-points and refills described as 'type A', which were within the patent field, and also referring to sales of similar articles, described as of 'type B' and 'type C', stated not to have been included in the returns because outside the patent field. The accountant asked to be supplied with specimens or specifications of types B and C so as to satisfy himself that they were indeed outside the range of the patent. The respondents refused, saying they were not obliged to give information of their business outside the patent.

By a clause of the deed of terms the respondents were bound to keep all necessary books containing entries necessary for computing the royalties payable to the licensors; to produce the books to the licensors' auditors; and to give all such other information as might be necessary or appropriate to enable the royalties to be ascertained, provided that, if so required by the respondents, the auditors should undertake to treat all such information as confidential and disclosed only for the purpose of verifying the amount of the royalties.

Lord Morton of Henryton said that the auditor could not ascertain the royalties payable without ascertaining whether types B and C were within or outside the patent. The word 'verifying' in the agreement afforded a strong indication that the auditor need not accept the statement of the respondents: that was merely a statement of their opinion. The use in the agreement of the words 'all such other information' meant that the auditor was entitled to receive information not appearing in the respondents' books of account, and there was inserted a clear limitation on the extent of that other information: it must be necessary or appropriate to enable the amount of the royalties to be ascertained. The information sought by the auditor fell within that limitation. Lord Keith of Avonholm and Lord Denning concurred. Lord Denning said that an auditor was not to be confined to the mechanics of checking vouchers and making arithmetical computations; he was not to be written off as a professional 'adderupper and subtractor'.

The lesson regarding audit evidence was re-emphasized in the Australian case **Pacific Acceptance Corporation Ltd** *v.* **Forsyth and Others (1971)**, which concerned allegations that the auditors were negligent in failing to discover fraudulent and irregular features in connnection with certain loans, supposedly against security. The judgement also provided a reminder of the need for proper control and supervision of the audit:

> '*Prima facie* the auditors' job is to check material matters for himself from available documents, and he does not ordinarily do his job . . . if he merely seeks the assurance of another as to the check that the other has made or as to his views as to the effect of documents . . . The essence of an audit . . . is for the auditor to check material documents or matters for himself, subject to exception on reasonable grounds.
>
> An auditor may properly rely a great deal on inquiries made and explanations sought of the company's staff and management at the appropriate level, but *prima facie* this is in aid of his vouching and checking procedures and not in substitution for them.
>
> If a material document ought to be inspected by an auditor the fact that inspection might put the auditor to some inconvenience is normally no excuse for not inspecting it.
>
> Upon any matter of substance . . . both the decision to make the inquiry, the making of the inquiry and the consideration of the answer would call for the attention of a person of experience and seniority . . . If clerks are allowed to make inquiries which may turn out to be material, at least close supervision is called for in order to counteract his inexperience . . . If the irregularities are numerous it is quite unreasonable to continue to be satisfied by explanations of the branch manager and assurances from him that there is nothing wrong because for this reason or that things are in order or he thinks they are. If in this kind of situation an inexperienced clerk is left to make decisions on such matters

and he uncritically accepts what the manager says without more inquiry, lack of care on the part of the auditors is likely to be inferred.

Reasonable care and skill calls for changed standards to meet changed conditions or changed understanding of dangers . . . If there are shortcomings in the work of the audit clerks or of the reviewers in the area of omission from the work programme, and undiscovered error or fraud occurs in that area, then any failure by the auditors to amend the programme will tend to indicate that the shortcomings were due to negligence.'

Conclusions

The conclusions to be drawn from the various cases upon this subject would appear to be as follows:

(1) An auditor must carefully examine his client's system of accounting and of internal control and must test it with vouchers and original records and make proper inquiries.

(2) He must verify the existence of assets as far as is reasonably possible and he cannot absolve himself from this duty by accepting the certificate of an official.

(3) He is entitled to rely upon the opinion of experts where special knowledge is required.

(4) He will not be held liable for not tracking down ingenious and carefully laid schemes of fraud, where there is nothing to arouse his suspicion and the frauds have been perpetrated by tried servants of the concern.

(5) He need not necessarily be suspicious, but when his suspicions are aroused he must exercise all reasonable care and skill before he satisfies himself that all is in order.

(6) As to what is reasonable care and skill depends on the circumstances of the case and the general standard adopted by the profession.

(7) If the auditor is not satisfied on any material points, he must report clearly to the shareholders.

(8) If an auditor is negligent he may be held liable to damages if his client or third parties have suffered damage which otherwise would have been prevented.

(9) If an auditor wilfully certifies accounts, knowing them to be false, he may be held criminally liable.

(10) The conduct of the directors of a company is no answer to any breach of duty by the auditors, although it is a circumstance which will be taken into consideration by the Court.

This question of the auditor's legal responsibilities is one of supreme importance to every practising accountant. It is, however, a most difficult one. The auditor's responsibilities are not clearly defined in the Acts and the principles evolved by case law are in several directions conflicting.

In conclusion, it may be said that it is very unlikely that an auditor will be held personally liable provided he is possessed of the requisite professional skill, and that he honestly exercises such skill in all cases, taking every reasonable precaution to satisfy himself upon every point before he certifies the accounts. In the event of his being dissatisfied upon any material point, he must report clearly in his audit report to this effect. It is thought that no better short definition of an auditor's duties can be given than the following, which we have already quoted as part of the judgment in *re London and General Bank* (1895):

> 'Such I take to be the duty of the auditor; he must be honest — that is, he must not certify what he does not believe to be true, and he must take reasonable care and skill before he believes that what he certifies is true.'

Appendix A

As its title implies, this book is concerned chiefly with the principles of auditing, and would become intolerably lengthy if it tried to examine in detail every question which can arise in practice. In any case, a great many of these have been dealt with in the Members' Handbook published by the Institute of Chartered Accountants in England and Wales, and of which both students and practitioners are recommended to study the relevant sections which are listed in this Appendix.

Statements of Standard Accounting Practice

M1 Accounting for the results of associated companies (issued January 1971)
M2 Disclosure of accounting policies (issued November 1971)
M3 Earnings per share (revised August 1974)
M4 The accounting treatment of government grants (issued April 1974)
M5 Accounting for Value Added Tax (issued April 1974)
M6 Extraordinary items and prior-year adjustments (amended June 1978)
M8 The treatment of taxation under the imputation system in the accounts of companies (amended December 1977)
M9 Stocks and work-in-progress (issued May 1975)
M10 Statements of source and application of funds (amended June 1978)
M12 Accounting for depreciation (issued December 1977)
M13 Accounting for research and development (issued December 1977)
M14 Group accounts (issued September 1978)
M15 Accounting for deferred taxation (issued October 1978)
M16 Current-cost accounting (issued March 1980)
M17 Post-balance-sheet events (issued August 1980)
M18 Contingencies (issued August 1980)

Accounting principles

N13 Accountants' reports for prospectuses: fixed assets and depreciation (issued March 1949)

N16 Accountants' reports for prospectuses: adjustments and other matters (issued November 1953)
N21 Retirement benefits (issued February 1960)
N28 The accounts of investment trust companies (issued August 1968)
N29 Trust accounts (issued November 1969)

Financial statements and reports

S13 Special reports required by accountants (issued July/August 1959, revised October 1968)
S18 Accountants' reports for prospectuses and similar documents: absence of detailed stock records (issued January 1972)
S19 Reports on accounts of sole traders and partnerships (issued July 1973)
S20 Valuations of company property assets and their disclosure in directors' reports or accounts of companies (issued February 1974)
S23 Accountants' reports on profit forecasts (issued November 1978)

Statements on auditing

U7 Verification of debtor balances: confirmation by direct communication (issued June 1967)
U9 Attendance at stocktaking (issued July 1968)
U11 Stock-in-trade and work-in-progress (issued April 1969)
U14 Internal control in a computer based accounting system (issued December 1969)
U15 The audit of computer based accounting systems (issued December 1969)
U16 The ascertainment and confirmation of contingent liabilities arising from pending legal matters (issued August 1970)
U21 Group accounts — reliance on other auditors (issued March 1976)
U22 Bank reports for audit purposes (issued August 1976)
U24 Guidance for auditors on the implications of goods sold subject to reservation of title (issued December 1977) [See also V24]
U26 Auditors' reports — registered friendly societies and industrial and provident societies (issued August 1978)
U27 Auditors' responsibilities under the Trade Union and Labour Relations Act 1974 (issued May 1979)

Legal and regulatory background to accountants' work

V3 Remuneration (issued September 1969)
V5 Books and papers (ownership and lien) (issued September 1953)
V6 Solicitors and accountants (issued February 1959)
V7 Acceptance of agencies for financial organizations (issued June 1959)

V8 Accountants' liability to third parties — the Hedley–Byrne decision (issued August 1965)
V9 Trustee Investment Act 1961 — Notes for guidance (issued May 1966)
V10 The interpretation of 'material' in relation to accounts (issued November 1968)
V12 Unlawful acts or defaults by clients of members (issued August 1957 — revised October 1968)
V14 Arrangements to cover the incapacity or death of a sole practitioner (issued November 1968)
V16 Engagement letters (issued May 1974)
V17 Financial and accounting responsibilities of directors (issued April 1970)
V18 Professional liability of accountants and auditors (issued August 1972)
V19 The personal interests of directors in the transactions of companies (issued November 1972)
V22 Changes in a professional appointment (issued December 1969)
V24 Accounting for goods sold subject to reservation of title (issued July 1976)

Appendix B
Auditing standards and guidelines

'Explanatory Foreword'

(Issued April 1980)

Introduction

This Explanatory Foreword explains the scope and authority of Auditing Standards and Auditing Guidelines approved by the Councils of The Institute of Chartered Accountants in England and Wales, The Institute of Chartered Accountants of Scotland, The Institute of Chartered Accountants in Ireland and The Association of Certified Accountants. It should be read in conjunction with the Standards and Guidelines to which it forms a collective preface.

An audit is the independent examination of, and expression of opinion on, the financial statements of an enterprise by an appointed auditor in pursuance of that appointment and in compliance with any relevant statutory obligation. The responsibility for the preparation of the financial statements and the presentation of the information included therein rests with the management of the enterprise (in the case of a company, the directors). The auditor's responsibility is to report on the financial statements as presented by management.

Scope of Auditing Standards and Auditing Guidelines

Auditing Standards prescribe the basic principles and practices which members are expected to follow in the conduct of an audit. Unless otherwise indicated in the text, Auditing Standards apply whenever an audit is carried out. Each Auditing Standard will consist of a text to which there may be added an explanatory note. Explanatory notes have the same status and purpose as Auditing Guidelines (see below).

It would be impracticable to establish a code of rules sufficiently elaborate to cater for all situations and circumstances which an auditor might encounter. Such a code could not provide for innovations in business and financial practice and might hinder necessary development and experiment in auditing practice. In the observance of Auditing Standards, therefore, the auditor must exercise his judgement in determining both the auditing procedures necessary in the circumstances to afford a reasonable basis for his opinion and the wording of his report.

Auditing Guidelines give, or will give, guidance on

(*a*) procedures by which the Auditing Standards may be applied;
(*b*) the application of the Auditing Standards to specific items appearing in the financial statements of enterprises;
(*c*) techniques currently being used in auditing;
(*d*) audit problems relating to particular commercial or legal circumstances or to specific industries;

but do not prescribe basic principles and practices.

Existing pronouncements
Existing pronouncements on auditing matters approved by the respective councils of the accountancy bodies listed above should be considered by their members as having the same status as Auditing Guidelines. They will remain in force until withdrawn.

Auditing Standards and Guidelines and the law
Members are advised that a court of law may, when considering the adequacy of the work of an auditor, take into account any pronouncements or publications which it thinks may be indicative of good practice. Auditing Standards and Guidelines are likely to be so regarded.

Detection of irregularities or fraud

The responsibility for the prevention and detection of irregularities and fraud rests with the management, who may obtain reasonable assurance that this responsibility will be discharged by instituting an adequate system of internal control.

The auditor's duties do not require him specifically to search for fraud unless required by statute or the specific terms of his engagement.

However, the auditor should recognize the possibility of material irregularities or fraud which could, unless adequately disclosed, distort the results or state of affairs shown by the financial statements. The auditor should, therefore, plan his audit so that he has a reasonable expectation of detecting material mis-statements in the financial statements resulting from irregularities or fraud.

Obligation for members to observe Auditing Standards

Members of the accountancy bodies listed above who assume responsibility as auditors are expected to observe Auditing Standards. Apparent failures by members to observe Auditing Standards may be enquired into by the appropriate committees established by the Councils of the accountancy bodies, and disciplinary action may result.

Personal standards

The personal standards relevant to the work of an auditor are described in the ethical guides published by the accountancy bodies.

Effective date

Auditors will be expected to observe Auditing Standards in the audit of any financial statements for a period commencing on or after the date specified in the standard. It is recognized, however, that for the most part Auditing Standards will represent only the formalization of existing good practice.

Glossary of terms

A glossary of certain terms used in the Explanatory Foreword, in Auditing Standards and in Auditing Guidelines forms an appendix to this Explanatory Foreword. This glossary may be extended as subsequent Standards and Guidelines are published.

Application of Auditing Standards overseas

Auditing Standards may not be appropriate to the audit of financial statements prepared in overseas territories solely for local purposes where different requirements of law or of general practice prevail. Where, however, the overseas financial statements are to be incorporated into UK or Irish financial statements the audit of the overseas enterprise should conform to Auditing Standards in so far as this is necessary to ensure that the audit of the UK or Irish financial statements as a whole is in accordance with Auditing Standards.

International Statements and Guidelines

The accountancy bodies listed above are members of both the Union Européenne des Experts Comptables (UEC) and the International Federation of Accountants (IFAC). The accountancy bodies have agreed to incorporate the principles on which UEC auditing statements and IFAC auditing guidelines are based into their own Auditing Standards and Guidelines.

Appendix: Glossary of terms

The following terms in the Explanatory Foreword to Auditing Standards and Guidelines, in the Auditing Standards or in the Auditing Guidelines, are used with the following meanings:

Audit — the independent examination of, and expression of opinion on, the financial statements of an enterprise by an appointed auditor in pursuance of that appointment and in compliance with any relevant statutory obligation.
Joint audit — where two or more auditors are responsible for an audit engagement and jointly produce an audit report to the client.
The auditor — the individual or firm carrying out the audit of the enterprise and the partners of such individual or in such firm. Where appropriate the term includes audit staff acting within delegated authority.
Audit staff — those members of the auditor's staff, who take a direct part in an audit engagement.
The enterprise — any body corporate or other organization on the financial statements of which the auditor is reporting.
Financial statements — balance sheets and profit and loss accounts (or other forms of income statements) together with such additional statements and notes as are identified as being within the scope of the audit opinion.
Reporting partner — the partner in a firm responsible for the conduct of the audit.
Internal control system — the whole system of controls, financial and otherwise, established by the management in order to carry on the business of the enterprise in an orderly and efficient manner, ensure adherence to management policies, safeguard the assets and secure as far as possible the completeness and accuracy of the records. The individual components of an internal control system are known as 'controls' or 'internal controls'.
Compliance and substantive tests — audit tests classified according to their primary purpose. Both purposes are sometimes achieved concurrently.

(*a*) Compliance tests — those tests which seek to provide audit evidence that internal control procedures are being applied as prescribed.
(*b*) Substantive tests — those tests of transactions and balances, and other procedures such as analytical review, which seek to provide audit evidence as to the completeness, accuracy and validity of the information contained in the accounting records or in the financial statements.

Approved Auditing Standards — those Statements of Auditing Standards which are approved for issue by the Councils of the accountancy bodies listed in the Explanatory Foreword and which are effective for the period covered by the financial statements on which the auditor is reporting.

'The Auditor's Operational Standard'
(Issued April 1980)

This Auditing Standard should be read in conjunction with the Explanatory Foreword to Auditing Standards and Guidelines including the Glossary of

Terms. General guidance on procedures by which this Auditing Standard may be complied with are given in Auditing Guidelines:

Planning, controlling and recording
Accounting systems
Audit evidence
Internal controls
Review of financial statements

This Auditing Standard applies whenever an audit is carried out.

Planning, controlling and recording

The auditor should adequately plan, control and record his work.

Accounting systems

The auditor should ascertain the enterprise's system of recording and processing transactions and assess its adequacy as a basis for the preparation of financial statements.

Audit evidence

The auditor should obtain relevant and reliable audit evidence sufficient to enable him to draw reasonable conclusions therefrom.

Internal controls

If the auditor wishes to place reliance on any internal controls, he should ascertain and evaluate those controls and perform compliance tests on their operation.

Review of financial statements

The auditor should carry out such a review of the financial statements as is sufficient, in conjunction with the conclusions drawn from the other audit evidence obtained, to give him a reasonable basis for his opinion on the financial statements.

Effective date

This Auditing Standard is effective for the audit of financial statements relating to accounting periods starting on or after 1 April 1980.

'The Audit Report'
(Issued April 1980)

This Auditing Standard should be read in conjunction with the Explanatory

Foreword to Auditing Standards and Guidelines including the Glossary of Terms. Qualifications in audit reports are dealt with in the Auditing Standard Qualifications in Audit Reports. *Examples of audit reports which will conform to this Standard are given in the Auditing Guideline* Audit Report Examples. *The considerations which arise when reporting on financial statements not required to give a true and fair view will be dealt with subsequently.*

Part 1 — Statement of Auditing Standard

This Auditing Standard applies to all reports in which the auditor expresses an opinion on financial statements intended to give a true and fair view of the state of affairs, profit or loss and, where applicable, source and application of funds. The Standard is not intended to override the statutory exemptions granted in respect of certain types of enterprise but is intended to apply to the audit reports relating to such enterprises in other respects.

The audit report should identify those to whom it is addressed and the financial statements to which it relates.

The auditor should refer expressly in his report to the following:

(*a*) whether the financial statements have been audited in accordance with approved Auditing Standards;

(*b*) whether in the auditor's opinion the financial statements give a true and fair view of the state of affairs, profit or loss and, where applicable source and application of funds; and

(*c*) any matters prescribed by relevant legislation or other requirements.

Effective date

This Auditing Standard is effective for the audit of financial statements relating to accounting periods starting on or after 1 April 1980.

Part 2 — Explanatory Note

Compliance with approved Auditing Standards

The auditor should comply with approved Auditing Standards and it is appropriate that his report should refer to this fact in arriving at his opinion. Approved Auditing Standards are defined as those Statements of Auditing Standards which are approved for issue by the Councils of the accountancy bodies listed in the Explanatory Foreword and which are effective for the period covered by the financial statements on which the auditor is reporting.

True and fair

The majority of audit reports are issued under the Companies Acts which normally require the use of the words 'true and fair view'. For the purpose of this Standard, therefore, the phrase 'true and fair view' has been retained. When expressing an opinion that financial statements give a true and fair view the auditor should be satisfied, *inter alia*, that:

(*a*) all relevant Statements of Standard Accounting Practice have been complied with, except in situations in which for justifiable reasons they are not strictly applicable because they are impracticable or, exceptionally, having regard to the circumstances, would be inappropriate or give a misleading view; and

(*b*) any significant accounting policies which are not the subject of Statements of Standard Accounting Practice are appropriate to the circumstances of the business.

Reference to accounting convention

The auditor should refer in his report to the particular convention used in preparing the financial statements if he considers it necessary in order to avoid misunderstanding.

Emphasis of matter

As a general principle the auditor issuing an unqualified opinion should not make reference to specific aspects of the financial statements in the body of his report as such reference may be misconstrued as being a qualification. In rare circumstances, however, the reader will obtain a better understanding of the financial statements if his attention is drawn to important matters. Examples might include an unusual event, accounting policy or condition, awareness of which is fundamental to an understanding of the financial statements.

In order to avoid giving the impression that a qualification is intended, references which are intended as emphasis of matter should be contained in a separate paragraph and introduced with a phrase such as 'We draw attention to . . .' and should not be referred to in the opinion paragraph. Emphasis of matter should not be used to rectify a lack of appropriate disclosure in the financial statements, nor should it be regarded as a substitute for a qualification.

Compliance with relevant legislation or other requirements

The auditor should comply with any reporting requirements imposed by legislation and any other reporting requirements relevant to the financial statements. It should be noted that the Companies Acts of Great Britain, Northern Ireland and the Republic of Ireland contain different reporting requirements.

Wording of report

Set out below is a form of audit report appropriate to a company incorporated in Great Britain which meets the requirements of this Standard where the auditor is able to report affirmatively on all the matters referred to above.

'AUDITORS' REPORT TO THE MEMBERS OF ....

We have audited the financial statements on pages .... to .... in accordance with approved Auditing Standards.

In our opinion the financial statements [which have been prepared under the historical cost convention as modified by the revaluation of land and buildings] give a true and fair view of the state of the company's affairs at 31 December 19 ..... and of its profit and source and application of funds for the year then ended and comply with the Companies Acts 1948 and 1967.'

An example of an unqualified audit report appropriate to a company incorporated in Ireland is given, together with other examples of audit reports, in the Auditing Guideline *Audit Report Examples*.

'Qualifications in Audit Reports'

(Issued April 1980)

This Auditing Standard should be read in conjunction with the Explanatory Foreword to Auditing Standards and Guidelines including the Glossary of Terms and the Auditing Standard The Audit Report. *Examples of audit reports which will conform to this Standard are given in the Auditing Guideline* Audit Report Examples. *The considerations which arise when reporting on financial statements not required to give a true and fair view will be dealt with subsequently.*

Part 1 — Statement of Auditing Standard

When the auditor is unable to report affirmatively on the matters contained in paragraph 3 of the Auditing Standard *The Audit Report*, he should qualify his report by referring to all material matters about which he has reservations. All reasons for the qualification should be given, together with a quantification of its effect on the financial statements if this is both relevant and practicable. Additionally, reference may need to be made to non-compliance with relevant legislation and other requirements.

A qualified audit report should leave the reader in no doubt as to its meaning and its implications for an understanding of the financial statements. To promote a more consistent understanding of qualified reports the forms of qualification described in this standard should be used unless, in the auditor's opinion, to do so would fail to convey clearly the intended meaning.

The nature of the circumstances giving rise to a qualification of opinion will generally fall into one of two categories:

(*a*) where there is an uncertainty which prevents the auditor from forming an opinion on a matter (uncertainty); or (*b*) where the auditor is able to form an opinion on a matter but this conflicts with the view given by the financial statements (disagreement).

Each of these categories gives rise to alternative forms of qualification depending upon whether the subject-matter of the uncertainty or disagreement is considered to be fundamental so as to undermine the view given by the financial statements taken as a whole.

The forms of qualification which should be used in different circumstances are shown below.

Nature of circumstances	*Material but not fundamental*	*Fundamental*
Uncertainty	'Subject to' opinion	Disclaimer of opinion
Disagreement	'Except' opinion	Adverse opinion

— In a disclaimer of opinion the auditor states that he is unable to form an opinion as to whether the financial statements give a true and fair view.
— In an adverse opinion the auditor states that in his opinion the financial statements do not give a true and fair view.
— In a 'subject to' opinion the auditor effectively disclaims an opinion on a particular matter which is not considered fundamental.
— In an 'except' opinion the auditor expresses an adverse opinion on a particular matter which is not considered fundamental.

Effective date
This Auditing Standard is effective for the audit of financial statements relating to accounting periods starting on or after 1 April 1980.

Part 2 — Explanatory Note

Introduction
There are occasions when, in order to convey clearly the results of his audit, the auditor needs to depart from the form of wording normally used for unqualified audit reports. Such departures are generally referred to as qualifications. The principles set out in this Standard are intended to make qualified audit reports more understandable by developing a consistent use of language to distinguish the types of qualification appropriate to different circumstances.

Reasons for qualification
As indicated in Part 1, circumstances which give rise to a qualification of opinion in an audit report may be in the nature of uncertainty or disagreement.

Circumstances giving rise to uncertainties include the following:

(*a*) *Limitations in the scope of the audit*. Scope limitations arise if the auditor is unable for any reason to obtain all the information and explanations which he considers necessary for the purpose of his audit; for example, inability to carry out an audit procedure considered necessary, or the absence of proper accounting records.

(*b*) *Inherent uncertainties*. Inherent uncertainties result from circumstances in which it is not possible to reach an objective conclusion as to the outcome of a situation due to the circumstances themselves rather than to any limitation of the scope of audit procedures. This type of uncertainty may relate to major litigation, the outcome of long-term contracts or doubts about the ability of the enterprise to continue as a going concern. Inherent uncertainties will not normally include instances where the auditor is able to obtain adequate evidence to support estimates and use his experience to reach an opinion as to their reasonableness; for example as regards collectability of debts or realizability of stock.

The wording in expressing the audit opinion describes the effect of uncertainties on that opinion and does not distinguish those arising from a limitation of scope from those which are inherent. The cause of the uncertainty will be described elsewhere in the audit report.

Circumstances giving rise to disagreement include the following:

(*a*) departures from acceptable accounting practices where:
(i) there has been failure to comply with a relevant Statement of Standard Accounting Practice (SSAP) and the auditor does not concur;
(ii) an accounting policy not the subject of an SSAP is adopted which in the opinion of the auditor is not appropriate to the circumstances of the business; or
(iii) exceptionally, an SSAP has been followed with the result that the financial statements do not present a true and fair view;

(*b*) disagreement as to the facts or amounts included in the financial statements;

(*c*) disagreement as to the manner or extent of disclosure of facts or amounts in the financial statements;

(*d*) failure to comply with relevant legislation or other requirements.

Small enterprises

The auditor needs to obtain the same degree of assurance in order to give an unqualified opinion on the financial statements of both small and large enterprises. However, the operating procedures and methods of recording and processing transactions used by small enterprises often differ significantly from those of large enterprises. Indeed, many of the controls which would be relevant to the large enterprise are not practical, appropriate or necessary in the small enterprise. The most effective form of internal control for small enterprises is generally the close involvement of the directors or proprietors. This involvement will, however, enable them to override controls and purposely to exclude transactions from the records. This possibility can give rise to difficulties for the auditor not because there is a lack of controls but because of insufficient evidence as to their operation and the completeness of the records.

In many situations it may be possible to reach a conclusion that will support an unqualified opinion on the financial statements by combining the evidence obtained from extensive substantive testing of transactions with a careful review of costs and margins. However, in some businesses such as those where most transactions are for cash and there is no regular pattern of costs and margins, the available evidence may be inadequate to support an opinion on the financial statements.

There will be other situations where the evidence available to the auditor is insufficient to give him the confidence necessary for him to express an unqualified opinion but this uncertainty is not so great as to justify a total disclaimer of opinion. In such situations the most helpful form of report may be one which indicates the need to accept the assurances of management as to the completeness or accuracy of the accounting records. Such a report should contain a 'subject to . . .' opinion. It would only be appropriate to use this form of report if the auditor has taken steps to obtain all the evidence which can reasonably be obtained and is satisfied that:

(*a*) the system of accounting and control is reasonable having regard to the size and type of the enterprise's operations; and is sufficient to enable management to give the auditor the assurances which he requires;
(*b*) there is no evidence to suggest that the assurances may be inaccurate.

Disclosure of reasons for qualifications

The audit report should include a brief recital of the reasons for a qualification and should quantify the effects on the financial statements if this is relevant and practicable. Whilst reference may be made to relevant notes in the financial statements such reference should not be used as a substitute for a description of the basic circumstances in the audit report.

The auditor should refer in his report to all material matters about which he has reservations. Thus, a qualification on one matter should not be regarded as a reason for omitting other unrelated qualifications which otherwise would have been reported.

The manner in which the reasons for qualifying are disclosed is for the auditor to decide in the particular circumstances of each case, but the overall objective should be clarity. The inclusion of a separate 'explanatory' paragraph before the paragraph in which the auditor gives his opinion is likely to be the clearest method of outlining the facts giving rise to the qualification.

Statutory requirements

The auditor will also need to consider whether the circumstances which give rise to his qualification impinge on his statutory duties to report. For instance, shortcomings in the sales records which give rise to a qualified opinion on the financial statements will generally mean that proper accounting records* have not been maintained. Similarly, limitations in scope may mean that the auditor has not obtained all the information and explanations he considers necessary.

Omission of statements of source and application of funds
SSAP 10 requires, with certain specified exceptions, that financial statements should include a statement of source and application of funds. Omission of such a statement from financial statements to which SSAP 10 applies presents a particular problem to the auditor in that the omission of a funds statement does not justify, on this ground alone, a qualified report on the profit and loss account and balance sheet.

It is considered that the standards set out in this statement will be met if the auditor reports the omission of a funds statement by adding a separate paragraph which follows his opinion. An example of the manner in which this matter could be reported is set out below:

> 'The financial statements do not specify the manner in which the operations of the company (group) have been financed or in which its financial resources have been used during the year as required by Statement of Standard Accounting Practice No. 10.'

Materiality
In deciding whether to qualify his audit opinion, the auditor should have regard to the materiality of the matter in the context of the financial statements on which he is proposing to report. In general terms a matter should be judged to be material if knowledge of the matter would be likely to influence the user of the financial statements. Materiality may be considered in the context of the financial statements as a whole, the balance sheet, the profit and loss account, or individual items within the financial statements. In addition, depending upon the nature of the matter, materiality may be considered in relative or absolute terms.

If the auditor concludes that, judged against the criteria he believes to be most appropriate in the circumstances, the matter does not materially affect the view given by the financial statements, he should not qualify his opinion.

Where the auditor has decided that a matter is sufficiently material to warrant a qualification in his audit report, a further decision is required as to whether or not the matter is fundamental, so as to require either an adverse opinion or a disclaimer of opinion on the financial statements as a whole. An uncertainty becomes fundamental when its impact on the financial statements is so great as to render the financial statements as a whole meaning-

*Described in some legislation as 'proper books of account'.

less. A disagreement becomes fundamental when its impact on the financial statements is so great as to render them totally misleading. The combined effect of all uncertainties and disagreements must be considered.

It is emphasized that the adverse opinion and the disclaimer of opinion are the extreme forms of the two main categories of qualification of opinion arising from disagreement and uncertainty. In most situations the 'except' or 'subject to' form of opinion will be the approprite form to use; the adverse opinion and the disclaimer should be regarded as measures of last resort.

Index